Revolution in Poetic Language
Fifty Years Later

SUNY series in Gender Theory
—————
Tina Chanter, editor

Revolution in Poetic Language Fifty Years Later

New Directions in Kristeva Studies

Edited by
EMILIA ANGELOVA

Cover art: Piet Mondrian, Study for a Composition, 1940–41. Art Institute of Chicago. Gift of Dorothy Braude Edinburg to the Harry B. and Bessie K. Braude Memorial Collection.

Published by State University of New York Press, Albany

© 2024 State University of New York

All rights reserved

Printed in the United States of America

No part of this book may be used or reproduced in any manner whatsoever without written permission. No part of this book may be stored in a retrieval system or transmitted in any form or by any means including electronic, electrostatic, magnetic tape, mechanical, photocopying, recording, or otherwise without the prior permission in writing of the publisher.

For information, contact State University of New York Press, Albany, NY
www.sunypress.edu

Library of Congress Cataloging-in-Publication Data

Name: Angelova, Emilia, 1962– editor.
Title: Revolution in poetic language fifty years later : new directions in Kristeva studies / edited by Emilia Angelova.
Description: Albany : State University of New York Press, [2024]. | Series: SUNY series in gender theory | Includes bibliographical references and index.
Identifiers: LCCN 2023047992 | ISBN 9781438498034 (hardcover : alk. paper) | ISBN 9781438498058 (ebook) | ISBN 9781438498041 (pbk. : alk. paper)
Subjects: LCSH: Kristeva, Julia, 1941–Criticism and interpretation. | Poetics. | Kristeva, Julia, 1941- Révolution du langage poétique. English
Classification: LCC PN75.K75 R48 2024 | DDC 801.95—dc23/eng/20240129
LC record available at https://lccn.loc.gov/2023047992

Contents

Editor's Acknowledgments ix

Introduction: Revolutionary Practice and the Subject-in-Process 1
   Emilia Angelova

Part One
Two New Texts by Kristeva

Chapter 1
Editor's Introduction to Julia Kristeva's "The Impossibility of Loss"
(1988) 31
   Emilia Angelova

Chapter 2
The Impossibility of Loss 41
   Julia Kristeva, translated by Elisabeth Paquette

Chapter 3
Of What Use Are Poets in Times of Distress? 63
   Julia Kristeva, translated by Elisabeth Paquette and Alice Jardine

Part Two
Beyond Feminism: Engaging Kristeva for Decolonial, Trans, and Disability Studies

Chapter 4
Julia Kristeva's Maternal Ethics of Tenderness 75
   Kelly Oliver

Chapter 5
Kristeva in a Trans Poetic Frame   91
   Sid Hansen

Chapter 6
Stranger than Other Strangers: On the Crossroads between
Subjectivity and Language in Kristeva and Anzaldúa   107
   Fanny Söderbäck

Chapter 7
Theories of Poetic Resistance: Julia Kristeva and Sylvia Wynter   141
   Elisabeth Paquette

Chapter 8
Proust among the Patients: Kristeva on Proust,
Psychoanalysis, and Politics   163
   Elaine P. Miller

Part Three
The Evolving Meaning of Ontological Loss: From Revolution to Revolt

Chapter 9
From Praxis to *Chōra*: The Filter of (In)Humanization in
Julia Kristeva's Early Work   189
   Miglena Nikolchina

Chapter 10
The Mental Image and the Spectacular Imaginary: Kristeva with
Lacan and Sartre   211
   Surti Singh

Chapter 11
Rhythm and the Semiotic in Revolution in
Poetic Language   233
   John Montani

Chapter 12
Excription and the Negativity of the Speaking Subject:
Reading Kristeva with Heidegger   253
   Emilia Angelova

Chapter 13
Kristeva and Arendt on Language, Sanity, and the *Sensus Communis* 283
    Anne O'Byrne

About the Contributors 307

Index 313

Editor's Acknowledgments

I would like to thank Julia Kristeva for contributing her journal article, "L'Impossibilité de perdre" in Les Cahiers de l'Institut de Psycho-Pathologie Clinique 8, November 1988, special issue on "Trauma réel, trauma psychique," along with her public address, "À quoi bon des poètes en temps de détresse?," presented at the Théâtre de la Colline in Paris, November 7, 2016, and for allowing these to be translated for this volume.

I also would like to thank the students in my graduate seminar in the Department of Philosophy at Concordia University, who made my own research on the work of Julia Kristeva, and its dissemination possible. My thanks especially to Bayonne Said, who not only completed a major research paper on Kristeva, but also edited the final manuscript, and to Shawn Huberdeau, Maxime Varin, Rosalind Jay, Jules Galbraith, and Mya Walmsley, who faithfully studied and reconstructed in their own writing the thought of Kristeva. Thanks to Ethel Gamache from Concordia's Webster Library, who contributed precious editorial advice in securing publication rights.

Thank you to Sara Beardsworth, Alice Jardine, Kelly Oliver, Fanny Söderbäck, and Sid Hansen for your seminal research, and creating, since 2011, the Kristeva Circle. Thank you to all the contributors to this volume, your enthusiasm and commitment to this project. In particular, my thanks to Elisabeth Paquette and Alice Jardine, for the selfless dedication, and labor of love in translating Kristeva's two texts included in this volume. I wish to express my thanks to two anonymous reviewers, and the editorial team, Tina Chanter, Rebecca Colesworthy, and Diane Ganeles, at SUNY Press, for their guidance and patience.

Finally, I could not have completed this work without the support, love and limitless expert advice of my partner and philosophical mentor,

David Morris, who helped me find the cover image. For instilling in me uncompromising respect for philosophical foundations, I am indebted to my doctoral supervisor Rebecca Comay. I thank my family, Veska, Snezhina, and Svetoslav, for their encouragement and love.

Introduction

Revolutionary Practice and the Subject-in-Process

Emilia Angelova

Julia Kristeva is our contemporary and one of the foremost intellectuals in the world today. This volume of essays by established scholars of her work celebrates the fiftieth anniversary of her magnum opus *Revolution in Poetic Language*. In the last fifty years, Kristeva has published nearly thirty volumes in semiotics, linguistics, literary theory and criticism, psychoanalysis, and feminist theory, not counting six novels and essays in film and art history. In an impressive recognition of her contributions as a public intellectual, in 2004, Kristeva became the first woman to receive the Holberg Prize, equivalent to a Nobel Prize for literature and humanities. Since then, Kristeva's stature as a public intellectual has risen astronomically. In 2021, she was inducted to the Légion de France for her lifetime achievement, following the international seminar at Cerisy on maternal reliance and revolt, just a year after the appearance of her long-awaited book on Dostoyevsky.

Capturing her astonishing rise to world-renowned philosopher and thinker, Alice Jardine, in a first intellectual biography, gives special role to the major significance of Kristeva's present practice of psychoanalysis. Kristeva's continued involvement with political thought reminds us of our duty to pay a debt the modern condition owes to the pain of psychic life under attack: "It is only through the process of what psychoanalysis calls *perlaboration*—a working-through, a reinvention, a *trans*figuration—of history and cultural memory that humanity can avoid a cataclysmic end"

(Jardine 2020, 186). There is nothing abstract or aloof in this demand that we transfigure through transforming our practices of our relations to others and that this shift is doubly dependent on beginning through transforming our relation to ourselves first. As I write these words, in August 2022, after two and half years of the COVID pandemic, the rise of autocracy in the West and its felt impact in climate, food, human trafficking, and racial violence around the world is becoming our extreme contemporary cataclysm. The unprecedented assault on women's reproductive rights rendering abortion illegal fifty years after *Roe v. Wade* (1973) in the US, this June opens up a new horrid reality leaving the rights of women in the hands of state legislatures—abortion after six weeks, including cases regardless of rape, is banned and subject to prosecution, in more than half the country. If we do not take stock of soft totalitarian practices that creep in and suffocate individual and collective lives together, we will keep repeating the mistakes of the past.

Kristeva's work since the 2000s is dominated by innovating psychoanalysis, as at the turn of the new millennium, not unrelated to the superpowers of the US and Britain bypassing the UN and unilaterally declaring a war on Iraq, she offered a diagnosis of a "society in depression." Concerned with the uncertainty in our contemporary psycho-political condition, she likened the crises of the then-globalization to ill will "that declares some humans expendable," echoing Arendt (Jardine, 186). As she restates in her 2012 address on New Humanism, in which she urges that the modern condition, its values, and new malaise of the soul has not yet finished with us, Kristeva signals the threat of inevitably slipping into genocide, and the mass "ending" of life is a constant preoccupation. She warns that, as a "humanity," we depend on the duty of revival and renewal of historical and cultural memory, to avoid the "death drive" at its "fullest and most horrific." The aim is precisely *not* to reject intellectual and cultural history, but much rather hermeneutically, it falls on remembering, re-understanding, re-inventing, redefining, reconceptualizing the past.

Over the span of fifty years, Kristeva remains a revolutionary, but she has shifted focus in order to more adequately take up the "politics of life"—through her psychoanalytically inflected term of "intimate revolt," a critique of soft totalitarianism. She has intervened with writing on myriad occasions of crisis, such as nationalism in Europe, America's war in Iraq, the Paris suburbs uprisings in 2011, and the immigrant wave in Italy in 2015. In 2011, Kristeva became the first woman to join, as nonbeliever, a group of eleven religious delegates to the Vatican, where she gave a famous speech: "No One Owns the Truth." Just one year prior to that, she wrote a manifesto, "Secular Humanism in 10 Theses," calling for a "new ethical language," "to be invented sooner," to promote rights for LGBTQ people, for recognition of non-normative subjectivity (Jardine, 284). In this collection, we draw from the sources that Kristeva proposes as New Humanism, to address the remarkable continuity from early into recent work.

What connects revolution to revolt?—this question orients all contributions in the collection. The theoretical approach to the psychic conditions of life in "revolt" culminated in her work in the 2000s marked by the trilogy on "female genius" (Arendt, Klein, Colette). The contemporary interest in Kristeva's enormous contribution to multiple aspects of social, cultural, and political importance could not have been possible, however, without the early work on "revolution" in "poetic language," in that a deep logical complementarity exists between the two domains, "revolution" and "revolt." I will slowly introduce this topic of a systematic interpretation of the terms of revolution-revolt after I first briefly introduce the ideas of the early work.

Leaving Bulgaria for France on a nine-month stipend by de Gaulle's government in 1966, the young Kristeva distinguished herself through a stellar success. In the same year of her first doctorate, 1969, with Lucien Goldmann, she publishes her first book *Semēiotike*, and in 1973, *Polylogue*. Immediately following, Kristeva defends a 645-page *doctorat d'etat* in 1974, published a year later in French (and just at 260 pages in 1984, in English), her major theoretical breakthrough, *Revolution in Poetic Language*. We celebrate the anniversary of Kristeva's text, yet this volume is focused on the (partial) translation and not on the original French text, *La Révolution du langage poétique: L'Avant-garde à la fin du XIXe siècle, Lautréamont et Mallarmé*. We owe the readers, and perhaps, not unrealistically, at this time of technological progress, a translation in full. In the meantime, Kristeva's legacy, in North America, and hence for this volume's primary audience, stands limited to the translated part. A future project to celebrate the magnum opus would rightfully in due fashion address the nontranslated sections that deal specifically with poetic language as it is manifest in Lautréamont and Mallarmé.

The intellectual achievement that *Revolution in Poetic Language* (1984) represents cannot be overstated. Kristeva names the dimension of producing meaning in language—a "poetic" dimension, namely, the capacity of the sign for literally "figuring" over and above being a mimetic faculty, in excess of the symbolic order of signification. By operating as temporally futural possibility of being yet-to-come, the poetic dimension invokes the radicalism of linguistic imagination as the sign of the subject already in "revolt." The radical linguistic text of the avant-garde poets at the end of the nineteenth century thus becomes a signifying practice confronting the limit of signification in language so as to disrupt bourgeois codes, much like the revolutionary forces confront late capitalism, for instance, in the Russian Revolution, to overthrow it. In this way, revolutionary practice and the avant-garde art and literature come to express both a necessity and limit in the production of language, as they reach out to a reality larger than the average understanding of everyday life and are aimed at metaphysical notions of time and justice, following ideas in Hegel's dialectic. As a linguist and innovator, Kristeva ties the semiotic text to Freud and Klein as having pointed to what lies beyond psychoanalytic processes of language acquisition, and simultaneously to Hegel's principle of the strength and resilience of the negative—namely, the manifestation of a semiotic authority as irreducible to past linguistic and cultural rituals.

Theorizing semiotic authority in excess of signification echoes Hegel's idea of rejecting the old while preserving it by other means, in the affirmation of the new but at the same time as a thought and judgment never reducible to an act, either linguistic or socio-political. For Kristeva, this opens to the interaction between the semiotic and symbolic levels of language as taking shape concretely through signifying practices embedded in the mother-infant semiotic matrix. This is to say that through its signifying power, language, which arches over both the symbolic order, and its semiotic, unfigurable dimension, reaches out to the bodily dimension of subjectivity that is outside of language. Indeed, the conditionality of revolution plays out as anterior to the symbolic order since it is its condition of possibility. However, this conditionality in no way pre-exists the symbolic order, although it precedes it in time, precisely because only the latter has the power to overturn it, by retrospectively revealing the effects of revolution within language.

Through her critique of language as structure, and the structure of subject formation in psychoanalysis, in *Revolution in Poetic Language*, Kristeva acknowledges language's timely power. This connects her, in the spirit of her contemporaries, to Derrida and Deleuze, and more primarily to a philosophical heritage developing a salvatory or messianic account of time, examining both the legitimate and illegitimate ways into foreclosure of temporal possibilities for modes of production of meaning in language. There is a horizon inherent in the aporetic structure of representation of language that draws from the unfolding of time and justice presupposed as metaphysically prior to symbol and rationality, which never can be outstripped by the power of language. The symbolic order of language for Kristeva, who follows Lacan and Freud, thus represents a horizon for revolutionary liberation, presuming that paternal law and patriarchal socio-historic order are opened up from the side of repressive illegitimate foreclosure, and from this Kristeva shapes her feminist theory. Not only is there an essential connection between revolution and revolt, but this collection also aims to contribute especially to theorizing Kristeva's account of time, which connects revolution and revolt, and how this can be retrieved out of the work in her magnum opus. The connection can be explained through a model of "revolutionary time," as Fanny Söderbäck recently argues (2012; 2019, 6, 9). This major idea about time as temporality and as well as explaining historical change is represented throughout the contributions in this volume.

In a bit more detail, work in recent years moving beyond feminist theory, which this volume ambitiously seeks to reposition under a broad umbrella unifying transgender, disability, and decolonial studies based on Kristeva, forges a link between revolution and revolt, and this means that the forcible linearity of paternal law and patriarchy becomes the focus of inquiry into the illegitimate foreclosure of temporal possibilities for modes of production of meaning in language. The resources for this are available in the early work but it has not always been easy to recognize them, specifically if and how this concerns reversibility and linear time.

To start with, Kristeva's explicit work on "revolt" does not begin until the 1990s trilogy (1997; 2002), which elaborates the "intimacy" of revolt—revolt as a form of the regaining of "lost" time, which includes treating time as a sign and "writing," for instance, in Proust (Kristeva 1998; see Miller 2014). As Jardine puts it, Kristeva's focus on revolt adds "time" over and above the early problematics of "history" and "subjectivity" (284). It takes Kristeva two decades to formulate the logic of this connection—namely, developing a "theory of time" through which to articulate this connection. Revolt, and that it is intimate, is not necessarily an action in the world, and so at first glance appears the opposite to revolution. The two are etymologically related, but revolt, insofar as it is essentially a retrospective examination, appears as the more conservative of the two signs. Revolt elaborates and renews meaning in psychic life, and Kristeva defines it on a tripartite temporal schema of transgressing-consummation-renewal (2002, 5, 8; 2014, 3; see also Hansen & Tuvel 2017, 1–13). Through displacement and alteration, the renewal of meaning becomes possible, and as Kristeva puts it: "There is a necessary repetition," "but beyond that, I emphasize its potential for making gaps, rupturing, renewing" (2002, 85).

Kristeva's confrontation from 1974 with "revolution," which in its ontological meaning assumes the possibility of a radical loss of significance, as I will explain below, also importantly signals the beginning of her turning away from negation and instead moving in a direction back "to" natality.

A systematic reading of Kristeva's lifetime of work does not yet exist, but bringing out a research project such as this, as this collection aims, appears quite timely. The contributions gathered here are momentous and quite needed given the current orientation in Continental philosophy and other areas and interdisciplinary interest, particularly work from liberatory natality in Arendt as opposed to "freedom" (Nancy, Badiou, and Heidegger), social and political philosophy generally, and critical disability, gender and transgender, and critical race studies specifically.

What does this mean in the terms of revolution as practice, and the subject-on-trial? Below, I indicate the main axes of the second and third scholarly divisions of this collection. The five chapters of division two engage Kristeva's lifetime development from the most recent and back through the 2000s of "New Humanism." The chapters logically trace out of the 1970s in French theory, the fate of the semiotic and symbolic in Kristeva's own path. They thoughtfully engage the task of reading Kristeva for the future, to reimagine the deepest potentiality for novelty and for transformative political agency. The authors jealously guard the heritage of Kristeva's thought, yet they rigorously inquire as well into complicating points of dissention. Adding new voices and challenges, the chapters push the boundaries of Kristeva's ethics, aesthetics, and psychoanalysis in a friendly encounter. These texts breathe the anguish and the cultural and historical turmoil of our current moment. Take, for example, the crisis of the present time we experience with normalizing transphobia, misogyny, racism, and extreme violence in the US, where critical race theory, critical gender and transgender studies, and Black history are targets under fire.

Five chapters in part 3 provide a lens through which we can revisit the contribution from the early work as already underway to the mid-1990s shift from "revolution" to "revolt," considered in depth for its theoretical proposals. This division opens with tracing the long arc of Kristeva's focus on the revolutionary power of poetic language, beginning with the very real political situation of coming of age in Bulgaria under communism. The leitmotif is how might language be employed to subvert a repressive order? To begin with, the mid-1990s find Kristeva looking for resources of subversion, and aligning herself with the critique of late capitalism available in Debord's society of the spectacle. The chapters work in concert to show how the resources of revolt's intimacy do not usher in discontinuity, specifically Kristeva opposes an egalitarian severing of ties between public and private, while engaging unorthodox psychoanalysis remains continuous with the core of *Revolution in Poetic Language*.

Beyond Feminism: Engaging Kristeva for Decolonial, Trans, and Disability Studies

Through her New Humanism, and on the basis of her philosophy of the subject, Kristeva is a great deal more than simply a resource in today's social and political philosophy and interdisciplinary critical studies, and most importantly, she matters for non-normative subjectivities, as well as decolonial and disability studies. We find this in the most recent developments of research on Kristeva—maternal love, care ethic, critical disability, decolonial subjects, transsubjectivity, Latinx feminisms, and more. Additionally, this makes it possible to rectify some misinterpretations connecting to the work from 1974, and especially the late 1970s, to instead show how Kristeva is quite useful beyond feminist theory. The initial unifying claim is that Kristeva outrightly refuses the rigid dichotomy between linear and cyclical time, and instead argues that, since this dualism rests on masculine-mind and feminine-body models that are not *actually* separate, we ought to also consider revolt in ontological and temporal terms.

It is important to note the contrast between second- and third-wave feminisms, and how Kristeva does not agree with either but might best fit in the fourth: affective materialisms. The activist movements of our era predominantly still rely on a notion of time of linear progress. Due to its historical period, the 1960s women's liberation was oriented by moving away from inequality and toward equality, and this is a program susceptible to appeals immanent to totalitarian regimes that render human lives disposable for the sake of securing a better future. Right-wing feminists today have presented indefensible conservative and harmful, exclusionary claims. Instead, Kristeva's theoretical approach urges for the constant renegotiation of values, what she early on understood and theorized as a complicitous approach of meaning creation, indebted to both semiotic and symbolic interaction. Her view of the Modern predicament is that it submits the human to "cyclical time," the so-called counterpart to linear time, to repression (cf. Kristeva 1981). But as she argues, without the perlaboration of trauma, the subject only returns to the repetition of past traumas. She warns that the denial and repression of cyclical time in the feminism of the 1980s (and repression of the feminine in fear of the body's being unto death) results in its unexpected and often unnoticed resurgence in our life, and the consequence of this is that "it is indeed deprived of a future" (Söderbäck 2012, 319).

Kristeva has not been always well received. A case in point concerns her now classic critical essays ("Women's Time" and "Stabat Mater") on second-wave feminism. Discussing the reception, Jardine rightly suggests that, like Foucault, Kristeva resists identity politics—for she believes that, with the onset of the Enlightenment, the dogmatic image of "Man" is finished. Being both a psychoanalyst and a poststructuralist, Kristeva believes that "woman has never been given existential worth," and "philosophically speaking she [Woman] does not exist"—and "yet, we must account for women sociologically, empirically, historically. But then, all identity models must shift in the name of revolt if not revolution" (Jardine 2020, 153). That is, since her earliest beginning, Kristeva is not theorizing the domain of political life (freedom, human rights, the rights of women) as structure, but nor is she theorizing something merely cultural (ethnos, the anthropological idea). This situates her work intricately at the margins of the signifier, at limits of material contiguity between metaphor and metonymy. Language, by itself, Kristeva argues, runs the risk of disconnecting from the very experience it sets out to articulate and reveals itself as unstable and dubious with regards to its revolutionary signifier. Hence, language rather accomplishes its revolutionary aim through the *mode* of retrieval of lost time by language, and not in the *content* of the language itself. Kristeva instead focuses on the proximity between the poetic and the decentered subject—and adding, since the early 2000s, the disabled subject (Jardine 2020, 166). On this radicalized social basis, she builds her model of a democracy of proximity, an ethic of care, rooted in the asymmetry of the alterity of the other, and not based in the mandate of obligation to care. She then anchors on this a "new humanism" (cf. Oliver 2009, 2020; McAfee 2005, 2020; Ziarek 2020; Hansen 2020; Sjöholm 2020).

The 1970s and the fate of the semiotic and the symbolic—the question as to where precisely Kristeva enters the debate—could not be more crucial to clearing misunderstandings of the early work. There is nothing apolitical or ahistorical in the early work, and a wide audience of interdisciplinary readers as well as the established community of Kristeva scholars have put significant labor into locating the classic work of *Revolution in Poetic Language* for its major primary findings, the difference between semiotic and symbolic, through the interests of intellectual and philosophical debates in the 1970s. It is significant, as Jardine points out, that by 1978, "the basic infrastructure of [Kristeva's] thought familiar to English-language readers was more or less in place" (179).

Kristeva's important interventions in the 1970s are her contributions to the theory of the materiality of the linguistic signifier, through the principle of the interaction of the semiotic and the symbolic. Some thirty years later, in her address to the Holberg Prize, appearing in a major collection of essays from 2005, *Hatred and Forgiveness*, Kristeva puts the distinction between the semiotic and symbolic this way: it "has no political or feminist connotation. It is simply an attempt to think of 'meaning' not only as a 'structure' but also as a 'process' or 'trial' . . . by looking at the same time at syntax, logic, and what transgresses them, or the trans-verbal" (2010, 11). The omission of feminism from Kristeva's definition of her work as French theory frequently baffles readers. How can we help not reading into Kristeva's theorizing of the materiality of the signifier a feminist connotation—in what way does this shed light on the early work? A quick response: She means narrowly that poststructuralist theories of language at the foundation of heated debates on interpellation and feminism of the 1990s remain tied to either pure "objectivity" (empiricism) or pure "subjectivity" (intellectualism) as targets of critique, while in reality much of the debate could benefit from arguments stemming from the unorthodox psychoanalytic theory she practices.

The easy answer is that since 1974, Kristeva differentiates herself from Lacan, who posits the symbolic as a metalanguage—akin to the word as an empty envelope, "genuine denomination of authentic speech," drawing from an inner operation of the mind, as in Cartesian introspection. Both thinkers help to break the tendency of theorizing to posit "that reassuring image that every society offers itself when it understands everything" (Kristeva 1984, 31)—a tendency of fetishizing Culture in all its colonizing and alienating forms, toward totalization and finality that is a product of the theoretical use of language. Both appeal in support of tearing down to the foundation, to Hegel's theory of desire and negativity as an antidote. Against Lacan, however, Kristeva posits that the semiotic, in that it evades the hold of the pure linguistic signifier—in excess over signification (her term is *signifiance*), just *is* this metalanguage; namely, there exists a gap between time and justice, the word in language and its history, such that no metaphysics can outstrip linguistic signifiers. Thus, the implication—there is no pure void of the signified, just as there is no pure linguistic signifier. All signifying practices and their institutions are, therefore, modalities of the materialization of bodies, the result of material bodily processes. As Kelly Oliver recognized, this point crucially engages Freud's theory of the drives differently, aiming to "bring the speaking body back into discourse" (1991, 6). The logic of language is already operating at the material level of bodily processes, and bodily drives continually, relentlessly reconstitute, make their way into language anew. Furthermore, on Kristeva's view, the speaking body's enunciating position may only be fully assumed through metaphorical and unstable processes—laying emphasis on the semiotic authority transgressing signification, and withdrawing to a futural promise of the past, to a messianic or heterogeneous, hidden objects, closed "text" dimension.

As Ziarek (2005; 2020), Sjöholm (2005), Söderbäck (2019), and Miller (2014) demonstrate, the early Kristeva's novel account of subjectivity, history, and time centers bodily intimacy and its folds: what sort of perspectives or standpoints place it beyond being, beyond abyss, for example, inscription of alterity at bodily borders, including semiotic meaning inscribing maternal abjection. In the 1970s, Kristeva introduces the semiotic as a perspective activating a double-bind view, which includes the possibility of the ethical relation to the Other, as the Other is beyond language, and so, beyond representation: the unfolding of time may only be accounted for in linguistic terms. However, alternatively, as it is a conduit of meaning created through signifying, language as it is available to the decentered poetic subject finds its essential aim through the accomplishment, ontologically, of a "temporal" revolution. In other words, over the span of fifty years, Kristeva maintains, there is something revolutionary, an important ambiguity at the root of normative egalitarian laws, attaching to the deferred, delayed action of dual retrieval of meaning as foundation, as both affect/structure and subject/outside structure at the origins of subject formation—and this definitely exceeds the logic of inauthentic being, binary gender, and we must add, colonization. In order to understand the interaction of both these dimensions, we must first understand the structures of subject formation, which *Revolution in Poetic Language* outlines. Indeed, in order for the semiotic to make its way to the symbolic, the subject must accept and assume its position as a fundamental lack, following the symbolic order, in Lacan (cf. Lacan 1977). However, as Kristeva differentiates her standpoint from Lacan, this position may only be fully assumed through metaphorical and metonymic unstable processes—laying emphasis on the semiotic authority transgressing signification "for the purposes of renewal" (1984, 29).

To restate: the symbolic in Lacan and Kristeva represents the structured aspect of language and subjectivity—the linear language of consciousness. But against Lacan, Kristeva maintains, the semiotic is that which evades such representative structures—that which "underpins language and, under the control of language, it articulates other aspects of 'meaning' which are more than mere 'significations,' such as rhythmical and melodic inflections" (Kristeva 2010, 11). The semiotic and symbolic are so utterly interdependent, such that the attempt to distinguish them easily runs into problems. In other words, the claim of the symbolic to any sort of logic or any sort of readability is hence definitionally unstable. For Kristeva, the symbolic itself inaugurates unavoidable violence; but in that, the symbolic is lawlike or inscription, a first founding violence, as it is at the same time procurement of the readability that makes the unfounded possible, that is, the semiotic as a second force, a law-enforcing violence, unreadability, the subject-on-trial necessary and unsurpassable. The symbolic, much like justice, amounts to an aporia that may not be surpassed, however, the thetic phase, Kristeva's third term (cf. Roudiez, 1984, "language leads to exteriority"), may not be negated without a remainder, even though it may be foreclosed, and surely it may not be a strictly symbolic apparatus (unlike the mirror stage might be for Lacan). More accurately restated, it is Derrida's *ārche*-trace that bears close comparison to the subject-on-trial in Kristeva (Kristeva 2010, 11).

That is, diverging from Lacan, Kristeva consistently claims since 1974, the thetic phase logically precedes (but does not pre-exist) meaning production, in that it draws on both symbolic and semiotic dimensions of language. In *Revolution in Poetic Language*, Kristeva defends that the inauguration of the symbolic order of language can only be carried out through a necessary separation between the subject and its primary bodily drives, what she calls the "thetic phase" (43–46). The thetic phase is hence the necessary separation in order for a "subject" and an "object" to appear as such and consequently, for an enunciation and an identification of the subject with these objects to be possible. The thetic phase implies both a rupturing of the preverbal subject and its drives, and is what allows the subject to build and produce a self-identification through its enunciation and relations. Enunciations may only refer to or represent their objects through specific meaning production, namely, through material contiguity, metaphors or metonymies—the chain of the network of signifiers is not closed, and the constant revision of the meaning of the word is part of the creativity of language as a sign system itself. However, diverging from Lacan's "trap" of linguistic science, for Kristeva, the thetic phase itself precedes logically and chronologically as the virtual fact of attribution of meaning to objects by the subject (49).

In Kristeva, as Sara Beardsworth helpfully suggests, this non-overlap or tension between meaning as actually present, and as virtual (e.g., affect subtending language), can be understood as a "tendential severance" (2004, 14). That is, separatedness yet connectedness (to the maternal body) is a formula to capture the self-production of subjectivity as a constant oscillation between semiotic and symbolic meaning. Moreover, these dimensions "need to be connected" in spite of severance "if self-relation, the other, and world-relation are to be possible" (2004, 14). Explaining along similar lines the theory from *Revolution in Poetic Language*, more recently Jardine clarifies that this oscillation, or "this symbolic/semiotic dance does not exist in the abstract, does not take place in a void, or only within an individual—but rather is grounded in an intensely interdisciplinary set of historical and material constraints" (Jardine 2020, 139). Thus, the *sújet-en-procès* denotes a process of signifying meaning "between," "within," and "among" two irreconcilable yet interwoven and interdependent modes of meaning. There can never be purely symbolic or purely semiotic language: the subject is always necessarily both, for the subject is constituted by the dialectic between the two and is "marked by an indebtedness to both" (Kristeva 1984, 24). To generalize, Kristeva then offers a philosophy of the subject in the 1970s, in a new key, in that she offers a philosophy of history through engagement with Freudo-Marxism reopening psychoanalysis and poststructuralism through Freud, Klein, and Lacan (Foucault, Deleuze, Derrida) and at the same time, radicalizing social-critical ontology in Heidegger (Husserl, Sartre).

As stated above, in *Julia Kristeva: Psychoanalysis and Modernity*, Beardsworth shows that from the outset Kristeva is centered on the modern problem of nihilism and her "*oeuvre* is best characterized as a philosophy of culture rooted in the psychoanalytic view of subjectivity" (2004, 2). This limiting to "philosophy of culture," though, is not the full scope of approaches to Kristeva. John Lechte, Kelly Oliver, Ewa Ziarek, Tina Chanter, Noëlle McAfee, Cecilia Sjöholm, William Watkin, Miglena Nikolchina, and others motivate recent engagement with Kristeva, by further examining the context of the 1970s, and situating her in epistemic-ontological and deconstructive, and affective materialisms' approaches to the subject.

The merit of Beardsworth's approach lies in demonstrating that Kristeva is not limited to a philosophy of culture. Its major contribution is that it explains Kristeva's method by situating her in the 1970s context of confrontation with modern nihilism as the "collapse of meaning, value, and authority—in the structures of the psyche" (Beardsworth 2004, 12). Kristeva is concerned that the prevailing institutions and discourses in Western society fail to symbolize the semiotic, which then deprives people of the ability to articulate love, loss, and separatedness. In order to experience values and meaning, there are pre-symbolic psychic structures developed in early infancy, which need to take on and be given symbolic form (this is why she often refers to the semiotic as rooted in "that unconscious 'language' found in children's echolalia before the appearance of signs and syntax" [2010, 81]).

The Evolving Meaning of Ontological Loss: From Revolution to Revolt

In order to evaluate two of the most salient proposals of *Revolution in Poetic Language*, it is important to place the extraordinary ideas of the early work within the context of the fifty years spanning the divide between us and the major advancements of Kristeva's genius, as it came to fruition in the doctoral dissertation. This collection aims to reconceive of the mainstay of impact of the early work through the prism of revolution-revolt. The meaning of ontological revolution is to usher in change, to reject the old and affirm the new. These iterations of change are, in addition, liberatory insofar as they depend on promise of return, what I call liberatory natality.

The main proposal at the heart of the account of time, then, treats liberatory natality as opposed to freedom and, as well, posits that *Revolution in Poetic Language* inaugurates Kristeva's thought on revolution, but also constitutes in the same breath a departure from it. It is well known that shortly after 1974, Kristeva begins a shift that will develop into a systematic withdrawal from the thesis on revolution and as early as 1980 recommence as a thesis more akin to revolt. I use William Watkin's fresh reading of Kristeva's major turn in 1974 as springboard for my introduction, specifically in that it contains, in implicit form, the tripartite temporal schema of revolt, and the bridge of transition to it. It is of interest to briefly reconstruct this reading to establish our starting point. This is because in the first place it provides one of the strongest claims to how there is a logical complementarity between revolution and revolt already in 1974. In the second place, it is of interest, since it ties to what Watkin calls Kristeva's lifelong commitment outright to "feminist revolutions" (Watkin 2003, 98; Lechte 1990, 34–35).

Current contexts in French philosophy, discussions of the material ontology of the coming-to-presence of being in Jean-Luc Nancy (or, the indifference of difference in Alain Badiou); and problematics on revolution in Hannah Arendt (egalitarian modernity and the invisible life of the mind)—constitute a two-party debate that distinguishes between freedom, for Nancy, and revolutionary liberation, for Arendt. Kristeva nurtures affinities with both, and is closer to Arendt. Kristeva, through Freud and Klein, turns up interestingly as mediator between the two conceptions.

In more detail, Watkin argues that around 1987, Kristeva clearly shifts from the original notion of "revolution" from 1974. She is willing to put to work the "potential of natality for undermining subjective certainty," that is, for emancipatory purposes, but like Arendt she is "afraid of living the life of natality/liberation, seeing birth rather as a limited event, a [mere] wiping the slate clean, an opportunity to begin rebuilding the subject once more" (Watkin, 95). In other words, in a world of severed ties between public and private domains, of repressive paternal symbolic law and patriarchal values for Arendt, and for Kristeva, "natality become[s] the precondition for foundation," "foundation as text." Birth serves to build foundation as precondition for it, "in the same way that the [semiotic] mark is the precondition for text," so far as it attacks, divests of subjective certainty, of the egoism of the isolated individual. In *Black Sun*, Kristeva is still quite close to the orientation of the main ideas from 1974, an ontological revolution. The "dead speech" of the melancholic disposition treats rejection analogically to the semiotic mark. "In *Black Sun* dead speech, the more similar it becomes to the revolutionary textual procedures [Kristeva] admires so much in the work of avant-garde writers like Mallarmé and Isidore Ducasse. . . . It is what happens to text when difference is renounced. Melancholic writing; to refuse differentiation" (92).

The question is: what was she shifting away from? Watkin puts it well in two lengthy passages, which I cite in full: "Yet Kristeva, having touched on the truth of the radical loss of significance as an ontological revolution in her early work, then systematically withdraws from it through a redefinition of terms and a re-consideration of the role of heterogeneous materiality. This means that when she returns once more to the issue of revolt in *The Sense and Non-sense of Revolt*, these issues are considered in a very different light" (Watkin, 92). "Freedom, for Nancy, is the foundational truth of the non-founded, that which can never be reduced to simple, basic foundational concepts, and that which will always exceed what has been founded. For Arendt, freedom is the return to a western myth of common origins, for Nancy it is the endless coming into being of events, subjectivity and community, that disallows such a single, common story totally to dominate. With this sophistication of approach to the basic idea of revolution leading to freedom, we can say that Kristeva's first interests were indeed in revolution not what she later calls 'revolt'" (94).

Watkin proposes that the turning point in Kristeva verges on her having arrived at the realization as to "the basic idea of revolution leading to freedom" (94). Contradicting Nancy's radical natality for Kristeva, what matters is that natality, pure and simple, is too weak to sustain opposition granted the unconditionality of freedom. Kristeva is contradicting a full-blown Kantian antinomian idea of groundless ground, a nonfounding concept, "the non-founded," as that which "can never be reduced to simple, basic foundational concepts, and that which will always exceed what has been founded." Like Arendt, Kristeva argues for an "extended thinking," also borrowing from Kant, but in his later period, the third *Critique*, "freedom is the return to a western myth of common origins." For Watkin, in *Revolution in Poetic Language* for Kristeva, text is generated always through the "sudden irruption of materiality into the sign whether from inside or outside the speaking subject" (91). The entire process of text production on this dialectical pattern of irruptive materiality overlaps with the process of putting the subject-on-trial. The semiotically divested subject, divested of its primary narcissistic subjectivity, is so put on trial. In 1974, fully fleshing out this view, Kristeva is forced to confront what it would be to experience revolution as near ontological loss of meaning.

"To deny difference both in what that means for the conservative and the radical, the right and the left, is to deny the condition of life itself. However impossible this might be in reality, this is, surely, the only condition which achieves a state anything like the total liberation from subjectivity that revolutionary and avantgarde practice strives for" (92).

While I need not discuss the Nancy and Arendt debate and the relation to Kristeva any further, for the purposes of this introduction I limit myself to a note. In the conception of 1974, Kristeva touches on the radical loss of significance as an ontological revolution. Suffice it to say, it is around this problematic of ontological revolution but tied to loss, mourning, and recovery in subject formation that Söderbäck's revaluation, through "temporal revolutions" (2012, 319) invites new approaches in recent work—the new productivity of Kristeva's "feminist revolutions."

In more detail, Kristeva's 1967 interview with Derrida in *Positions* (Derrida 1974) is worth revisiting with these ideas in mind. Temporal revolutions, in Söderbäck's interpretation of Kristeva, do not give in on the importance of the symbolic order for revolution. The renewal of meaning in its effectivity may only be revealed in the future, in retrospect. In this sense, the later Kristeva perhaps even more strictly aligns with Derrida's aim in his 1985 "Force of Law" (1992) to reimagine the locus of the unfolding of justice. Justice in its totality, for that matter, is played out on the grounds of the very laws on which foundations are violent (as only law-founding violence is revolutionary in definition), without referring to justice as an outside and exterior concept. Likewise, Kristeva's use of psychoanalysis as "counterdepressant" in 1987 and onward (shifting to subjective revolt), is restricted to necessary repetition, without referring to time as an outside and exterior concept, and retrospectively recollecting, and reconceptualizing the past.

By the 1980s, the benefits of good mental health are too useful for reconceptualizing natality by Kristeva as a practicing psychoanalyst to dismiss. Her interventions for feminist revolutions and regaining "lost" time in the 1980s and 1990s are predominately work from her psychoanalytic practice. Freud's ill-formed fable of *Totem and Taboo*, founding the "cultural/mythical/subjective on the original crime of patricide," as Watkin notes, in Kristeva's much revised unorthodox and feminist direction, is simply an opportunity "too useful to dismiss," "the two acts of murder and consumption of the body" "match the dialectic of the semiotic and the symbolic" (Watkin, 96). These transformations, then, tie Kristeva's systematic withdrawal from the term *revolution* instead to favor a psychoanalytic discourse of revolt, and in concert her withdrawal from a monolithic notion of the semiotic, instead to favor plurality (cf. Chanter & Ziarek 2005; Oliver & Keltner 2009; Hansen & Tuvel 2017).

It is appropriate at this point to briefly introduce the notion of the speaking subject as a site of the consolidation of loss, negativity, and mourning through the model of the Kristevan foundation of "motherhood," which represents object-less love. These only deepen with the theory of a subjectivity in revolt in Kristeva's later development, and this makes fuller sense of the turning point after *Revolution in Poetic Language*. I next outline three argumentation points, accordingly: mimesis; significance [*signifiance*] as historic-social effects since "language only leads to exteriority" (cf. Kristeva 2002, 57); and what this has to do with object-less love—all three help explain the construction of the speaking subject in Kristeva.

Kristeva's argument through mimesis in *Revolution in Poetic Language* is similar to Derrida's work on structural contamination between the metaphysical value of the address of justice as such, on the one hand, and its always singular addressee, non-metaphysical and empirical application, on the other hand. The double bind of *signifiance* in Kristeva's semiotic dimension of language with regard to justice is analogical to contamination, that is, it plays out as mimetic in so far as it is a repetition. As a generality, the law structures as foundation its future possibility as an installment, as a singularity (Derrida 1967; 1974; 1992). The presence of justice, like the presence of other metaphysical entities (such as, e.g., deconstruction or democracy), may only make its way into manifesting within laws by the messianic structure of time, by "withholding" total releasement. Accordingly, *signifiance* for Kristeva reveals that the semiotic dimension of language may only make its way into the symbolic order as the releasing, by the subject, of temporally discontinuous and maternal pre-Oedipal drives. Hence, revolution, the retrieval of "lost" time by *signifiance*—is never fully completed and always to-come (cf. Miller 2014). This temporal openness is retained in the Kristevan revolt.

The second argument concerns the exposure of the sign in language to a "transcendental" dimension of signification in the thetic phase as a fundamentally figurable and transcendental dimension of language—without which we lose the very possibility of language to signify. Söderbäck rightly insists that, unlike an ahistorical orientation in deconstruction, Kristeva's archaeological approach acknowledges a distinction between the *mode* of retrieval, that is, archaeology, and the *object* of retrieval, the *archē* being paradigmatically inscriptive (Söderbäck 2012). Indeed, according to Kristeva, the reintroduction of the previously repressed maternal drives is a break from the previous syntax and inaugurates a new symbolic order.[1]

Only through language and the analysis of its signifiers is Kristeva's archaeological work possible, since lack always reveals itself as such or as such, that is, metaphorically. Representation, for Kristeva, is a second nature within which the psyche lives. The rule of representation holds throughout, since *signifiance* must have a socio-historical function in order to be revolutionary. The socio-historical function of significance may only arise as a break or a breaching within the narcissistic fixations of the psyche, and narcissism is a condition of possibility of *signifiance* itself. Kristeva works with the mother-infant dyad and genesis of narcissism at the boundaries and at margins, since *signifiance* only arises from there. Kristeva strongly defends the necessity of the split, that is, two aspect view, and argues that "only a subject, for whom the thetic is not a repression of the semiotic *chōra* but instead a position either taken on or undergone, can call into question the thetic so that a new disposition may be articulated" (1984, 51). On this point, Söderbäck writes, "what is at stake here is renewal, not absolute destruction. Later in *Revolution in Poetic Language*, she reminds us that while the thetic is 'absolutely necessary,' it is nevertheless 'not exclusive: the semiotic [. . .] constantly tears it open, and this transgression brings about all the various transformations of the signifying practice" (Söderbäck 2011, 86f18).

The third argumentation point is implied by the preceding exposition on breaching representation and narcissism, namely, the two components of the divide or split: the speaking subject is founded on negativity; this implies the role of liberatory natality in later Kristeva, and the centrality of feminist revolutions. She posits via Klein that in the early state of infancy, the child directs all their desires onto the mother's body, experiencing both pleasure and suffering. Yet, the child, in this state, does not distinguish between self and mother—there is no identity yet. Only when the child experiences the mother directing desire elsewhere do they identify with the "object." Mother's erotic desire points to an elsewhere, a third term (the Freudian imaginary Father of individual pre-history, see *Tales of Love*) that inaugurates the entrance into language, which is a positing of position or identity. Thus, primary narcissism is a drama that relies on a third term to establish an identity that allows one to construct a productive relationship with otherness. As adults, object-less love is always with a bit of a distance, a little nostalgic, a little sad; it inaugurates that we cannot access the pre-Oedipal space to negotiate this structure or feel the states, so we must return to it, reimagine it, and reconstruct so as to produce something like those states in adulthood.

Division into Chapters

The volume is comprised of three parts, in which the contributors engage with the legacy of Kristeva's ideas from the doctoral dissertation and onward, but the center of each essay organizes its starting point from out of *Revolution in Poetic Language*. What further distinguishes this collection is that the first part offers two texts from Kristeva, here first published in English.

The first text in division one is Kristeva's article from 1988, "*L'impossibilité de perdre*," translated by Elisabeth Paquette. This concentrated text, presented at a conference, comes with a ten-page lengthy question-and-answer period following the talk, in which the reader will find a wealth of technical terminology made accessible. Importantly, this brief talk given just a year following her main publication on melancholia and the depressive position from *Black Sun*, underlines Kristeva's affinity with and transformation of Freud's psychoanalysis; her divergence from Lacan (especially on sublimation); and her agreement, and as well disagreement, with Klein (in theorizing separation and the earliest mother-infant dynamics of psychic life). Since this collection aims at situating the contribution from the early work in Kristeva's overall intellectual trajectory, and more specifically, attends to her shift to the intimacy of a subjectivity in revolt around the 1990s, this text from 1988 is crucial as it represents a watershed point.

Kristeva's second text, "Of What Use Are Poets in Times of Distress?," is an address from 2016, co-translated by Elisabeth Paquette and Alice Jardine. The title of this address is the question to which Kristeva, along with other invited philosophers, filmmakers, historians, and writers responds, as part of the colloquium on November 7, 2016, at the Colline National Theater, as part of the movement "*Fraternité génerale!*" [Fraternity for All!]. The colloquium was organized by the French Ministry of Culture and Communications, commemorating the first anniversary of the arrival of the Syrian immigrant wave in 2015. Both these newly translated texts are discussed in more detail, outlining their significance, in the editor's introduction to part 1.

The second part offers a perspective on the work from 1974 by a fresh engagement emphasizing the proximity of de-centered subjects: the poetic subject aligns with maternal ethics, disability, decolonial subjects, including nonbinary and transgender subjectivity. Kristeva's *polis*, in the most recent development of a more complex New Humanism, translates the political dimension of revolution into a politics of intimate revolt. Today's geopolitical crisis puts pressure on recalibrating the psychoanalytic aspect and whether its semiotic process is delimited within the individual psyche, or even nation's psyche, or Europe, and evidently new vantage points take on some critical and unresolved problematics, as well.

Kelly Oliver's essay offers an energetic and passionate involvement with Kristeva. She traces Kristeva's evolving discussion of the maternal in relation to ethics, and breaks new ground by showing how an ethics of tenderness in Kristeva grows out of her engagement with disability and her exchange with Jean Vanier, founder of *L'Arche*. From Kristeva's early suggestions of an *herethics* of love and into more recent discussions of democracy of proximity, as Oliver argues, the maternal ethics of tenderness revolves around complex affective connections, which are always ambivalent and requiring critical interpretation. By emphasizing Kristeva's call for attending to ambivalence-ambiguity, Oliver proposes that Kristeva posits this critical love as the basis of an ethics of tenderness, which goes beyond care or ethics of care, and goes to what Oliver describes, is an ethics of *being with*.

Sid Hansen corrects two popular 1990s misunderstandings, by Judith Butler (who situated Kristeva along with a similar misunderstanding of Foucault's *Barbin*), and then by Nancy Fraser—both of which isolate a blank slate concept of sex as opposed to gender as the social construction discursively performative of it. It is a misunderstanding to treat Kristeva's interaction between semiotic and symbolic developed in the *Revolution in Poetic Language* (and similarly Foucault), as leaving out the body as signifiable, as if it were situated outside of the socio-historic and therefore bearing no implications for the political. In emphasizing the socio-historic embeddedness of the signifiable body, Hansen appreciates Kristeva's theory of abjection as a useful resource in transgender studies. However, Hansen wishes to know if Kristeva might be open to repositioning trans studies from out of an intersectional perspective. The socio-historic and symbolic context of the oppression of trans youth and trans bodies does not exist in a vacuum but is the development of a bio-necropolitical capitalism, as we blatantly witness in the United States. Disturbed by

Kristeva's position as reported in 2016, regarding the "fabrication of gender by overly sympathetic gynecologists and endocrinologists," Hansen adopts Sheila Cavanaugh, questioning whether the transgender body also for Kristeva might "hang in midair as well." If so, as Hansen argues, what of heterogeneity, the embodied poetic experience of trans people searching for "possible new identities and new ways of talking about ourselves"? Hansen turns to Gill-Peterson to argue that in the United States during the 1940s and 1950s, it was increasingly possible that human life "might not be binary, that intersex and trans embodiment were but two facets of life's natural variation." On these grounds, Hansen invites Kristeva to an open dialogue as they write: "The universalization of this understanding of sex and gender worked to marginalize those patients whose dysphoria or gender performance did not cohere with dominant understandings, especially patients of color whose gender identity expression is often perceived as non-normative."

Fanny Söderbäck explores the long-standing theme of the stranger in Kristeva in a new key, to test pressure points in its political dimensions today. She argues that staging a dialogue between the poetic subject and the rapidly changing global South perspective, including Latinx feminisms, might detect a potential Eurocentric bias in Kristeva's notion of heterogeneity. In *Revolution in Poetic Language*, Kristeva introduced several concepts centering on heterogeneity, which she later equated to an internal foreignness or strangeness. The rapport between Kristeva and Gloria Anzaldúa is, as of now, unexamined in the secondary literature. Yet, Kristeva's model of subjectivity as opaque and internally divided allows for thinking in parallel with Anzaldúa, in her defense of the ambivalent-ambiguous, in a new consciousness refusing boundaries-as-separation, and in insisting instead on the Borderland as an opening. The subject-in-process, on the one hand, and the shadow beast, the new mestiza, the *nepantla*, on the other hand, both refuse stability, universality, and homogeneity. However, situatedness matters, for Kristeva and Anzaldúa are differently situated. In this staged encounter, Sara Ahmed's nod that strangeness is in fact unevenly historically politically distributed can help transform this dialogue, especially because Kristeva remains an important interlocutor.

Elisabeth Paquette examines the strength of the poetic within theories of resistance, with Julia Kristeva and Sylvia Wynter at the center. Both engage in common projects, in part evidenced by Wynter's various references to Kristeva. But Wynter's decolonial project at times strains or disrupts the limits of Kristeva's work. The political implications of their respective articulations of the *operation* of poetry and the poetic take on a mode of being for the purpose of revolution. This allows a nuanced focus on the extent to which Kristeva's theory of poetic revolution can be useful for decolonial theory. The chapter argues that Wynter's engagement with Frantz Fanon's conception of sociogeny, which serves as a critique of psychoanalysis and the writings of Sigmund Freud, can be extended to Kristeva's project. This keenly brings Kristeva's project into conversation with the writings of Wynter and Fanon, as invitation or intervention.

The concluding fifth chapter, by Elaine Miller, brings into dialogue *Proust among the Nations*, Jacqueline Rose's book of 2011 and Kristeva. For Rose, Proust's discussion of the late-nineteenth-century "Dreyfus Affair" frames her own analysis of the legacy of the Israeli-Palestinian conflict. Kristeva, though, whose pioneering work on Proust has influenced Rose, only focuses on the individual dimension of this kind of history. Both Rose and Kristeva are well aware of the danger of the equivocation between psyche and *polis*, and see it as a common problem of both individuals and nation-states. In addition, both recognize that art has the capacity to impel humans to take responsibility for personal and political trauma. However, whereas Kristeva believes this project must be undertaken on a one-on-one basis that resembles the psychoanalytic session, Rose argues that countenancing the entire historical and political context of trauma can and must form part of the "treatment." Rose prioritizes structural violence, including the pressing contemporary crisis of Palestine-Israel that needs to be addressed, and to which psychoanalytic insights can be productively applied. By contrast, since 2015, Kristeva is concerned with Islamic activism and terrorism in France, a crisis she attributes to globalism, and a "need to believe" rather than to any historical-political context out of which it emerges. Miller concludes that Kristeva's *Revolution in Poetic Language* held much more promise as a political analysis than her current efforts at addressing Islamic fundamentalism in France.

The third part of this volume brings into perspective the context in which the semiotic and the symbolic in the 1970s, position Kristeva as a revolutionary of her own right. This division gives a comprehensive discussion of the evolving meaning of the turn from revolution to "intimate" revolt, by more closely assessing the theoretical achievements proper of the text from 1974. Here the meaning of revolution as involving ontological loss and as well the negativity of the speaking subject both serve to focus on the formidable accomplishments that the doctoral work represents. The opening chapter takes up Kristeva's ideas prior to 1974, and through the prism of the Eastern European sociohistorical and intellectual scene these are brought to focus. The second chapter discusses Kristeva's indebtedness to both Lacan and Sartre, through a specific angle, in how it prepared Kristeva's turn from revolution to revolt. The third, fourth, and fifth chapters theorize predominantly the concept of rejection/negativity, what Kristeva calls Hegel's fourth negation. These chapters bring to focus the work on revolution and the systematic shifting away from a monolith semiotic in order to take up the challenge that becomes Kristeva's own point of reinvention, involving liberatory natality, and conditions of plurality, the *polis* and action.

Miglena Nikolchina gives a logical and chronological account of the swift turns prior to 1974, of several major terms in giving a roadmap from *praxis* to *chōra*. Between the essays collected in *Semēiotike* (1969) and the magnum opus *Revolution in Poetic Language*, some of Kristeva's earliest concepts undergo considerable transformations. One remarkable makeover involves the subsumption of the concepts of *nombre* and *nombrant* by Kristeva's 1974 influential conceptualization of the semiotic and the *chōra*. While both pairs of concepts explore the continuous making and unmaking of the subject that she terms *signifiance*, the reasoning behind this subsumption is to address the "filter of (in)humanization" inflecting the passage from the mathematical infinity of all possible combinations to the infinite generation in artistic production as the true *praxis* of social change. The shift from *nombre/nombrant* to semiotic/*chōra* is revealed as subtended by another conceptual transformation: Kristeva's rethinking of the Marxian term *praxis* at a time when it is contested by thinkers like Lucien Goldmann, Jean-Paul Sartre, Louis Althusser, the Frankfurt School, the Yugoslav "Praxis" group of philosophers, and so on. The coupling of praxis (practice, *pratique*) with *signifiance*, which will ultimately take Kristeva to the *chōra* and to her theory of the feminine, is thus seen as indicative of the profoundly altered and yet irreducible imprint of Marx on Kristeva's work.

Surti Singh returns to the short but crucial chapter devoted to Lacan's theory of the mirror stage and castration in *Revolution and Poetic Language*, with the aim of tracing its impact on the later work. Kristeva here develops a view of subject formation that evolved in an enduring, methodological concern, particularly in her 1990s discussion of the fate of the imaginary in the "society of the spectacle." Kristeva, at that point, turns to Sartre in *Intimate Revolt* through analysis of the imaginary, but as Singh argues, the move traces to 1974. In Sartre's conception of the imaginary,

Kristeva remarkably finds avenues for resistance to the society of the spectacle, which were unavailable through the purely Lacanian schema. In other words, she posits Lacan's and Sartre's works to be complementary. Kristeva's connecting through 1974 to Sartre's phenomenology, against the backdrop of Lacanian psychoanalysis, allows her to present a view of the imaginary in the society of the spectacle that demonstrates its connection to both repression and resistance.

John Montani offers an original study of rhythm in Kristeva's *Revolution in Poetic Language* and less centrally, *Desire in Language*. He argues, first, that rhythm is what traverses the boundary between the semiotic and the symbolic, and he defends the essential role that rhythm plays in the process Kristeva calls transposition. Kristeva's argument underscores that, far from being a metalinguistic notion, rhythm is instead a practice. In operating as a practice, it helps organize instinctual drives within the signifying process and transpose significations. Second, rhythm is the clue to Kristeva's understanding of "text" or writing as practice, for it provides a structural account of her notion of "semiotic rhythm," from both a phenomenological and a psychoanalytic perspective. Furthermore, rhythm and the semiotic are, then, integral not just to practices of experimental art and poetry, but to philosophical thinking as well. These three arguments retrieve and clarify the often-neglected role of rhythm in Kristeva as crucial for substantiating the notion of the semiotic.

Emilia Angelova posits that in *Revolution in Poetic Language*, Kristeva's philosophy of time depends on affirming the importance of language as a symbolic order. Following psychoanalysis, only through metaphorical processes is it possible that the subject accepts its position in language as a fundamental lack. For Kristeva, in order for the semiotic to make its way to interaction with the symbolic, the very structure of subject formation, or what she calls the subject-in-process, depends on a receding of *alethēia* as truth or justice structured as a metaphorical concept. Specifically, the recession is premised on the withdrawal, withholding, dispersal of lost or "just" time. Regaining "lost" time is a promise of a possibility, which may not outstrip the gap between a metaphysical concept of time and justice, and its a priori presupposition, on the one hand; and the analysis of symbolic law, one step at a time, structuring the world of a phenomenologically constituted intersubjectivity, on the other hand. Furthermore, following Klein, Kristeva proposes that fear of collapse of a phenomenologically constituted subjectivity is "experienced" as anxiety of persecution, and it manifests as that which ruptures the beautiful at its limits, analogous to the model of foundational violence done to the imagination. Finally, this capacity for experience of form, "in advance" of time taking on linguistic form, assumes the shape of releasement of semiotic internal tension, and in this way, through embodied appropriation, points to "other times" inherent in the radically finite time of a "future past," a futurity yet-to-come. This examines how, on these premises about time and language, Kristeva already connects the semiotic-symbolic with the pre-Oedipal abject-object.

Anne O'Byrne turns to Kristeva's encounter with Arendt. At the conclusion of her book on Hannah Arendt, Kristeva notes that, for Arendt, "language cannot go mad." Language and humanity are Arendt's version of Being, and when asked in later years what remained for her of pre-Holocaust Germany, she famously replied that the language remained, adding: "It was not the German language that went crazy." Kristeva finds here a remarkable and unjustified faith in language as it conditions the subject and constitutes the bonds that tie the subject to its shared community. After all, was this not a case where a language that tied Arendt to a specific community, the *sensus communis* of a people, *did* go mad? If this is the case, what follows? This chapter offers a rereading of the operation of *sensus communis* in and as language, not only language as such but also the historical and communal experience of mother tongue. When Arendt takes on Kant's aesthetic notion of enlarged mentality as the basis for political community, she asks us both to understand it as the transcendental exercise of thinking from the point of view of all possible others, and to practice it as the worldly exercise of thinking from the point of view of particular others. Taken together, these are perplexing requirements of different orders. Kristeva's semiotics in *Revolution in Poetic Language* does not clear up the perplexity, but it does lead us deeper into the problem and make us rethink the stakes by shifting focus from subjects and their positions to the mobility and *poiesis* of language.

Notes

1. For further details, see Kristeva 1984, 63–64.

References

Beardsworth, Sara. 2004. *Julia Kristeva: Psychoanalysis and Modernity*. Albany: State University of New York Press.

———. 2020. *The Philosophy of Julia Kristeva*. Edited by Sara Beardsworth. Chicago, IL: Library of Living Philosophers.

Chanter, Tina, and Ziarek, Ewa Płonowska, eds. 2005. *Revolt, Affect, Collectivity: The Unstable Boundaries of Kristeva's Polis*. Albany: State University of New York Press.

Derrida, Jacques. 1967. *De la grammatologie*. Paris: Les Éditions de Minuit.

———. 1974. "Sémiologie et Grammatologie: Entretien avec Julia Kristeva," in *Positions*. Paris: Les Éditions de Minuit.

———. 1992. "Force of Law: The 'Mystical Foundation of Authority.'" In *Deconstruction and the Possibility of Justice*, edited by Drucilla Cornell, Michel Rosenfeld, and David G. Carlson, 3–67. New York: Routledge.

Hansen, S. K. 2020. "Intimate Revolt at the Margins of Community and the Hope of Postcoloniality." In *The Philosophy of Julia Kristeva*, edited by Sara Beardsworth, 573–89. Chicago, IL: Library of Living Philosophers.

Hansen, S. K., and Tuvel, R., eds. 2017. *New Forms of Revolt: Essays on Kristeva's Intimate Politics*. Albany: State University of New York Press.

Jardine, Alice. 2020. *At the Risk of Thinking: An Intellectual Biography of Julia Kristeva*. Edited by Mari Ruti. New York: Bloomsbury Publishing.

Kristeva, Julia. (1974) 1984. *Revolution in Poetic Language*. Translated by Margaret Waller. New York: Columbia University Press.

———. (1980) 1982. *Powers of Horror: An Essay on Abjection*. Translated by Leon S. Roudiez. New York: Columbia University Press.

———. (1979). "Women's Time" (translated by Alice Jardine and Harry Blake). *Signs: Journal of Women in Culture and Society* 7, no. 11: 13–35.

———. (1987) 1989. *Black Sun: Depression and Melancholy*. Translated by Leon S. Roudiez. New York: Columbia University Press.

———. (1996) 1998. *Time and Sense: Proust and the Experience of Literature*. Translated by Ross Guberman. New York: Columbia University Press.

———. (1996) 2001. *The Sense and Non-sense of Revolt*. Translated by Jeanine Herman. New York: Columbia University Press.

———. (1997) 2002. *Intimate Revolt: The Powers and Limits of Psychoanalysis*. Translated by Jeanine Herman. New York: Columbia University Press.

———. (2005) 2010. *Hatred and Forgiveness*. Translated by Jeanine Herman. New York: Columbia University Press.

———. (2012) 2014. "New Forms of Revolt." *Journal of French and Francophone Philosophy* 22, no. 2: 1–19.

Lacan, Jacques. (1949) 1977. "The Mirror Stage as Formative of the Function of the I," in *Écrits*, translated by Alan Sheridan, 1–8. New York: Norton.

Lechte, John. 1990. "Art, Love, and Melancholy in the Work of Julia Kristeva." In *Abjection, Melancholia and Love*, edited by John Fletcher and Andrew Benjamin. London: Routledge.

McAfee, Noëlle. 2005. "Bearing Witness in the *Polis*: Kristeva, Arendt and the Space of Appearance." In *Revolt, Affect, Collectivity: The Unstable Boundaries of Kristeva's Polis*, edited by Tina Chanter and Ewa Płonowska Ziarek, 113–27. Albany: State University of New York Press.

———. 2020. "Kristeva's Latent Political Theory." In *The Philosophy of Julia Kristeva*, edited by Sara Beardsworth, 753–69. Chicago, IL: Library of Living Philosophers.

Miller, Elaine P. 2014. *Head Cases: Julia Kristeva on Philosophy and Art in Depressed Times*. New York: Columbia University Press.

Oliver, Kelly. 1997. *The Portable Kristeva*. New York: Columbia University Press.

———. 2009. "Meaning against Death." In *Psychoanalysis, Aesthetics, and Politics in the Work of Julia Kristeva*, edited by Kelly Oliver and S. K. Keltner, 49–65. Albany: State University of New York Press.

———. 2020. "The Democracy of Proximity and Kristeva's New Humanism." In *The Library of Living Philosophers, Volume XXXVI: The Philosophy of Julia Kristeva*, edited by Sara Beardsworth, 769–85. Chicago, IL: Library of Living Philosophers.

Sjöholm, Cecilia. 2005. *Kristeva and the Political*. New York: Routledge.

———. 2020. "From Denial to Forgiveness: Kristeva, Arendt, Radicalization." In *The Library of Living Philosophers, Volume XXXVI: The Philosophy of Julia Kristeva*, edited by Sara Beardsworth, 719–35. Chicago, IL: Library of Living Philosophers.

Söderbäck, Fanny. 2011. "Motherhood According to Kristeva: On Time and Matter in Plato and Kristeva." *PhiloSOPHIA* 1, no. 1: 65–87.

———. 2012. "Revolutionary Time: Revolt as Temporal Return." *Signs: Journal of Women in Culture and Society* 37, no. 2: 301–24.

———. 2014. "Timely Revolutions: On the Timelessness of the Unconscious." *Journal of French and Francophone Philosophy* 21, no. 2: 46–55.

———. 2019. *Revolutionary Time: On Time and Difference in Kristeva and Irigaray*. Albany: State University of New York Press.

Watkin, William. 2003. "Melancholia, Revolution and Materiality in the Work of Julia Kristeva." *Paragraph*: 86–107.

Ziarek, Ewa Płonowska. 2005. "Kristeva and Fanon: Revolutionary Violence and Ironic Articulation." In *Revolt, Affect, Collectivity: The Unstable Boundaries of Kristeva's Polis*, edited by Tina Chanter and Ewa Płonowska Ziarek, 57–77. Albany: State University of New York Press.

———. 2020. "A Materialist Ethics of Psychoanalysis? Reflections on Matter, Forgiveness, and Vulnerability." In *The Library of Living Philosophers, Volume XXXVI: The Philosophy of Julia Kristeva*, edited by Sara Beardsworth, 735–53. Chicago, IL: Library of Living Philosophers.

Part One

Two New Texts by Kristeva

Chapter 1

Editor's Introduction to Julia Kristeva's "The Impossibility of Loss" (1988)

Emilia Angelova

In the concluding parts in division four of *Revolution in Poetic Language*, Kristeva incessantly returns to the productivity of language and that it is generative, a heterogeneous production. How do we reconnect liberatory natality, the conditions of being singular and the plurality of the human condition, in Arendt—with Kristeva's own borrowing of resources from Klein? Kristeva's trilogy on Arendt, Klein, and Colette appeared separately within three years in the 2000s. The early work prepares Kristeva for a shift, in the late 1980s and the 1990s, to focus on the subjectivity of intimate revolt and the politics of time. Linguistic negativity leads her to develop a construction of the speaking subject as premised on the theory of sublimation, she posits that in the analytic session it is possible to work through psychic violence and make room for "new things," and "new beginnings."

This text from 1988 puts forth a main argument about the "impossibility" of mourning archaic loss. It builds on a thesis about the depressive position, part of Kristeva's illustrations of feminine depression more fully developed within 1987. The text is very close to multiple dispersed sections in *Black Sun* (1987), but it deserves mention that several dense endnotes from this book make their way into this paper. The paper quickly restates a dense philosophical problematic on the classic definition of melancholia from the fifteenth and sixteenth centuries of central interest in *Black Sun*. The paper departs from the relationship philosophers have maintained with melancholia, for it simultaneously makes a case for revising and reformulating Kristeva's own position, which she distinguishes from classic melancholia. As is evident, the paper stirred up significant discussion, here translated in full, which is especially helpful for clarifying terminological notions. The discussion uses accessible language to draw connections, for example, between Sartre and Kristeva, and shows how daringly Kristeva intended for her semiotic theory of a "revolution in language" to become the dangerous supplement overthrowing an outdated cis-normative European classic psychoanalysis. Kristeva's paper, together with the discussion presented at a psychoanalytic conference in Lyon, was included in the proceedings specifically on real *versus* psychic trauma, published in a special journal issue dedicated to it.

In the first place, the paper is unique theoretically—on the question of sublimation Kristeva states in robust terms her most important difference from Lacan. This alone suffices to justify this worthwhile translation by Elisabeth Paquette. This excellent translation, additionally, takes on several important modifications of terms, different than the ones in Leon Roudiez. Kristeva's text provides a valuable terminologically succinct formulation of the argument in a nutshell from *Black Sun*. The paper opens with a *tour de force* entry, bringing together into one cluster the triad of Kant, Heidegger (via Arendt), and Freud, and directly links this onto Kristeva's own term, psychic trauma. Taken together, in 1988, time and temporality, and psychic trauma, form a new complex, a notable advancement in Kristeva's own development. This novel center, psychic trauma, provides a precious glimpse into nascent ideas looking forward to the "timeless" unconscious, negativity tracking the evolution of her theory of meaning and the symbol, and anticipating the work on the intimacy of revolt in the 1990s—notable on these pages is the absence only of Proust.

The brief introduction below mainly intends to clarify in a preliminary way the difference from Lacan regarding the concept of sublimation, which Kristeva links to her 1980 theory of abjection of the archaic maternal. I will introduce three themes guiding Kristeva in that moment: a distancing from Lacan; a distancing from Freud; and a distancing from Klein.

The first central contribution, found in 1988, is Kristeva's distancing from Lacan on the theory of sublimation. This began in 1974, as a distancing on the process of subject formation as premised on the mirror stage (Lacan 1977) and Lacan's notion of discourse functioning as metalanguage. Sublimation is part of the logic of transference love, and what Kristeva will gradually next begin to develop into the notion of forgiveness and meaning as its horizon. Drawing on *Intimate Revolt*, transference love does not simply take support from preverbal significances: these allow complex and intraverbal experiences "to be brought to the other"; "they help in forgiving, in transferring," giving pardon (2002, 19). The most notable piece of her notion of sublimation is that its logic takes on a process and that it leads to transference, which is like forgiveness, and is not given by another. She writes: "Remission and rebirth are . . . acquired through the putting into words of the unconscious; they are acquired by giving conscious and unconscious meaning to what did not have any, for it is precisely this absence of meaning that was experienced as ill-being. Forgiveness is not given by another" (18–19). Thus, paradoxically, "one forgives oneself with the help of another (the analyst), by relying on his or her interpretation and on his or her silence (and on his or her love), in order to make sense of the troubling senselessness" (19). Intimate revolt abides by a logic of wanting to "return" that is tied to an impossibility of doing so, to a threat of annihilation.

We now can glean into why the idea of sublimation leads the transformation and makes for this crucial contribution. In "*L'Impossibilité de perdre*," Kristeva distances herself from Lacan and his view of sublimation, specifically through engaging psychic trauma (as opposed to real trauma). She articulates her view of traumatism in relation to the archaic maternal: "In commenting on the notion of [the thing] *das Ding* in Freud's *Entwurf*, Lacan claims that however withdrawn the Freudian Thing may be from judging consciousness, it is always already given in the presence of language." Kristeva tells us that affect is anterior to, and subtending language, that it is generative of *signifiance* and yet cannot be signified in language. How do we conceptualize affect via the return of the maternal semiotic repressed in literature and the arts (as the early work established), and which becomes the maternal archaic repressed? This is necessarily predicated on the major gains made by Kristeva's essay on abjection. Below, I dwell for a moment on the contributions from abjection.

The work in 1980 *Powers of Horror* provides the major theory explaining this connection between semiotic excess over signification or affect, and the maternal archaic repressed. The power of language is its capacity for generative labor, primarily understood as a mode of the production of meaning in language while relating to an "outside." The very force of conditionality of "binary logic" is anterior to the symbolic, predicated on linguistic imagination's capacity for "revolt," and yet, as Kristeva argues, in no sense preexists it—this force is "not that of *linguistic* signs nor of the *symbolic* order that these signs found" (1982, 72). The Freudian paternal metaphor is that source relating the verbal to the real or the outside, hence it is power, embedded in structures, culturally and socio-historically symbolic. And yet, on Kristeva's bold construal, it is the conditionality of the force of the semiotic or the primal mapping of the body as itself older than paternal law, which is secondary to it. "While being the precondition of language, [the maternal semiotic] is dependent upon meaning," and yet it is a dependency on the maternal body as trustee—which is "distinguished from paternal laws" (72).

The major achievement of the writing on abjection in 1980 is Kristeva's position concerning the illegitimate, human-derived foreclosure of mourning maternal loss. Loss and the impossibility to lose/mourn the maternal archaic is explained by appeal to conditions of socially imposed abjection. (70) Kristeva speaks of abjection as what takes shape owing to a subjective benefit derived from it on the level of libidinal economy. Additionally, within these laws, however, this becomes the "royal way" to progress in history—that is, "with the phallic phase and acquisition of language, the destiny of man will take shape" (72). On these very premises, working-through the loss of the repressed archaic maternal is impossible: "Through frustrations and prohibitions, this [semiotic] authority shapes the body into a *territory*, having areas, orifices, points and lines, surfaces and hollows, where the archaic power of mastery and neglect, of the differentiation of proper-clean and improper-dirty, possible and impossible, is impressed and exerted. . . . Maternal [semiotic] authority is the trustee of that mapping of the self's clean and proper body; it is distinguished from paternal laws" (72). We can generalize the conclusion from the essay on abjection as introducing the mainstay of psychoanalytic insight in Kristeva's work on trauma, what will become known by the end of the 1980s under the heading "illustrations of feminine depression."

The main point from the essay on abjection, its "horror" in "dual war," is that a dual *semiotic authority* carries negative signifying power for it presides over a mapping of the maternal body and that of the future subject. Without this transgressive and even regressive yet durational, timeless presiding authority, the symbolic "exclusionary prohibition" constitutive of collective existence would not have sufficient strength over the "binary logic" of either/or negations. The exclusionary value of the symbol would not have sufficient strength "to dam up the abject or demoniacal potential of the feminine" (65).

In other words, setting up a separation, as language—like culture—does, implies that suppressing this insufficiency of strength is dependent on an archaic repressed; and, above all, the authorization of a fiction, illusion, of the return of the maternal archaic repressed. "Such an archaic relationship to the *object* interprets, as it were, the relationship to the *mother*" as an unnamable maternal (64). And in some societies, Kristeva notes, the "abject" points to attributes of women, to matrilineal or related filiation, or endogamy.

Kristeva's psychoanalytic work since 1980 remains focused on this semiotic-symbolic tension, and it takes the form of the abject as the archaic maternal. Abjection, operating in retroaction on the archaic maternal (as indicated in her discussion of act and inscription in the anthropological context), and playing out in bodies and on the couch (as in her analysis of Little Hans and Narcissus), is, for Kristeva, what sustains and drives psychic life. Yet, as she goes on to claim, that which sustains psychic life (abjection) simultaneously also always threatens to explode the symbolic from within, shattering it. Imploding within the symbolic are the breaching efforts to separate from and master the semiotic. This shattering is central throughout and into the 1990s Kristeva's concept of intimate revolt. Affect as oppositional force, as a capability of psychic or semiotic retroaction, by the 1990s is the port through which traumatism enters, breaching the symbolic.

In 1988, Kristeva focuses on the "infantile event" as structural precondition of trauma, and she contrasts this to Lacan's view of the subversion of the subject—specifically in the structure of "subject/other." This is, as Kristeva argues, reviving the point of the "original unknown" of the origin of so-called trauma: "*ce n'est pas un événement originaire, mais un second, réactivant le premier, qui constitue de cet 'inconnu originaire' un trauma*" (30, in the French).

Trauma reel and *trauma psychique* is the central feature of this claim. For Freud (and Lacan), the death instinct or drive, much like was established in 1927 in Heidegger's being-for-death (cf. Kristeva in *Black Sun*), introduces the "I" to the vital necessity of embarking on an existential choice, individuation as subject, living in the world with others. This implies affirming the law of the socio-historic symbolic order and subordination to its consequences—as a speaking being, the capacity to live an independent life with others depends on the ability to renounce difference yet refuse a differentiation from the perceived and real object of one's being a whole; a connectedness with being having-been. At the foundation of the productivity of symbolic equations, Kristeva will place the story of the fourth negation, *rejete*, as productive rejection, and the cooperation of symbolic, semiotic, and thetic.

Below, I situate in a bit more detail the second main theme, Kristeva distancing her concept of trauma from Freud. The notion of trauma in Freud (and Lacan's mirror stage) refers to the (return of) irrepressible psychic trauma. For 1920 Freud, the beyond in *Beyond the Pleasure Principle* as origin and ground of repetition-compulsion, which is the Oedipal model of the ego based in a neurosis, is tied with a constitutive trauma. Trauma is defined as "any excitations from outside which are powerful enough to break through the protective shield [of the interior]" (1961, 31). Trauma thus functions as a "breach in an otherwise efficacious barrier against stimuli," which thus suspends the function and mastery of the pleasure principle (33). The pleasure principle, then, no longer holds its position of primacy—its unbounded cathexes are, thanks to the arrival of the sign, punctured, barred, negated. The death instinct, a latecomer and akin to Nietzsche's model of the slave morality and imagined as a temporally ontic individual, is set as a response to breaching stimuli powerful enough to break through. By virtue of resisting and then, in consequence, producing bounded cathexes, and protecting, paradoxically, what emerged in effect as a second field force stands to gain mastery, the model of the Oedipal ego (bounded energy) as mastery of the reality principle is that which gives the psyche the very possibility of persisting.

We could venture that the individual principle on which the death drive is based, in Freud, remains ontic. This changes in Kristeva via Lacan—through dependency on Heidegger (the theory of anguish, mood, in *Being and Time*)—it deepens into epochal discordance, the "crossing out" of Being, a negativity presenting as historicity, ontic-ontological thinking. The matter of negation concerns the propriation of the signifier of the *Temporalität* of Being, a negativity as a principle whose displacement and substitution promotes that language has a history based of a philosophical anthropology of conscience and values, and as well culture's rise and fall in decline, the affirmation that ontological Being is not a being.

In Freud, as a negative drive force, the death instinct (as not biological) invests efforts to reduce psychic tension through the dual function of both release and inertial self-preservation, in attempts to lower tensions in and of the psychic system in the process of somatization. The binding-unbinding dual function of both release and inertia leads Kristeva to her "energy" reference in *Black Sun* (1989, 45). In her comments on negation and denial and its symptoms in causing a neurosis (e.g., in repudiation) in Freud's *Verneinung* (1926), in similar fashion approaching trauma, she however distinguishes that the mental life of the ego (1989, cf. 10, 25–27, 40–50), is a *Bejahung*. Indeed, in Freud the "dominating tendency of mental life [. . .] is the effort to reduce, to keep constant or to remove internal tension due to stimuli" (1961, 37). In Freud (and Lacan), the death drive in this binding-unbinding-rebinding function demonstrates an *increase* in psychic tension encountered in the repetitions of traumatic stimuli. Thus, the death instinct understood as a response to trauma generates an *increase* in psychic tension, establishing the link between (unbound) repetition and (bound) Ego cathexes in traumatic neuroses.

That is, in contrast, Kristeva is drawn to Freud's hint at the *Bejahung*, affirmation (as part of the symbol, labor of negation, *Aufhebung*). She suggests that the destroyal of the maternal bond of mother-infant from the earliest stage of psychic life has the right to serve as precondition anterior to subject formation as Oedipal. Through the positionality of the Kleinian mother-infant dyad she implies the possibility of an assumption of identity prior to, and on the preservation of whose remainder, *reste*, trace, depends the installment of the subject at the roots of the Oedipal stage.

In the last section of this introduction, we look at the theme of how while distancing herself as well from Klein, Kristeva nonetheless aligns most closely with her. How does Kristeva enlarge to the social (comparable to Arendt's enlarged thinking, 1961) Freud's theory of the death drive? Kristeva sets her theory apart from Freud in 1988—"I propose to speak" of older-time, archaic attachments to the libido, recounting Freud's 1915–1917 lectures of "the infantile event." The emphasis lies on reactivating the impact of breaching, stimuli external or internal. This is to say, reactivating return introduces an additional premise to Freud. On this retrieval of an earlier experience of splitting in the interior life of psyche, functioning like a counterturning truth, a quickening, the withdrawal of a time unavailable for mourning and healing, Kristeva builds the theoretical construction of the speaking subject. The negativity of the speaking subject, as she puts it in *Black Sun* (42–43, 48), as based on the possibility of sublimation (but not Freud and Lacan) via the semiotic-symbolic-thetic, enters via Klein's pre-Oedipal dynamic.

Kristeva accepts from Freud and Lacan the death drive as introducing in the symbolic the "negativity" of repetition and its origin situated in the psychic life of the individual. Repetition is traumatic, and in 1974 Kristeva demonstrates this: it "constitutes the logical impetus beneath the thesis of negation and that of the negation of negation, but is identical to neither since it is, instead, the logical functioning of the movement that produces the theses" (1984, 109). It is "the liquefying and dissolving agent that does not destroy but rather reactivates new organizations and, in that sense, affirms" (109). In *Black Sun*, Kristeva revisits *Bejahung* as she draws from Segal, Klein, Green, and Edith Jacobson. "Not nothing, but symbolic equivalents" (1989, 23).

This stress on *psychique* versus *reel* enforces the (im)possible mourning of loss; Kristeva activates a plea for proper burial rights denied to the feminine: the "unburied" and "undead mother," as in 1988 she further pursues what she formulates with Ferenczi and the maternal bond in *Black Sun*. Similarly, in 1997, in the essay on Freud titled the "Scandal of the Timeless," the "scandal" leads her to argue that the right to love/sublimation is premised on the complex of "perversion of the mother-child link." She writes that "there is necessary repetition," but "beyond that, I emphasize its potential for making gaps, rupturing, renewing," a meaningful retrospection, revolt (2002, 85).

Thus, in short, in 1988, "reactivating" pertains to opening deeper into the organizational negativity, which is a necessary structural condition of and for the psyche and its relation to the ecosystem of the outer world, and to the alterity of the o/Other. Klein locates this sense of relatedness *to* a world (and its "whole" objects, viz., the imaginary), and its primary figuration commencing with the subject's early object-relations. The Kleinian subject formation posits, like Kristeva does, a subject not condemned to the linguistic closed signifying structure.

By 1988, Kristeva posits that every sense of coming into the (historical) socio-symbolic, and in adult life, emerging out of the atemporality of the present, has at its foundation the *capacity* for assimilating love and hatred in the process of relationality in the meaningful connection to the world. Kristeva and Klein elevate this into precondition of the disruption into presence from return of the archaic maternal (semiotic) repressed; in turn, this non-founded foundation at the beginning of each new beginning is what then gives sense and representation in language in the Oedipal stage of life.

For Kristeva, the unstable ground from which "illustrations of feminine depression" develops owes to Klein, as the movement (labor of mourning, quickening) takes place between two developmental "positions": the schizoid-paranoid and the depressive position. Klein's construction of *phantasy* in the depressive position occurs at around six months of infancy in so-called normal development. As Hanna Segal puts it, these positions are "a specific configuration of object relations, anxieties and defences which persist throughout life" (1988, ix). This notion of "positions" allows us to carefully consider the sense of flexibility of the developmental process. Flexibility characterizes Klein's "positions" as plastic and malleable. As Kristeva will complicate through her semiological work the psychoanalytic frame of Klein, "speech" and its poetic form make the form of delivery of meaning at the threshold of signification, rendering the limits of language plastic and malleable.

This is paramount because "the function of desire must remain in a fundamental relationship with death" (Lacan 1997, 303). As Kristeva puts this—the relation of the subject to the Thing is enabled through experience of embodied symptomatic complaint of a Kleinian psychic trauma. Then, in 1988, Kristeva argues trauma is that which positions the subject in relation to the Thing.

For Kristeva, prior to signification and prior to whole-object relations, there begins a genesis of the partial-object of the maternal breast of ambiguity, as the Thing *and* object, which sets the groundwork of the threshold of signification as plastic and malleable. It is plastic and malleable since it is operating as valuation and value positing, the split between good or bad ("it is *good* when it feeds me, but when it is gone it is *bad*"). Because this precarious positionality occurs developmentally prior to (although returns to this position are in fact possible, as in, for instance psychosis, which forecloses the thetic) a more organized egoic subject/object distinction, its affirmation (*Bejahung*) allows the "schizoid-paranoid" position to give the grounds for symbol-formation and therefore communicability. Such a dynamic reveals that from the earliest stages of infancy—which crucially take place *before* the integration of the ego—the infant is capable of constructing the basis for introjective and projective functions in integration (of the partial object) and external evaluations of binary logic and chronology, of "good" and "bad" values. Kristeva's recovery of this pre-Oedipal "binary logic" in abjection will offer its semiotic correlate in linguistics as "a primal mapping of the body," which, "while being the precondition of language, it is dependent upon meaning, but in a way that is not that of linguistic signs nor of the symbolic order they found" (1982, 72).

As I come to the end of this introduction, I want to emphasize the labor of the negative, the *rejete* or "fourth" negation as the productive operation of the death drive in the symbolic-semiotic formation. Kristeva's main thesis in 1974 concerns the form of a linguistic or inscriptive bodily trace or remainder (*reste*) of the semiotic. This impossible to collapse, inassimilable remainder implies, among other things, that the oppression and dominance of the laws of language may never fully repress the power of language to signify "new" things. Semiotic trace or the *archē* is unstable, but it nonetheless constitutes a *horizon* for the work of time retrieval by *representing* the limit of time within language. But as Kristeva shifts in the 1980s and 1990s, from a monolithic semiotic to a social plurality of the human condition, we can think of the semiotic as the effectiveness of revolution—as effectiveness and as well inertia, of the self-preservation and protection, against the odds, paradoxically harnessed by the death drive in language.

References

Freud, Sigmund. (1920) 1961. *Beyond the Pleasure Principle*. Translated by James Strachey. New York: Norton.

Kristeva, Julia. (1974) 1984. *Revolution in Poetic Language*. Translated by Margaret Waller. New York: Columbia University Press.

———. (1980)1982. *Powers of Horror: An Essay on Abjection*. Translated by Leon S. Roudiez. New York: European Perspectives: Columbia University Press.

———. (1987) 1989. *Black Sun: Depression and Melancholy*. Translated by Leon S. Roudiez. New York: Columbia University Press.

———. (1997) 2002. *Intimate Revolt: The Powers and Limits of Psychoanalysis*. Translated by Jeanine Herman. New York: Columbia University Press.

Lacan, Jacques. (1949) 1977. "The Mirror Stage as Formative of the Function of the I." In *Écrits*. Translated by Alan Sheridan, 1–8. New York: Norton.

———. (1957) 1997. *The Ethics of Psychoanalysis, Book VII*. Translated by Dennis Porter. New York: Norton.

Segal, Hanna. 1988. *Introduction to the Work of Melanie Klein*. London: Karnac Books.

Chapter 2

The Impossibility of Loss

Julia Kristeva

Translated by Elisabeth Paquette

It is of *psychic* trauma, and not of the *real*, that I propose to speak to you today.

The Freudian concept, whatever its evolution, is essentially economic: there is trauma when the psychic apparatus fails to eliminate or work out an excess of excitations. However, since the *Introduction to Psychoanalysis* (1915–1917), Freud associates the "accidental (traumatic) event" situated seemingly late in the experience of the neurotic, with an "inclination towards a fixation with the libido." This consists of two parts: one pertains to "The sexual constitution or prehistoric experience"; the other to "Infantile experience." Speaking to this development, Laplanche and Pontalis state that "The trauma's import is reduced and at the same time its singularity diminishes" and it tends to become synonymous with "frustration" (*Versagung*).[1] Certainly, this seems to be Freud's explicit intention. Nevertheless, this kind of connection of trauma with, on the one hand, the sexual constitution (we would add here today biology) and, on the other hand, the events of infantile experience, invites us to think of trauma with respect to the field of biology and the psychic apparatus that induces trauma from an event. Leaving the neurosciences aside, I would like to reflect on "infantile experience" and the "inclination towards a fixation with the libido." Rather than focusing on the indelible destination that the intersubjective shock inflicts on the individual (Freud himself circulates this temptation by introducing the idea of the "*après coup*": it is not a primary event, but a secondary one, reactivating the first, that constitutes this "unknown origin" of *trauma*), I would like to investigate the type of relation that the subject builds with the other from a very young age. I propose that "infantile experience" and the "inclination towards a fixation with the libido" that Freud speaks of as the precondition of trauma *is itself a structure*, in particular the *subject/other structure*. It accumulates subsequent wounds and confers upon them—or not—a sense of trauma.

To illustrate my point, I approach depression as setting itself up precisely only if the traumatic event that triggers it (once it is present, once it is identifiable) encounters a specific "terrain." I will not consider the biological aspects of this terrain. I would like to direct you to reflect on *the object-relations of the depressive or the depressed*, and in particular on the depressed narcissist.[2] Even if the two classes do not have entrenched borders, I believe that there exists a depression that is a hatred for the other inverted onto oneself; and another, more specifically narcissistic (see the work of E. Jacobson and A. Green in this sense). This depressed subject feels affected by a fundamental failing, an innate deficiency. Their grief does not hide the guilt or the fault of a secret vengeance summoned against the ambivalent object. Their sadness would also be a more archaic expression than a nonsymbolizable, unnameable, narcissistic wound, so precocious that it has no referent outside of language. For this type of depressed narcissist, sadness is in reality the sole object: the subject attaches to, specifically, an ersatz object, that they tame and cherish, as someone else's fault. In such an instance, suicide is not an act of camouflaged war, but a reunion with sadness, and—beyond the subject—with this impossible love, never touched, always elsewhere, like the promises of nothingness, of death.

Thing and Object

The depressed narcissist is in mourning not for an Object but for the Thing. I am calling the Thing the real that does not lend itself to signification, the center of attraction and repulsion, the seat of sexuality from which the object of desire will become separated.

In philosophy, we do not distinguish between "object" and "thing." In a fundamental text, *What Is a Thing?*[3] Heidegger recalls that, since the dawn of Greek philosophy, the emergence of the *thing* is bound up with the utterance [*l'énoncé*] of a *proposition* and its *truth*. However, Heidegger opens the question of the "historied" character of the thing; logically and chronologically speaking, there has never been, and never will be a "thing," "proposition," or "truth." "The question of the thing again comes into motion from its beginning" [*"La question en direction de la chose se remet en movement du fond de sont début"*].[4]

Without going into the history of this conception of the *thing* but opening it up to the interval that plays itself out between *man* and the *thing* Heidegger notes, in conversation with Kant: "that this *between* [between man and thing] as an anticipation reaches beyond the thing and back behind us."[5]

In the gap opened by Heidegger's question and followed by Freud's elaboration of rational certitude, I speak of the *Thing* as being the "something" that the subject has already constituted, but whose being appears as indeterminate, inseparable and elusive, even in its determination as the sexual thing. I reserve the term *Object* for the spatiotemporal constant that verifies [*vérifie*] the position enunciated by the subject as a mastery of one's speech [*son dire*].

Of what I call a *Thing* as opposed to an *Object*, Gérard de Nerval offers a stunning metaphor suggesting an insistence without presence, a light without representation; The *Thing* is an imagined sun, bright and black at the same time. "It is a well-known fact that one never sees the sun in a dream, although one is often aware of some far brighter light."[6]

Following this archaic attachment, the depressed person has the impression of having been deprived of an unnameable supreme being, of a supreme good, of something unrepresentable, that perhaps only figuratively devouring might represent, or an *invocation* might indicate, but no word could signify. Furthermore, no erotic object could replace for them the perception of a place or a *pre-object* that confines the libido or severs the bonds of desire. Knowingly disinherited of the Thing, the depressed person wanders in pursuit of continuously disappointing adventures and loves; or else retreats, disconsolate and aphasic, "alone with the unnamed Thing." The "primary identification" with the "father of individual prehistory"[7] would be the means, the link that might enable one to commence the work of mourning the Thing. Primary identification initiates a compensation for the Thing and at the same time secures the subject to another dimension, that of imaginary adherence, reminding one of the bond of faith, which is precisely what crumbles within the depressed person.

For those affected by melancholia, primary identification proves to be fragile and insufficient for securing other identifications, which are symbolic this time, on the basis of which the *erotic Thing* might prove susceptible to becoming a captivating *Object of desire* by ensuring continuity in the metonymy of pleasure. The melancholy Thing interrupts the metonymy of desire, thereby opposing a working through of intrapsychic loss.

I should differentiate my position from that of Lacan, to whom it is indebted. In his discussion of the concept *das Ding*, starting from Freud's *Entwurf*, Lacan postulates that there is something concealed in the self of the Freudian Thing before the presence of a judging consciousness that is experienced as always already there in the presence of language [*langage*].[8] Lacan's formulation does not miss the contradictions at the heart of the Freudian Thing. Lacan prioritizes affect over language and at times language over affect, but eventually and definitively he affirms a certain hold on the speech [*parole*] of the *Thing*; a precise and sad hold over the depressed suicidal silence which, supposing they are a lover of the *Thing*, becomes disavowed. "*Das Ding* is originally that which we call outside of signification. It is in the function *of this outside-signification and a pathetic reaction to it that the subject maintains its distance and constitutes himself in this world of relations, of primary affect anterior to any repression.* The entire primary articulation of the *Entwurf* is made around that."[9] However, whereas Freud insisted that the *Thing* shows up as a *cry*, Lacan translates it as *word*, playing on the ambivalent meaning of the term *mot* in French ("*mot*, is that which remains silent," "no *mot* is spoken"). "The things in question are things insofar as they are silent. . . . And silent things are not exactly the same as things that have no relationship to words."[10]

Rebellious to language, would not the bond between the Subject and the Thing be an inaccessible domain? How would one approach this domain? Sublimation makes an attempt in that direction: by melodies, rhythms, polyvalences, semantics, the form spoken poetically that undoes and remakes the signs is the only "container" [*contenant*] that appears to ensure an uncertain yet adequate hold on the Thing.

One could assume the depressive person an atheist; deprived of sense and meaning, deprived of values.[11] For them, to doubt or ignore the Beyond would be a cause for self-deprecation. Although atheistic, there are those in despair who are mystics: they adhere to their *pre-object*, not believing in Thou, but are silently adept and unshakable in their own proper inexpressible hold [*contenant*].¹² To this aura of strangeness, they consecrate their tears and *jouissance*. In the tension of their affects, muscles, mucus membranes, and skin, they experience their belonging to, and at the same time separation from, an archaic other that again escapes representation and naming, but whose corporeal discharges, and their automation, still protect the mark. Unbelieving in language, depressive persons are affectionate, wounded to be sure, but captive to affect. Affect, that's their thing.

The *Thing* inscribes itself on us without memory, a subterranean accomplice to our inexpressible anguish. One can imagine the delights of reunion that a regressive dream promises through the nuptials of suicide.

The emergence of the *Thing* is summoned in the subject by way of the constitution of their élan vital: the prematurely born self that we all are survives only if it succeeds in attaching itself to an other, like a supplement, a prosthesis, or a protective wrapping. However, this life drive [*pulsion*] is radically that which *simultaneously* rejects me, isolates me, and rejects [*rejette*] him (or her). The ambivalent drive is never more formidable than in this commencement of alterity where, lacking the filter of language, I cannot inscribe my violence in the "no," no more than in any other sign. I can't expel it but through gestures, spasms, screams. I propel it, I project it. My *Thing* is a necessity but also absolutely my enemy, my foil, the delightful opposing pole of my hatred. The *Thing* falls from me just outside the outposts of significance, where the Verb is not yet my Being. A nothing, which is a cause, but at the same time a fall, before being an Other, the *Thing* is the vessel [*vase*] that contains my *dejecta* and everything that results from *cadere* [Latin: to fall]: it is a waste with which, in sadness, I merge. It is Job's ash pit in the Bible.

Anality summons itself in the process of setting up this Thing, one that is as much our own and proper Thing as it is unclean, improper. The melancholy person who extols this border where the self emerges, but also collapses in devaluation, fails to summon the anality that could construct separations and frontiers as is normally done, or as a bonus with obsessive persons. On the contrary, the entire ego of those who are depressed is engulfed in the diseroticized and yet jubilatory anality, as the latter becomes the vector of jouissance fused with the archaic Thing, perceived not as a signifying object but as the frontier element of the self [*moi*]. For those who are depressed, the Thing, like the self [*moi*], is a downfall that carries them along into the invisible and the unnameable. *Cadere*. Waste and corpses all.

Now, I would like to present the depression of a patient who was triggered, in a rather banal manner, by trauma suddenly revealed by the infidelity of her spouse. This trivial abandonment was entered into through a resonance with an object relation, which I describe as a link to a *Thing* and not a link to an *Object*; this was highlighted in analysis, and this is what I would like to demonstrate to you. Let us attempt, perhaps, to pull from these fragments a conclusion that might advance a cure.

I would like to speak to you of feminine depression and the impact of object relation on the traumatic event and on its development.

The Act Would Be Merely Reprehensible

The traumatized person does not speak, but when she is not devastated, she can act [*agit*]. The wounded speaking being survives in action; insensitive, hallucinating, sometimes murderous. Feminine depression is occasionally concealed under a feverish activity that gives to the depressed person the appearance of a practical woman, at ease with herself, who thinks only about being useful. To such a mask, which many women wear either deceitfully or unwittingly, Marie-Ange adds a cold urge for vengeance, a veritable mortifying plot, of which she herself is surprised for having the brains and the brawn, and which brings her suffering because she experiences it like a grave wrongdoing. Having discovered that her spouse was cheating on her, Marie-Ange succeeds in identifying her rival and engages in a series of more or less infantile or diabolical schemes in order to simply eliminate the troublemaker, who happens to be a friend and a colleague. This mostly amounts to pouring sleeping pills and other harmful products into coffee, tea, and other drinks that Marie-Ange offers her freely. But she will also go so far as to slash her car's tires, cut her brakes, etc.

A kind of intoxication dwells in Marie-Ange when she undertakes these retaliations. She forgets her jealousy and her injury and, even though ashamed of these acts, she almost feels satisfied. To be at fault causes her to suffer because being at fault brings her joy, and vice versa. Does not hurting her rival, disorienting her, or even killing her, also amount to inserting herself into the other woman's life, giving her enjoyment [*faire jouir*] to the point of death? Marie-Ange's violence confers on her a phallic power that compensates for the humiliation and, even more so, gives her the impression of being more powerful than her spouse: more decisive, so to speak, over his mistress's body. The recrimination against her spouse's adultery is only a superficial cover. While hurt by her spouse's "wrongdoing," what rouses Marie-Ange's suffering and avenging mood is neither moral castigation nor the complaint about the narcissistic harm ("trauma" = harm in Greek).

At a more primary level, *any possibility for acting* appears to her, it seems, fundamentally a transgression, a wrongdoing. Trauma is positively doing something. To act would be to compromise herself (like the other who compromised me by traumatizing me), and when the underlying depression hampers the inhibition hindering all other possibilities of realization, the only possible act for her becomes the action of capital wrongdoing: to kill or to kill herself. One can imagine the complicity of the traumatized with the traumatizer.

A Blank Perversion

Trauma that triggers depression is not experienced solely as castration. Certainly, the loss of the erotic object (through infidelity or abandonment by the lover or spouse, divorce, etc.) feels to a woman like an attack on her genitality and, from that point of view, is equivalent to castration. At once, the feeling of castration starts resonating with the threat of destruction of bodily integrity, body image, and entire psychic apparatus as well. As a result, feminine castration, rather than being diseroticized, is recovered by a narcissistic anguish that houses eroticism like a *shameful secret*. Even though a woman has no penis to lose, it is everything—body and certainly soul—that she feels is threatened by castration. *As if her phallus were her psyche*, the loss of the erotic object fragments and threatens to empty out her entire psychic life. The outer loss is immediately and depressively experienced as an inner void.

This means that the "psychic void" and the painful affect that constitutes its miniscule yet intense manifestation, installs itself in place of shameful [*inavouable*] loss. Depressive behavior [*l'agir depressif*] is inscribed from the start in this void. Blank activity, exempt from signification, may just as well follow a death-bearing path (killing the rival that ravishes the partner) or a harmless one (exhausting oneself by revising the children's lessons). She dwells, always retained by an enveloping psychic pain, anesthetized, like "death." (We can think of this using the same logic as with certain adolescent rebels who traumatize others in order not to love their own proper trauma-object.)

In the early stages of analysis, the depressive woman welcomes and respects her emptiness as a living dead. Only through establishing a friendly collusion, free from superego tyranny, is her shame spoken and does *death* find its domain as a death wish. Marie-Ange's desire to kill (the other) so as not to pretend to be dead (herself) can be narrated as a sexual desire for joy in her rival or to give her joy. For this reason, depression—and its mortifying and vengeful act—appears as the veil of a *blank perversion*: one that is dreamed of, desired, even thought of, but unnameable and forever impossible. As such, we understand the depressive course [*l'agir*] as precisely carrying out the economy of perverse acts [*passage a l'acte*]: it empties out the painful psyche and blocks the experience of sex understood as shameful. The unbounded activity of the depressive person is somewhat hypnoidal, enclosing in a secret the perversion within an inflexible feature of the law: in the constraint, duty, destiny, and even the fatality of death.

Making the traumatized person speak of this inconsistent perversion that the trauma encloses within her, already takes a step toward trauma. By revealing the (homosexual) sexual secret of the depressive course that causes the melancholic person to *live with death*, analysis gives back its place to desire within the patient's psychic space (since the silenced *death drive* is not the spoken *desire for death*). Therefore, the cure demarcates a psychic space that becomes capable of integrating traumatic *loss* as a signifiable and eroticized *object*. Henceforth, the separation appears no longer as a threat of disintegration, but as the *bridge* [*relais*] toward someone else; conflictual, carrier of Eros and Thanatos, susceptible to Sense and Non-Sense.

Don Juan's Wife: Sorrowful or Terrorist

How have infantile experiences contributed to constructing these bonds to the Thing that renders the depressive person also vulnerable to "secondary" traumas? Marie-Ange has an older sister and several younger brothers. She has always felt jealous of her older sister who was her father's favorite, and she retains from her childhood the certitude of having been abandoned by her mother, who was monopolized by her numerous children. No hatred toward her sister or her mother seems to have been made manifest in the past, no more than now. Marie-Ange, on the contrary, comported herself like a well-behaved child, sad, always withdrawn. She was afraid of going out, and when her mother was running errands, she would wait anxiously at the window. "I lived at the house as if I were there in her stead, I conserved her fragrance, I imagined her presence, I kept her with me." Her mother considered this sadness abnormal: "This nun's appearance is deceitful, she is hiding something," the matriarch would say disapprovingly, and these words would discourage the little girl even more as she withdrew to her inner hiding place.

It took Marie-Ange a long time before speaking of her present depressive states. Under the surface of the always punctual, busy, and faultless teacher, appeared a woman who sometimes took extended sick leaves because she did not have the desire or the ability to leave her house: in order to imprison what fleeing presence?

Nevertheless, she succeeded in controlling her states of total dereliction and paralysis by identifying with the maternal figure: either with the hyperactive housewife, or even—and this is how she arrives at the passage of the murderous act—with a desired phallic mother, whose homosexual passive partner she would like to be or, conversely, whose body she herself would like to arouse by putting her to death. So Marie-Ange told me about a dream that gave her a glimpse into the kind of passion that was feeding her hatred of her rival. She goes to open the car of her husband's mistress to hide a bomb [*un explosif*] in it. But in fact, it is not a car, it is her mother's bed; Marie-Ange is nestled against her, and she suddenly notices that this mother, who so generously gave her breast to the swarm of little boys that came after Marie-Ange, possessed a penis.

The heterosexual partner of a woman, when the relation proves satisfying for her, often possesses the qualities of her mother. The depressive woman only deviates indirectly from this rule. Her preferred partner or her husband is a fulfilling yet unfaithful mother. The depressive woman can then be dramatically, painfully attached to her Don Juan—the traumatizer. For, beyond the fact that he gives her the possibility of possessing an unfaithful mother, Don Juan satisfies her greedy appetite for other women. His mistresses are her mistresses. His exploits [*passage a l'acte*] satisfy her own erotomania and provide her with an antidepressive, a feverish excitement beyond pain. If the erotic desire underlying this passion were repressed, murder might take the place of embrace and the depressed woman might change into a terrorist.

To the contrary, taming sorrow would not immediately evade sadness, but would leave it some time to install itself, flourish even, and only here discharge itself: that is what could have certainly been one of the temporary yet indispensable phases for the analysis. Could the richness of my sadness be my way of protecting myself against death—the death of the desired/rejected other, the death of myself?

Marie-Ange stifled within herself the distress and devalorization where the real or imaginary maternal abandon resided. The idea of her being ugly, worthless, and insignificant did not leave her, but it was more an "*atmosphere*" than an "*idea*," nothing obvious, just the dreary coloring of a gray day, which camouflaged her death drive. However, the *desire for death*, of her own proper death (for want of avenging herself on the mother) infiltrated her phobic symptoms: fear of falling from the window, from the escalator, off a rock side, or off the slope of a mountain. Fear of finding herself in a void, of dying from the void. A permanent fear of heights. Marie-Ange protected herself from it for the time being by displacing it onto her rival, who was supposed to disappear by poisoning or by vanishing in a car rolling toward an open tomb. Her life was unharmed at the cost of sacrificing another's.

The terrorism of such depressive hysteria is often manifest by aiming for the mouth. Many stories involving harems and feminine jealousies have consecrated the image of the poisoner as a privileged image of feminine Satanism. However, poisoning drink or food reveals, beyond the unruly sorceress, a little girl deprived of the breast. And if it is true that little boys are also deprived, everyone knows that men find their lost paradise in the heterosexual relation, but also and certainly through diverse roundabout means that lavish oral satisfactions on him or do so by means of orality.

Women's exploits [*passage a l'acte*] are more inhibited, less elaborate, and consequently it can be, when it takes place, more violent. For the loss of the object seems irremediable for a woman (only the homosexual will find a woman as a sexual object), and its mourning more difficult, if not impossible. But, if the mourning is not done, the object is not lost: the depressed is in the impossibility of loss. So, objects of substitution, perverse objects that should direct her to the father, appear laughable. She often succumbs to heterosexual desire by repressing archaic pleasures, even pleasure itself: she yields to heterosexuality in frigidity. Marie-Ange wants to keep her husband for herself, for herself but not for erotic pleasure. Access to jouissance is affected only through man's perverse object: Marie-Ange's pleasure comes from the mistress, and when her husband does not have one, he no longer interests her. The depressive woman's perversion of the depressed is devious; she needs an intermediary and screen of man's object-woman in order to find the other sex. But, once installed on this path, the extenuated desire of the melancholy woman knows no bounds: it wants everything, to the end, until death.

The sharing of this mortifying secret in analysis is not merely a test of their reliability or of the difference between their discourses and the domain of law, condemnation, or repression. Such confidence is an attempt to win over the analyst into a common jouissance: the one that the mother refuses, that the mistress steals. In revealing that this confidence is an attempt to gain ascendency over the analyst as a *Thing*, following which, as an erotic *Object*, the interpretation then maintains the patient in the truth of her desire and her attempts at manipulation. Yet following an ethic that is not to be confused with punitive legislation, the analyst recognizes the reality of her depressive position and, in affirming the symbolic legitimacy of her pain, permits the patient to find other means, symbolic or imaginary, of working out her suffering.

To briefly conclude this fragment of analysis, let's say that trauma doesn't efface itself. Let it stand that there are actual brutal events, where she rekindles infantile wounds, and the trauma puts into place the relation of the Subject with the Thing. Internal to language but denied by it, this relation often passes as an act [*s'agir*] rather than in speech [*parole*]. In treatment, we should find it, and its effects are recited: the time of grief, of complaint, of resentment. It is therefore that the Subject detaches itself from the Thing and creates an Object: nameable, desirable or detestable. Only in the third moment, that is, in analysis, can we imagine the loss of this love-hate object: to eliminate or to work through the trauma. Analysis can come to move beyond it. In time, we ought not attempt to too quickly relieve the patient of their trauma. It is their Thing of which they need to speak.

Roundtable

JEAN-JOSÉ BARANES: Thank you, Julia Kristeva. The silence that has taken over the room is a testament to the interest stirred by your talk and its concentrated contribution. A prior remark: our audience have probably noted that Jean "*Corps nu*"[13] [naked body] has found his "*cournut*" as the body of the body put into words, and that his patients have found the possibility of formulating their passion with Julia Kristeva!

First question: Would it have been necessary that Ferenczi be a woman in order to succeed at "passing"? I believe that it is indeed a register that Julia Kristeva explores. This register brought me to think about another possible title for this colloquium, which I had thought about before the start of the event, and which returned to me while listening to you: rather than speaking of the "real trauma—psychic trauma," maybe there is a way to speak of completed trauma—endless trauma, finite trauma—infinite trauma, and finite trauma—indefinite trauma. Yet, Julia Kristeva proposes other formulations, another theorization, different from the economic, a different arrangement from the point of view of history, under the angle of the articulation between history and structure.

In this regard, another question could be: is there a structure of affect? Because you have evoked intoxication, shame, jouissance, all in situating things in the register of alterity and structure, pre-alterity rather than the game between the "not yet constituted" of the I and the "coming to be of the object" starting from the Thing.

GEORGES BAAL: It seems to me that, while speaking of a clinical case about a woman, Julia Kristeva has proposed at least two issues. I would like to ask a couple of questions on this subject.

I believe I have understood your distinction between thing/object from the point of view of ontogeny, but you have also said that once the object and language appear, trauma can be situated always elsewhere than where there is language. This poses a big problem. I have always understood that the disastrous effects of traumas passed through the phenomena that Freud named condensation, displacement, representability, etc., and that all this was connected to work, to a working through [*perlaboration*] (if one must keep this French term), a process that cannot pass outside of language. Must we understand that you are developing an entire domain, an entire field where these phenomena do not operate, but where traumas pass? Otherwise, how would you articulate this with the three mechanisms that you have evoked?

I have a second question that is very short and completely connected to my first question. You speak sometimes of "acts" as opposed to speech [*parole*]. Speech [*la parole*] is not language, but where is this act situated compared to the field of language? And what is the difference between the "act" [*l'acte*], "action" [*l'agir*], and "the carrying out of acts" [*le passage à l'acte*]?

JULIA KRISTEVA: I thank you for these questions. I will try to respond to both speakers. The distinction that I am attempting to establish between thing and object can in effect be seen in the diachronic view, in the evolution of the psychic life of the subject. But I think that it is also structural and that in our normal functioning we have, on the one hand, a relation to the object where the limits of the subject-object are discernible (it is perhaps there that neuroses play), and, on the other hand, a relation to the other that is in the register of the thing (it is in this sector that we find instead the borderline, depressive states and probably also certain somatizations). That which is historical can also be found to be structural.

When you say that we can infer from my talk that trauma does not pass through language, I would like to offer a correction. It is probably my clumsiness of expression that led to this idea. It is evident that for all, speaking brings trauma to pass through a verbal relation, including when it is a young child who does not have active use of speech [*parole*] because he is enveloped by language. My point is that the disorganization of language is what touches this more archaic relation where the presubject object relation is situated and where what is submerged in the traumatized individual is a prelinguistic semiotization (this is a term of my semiological language). One does not speak [*parle*] but this is not to say that there is no meaning. There is meaning here, but it does not have signification. What I call signification is what I communicate to another by a language articulated with signs, syntax, and a logic that recites in order to communicate, to liberate myself in some way. Even if there is no possibility of signification, there is a sense or meaning that can remain traumatized or "encrypted," as Maria Torok and Nicolas Abraham stated, often in the prelinguistic material: in the tone of a voice, in certain gestures, in the phenomenon of comportment, in tears, in the expressions of affect more archaic than their verbal expression. What I am attempting to say is that with this type of patient, who can be depressed but also borderline, we are often reticent to interpret these prelinguistic phenomena. Throughout this colloquium on the voice—I have said that I interpret the voice of the depressed, because their discourse has been inexistent, opaque, defensive, and that the depressive trauma seemed to me encrypted in the voice—I was told that this was intrusive. However, in this instance, I think that the role of the analyst is to attempt to bridge this rudimentary meaning, encrypted in rudimentary expressions and often kept secret, and to clear the way toward desire and toward the other. Is this a "holding"? I think that if this is a holding, it is a holding at the level of logic—it is not a sentimental mothering. It is a kind of transplanted speech [*parole*], it is a way to teach, to acquire for the traumatized, who has lost the means of expressing their trauma or who never had the opportunity to verbalize it.

Act and speech [*parole*]? I believe that I have somewhat responded to this question. There are acts that are not conscious acts and are therefore not assimilable with the logic of the conscious act. Earlier I had cited the history of philosophy. As you know, for phenomenology there is an act, or action that aims at an object, a goal, when there is a judgment, when the subject is capable of judgment and action. But in the states of the unconscious act, the carrying out of the act [*passage a l'acte*], can we speak of the act in the logical sense of the term? I believe not. We must look for other terms to designate the specificity of this act. It is for this reason that for the traumatized who takes action, I proposed the hallucinatory act, the hallucination matrix, the preliminary act, etc. Freud made allusion to these obsessive acts understood as acts of magic. To elaborate extensively on this would require attempting to understand in what way these acts are not mastered and from this point of view escape speech [*parole*] and a clear conscious aim.

JEAN-JOSÉ BARANES: Julia Kristeva's response introduces something that is without doubt a reprise from the roundtable debate earlier, to know the conditions of the interpretation and the conception that we can have about the interpretation within these situations of trauma. That said, I find that ambiguity lives on in this question of knowing whether you speak very specifically about trauma or if it consists of something that concerns more generally the feminine, or the woman, or the feminine in each of us.

JULIA KRISTEVA: This connects to your question about Ferenczi, to which I never responded.

Question: You have clinically situated the history of the cheating on one's wife between the register of clinical emotions and the register of psychopathology. Can we suggest that alcohol, which was not brought up, could have been a representation of "the thing"?

JULIA KRISTEVA: Yes, in effect, one drowns in a lack of distinction, with something that is neither me nor other, and which makes us obliterate the trauma without working through it.

Question: To return to Shakespeare, at the start of *Hamlet*, the people responsible for depicting the ghost hesitated a lot between not showing it or, on the contrary, showing a passing shadow. Is this thing inscribed in the register of "the thing" as you understand it?

JULIA KRISTEVA: I am very flattered that you find a shadow of what I said in Shakespeare. I find these kinds of interpretations very beautiful; the ones that [André] Green makes of *Hamlet*. It is the story of the mother as the ultimate object of desire, but who is never symbolized that way, who may remain this melancholy thing from which we do not want to separate; compared to searching for eroticized bias in a masculine figure, represented in the occurrence by the shadow of a father. This latter, Green suggests, is, in the last instance, a maternal shadow.

Written question: It seems to me that Roquentin, the hero of [Jean-Paul] Sartre's *Nausea*, expresses a fair literary institution, if not an illustration of what Mrs. Kristeva develops in the section of her talk on the depressive narcissist. In particular, the experience of nausea of being face to face with a tree would depict a suitable literary illustration of an undecidable alternative between the philosophical theme of facing "the thing" (according to Heidegger, cited by the conference presenter) and the psychoanalytic theme of the depressive narcissistic subject and an inaccessible object, facing the loss of the thing.

JULIA KRISTEVA: Quite. I am very sensitive to this remark because it reminds me of my work on [Louis-Ferdinand] Céline and his relation with the material object and horror, the abjection of this triggered relation. It would appear that there is a clear-cut and clean relation, at the level of the critique of the sources, as we like to say in literature, between Roquentin and Sartre and, then likewise, all those who problematize Céline. In psychoanalysis we are too tied to the idea of the object that will always be there, even if all Kleinian theories try to constitute outposts in the constitution of this object. With Lacan in particular, the concept of the *objet petit a*, even if it was not Lacan's intention, left out the fact that there are objectless states [*etats inobjectaux*], in the sense that the subject is not separated from the object. The psychosis of certain traumatic phenomena plays out well in this interpretation. When we try to describe these situations, we speak of the merger, of the hold, and yet the term *merger* supposes that the two are there since they merged: similarly, in the hold, one holds the other. What I have been attempting to make evident with this reflection on the thing and object is the question concerning states where limits are not posed: as in certain obvious pathologies, but also in the individual states constituted normally and the states that are reactivated in traumatic situations.

Certain philosophies have attempted to point out these situations by referencing mystical experience, for example. One might ask to what extent these socially limited states that are waring, confining, etc. do lead us to analogies with what philosophy has thematized across these mystical and limitless states [*des états de non-limite*].

ELIANE ALLOUCH: My first question pertains to the distinction you made between the concept of the thing and the concept of the object. Not once in your talk did you relate your concept of the thing to a Freudian conception of "thing-represented." Moreover, it seems as though the concept of the thing that you presented is closer to the concept of object than to thing-represented. Could you provide us with some additional details concerning the links or the differences that you establish with the Freudian notion?

The second question bears on this nonrepresentation, on this inscription to which you have alluded. While listening to you, I was asking myself if this nonrepresentation, this nonverbalizable material (if you said this) was not the underlying "cause" of this very singular aspect of your method. Your method consists of (if I have understood what you have said in one of your texts) "encouraging," more or less, some of your patients—if the opportunity presents itself—to engage in personal artistic endeavors? Is this not also what some hasten to decry, by saying that Julia Kristeva goes beyond the framework of psychoanalysis?

AURÉLIA MESTRE: I would like to intervene in relation to Julia Kristeva's remark on Kleinian psychoanalysis to make a personal association based on the problem that the object poses. I think that what Kleinians forget is that there is always a relation to the object, but more precisely the relationship is made during the processes where the maternal takes place and the object is not found before, it will gradually establish something between this mother and this child in the order of an object relation. It is true that if there are some slippages in this relation to the object, we might also speak of traumatization in a certain sense. What you have evoked in this clinical case, that I personally found to be very handsome and rich, reminded me of the method through which you expressed it. It also made me think of Melanie Klein's idea of projective identification. For me, this evoked the way this patient could have evaded her mother—who did not permit at the time the working out of her identity and a sufficiently rich relation—the continuous sentiment of abandon preventing the working out of her depression; nothing was left to her other than to stick to the object, in the most vampiric sense of the term. Thus, she projects inside her husband's mistress the pasted image of her primitive mother. She wants to effectively relinquish this object in order to recuperate her own proper/clean identity. My question for you is: Isn't the case that you have presented ultimately a sufficiently striking illustration of this concept of "projective identification"? Even if we don't call it that, what we call it is not very important.

BÉATRICE ANG: Would you agree with the idea that it rests less on an interpretive function with these patients than on a transplant of the senses and meaning taking shape in the *content* of countertransference? Is it, then, a regressive support that brings us to being content with merging or indifferent states, transplanting sense and meaning but above all *transplanting the libido*?

"Poetic" reverie serves this wording because it allows for surprises, ascending creations that name the affect and above all *de-confine it from libidinal representation*.

Is not the representation of the thing within melancholy first a dead thing, cooled, interred that the analyst *constitutes* as a representation of affect, spawning support, supporting a possible representation of the word. It is perhaps less a function of interpretation that one must speak than the *poetic function* in the analyst.

Otherwise, I wonder about the content of this countertransference for these patients. And because it consists of trauma, is not the actual form that it takes in the cure sometimes a *traumatic seduction* that breaks and crashes into a moment of psychic work in action, at the time when one is trying to constitute oneself like a containing and maternal wrap.

JULIA KRISTEVA: I don't know if I will be able to respond to all these questions, but I think that we are picking up certain themes this afternoon. First, regarding the representations of things: for Freud the notion is sufficiently polyvalent, thinking of two definitions; for example, one is found in *Instincts and Their Vicissitudes*, wherein the representation of thing and the representation of the object are two variants of the text, which recover the same reality and are opposed to the representation of word [*mot*].[14] There Freud does cleanly and clearly distinguish between object—separated from the subject, and existing in the real world—and word—that coming from the psychic apparatus will try to capture this external reality. I see myself as being closer to what Freud said and that I have cited in my own text (and that Lacan picks up), when he speaks of an initial apprehension. We have returned to the outposts of subjectivity, where the subject is not yet constituted as such and neither is the thing, keeping in mind that it is the initial apprehension of the thing. He states that the conduit [*vecteur*] that comes from the individual to signal the presence of this thing is the scream [*cri*]. And this is what is so interesting: it is not language, but the scream. When Lacan takes up this case, he says that the scream, calls out, but we only perceive the scream as coming across as speech [*parole*], the scream is word. In effect, word can be nothing; for example, in French we say "*qui ne dit mot*" [who does not say a word], this means "*qui ne dit rien*" [who says nothing], consequently word, speech can be returned to the scream. This is true, but I have the impression that Lacan makes an amalgam that misses the distinction between Freud's prelinguistic, on the one hand, and language, on the other hand. So far as the prelinguistic goes, Lacan insists that the scream would be fixed to the thing, this carries us toward the issue under consideration in the register of the voice, so other phenomena that are in a traumatic situation have a considerable importance.

What you said regarding my interest in elaborating across metaphors, alliteration, and other "poetic" modulations of the unconscious—that in doing so I would not be doing psychoanalysis but aesthetics—this does not trouble me at all. I suppose that it is a compliment and I take it as one. It seems to me that we have lots of problems concerning the style of interpretation that we should take, with respect to these cases of trauma, borderlines, and the psychosomatic. . . . Too often we have an impression that drives interpretation, under the guise of rational judgment we enclose the unconscious in a mentalization. Mentalization, even if it is fruitful in neurosis, finds itself mutilated in depression. In this moment here, as Béatrice Ang stated earlier, certain dreams, a certain metaphoricity of interpretation, a certain poetics—why not?—appears advantageous in reconnecting trauma and represents the first step prior to a working out and comportment toward the truth that one must face as a last resort.

I am completely in agreement with what has been said about Kleinians. In the work I have done around depression, I am using a lot of the work of M. Klein and of H. Segal on the depressive position and different types of language, symbolization, symbolic equivalents, symbolic access, etc. Regarding projective identification, in effect we can interpret what I described earlier as relevant to this mechanism. If I don't employ this term, it's for a simple reason. It seems to me that when the patient, for example, attempts to accomplish the act of murdering her rival, we can say that she is projecting, but she projects something which did not exist. She created it. The concept "projection" assumes that she already had a hatred or a desire for murder that was already there and that she wills to externalize it. Yet, I get the impression that this posttraumatic situation consists of a working out that is not the external manifestation of what has already taken place. It produces there a supplementary psychic activity a bit different from the mechanism of projection, properly speaking.

JEAN-JOSÉ BARANES: The discussion on the projective identification could be continued another day. In effect, it seems to be difficult to export the concept of projective identification outside of a Kleinian theorization without risking saying anything. For example, projective identification would go together with existence, postulated from the outset by Mélanie Klein, of an object and of a preconscious relation to the object. This implies the existence of a differentiated inside and outside, albeit in a piecemeal manner. Is everything that you are saying compatible with such a conception of object relation?

JULIA KRISTEVA: In the projective identification, there is already an overtaking of this uncertainty to which the traumatized is incapable of reacting.

Question: Is projective identification already an attempt at overtaking?

JULIA KRISTEVA: Yes, but one that is not in a state of working out. For this, one needs only to place oneself aside, and attempt to be neither the mere projection of a victim nor the perpetrator of a traumatic act. It seems to me that putting into words the dream and the implementation of sense and meaning is necessary for certain situations. This brings us back to Baranes's question, to discern whether there is a structure of affect—a structure of word? In effect, in the cure for this type of patient, there is a call for an intense identification with the other beyond speech [*paroles*] that she either says or not (especially those who do not speak since they are often feeling mute). This identification is a constructive act, and one is perhaps never more than in this case, the constructive-analyst, as Freud calls it. Through the words that I provide—be they metaphoric, poetic, etc.—I bring about not only the affects that are in the form of suffering, of tears, but I also differentiate [*différencier*] them, I construct a structure of affects. All this is to say that the structure of affects is without a doubt dependent on the structure of language, and that the subject who is flooded with affects does not have a structure of affects. The first level of analysis would be through the words that are proposed by the analyst that permit her to better locate these affects, to sort out what is joy, suffering, tears, laughter, in order to make a primary identification. But if words permit one to do so, affective reality comes through an identification with this substrate and, for me, that is an indispensable reality for analysis. We often say, for our generation, which was formed by Lacan, affect is the distinctive feature, the opening, but I think that the analysts must put themselves in the place of this distinctive feature, of this opening, and fill it by providing the words. One must not leave it in the state of this feature, otherwise trauma will endure.

JEAN-JOSÉ BARANES: On May 6, 1931, Ferenczi held an extraordinary conference on the occasion of Freud's seventy-fifth birthday. On the sixth of May 1988 [today], it is not futile to recall the following excerpt: "I assumed that one has no right to be satisfied with any analysis until it has led to the actual reproduction of the traumatic occurrences associated with the primal repression, upon which character and symptom-formation are ultimately based."[15]

One must carefully weigh and argue such an affirmation, given that we know it has brought Ferenczi to his technique of game and play, with the goal of repairing the damage that led to traumatic infantile alienation: it was postulated as a primary infantile goodness in which no one can believe.

But the problem posed by taking into account the fact of trauma remains more than ever a concern for the clinical analyst. Admittedly, this is the aim of all analytic treatment, wherein lies the recovery of the subject's real history in their dialectic of desire. And the event that becomes the memory trace can thus be redesigned [*réélaboré*] afterward in a process of successive signification that relativizes historic truth, to the benefit of lived history and the truth spoken [*parlée*] by the analyst.

But in this case, if it is always a question of flushing out desire (and drive), precisely there where the patient would like to see named—and accused—the reality, the traumatic event, or the external deficiency as causal agent of their actual suffering, the recognition of the reality of such violence to the psyche can be a necessary anchor within narcissistic structures or for certain psychotics. It is this recognition that we see as indispensable for the efficacity of interpretive work. In this respect, in a progression toward the cure, preventing a repetition of the alienating experience of a denial by another (of the lived reality by the subject), thereby dispensing with the time-consuming analytic working out of the hallucinatory activity, would trigger trauma (F. Brette).

Trauma has been a theme for the important work of the speakers from Lyons, including Claude Janin. He will now present for us his paper titled: "From the Reality of the Seduction to the Seduction of Reality: The Qualitative Trauma."

As I noted earlier, Claude Janin is a member of the Psychoanalytic Society of Paris, Lyons. He has already published a number of works such as: "On the Constructive Interpretation in Analysis"; "The Hot and the Cold: The Logics of Trauma and Their Administration of the Cure"; "The Indecision of Interpretation."[16]

Trauma, according to Ferenczi, will probably be present in his next text, appearing in *Journal clinique*.

Notes

Originally published as "L'Impossibilité de perdre" in *Les Cahiers de l'Institut de Psycho-Pathologie Clinique* 8, November 1988, special issue on *"Trauma réel, trauma psychique."*

Professor, University of Paris VII, place Jussieu, 75005 Paris.

1. Translator's note: This translation comes from Laplanche et al., 1988, 468.

2. I [Kristeva] develop this problematic in detail in *Black Sun: Depression and Melancholia* (originally published as *Soleil noir, depression et mélancolie*), Paris: Gallimard, 1987 (published in English by Columbia University Press in 1992, and translated by Leon S. Roudiez), wherein many of the following passages can be located.

Translator's note: For the sake of consistency, I drew upon Roudiez's translation however significant differences remain. Any errors in this translation are my own.

3. Translator's note: Kristeva drew from the French translation of this text, published by Gallimard in 1965. As translator, I drew from the following English translation: Martin Heidegger, 1967, *What Is a Thing?*, translated by W. B. Barton Jr. and Vera Deutsch, South Bend, IN: Gateway Editions.

4. Translator's note: Kristeva cited page 57 of the French Gallimard translation of *Qu'est-ce qu'une chose?* As translator, I have turned to the following English translation: Heidegger, *What Is a Thing?*, 48.

5. Translator's note: Heidegger, 1967, *What Is a Thing?*, 243.

6. Translator's note: Kristeva cites the following: Nerval, "Aurélia," I *Oeuvres complete*, Paris: Gallimard, 1952, 377. Following the Roudiez translation, I cite the following: Gerard de Nerval, 1957, "Aurelia," *Selected Writings*, trans. Geoffrey Wagner, Ann Arbor: University of Michigan Press, 130.

7. Translator's note: Kristeva cites S. Freud, 1923, *"Le soi et le ça,"* Essais de Psychoanalyse, Paris: Payot, 1976, 200; SE, t. XIX, 31; Gesammelte Werke, t. XIII, 258. In S. Freud, 1989, "The Ego and the Id," translated by Joan Riviere,

edited by James Strachey, New York: W. W. Norton, 26—"father of individual prehistory" is translated as father of "personal prehistory."

8. Translator's note: In every instance, language has been translated from *langage*.

9. Translator's note: Kristeva drew from J. Lacan, *Ethique de la psychoanalyse*, 67–68 for this quote. As translator, I drew from *The Seminar of Jacques Lacan: The Ethics of Psychoanalysis* 1959–1960, Book VII, 1997, translated by Dennis Porter, New York: W. W. Norton 55—translation adjusted.

10. Translator's note: Kristeva drew from J. Lacan, *Ethique de la psychoanalyse*, 68–69 for this quote. As translator, I drew from *Seminar of Jacques Lacan*, 55—translation adjusted.

11. Translator's note: Kristeva's use of "*sense*" is at times ambiguous, that is, having a double meaning. As such, throughout her essay, I have translated *sense* as both sense and meaning, and at times both sense and meaning are included in an attempt to capture the ambiguous use of this term.

12. Translator's note: Kristeva's use of the term "*propre*" is (again) ambiguous. It invokes a sense of one's own (i.e., mine) and also is imbued with a sense of cleanliness. In this instance, and throughout, I have attempted to maintain this ambiguity by using *own*, *clean*, and at times *proper*, in the later instance, my intention to invoke a sense of "norms" that mirrors the cleanliness I take Kristeva to be utilizing.

13. This refers to a slip repeated by J. Kristeva on Jean Cournut's name.

14. Translator's note: In this instance, Kristeva notes *Supplément de la Metapsychologie* by Freud. This seems to be a reference to the text *Preliminaries to a Metapsychology* that Freud had intended to publish as a standalone text, but was ultimately not published as such.

15. Translator's note: Kristeva references S. Ferenczi, "Analyse d'enfants avec des adultes." As translator, I located in the quote in the following location: Sá Ferenczi, 2002, "Child-Analysis in the Analysis of Adults," in *Final Contributions to the Problems and Methods of Psycho-Analysis*, edited by Michael Balint, translated by Eric Mosbacher and others, New York: Karnac, 131.

16. The French titles of these essays are as follows (following the same order): "Sur l'interprétation construction en analyse," "Le chaud et le froid: Les logiques du traumatisme et leur gestion dans la cure," and "L'indécidable de l'interprétation."

Chapter 3

Of What Use Are Poets in Times of Distress?

JULIA KRISTEVA

TRANSLATED BY ELISABETH PAQUETTE AND ALICE JARDINE

Ladies and Gentlemen, Dear Friends,
Thank you so much to the organizers for providing me with this time, thanks to you all for being here.
"Of what use are poets in times of distress"?
What could I tell you—given the culture of *speaking*, of how to say things—that you don't already know? Perhaps an invitation to travel, departing from Hölderlin's elegy, relying on my present actuality which, I hope, intersects with yours.[1]
The poem [by Friedrich Hölderlin] "Bread and Wine" dreams of Greek gods, of heavens, of absent friends, of the Eucharist without Jesus, and even a Syrian who arrives smiling . . . a radiant image that exists at a distance from the flux of today's Syrian migrants.
Hölderlin's melancholic question dates back to 1800. It formulates the disillusionment of those who saw the Enlightenment of the French Revolution extinguished in the Reign of Terror, and the Absolute Spirit, galloping by horse under their window, disappear during the war of nations (Hegel).
Hölderlin is not addressing those disappointed by history, but those "abandoned by God." He notes the historical and spiritual collapse, the

eclipse of transcendence, and he responds by way of this astonishingly simple formula: "Living is defending a form" (1804); and, three years later, he charges poets with an incommensurable task: "the poets ground that which remains/dwells" (see Souvenir/*Andenken*, 1803). Can poetry serve as a substitute for Greek gods, for evangelical intoxication, for the influence of the Quran? This is an untenable expectation! From which arises the anxious tone: Why? Of what use?

More serious and more rebellious, Theodor W. Adorno invites us in the twentieth century to think about whether it is possible to write poetry after Auschwitz. The poets /*Dichter* facing distress (the German term *Dürftiger* denotes *indigence, misery, lack*, and more commonly *distress*): the word seems weak when referring to the death of God, indefensible faced with crimes against humanity. However, the question is posed anew today in this new phase of the breakdown of relations and values: entrepreneurial nihilism, hyperconnected illiteracy in the empire of *selfies*, gangstro-Islamicist-radical-fundamentalism, eroticization of the death drive—with its "human bombs," decapitations—and democracies within states of exception, . . . Why poets . . . And furthermore, is this really their place, their vocation? This interrogation, this anguish touches me, and I will try to respond to it . . . in my own way.

∼

Of Bulgarian origin, of French nationality, European citizenship and American adoption, drawn to India and China . . . I learned your language, our language, in the texts of French poets and novelists. It was traveling through writing that has constructed me, and some of my stops along the way include:

> "But the true voyagers are only those who leave / Just to be leaving / . . . / And without knowing why they always say: 'Let's go.'" (Baudelaire)[2]

> "I am a far more deserving inventor than all those who went before me; a musician, in fact, who found something resembling the key of love." (Rimbaud)[3]

> "Destruction was my Béatrice." (Mallarmé)[4]

"In my own country, a foreign nation." (Aragon)[5]

"[T]o stand, in the shadow / of a scar in the air." (Paul Celan)[6]

"To be reborn has never been too much for me." (Colette)[7]

Tonight, I prefer to recall Celan: ". . . to stand, in the shadow of the scar in the air"; and Colette: "To be reborn has never been too much for me." It is necessary, after all, to have a woman in this fraternity!

For me, the poet is above all a musician of language, he[8] upsets the maternal and/or national language because he takes hold of its nerve—the voice and meaning accorded, and he excels in what the first Stoics called the "inner touch": the *oikeiois*, that impalpable sensation that connects each of us to the most intimate parts of our self and of the other, thus constituting the first sketch of what will be called a "conciliation," an "*amor nostri*" and later, the "human race" and "fraternity." The poet is at the root of this "inner touch," he is the carrier wave of incarnated universality. Why the poet? Because by readjusting sense and sensibility, by testing unspeakable passions, the poet crosses through identities, borders, and foundations, and he makes co-presence sharable. I am telling you that the alchemy of the poetic verb is an inseparable lining of the *fraternity* that has inspired our meeting tonight. It was inevitable, therefore, indispensable, that we should seek the poet when humanity collapses, and that we ask of him, and of him in the first instance, not *to be or to not be*, but quite simply just to begin again. For without him, there will be no more "inner touch" to be shared, there will be no more humanity.[9]

But as you know (Wajdi Mouawad has worked on the subject): to explore the "inner touch" and to bring it into existence socially, requires the timelessness of solitude, at a vertical axis to social time as the time of the production of goods and of sexual reproduction. Explosion of desires and of violence, relations and ruptures, destructiveness acted upon and suffered, death experienced and avoided. And this permanent travel of timelessness in time, of insurrection and resurrection of self and not-self, is possible if and only if I am able to *invest* (remember this word) in the act and the medium of expression itself (speech, sound, gesture, image, scenic space, and new technologies because there is a "poet" in every artist), and to hold myself thus in the present moment of poetic speech.

Let's take a step further into the memories of words that will bring us to the scars of modernity. To *invest* in Sanskrit is *kred, and implies a gift in reciprocity, you hear it also in the Latin *credo* ("*I believe*") and even in the financial "credit." A kind of love that flourishes in the very shadows of love: isn't this what Rimbaud called "the key of love"? As you know, it is only when someone has believed in a child and the child has come to believe in someone, that the child bursts with questions: he is searching for "the key" to open meaning, of death and of love, and he reinvents them: "I am an inventor more deserving than all who went before me." . . .

I invite you to think of poetic *speech* as arising at the dawn of this mutual "inner touch," of this prereligious and prepolitical *anthropological* need to believe, and in this sense, it is anterior to the religions that have exalted or censured it.

But only the musician of "inner touch" authorizes himself to vary his medium and his media; and to signify to the believers or to the atheists among us, that he does not depend on any *Sens Absolu* [absolute sense/meaning] nor on some sovereign foundation, whatever it might be; since the poet is an "inventor," with his own "wonderful and unexpected measure." And you will be inventors, with him.

A poet's solitude (in the broadest sense of the term) is a *traveling* that precedes and exceeds the religious, because this traveling convinces me that, to live, it is not sufficient only to "defend a form": because being alive is to begin again the unexpected and the wondrous, to convey this "inner touch" that specifies speaking beings: thus to give time to the only universal freedom that is worthwhile, the audacity to invent.

I am moving away from Hölderlin's quotes; however, the polyphony of his texts still accompanies me. And I want to emphasize that for the last two centuries, the *Why* of the Poet [*le* Pourquoi *du Poète*] (the two *P*'s capitalized) has surrendered to the *How* of writing (in the generic sense that modernity has given to the word in all the arts): the drunken boat[10] of sensual undoing, the illumination of sense and non-sense. Poetic writing does not provide us with any foundation, it just wakes us up enough to remake the foundations, including the foundations of the Enlightenment and the Rights of Man. It reveals to us the multiverse (as cosmologists say) of the interior experiences it renews without end. Therefore, given the effectiveness of the Rights of Man in leading to the fulfillment of singularities, over and above the clash of religions, can poetic writing be the language of sharable singularities? That is my wager. As a result, it is up to us to better grasp the psychosocial dynamics of poetry and especially to encourage its dissemination in the multiple forms that, in particular, our digital modernity offers to us. This will be a bold and long-term engagement. However, if we are incapable of this, transhumanism will only have been a tool of banalization and the automatization of the human species.

~

Examples of these poetic multiverses, multiverses of life-giving power?
There are some examples, on the part of those who are fragile: my son David Joyaux proves it; he publishes some of his poems in the newspaper, *Le Papotin*, open to people with disabilities. This is how he confides and confirms his sur-vival (with a dash) after a long coma at the hospital:

Writing

From the white point to the point / black where is written / without / the day, without the night, the attraction / of words for the withdrawal / of the seas . . . The hidden objects / are sentences / Where I'm hiding so as / not to forget love. / The envelope, / it's silence. To perform / your writing / listen to the silence of the books. Writing allows / thinking. It is the / memory of life. / It allows the forgetting / of suffering, it allows / to love, it allows / to be together / surrounded /, in the / solitude. / Writing allows travel / When one wants / or does not want / . . . / Writing . . .[11]

Usually more at ease in music than in words, David gave us his first sign of life when coming out of a coma through this resonance titled "Writing." I also perceive the sur-vival of writing in blogs and other forums of global internet users who are today reappropriating the memory of cultural diversity, and in countercurrent to the sterile nostalgias like those of our politicians' one-upmanship on austerity—these *internautes* inhabit the infinitude of language through their new and incalculable creativities.

Can the politician hear this "inner touch," enroll in this new temporality of renewal? It is said that he lacks vision, even incarnation. And what if the remedy for our elected representatives was to cultivate themselves and to encounter more poets and artists? What would we risk? That a president of the Republic would start speaking like Paul Claudel, Michel Deguy (present here), Guyotat, or Sollers? Not likely! But let's try, let's take the risk.

Intellectuals, for their part, have a tendency to blind themselves as ideologues, and playing with power heavily distances them from the possibilities of poetic language.

For my part, it is in psychoanalysis that I have found a kind of *poïetics*, when I hear and interpret the new beginnings of singularity on the part of those analysands whose trust I have gained.

Another example: I moved my seminar on the "Need to believe" from my university—Université de Paris 7—to the Home for Adolescents, the Maison de Solenn, at the Cochin Hospital [Paris]. There we receive depressed, suicidal, anorexic, and addicted adolescents. Or those in the process of radicalization. Souad is a young girl of fourteen years, from a Muslim family. She was admitted for anorexia: her body was slowly dying, killing the young woman and the mother in herself, both abandoned and misunderstood. Burqa, silence, and Internet where, with unknown accomplices, she accuses her family of being "apostates, worse than unbelievers" and prepares for her travels "over there," to become an occasional wife to polygamous fighters, a fertile mother of martyrs or a kamikaze herself.[12]

Souad started the interviews with the multicultural team of mixed analytic psychotherapists by provocatively saying that she had a "scientific mind," strong in math and physics-chemistry, but that "only Allah spoke the truth and could understand her." Literature "did not speak to her" and she "detested courses in French and philosophy," which she "skipped whenever possible." But Souad found pleasure in telling her story, in playing with the team as with a newly blended family, in laughing with others and at herself. And in re-engaging with French: in using the language to tame her destructive drives and her sensations of suffering. Other teens accompanied by the team frequented writing and theater workshops. Souad borrowed from them a book of Arabic poems translated into French. She skipped fewer French courses. And she put her jeans back on.

Roland Barthes wrote that if you rediscover meaning within the fullness of a language, the "absence of the divine can no longer be menacing." I would add: the totalitarian hold of the divine would also no longer be menacing. Souad isn't there yet. It will be a long journey for her. But how many young women won't ever have the opportunity to encounter the poetics of listening? And to reconnect with an identity in movement?

You will say to us this evening: How can one be a poet today? Who are your readers, your journals, their distribution, your discoveries, your limits? I would like to finish by adding to the debate one final and inevitable question.

By opening up a maternal and/or national language, poetic language opens up and remakes identity, notably national identity. Far from being a reactionary archaism, identity is an antidepressant (it is perhaps what Hölderlin was looking for in a "form"?). For the poet, however, as I understand it, identity remains a scar where he inscribes his singular inspiration, which allows him to hold on during the time of identities.

As for European identity, this *poïetic* memory reminds us that, despite our current sense of powerlessness and our past or present crimes, we are a civilization, perhaps the only one, within which identity is not a cult, but rather a large question mark. And a civilization in which an evening like this one is possible, where poetry confronts nihilism and transcendence, the politics of the "least horrible" and sacred barbarism. When neither tweets nor the social networks nor distress itself speaks to you, when you have nothing left to say—you look for the "great voices": poems, novels, theater, movies, concerts. I do as you do. And then I can understand better the frail trembling of David and of Souad.

JULIA KRISTEVA
November 7, 2016, Théâtre de la Colline

Context of Julia Kristeva's Public Lecture, in Minutes of the Ministry of Culture and Communications

"Of what use are poets in times of distress?" It is to this question posed by Friedrich Hölderlin in his "Élégies" that the Minister of Culture and Communication and the Colline National Theatre invited, on November 7, philosophers, filmmakers, historians, and writers to respond as part of the movement *"Fraternité génerale!"* [Fraternity for All!].

"To find the necessary words and gestures faced with the evils that surpass us." With these words, Wajdi Mouawad, director of the Colline National Theatre, welcomes the vast public audience attending the colloquium. In effect, there is no need to say more. The playwright, who calls on the ideas of the philosopher Jan Patočka—"a unity between humans that relies on the idea of disruption"—knows perfectly well those evils are on everyone's mind in advance of the thirteenth of November 2015 commemoration. "While we do not know yet if we are beyond the time of worry, we do know, nevertheless, that we have to make more room for thought and beauty," responds, in echo, Audrey Azoulay, but also the writer and the psychoanalyst Julia Kristeva, who after recalling the words of Theodor Adorno—how could one write poetry after Auschwitz—launches into a vibrant plea in favor of poetry: "If you rediscover the meaning of the world within the fullness of a language, totalitarianism will no longer be menacing for you."

Julia Kristeva: "La culture française permet d'intégrer et de montrer l'étrangeté dans l'identité." (French culture permits the integration and demonstration of strangeness/foreignness in identity.)

I am a child of the Alliance Française, since I learned French in Bulgaria and came to France to write a thesis on the New Novel. Literature and poetic language molded me. I am fortunate to be invited abroad [*à l'étranger*] to speak about French literature and poetry, and I sense everywhere a desire for French language and culture. I have just published a book in which a young psychologist, Samuel Dock, interviews me about my life story and my relationship to the French language. The title, *Je me voyage* (*Traveling through Myself*), is a nod to the fact that French is not my first language. It seems to me that people who, like me, come from other cultures and learn French, can carry rhythms, vibrations, and neologisms that enrich the language. I often say that national identity is not necessarily an archaism, but it is an antidepressant. The poet shows us that we should not abuse it, but bring to it innovations that will enrich tradition. French culture permits the integration and demonstration of strangeness/foreignness within identity. It is in France that a theater like La Colline can organize an evening where it is poetry that interpolates nihilism, integrationism, and politics.

Minutes from the evening are on the site of the Minister of Culture and Communication: https://www.culture.gouv.fr/Actualites/Le-XXIe-siecle-sera-poetique-ou-ne-sera-pas.

Notes

Originally presented as a public address, "À quoi bon des poètes en temps de détresse?," presented at the Théâtre de la Colline, November 7, 2016.

Editor's note. Lecture given by Kristeva on November 7, 2016, at Colline National Theatre. Below all endnotes are made by the translator, Elisabeth Paquette. Translation first begun by Alice Jardine, who published parts of it in Jardine (2020, 313–14). This is a co-translation as Jardine joined Paquette to translate the text in full for this volume.

1. The use of *travel* here and throughout this essay corresponds to Samuel Dock's interview with Julia Kristeva, titled *Je me voyage: Mémoires* (Paris: Fayard, 2016). The title is translated by Alice Jardine as *Traveling through Myself*, in Jardine (2020, 18). I have opted to use *travel* instead of *voyage* for the French *voyage* in an attempt to ensure consistency. In addition, in many instances, I have utilized the gerund of *travel*, wherein the verb *to travel* operates as a noun, that is, *a traveling* again, to ensure consistency with Kristeva's text and other translations.

2. The poem referenced here is Charles Baudelaire's "Le Voyage" collected in *Les Fleurs du mal*, published in 1857. This translation comes from Aggeler (1954).

3. The poem referenced here is Arthur Rimbaud's "Vies" which can be found in *Illuminations*, published in 1886. This sentence was translated by Wallace Fowlie, and can be found at https://www.poetryfoundation.org/poems/55037/lives.

4. Stéphane Mallarmé, "Lettre à Eugène Lefébure," May 27, 1867. This sentence is translated by Mary Ann Caws (Mallarmé, 1982, 88).

5. Louis Aragon (1945). My translation.

6. Paul Celan, *Atemwende*, a 1967 German-language collection of poetry published in German in 1967, translated into the French as *Renverse du souffle* that same year. Translated by John Felstiner (Räsänen 2007, 289).

7. Colette (2002, 110).

8. The use of the masculine pronoun *him* in this instance refers to a universal position, a move that is consistent with the original French, and as the French language often utilizes the masculine to denote universality.

9. This paragraph was translated by Alice Jardine (2020, 313). This translation was taken from that text.

10. This seems to be a reference to Arthur Rimbaud's "The Drunken Boat."

11. From Jardine, *At the Risk of Thinking* (314).

12. Parts of this paragraph were translated in the essay titled "Reconstructing Identity in Times of Existential Crisis," which can be found at http://www.kristeva.fr/reconstruire-l-identite.html. I drew in part from this translation.

References

Aggeler, William. 1954. *The Flowers of Evil*. Fresno, CA: Academy Library Guild. Retrieved from https://www.poetryfoundation.org/poems/55037/lives.

Aragon, Louis. 1945. "En étrange pays dans mon pays lui-même." In *Collection Poesis 47*.

Colette. 2002. *Break of Day*. Translated by Enid McLeod. New York: Farrar, Straus and Giroux.

Jardine, Alice. 2020. *At the Risk of Thinking: An Intellectual Biography of Julia Kristeva*. New York: Bloomsbury Press.

Kristeva, Julia. 2016. *Je me voyage: Mémoires*. Paris: Fayard.

———. 2017. "Reconstructing Identity in Times of Existential Crisis," Keynote lecture, Reconstructing Identity in Times of Existential Crisis from The Jack, Joseph, and Morton Mandel Institute for Social Leadership at Ben-Gurion University of the Negev. Beersheba, Israel. Retrieved from http://www.kristeva.fr/reconstruire-lidentite.html

Räsänen, Pajari. 2007. "Counter-figures: An Essay on Anti-metaphoric Resistance: Paul Celan's Poetry and Poetics at the Limits of Figurality." PhD diss., University of Helsinki.

Stéphane Mallarmé. 1982. "Lettre à Eugène Lefébure." In *Stéphane Mallarmé: Selected Poetry and Prose*. Edited by Mary Ann Caw. New York: New Directions.

Part Two

Beyond Feminism: Engaging Kristeva for Decolonial, Trans, and Disability Studies

Chapter 4

Julia Kristeva's Maternal Ethics of Tenderness

KELLY OLIVER

Introduction

From the beginnings of her writings, Kristeva has attempted to bring the body back into philosophies of language, which she maintains only consider a fixed body in repose. More specifically, as a corrective to both philosophy and psychoanalysis, Kristeva complicates the *maternal* body, refusing to accept its reduction to mere reproduction or animal instinct. Against Freud in particular, she argues that the mother is a speaking being who introduces her child to the rhythms and tones of language (the semiotic), even before giving birth. Straddling biology and culture, the maternal body becomes an icon within Kristeva's thought, a model for relationships, and an ideal for our very humanity.[1] It is difficult to overestimate the importance of the maternal—in terms of both function and body—in Kristeva's work.[2] Her most influential concepts, especially the semiotic and the abject, are linked to the maternal body. Indeed, of all of her notions, the centrality of the maternal body is as evident in her work today as it was almost fifty years ago.

In this essay, tracing Kristeva's evolving discussion of the maternal in relation to ethics, I propose an ethics of tenderness that grows out of her engagement with disability and her exchange with Jean Vanier, founder of *L'Arche*.[3] From Kristeva's early suggestions of a heretics of love to more recent discussions of democracy of proximity,[4] the maternal ethics of tenderness revolves around complex affective connections, which are always ambivalent and require critical interpretation. Ultimately, this critical love is the basis of an ethics of tenderness, which goes beyond care or ethics of care, to what I will describe as an ethics of *being with*.

In her seminal essay, "Stabat Mater," Kristeva (2002) concludes with the provocative suggestion of a *Herethics* born out of a new discourse of maternity, one that does not reduce it to either biology (science) or the sacred beyond (religion), but rather fuses a phenomenology of maternity with an account of the structure of maternity that both logically and chronologically precedes and supports the child. Thirty-five years later, in her discussion of *maternal reliance*, she (2013) again invokes this *Herethics* when she provocatively claims, "Without that [discourse of maternal eroticism], the emancipation of the woman-subject is fated to be only an ideology without ethics. . . . There will not be a free woman as long as we lack an ethics of the maternal. But this ethics is just being born; it will be a herethics of reliance" (82–83).

But what is this herethics born from reliance? In this essay, I will focus on the relationship between reliance and ethics, specifically the maternal support that allows the child to feel safe and be itself. I suggest that Kristeva's notion of maternal reliance takes us back to her early discussions of herethics and her analysis of the paintings of Giovanni Bellini. What she describes as the sublimatory process of passioning and depassioning maternal eroticism into tenderness is prefigured in her analysis of Bellini's paintings. In "Motherhood According to Bellini," she (1980) interprets the placement of the Virgin's hands around the child, and her gaze outside the frame of the paintings, to describe a maternal jouissance as sublimation of eroticism, that is, "eroticizing without residue and a disappearance of eroticism as it returns to its source" (240).

This "objectless" jouissance is at the heart of Kristeva's recent notion of maternal reliance, which she describes as the passioning and depassioning of maternal eroticism. In *Hatred and Forgiveness* (2010), she goes so far as to suggest that maternal reliance as objectless love can provide a counterbalance to fundamentalism, which she describes as obsessed with an absolute object (169). Maternal eroticism, rather than directed at one object, dissolves both subject and object into a fluidity that defies categorization, the fluidity of the subject-in-process that she describes in *Revolution in Poetic Language*. Maternity, however, is not the only form of objectless love that dissolves both subjects and objects. Psychoanalysis, art, writing, and mysticism are all places where this "objectless love" can take place (chapter 12).

At the end of "Stabat Mater," Kristeva (2002) links herethics to "flesh, language, jouissance" and ultimately to objectless love (332). She describes this heretical ethics as separated from morality and law. It is "that which in life makes bonds, thoughts, and therefore the thought of death, bearable" (332). Love as the counterweight to death, *amour* and *a mort*. With her notion of maternal reliance, Kristeva further elaborates how this ethical love operates. Thus, in order to understand herethics or the ethics of maternity, we need to investigate what Kristeva means by reliance.

Kristeva (2014) defines reliance: "Reliance: to link, to gather, to join, to put together; but also to adhere, to belong, to depend on; and therefore to trust, to feel safe, to share your thoughts and feelings, to assemble together, and to be yourself" (79). As I've mentioned, her notion of maternal reliance (maternal bind or hold) can be interpreted an extension of her early analysis of the placement of the Virgin's hand in the iconography of Giovanni Bellini. In "Motherhood According to Giovanni Bellini" (1980), she contrasts Bellini's identification with the position of the mother, who supports her child even as her gaze is elsewhere, and Leonardo da Vinci's representation of the Virgin as completely absorbed by her child (245). She sees in Bellini's art the representation of a mother "split" between possession and separation, but ultimately maternal jubilance expressed through color and light (248–49). Whereas da Vinci is obsessed with the object and its mastery, Bellini takes us beyond the object to an objectless love, which comes to represent maternal eroticism or the process of passioning and depassioning (246–47; cf. 2010 71–76).[5]

In her later work on reliance, the maternal split that gives way to objectless love becomes maternal eroticism as passion and depassion, which corresponds to the movement between holding on to and letting go. The mother is called on to support her infant, and yet eventually she must let go of it so that it can be weaned and have a life of its own. Both attachment and separation are necessary elements of the maternal function that operate in a fragile equilibrium that, *in the ideal*, avoids either overprotection or neglect. For the sake of both the well-being of the mother and the child, the mother must perform this delicate balance, providing just enough support. Her hold on the child needs to be reassuring but not suffocating, light but not lax.[6]

Kristeva proposes the maternal as a structure—or we could say model—for human relationships, what she also calls a prototype.[7] This *ideal* of human relationships is one that is based on an affective connection and an affirmation of the singularity of each individual. As an ideal, the maternal function includes not only passionate attachment to the other that is her child, but also depassioning as she lets the child become its own person. The ideal mother loves her child for itself and not as an extension of herself. The ideal of motherhood that Kristeva proposes as a prototype for of human passion—and the basis for a new humanism—is based on a loving affirmation of the singularity of her child. The mother attends to her child's responses, especially encouraging its baby talk, which she enjoys.[8] This joy in the very being of the other, is the basis for an other-directed ethics. The ideal mother's radical acceptance of the other becomes the model for all ethical relations. Kristeva (2010) describes the mother's relation to her child as the "beginning of this otherness, of this enigmatic love of difference" (55).

Obviously, real motherhood is complex and always filled with ambiguity and ambivalence. The mother-child relationship is fraught with tensions and power dynamics and decidedly asymmetrical.[9] Yet, this asymmetry is necessary for the ethical demand at its heart. For, herethics is not based on laws or principles, but rather on love and acceptance that found an ethics of response to the otherness of the other. This is an ethics of difference based on an asymmetrical responsibility to the response of the other. In this regard, herethics resonates with Levinasian ethics as responsibility to the other's response. Whereas Levinas proposes what he calls paternal election of the son as radical other as a model for this affirmation of the otherness of the other, Kristeva proposes maternal eroticism as passioning and depassioning.

In a sense, both Kristeva and Levinas suggest that giving birth to one's child leads to a process, which is necessarily ongoing, of being born and reborn oneself, through this uncanny stranger who is elected but never chosen. This strange relation requires relinquishing any illusions of control or identification in order to love this other who is "my child," but never mine. The process of negotiating—or better yet, undergoing or suffering—the passion and dispassion that constitute the Eros of paternity and maternity, can awaken the uncanny stranger within the parent. The arrival of the little stranger gives birth to an uncanniness that disturbs the parents' sense of self-control, self-identification, and self-ownership. For Kristeva, this awakening of the stranger within is a process of rebirth that comes through various forms of sublimation not limited to maternity or paternity.

Yet it is Levinas who reminds us that the little stranger, this newcomer born out of the bodies of women, can be chosen only after the fact, which is to say as a gift beyond any economy of exchange or reciprocity. The structure of maternity and paternity, when they approach the ideals described by Levinas and Kristeva, the ideals of Eros and love beyond sovereignty and self, teach us that even as we try to repress or ignore them, we do not choose the others or otherness that calls to us, but we can elect to embrace it. Although we may not choose the stranger, we can embrace him or her. For Kristeva, this is the transformative power of maternal eroticism sublimated into tenderness.

Following biologist Jean-Didier Vincent, Kristeva defines passion as specific to humans in that it requires reflexive consciousness and the capacity for encountering the other. Passion is the crossroads or interface between emotions, which are bodily or somatic and shared by all vertebrates, and reflexive consciousness, which is the result of both the symbolic pact that founds human civilization (that is to say, the murder of the father and substitution of the totemic animal) and the formation of the unconscious as a result of the repression of this criminal act on which the pact originates (2010). In other words, passion is both what makes human experience uncanny or strange and allows us to live with that strangeness. Maternal passion is a prototype of all human passion (2011).

In a chapter of *Hatred and Forgiveness* titled "The Passion according to Motherhood," Kristeva (2010) says, "allow me to take the mother's side" and proceeds to describe "the extraneousness of the pregnant woman" as the narcissistic withdrawal wherein "the future mother becomes an object of desire, pleasure and aversion for herself" (85). In this state, which Kristeva claims is not unlike "possession," the pregnant woman is "incapable of taking into account an existence separate from her own" (85). She is completely absorbed by emotions invested in her own body as the "hollow" habitation of a future love-object that she will have to allow to become a subject.

Kristeva describes this maternal progression toward what she calls the "miracle" of love as a progression from the pregnant woman's destabilized sense of self due to the literal other within, followed by her investment in her own body as the site of her instability in a passion turned inward, toward her own body. Next, when the child is born, the mother must redirect that passion outward and onto her child as separate from herself: "This first stage [pregnancy] of inwardly turned passion is followed by the mother's passion for a new subject, her child, provided he stops being her double and that she detaches herself from him so he gains autonomy. The motion of expulsion, of detachment, is essential. . . . [It] allows the affect to turn to tenderness, caretaking and benevolence" (Kristeva 2011).[10] This move from self-absorption to love of the child and then eventually release or weaning of the child is the "miracle" of maternal passion become tenderness. The mother embodies both passion and depassion, or passion and working through passion, such that eroticism gives way to tenderness.[11]

On Kristeva's account, then, it is not primarily passion that is uniquely human but rather depassion, and ultimately the sublimation of passion, which is essential to maternal passion as successful mothering. Depassioning as de-eroticizing is necessary for sublimation of sadomasochistic drives that simultaneously threaten and inaugurate speech. This depassioning is also a form of repassioning insofar as it is necessary for the rebinding or reliance that Kristeva associates in her later work with maternal eroticism (2014). Considering her notion of maternal reliance, or the maternal bind, highlights her shift from the Freudian emphasis on the paternal to the maternal. In addition, her theory of reliance as a rebinding of affect illuminates how she understands sublimation as a rebinding rather than merely a binding.

Furthermore, the mother's passion for her child as a depassioning becomes a model for sublimation that informs Kristeva's theory of representation and her aesthetics. Thus, in order to fully appreciate the novelty of her turning away from the Freudian and Lacanian father of the law and toward the face of the mother and maternal affect, we need to explore Kristeva's latest thinking on the maternal hold, not just the maternal hold on the child, but also the maternal hold on our culture. In some sense, we could say that for Kristeva, sublimating the affective bind to the maternal is the fundamental task of all representation, which operates as a rebinding of that affect into signification, which for Kristeva is a hallmark of our humanity.

Thus, the model of maternal eroticism as the basis of Kristeva's new humanism involves three stages: binding, unbinding, and rebinding.[12] The mother is passionately attached to the child. Then the mother must detach herself to wean the child and let it become its own person. Finally, the mother must reinvest her passion through sublimation and bind that passionate energy to signification itself. By so doing, the mother not only "teaches" the child to love through language, but also learns to do so herself. The affective bodily connection between mother and child finds a necessary supplement in representation. All of these stages involve negativity and ambivalence. The push-pull of attraction-repulsion between self and other is operating at every stage, which makes it all the more "miraculous" that the mother can emerge from this process loving the other qua other. Through motherhood, the negativity, ambivalence, and aggressiveness inherent in all human relationships is transformed into love; "It is in motherhood that the link to the other can become love" (Kristeva 2010, 87).

At this point, it is important to reiterate that Kristeva's analysis of these structural features of motherhood are intended to tell us something about all human relationships, which is why she (2010) insists, "I am emphasizing *the structural* experience of motherhood: I am not fundamentally 'pro-birth'" (87; emphasis mine). She also maintains that other signifying practices can transform passion into depassion and rebind erotic drives to representation through sublimation (2011). Still, while Kristeva is clear that she is using maternal Eros as a structural model of loving compassion and depassion, there are problems with using the maternal model, including the power dynamics in the mother-child relationship, the fact that most people aren't mothers, and most importantly that many if not most mothers cannot live up to this ideal. Still, the emphasis on the affective bind between mother and child is very powerful and evocative as a model of love and affirmation. The emblematic elements of maternity are its openness and responsiveness to the difference of the other, and its acceptance, even love and embrace, of that difference.[13] Kristeva is asking us to emulate this ideal of affirmation of otherness in all our relationships. An ethics based on the singularity of each demands it.

Ethics of Tenderness

In "Tragedy and Dream: Disability Revisited," Kristeva (2013) again turns to maternal love as the basis for ethics. Here, however, her concern for an ethics of singularity based on love also inflects politics. She says, "Through my love for the other singular, I carry him or her to their specific, singular, development—and to mine, equally specific and singular" (227). The love that Kristeva identifies is not love with a capital *L*, nor is it romantic or romanticized love (224). Rather, it is analytical love, which is infused with transferential affect and critical analysis. The love she proposes is a critical love that demands vigilant investigation into our own investments in violence and our own ambivalent desires. This critical love brings with it obligations, not just for what we do or say, not just for what we feel or believe, but also for our unconscious fears and desires and the effects they have on others.

In her discussion of love at the end of "Tragedy and Dream," Kristeva (2013) associates this love of the singular with what she calls "vigilant transfer" in the maternal relationship, or, in other terms, the transfer of affect. This vigilant transfer points to the centrality of transference in human relationships (229). Transference, specifically the transfer of affects, is what is missing in integration and present in interaction. This is why Kristeva insists on interaction and not merely integration when it comes to people in the situation of disability. The "transferential encounter" revitalizes and jubilates. Operating on the affective level, it imbues signification—and human life itself—with meaning (229).

Kristeva (2013) goes so far as to suggest that caregivers be trained in transference to better understand the needs of the ones they care for and their own relationship to them: "I am thinking of the *training of caregivers* in place of psychoanalysis in this complex and controversial area when broaching the question of love, understood as a continual and elucidated transference, in caring for the disabled person" (223). Part of this training might involve the benevolent listening that Kristeva identifies with psychoanalysis.

Analytic listening is not only an attentiveness to the circulation of affect as manifestations of unconscious fears and desires, but also, and moreover, nonjudgmental listening, which is why Kristeva also associates analytic listening with forgiveness or pardon as the giving of psychic space and time necessary to make traumatic experiences meaningful (2010, 191–94).[14] The goal of psychoanalytic listening is to suspend judgment and allow the subject space and time to connect her affect to words. In addition, analytic listening is attentiveness to one's own desires and fears as they are evoked by encounters with others. By both suspending judgment and analyzing one's own fears and desires, psychoanalytic listening opens the political onto the ethical. In fact, analytic listening's suspension of judgment opens up the possibility of analyzing our own investments in violence, abjection, and exclusion.

Kristeva (2010) argues that traditional humanism has excluded people with disabilities because it is "incapable of traversing the fears and anxieties that control the unconscious—and often conscious—rejection of the disabled by those who are not. It is precisely here that psychoanalytic listening to vulnerability could take on political meaning, addressing not only those affected by a disability but the society of others, who, instead of integrating them, might have real interaction with them" (191–94).

Moving transference from the psychoanalytic setting into everyday relationships would mean critical reflection on the ways in which we project our own fears and desires onto others. Furthermore, it would require taking responsibility for the ways in which our responses to others engender their responses to us, particularly emotional responses. Taking responsibility for the other's response is a hallmark of Levinasian ethics as first philosophy. It is also the basis for what I have called *witnessing* as attention to a pathos beyond recognition that binds us and obligates us to respond.[15] An ethics of psychoanalysis is even more radical than Levinasian ethics, which makes us responsible for the other's response, in that it makes us responsible for our unconscious desires and fears and the process of transference and countertransference, which encompasses our response to others and otherness in ourselves.

Kristeva (2013) suggests moving this ethical attention to the singularity of each supported by psychoanalytic listening and attention to the transfer of affects into the political realm, in "a politics that has become ethics, in expanding the political pact as far as the boundaries of life," which places "utter singularity at the heart of the political pact" (224). What happens, then, when love of the singular moves into—and moves— the political pact? Can we learn to love others, even those most different from ourselves, even those whom we fear? Can we work through our own projections and abjections and come to terms with others in our midst?

Kristeva proposes love over solidarity to transform social bonds and the political pact and make them more inclusive. We need to: "reinvent love as *union with singularity* of all others. In other terms: the *love of singulars* must be substituted for *integrating solidarity* with the weak. What love? Love as desire and will so that the singular can elucidate, be recognized, and develop in sharing his own singularity. Far more than solidarity, which itself still has trouble existing, only this love can drive the constitutive singularity" (2019, 222–23). Solidarity with others or the disabled is not enough. Integration is not enough. We must do more than tolerate others. We must embrace them through interaction and ultimately critical analytic love. In other words, we must desire and will their existence and not just tolerate it. We must want them to be . . . to be as they are and not how we might wish. This love of being goes beyond mere acceptance and integration of "deficient" others.

Again Kristeva (2013) turns to a mother's love of her child, and more personally, her own love for her son, when she says, "I want you to be . . . I love that you be" (229). This is not mere acceptance of, or solidarity with, those seen as lacking. This love goes beyond accommodating for privations and defects, which Kristeva associates with both the Aristotelian and Christian approaches to disability (226). Rather, this love embraces the positive in the person in the situation of disability and wants them to be as they are and not otherwise. It is through interaction with the singularity of each as an act of love that embraces them as they are and thereby transforms the norms of culture. In this dynamic relationship, new political subjects emerge "who push back the limits of former norms and engender new ones," proving that "the norm is no longer an a priori fixed concept but a dynamic one" (226).

In her exchange with Jean Vanier, Kristeva (2011) identifies affective connection as fundamental to what it means to be human: "I maintain that the *difference* of disabled people, contrary to all other differences, takes us back not to a struggle for power, but to the meaning we give to the human species. Even when a person doesn't have access to the signification of language and thought, s/he is inhabited by affective meaning: infinitesimal, incommensurable joy and suffering. This meaning inhabits the pre-political and pre-religious foundation where, in effect, the ties of tenderness hide the secret of survival" (140). To live with others is to learn tenderness as a lesson in loving the uniqueness of each person. Again, for Kristeva this lesson in love comes through transference and the dynamic of unconscious affect. She (2019) says, "The Freudian discovery of the unconscious . . . makes it possible to rethink the work of the signifying process through love in the singularity of the human adventure" (80). This human adventure is learning to embrace the singularity of each one through tenderness.

Kristeva associates this tenderness with maternal passion, more specifically, with the sublimation of maternal passion. Maternal eroticism is sublimated into tenderness (Kristeva, 2011). The ambivalence and aggressive drives, both Eros and Thanatos, are sublimated into tenderness toward the other as an affirmation of the child's being. This tenderness is what makes the child feel safe and allows it to be or become who it is. Thus, Kristeva concludes(2014), "But while the lover's libido is dominated by the satisfaction of drive, maternal eroticism deploys (or 'sprouts') its libidinal force as tenderness. Beyond abjection and separation, tenderness is the basic affect of reliance" (75).

Tenderness cannot be reduced to some kind of maternal instinct. In her exchange with Vanier, Kristeva (2011) says, "More so than female cats or tigresses [who also cares for their young] humanity's mothers, because they are endowed with language, manage to sublimate their erotic and destructive drives through tenderness." Also, tenderness cannot be reduced to care, although caring for can be an expression of tenderness. This ethics of tenderness is a way of being with, a disposition toward the other, rather than a set of particular actions or even intentions toward the other.

Like feminist care ethics (e.g., Gilligan, Noddings, Kittay), ethics of tenderness starts from a deeply relational notion of the self wherein duties and obligations originate from our interdependence and mutual vulnerability rather than from some presumed autonomy. Care ethics emphasizes our interdependence as its foundation. For example, Eva Kittay (1999) maintains that our obligations to each other are grounded in our interdependence and, therefore, an individual who "refuses to support this bond absolves itself from its most fundamental obligation—its obligation to its founding possibility" (131). As Kittay points out, we all begin our lives entirely dependent on others, and most of us will end our lives in nearly the same way, with varying degrees of dependence in between.

Whereas in care ethics our interdependence and vulnerability are based primarily on our bodies, for Kristeva, herethics is based on the fact that we are speaking beings. For Kristeva, vulnerability is not primarily the consequence of our embodiment or the fact that we can be physically wounded or become ill. Furthermore, her notion of vulnerability cannot be reduced to our dependence or interdependence or that we require or give care—although giving and receiving care are essential for human life and flourishing. Rather, for Kristeva (2010), vulnerability is the result of the fact that we are "speaking beings" (41).

As speaking beings, we straddle biology and culture, *zoë* and *bios*, such that this split forms a primary wound (to use Kristeva's description from "Stabat Mater"). We are vulnerable because we are beings who mean. As beings who mean, our very biology is innately social. She (2010) claims that the discovery of the unconscious as the place where biology meets culture is a discovery of "the essential vulnerability of the speaking body" (41). Human vulnerability, then, is the unique consequence of our place between nature and culture as speaking bodies, or more generally, as beings who mean. The vulnerability of the speaking being—or being who means—is its radical dependence on belonging and being accepted.

This vulnerability is the psychic vulnerability that comes with occupying a place between being and meaning such that we can never fully articulate or communicate our bodily experience.[16]

This vulnerability points to the centrality of emotions in meaning making, which is possible only by virtue of our relationships with others and otherness. Without considering the ways in which emotions affect our relationships, we risk acting out unconscious desires and fears and projecting them onto others. When we merely project our fears and desires onto others, we are not truly interacting with them. Interacting requires attention and the nonjudgmental listening that Kristeva attributes to psychoanalysis. Moreover, interacting with tenderness requires going beyond withholding judgment and toward a positive affirmation of the singular difference of the other. As we have seen, the sublimation of maternal eroticism into tenderness is the model for not only accepting the other as they are, but also and moreover, embracing or affirming their singularity: "I want you to be. I love who you are."

In her clinical practice, this affirmation and suspension of judgment are part of what she calls "accompanying."[17] For example, in a recent piece in *Slate* magazine in France, discussing the radicalization of youth into violent fundamentalist groups, Kristeva claims that psychoanalysts and others need to "accompany" on their need to believe in order to assist their "reconnection" to language and signification that can absorb their violent drives and quell the urgency of their quest for the absolute.

She gives the example of a girl she calls Souad, who was hospitalized for serious anorexia and had been radicalized online by Islamic extremists. Her hospitalization resulted in psychotherapy, which eventually lead this "girl of few words" to enjoy telling stories and sharing with the group, thereby reconnecting her suffering to language: "taming through language the drives and sensations of suffering, finding the words to make them exist, to unmake and remake, to share them: language, literature, poetry, theater filled the lack of meaning and undid the nihilism" (Kristeva 2016). Kristeva maintains that therapists and others must listen and recognize wounded young people by "accompanying" them and thereby supporting the reconnection of their suffering to words and the rebinding of their affects to signification.[18] Only by rebinding aggressive drives can we prevent violence and destruction.

There is much more to say about the sublimation of violence, but in conclusion, I want to emphasize Kristeva's use of the word *accompany*. Tenderness is a way of accompanying.[19] Tenderness is not an activity or set of activities, including caregiving. Rather, tenderness is an orientation, a way of being in the world, a way of accompanying suffering. The ethics of tenderness, then, is a mode of being with, of accompanying that supports the movement of suffering into signification.

Kristeva proposes motherhood as a model and prototype of this ethics of tenderness. The ideal of motherhood she imagines is based on the acceptance and embrace of the child as other and different. The mother's love provides the support for the child's entrance into language. She both holds on and lets go. She attends to her child. And she enjoys the child's response. Her way of being toward this other is one of tenderness. If love "is the intimate side of ethics," then maternal eroticism is the model of this ethics of tenderness (2014, 82).

From herethics to ethics of tenderness, Kristeva complicates the maternal function and gives us a model of motherhood that goes beyond Freud's oceanic feeling, or the reproduction of the species offered by biology, or the sacred beyond of the Catholic Virgin. Pierced by negativity, charged with drive energy, and full of ambivalence, Kristeva's ideal mother sublimates both Eros and Thanatos into tenderness. Kristeva asks us to imagine that tenderness as the hallmark of humanity, and ultimately of a new ethics, an ethos of tenderness.

Notes

1. In 1975, Kristeva (2002) calls the maternal body "a filter . . . a thoroughfare, a threshold where 'nature' confronts 'culture' " (329). Thirty years later, in "Motherhood Today," she says, "The mother is at the crossroads of biology and meaning as early on as the pregnancy: *maternal passion debiologizes* the link to the child, *without becoming completely detached from* the biological, yet already the emotions of attachment and aggression are on the way towards sublimation," 2011, http://www.kristeva.fr/motherhood.html.

2. For a critical take on Kristeva's notion of maternity, see Bruzelius (1999). For more positive expositions, see Hopfl (2003), Hawthrone (2013), and Lemma (2009).

3. In 1964, after a visit to an institution in France were disabled men were kept locked up, Vanier gave up teaching philosophy at the University of Toronto and bought a small house in northern France, where he lived with two disabled men from the local psychiatric asylum. That was the beginning of *L'Arche*—named for Noah's Ark—which now has communities in thirty-five countries.

4. For an expanded treatment of Kristeva notion of democracy of proximity, see Oliver (2020).

5. Kristeva (1980) says of da Vinci, "The artist, as servant of the maternal phallus, displays this always and everywhere unaccomplished art of reproducing bodies and spaces as graspable, masterable objects, within reach of his eye and hand" (246). Describing Bellini's painting *The Ecstasy of St. Francis*, she maintains that color and light "are the real, objectless goal of the painting" (248).

6. Benigno Trigo (2016) translates *maternal reliance* as *maternal hold*.

7. In "Motherhood Today," Kristeva (2011) says, "We see that while being a prototype of human passion, maternal passion is also the prototype of letting go of passion which allows the speaking subject to take her distance in relation to the two tormentors of the human psyche which are also passion's aids: drives and the object." She also maintains that there are other ways maternal passion manifests itself other than literally giving birth: "through psychoanalysis, self-analysis, or sublimating work a woman can also live out her maternal passion without gestation and giving birth."

8. In "Motherhood Today," Kristeva (2011) claims, "When the mother and child exchange signifiers . . . the withdrawal of the mother's drives; her attentiveness to the reaction of her child alone; and the surplus of pleasure created, or the encouragement given to the child's response. The mother does not invest her own message, but only the child's response from which she procures even greater jouissance and which in turn she magnifies and encourages."

9. For criticisms of Kristeva's essentialism when it comes to maternity, see, for example, Butler (1990) and Bruzelius (1999).

10. Kristeva (2014) describes maternal reliance as the work of the negative: "Reliance is clearly the work of the negative. But it couples it with that negativity a *fabulous investment in the state of emergency in life*; it is linked to a cathexis on physical and psychical *survival*, on the *care* of the living and concern for transmission. To put it simply, the negative is at work if and only if its *unbinding* is immediately recathected and reattached" (77).

11. She (2010) calls the sublimation of maternal eroticism into tenderness a miracle: "Miraculously ('miraculously,' because even though it seems impossible, this alchemy manages to take place, and consequently, humanity exists, thinks, speaks, lives), motherhood is a passion in the sense that the emotions of narcissistic attachment and aggressiveness, filtered through reflexive consciousness and through the unconscious that speaks of Eros and Thanatos, are transformed into love (with its more or less attenuated correlate of hate). I would even say that in this experience of motherhood, passion takes on its most human aspect, which is to say, the furthest from its biological foundation, which nevertheless accompanies it (the famous drives of attachment and aggressiveness), and that it takes the path of sublimation without ceasing to be a passion" (86).

12. For a discussion of rebinding in relation to binding and unbinding, see Oliver (2014).

13. For example, speaking of openness, Kristeva (2014) says, "maternal eroticism renders the fixation of the life and death drives both problematic and

available, and places them together in the service of the living as an 'open structure,' related to others and to the environment" (71). More specifically, she describes maternal eroticism as opening onto new beginnings: "[Maternal reliance] regulates the time of death into a temporality of new beginnings: jubilatory affirmations and anxious annihilations that literally put me beside myself, outside myself, and, without annihilating me, multiply me" (73).

14. For a discussion of Kristeva's notion of forgiveness in relation to the history of philosophy, see Oliver (2003, 280–92).

15. See Oliver (2001 and 2018).

16. In the case of people with disability, Kristeva makes the controversial claim that we need to learn to live with the mortality we encounter through interactions with them. For criticisms of Kristeva's association between disability and mortality, see Grue (2013) and Bunch (2017). For a sustained critical engagement with theories of vulnerability, see Oliver (2018).

17. Thanks to Benigno Trigo for pointing out that Kristeva repeatedly uses the words *accompany* and *accompaniment* when describing her analytic journey.

18. For example, Kristeva (2016) says, "*Il importe d'accompagne les candidats au djihad en voie de radicalisation, avant qu'ils ne rejoignent les camps de Daesh, pour revenir en kamikazes ou, éventuellement, en repentis plus ou moins sincères, pour une éventuelle déradicalisation.*" (It's important to accompany would-be jihadists in the process of radicalization, before they join Daesh camps, only to return as suicide bombers or, possibly, as more or less sincere repentants, for eventual deradicalization.)

19. For a discussion of Kristeva's theory of sublimation of violence, see Oliver (2013).

References

Bruzelius, Margaret. 1999. "Mother's Pain, Mother's Voice: Gabriela Mistral, Julia Kristeva, and the Mater Dolorosa." *Tulsa Studies in Women's Literature* 18, no. 2: 215–33.

Bunch, Mary. 2017. "Julia Kristeva, Disability, and the Singularity of Vulnerability." *Journal of Literary & Cultural Disability Studies* 11, no. 2: 133–50.

Butler, Judith. 1990. *Gender Trouble: Feminism and the Subversion of Identity.* New York: Routledge.

Grue, Jan. 2013. "Rhetorics of Difference: Julia Kristeva and Disability." *Scandinavian Journal of Disability Research* 15, no. 1: 45–57.

Hawthorne, Sian Melvill. 2013. "An Outlaw Ethics for the Study of Religions: Maternality and the Dialogic Subject in Julia Kristeva's 'Stabat Mater.'" *Culture and Dialogue* 3, no. 1: 127–51.

Hopfl, Heather. 2003. "Of Mothers": The Maternal Body and the Organization." In *Organization Theory and Postmodern Thought*, edited by Stephen Linstead. Thousand Oaks, CA: Sage.

Kittay, Eva Feder. 1999. *Love's Labor: Essays on Women, Equality and Dependency.* New York: Routledge.

Kristeva, Julia. 1980. "Motherhood According to Bellini." In *Desire in Language*, edited by Leon S. Roudiez, translated by Thomas Gora, Alice Jardine, and Leon S. Roudiez. New York: Columbia University Press.

———. 1984. *Revolution in Poetic Language*, translated by Margaret Waller. New York: Columbia University Press.

———. 2002. "Stabat Mater." In *The Portable Kristeva*, edited by Kelly Oliver. New York: Columbia University Press.

———. 2010. *Hatred and Forgiveness.* New York: Columbia University Press.

———. 2011. "Être mère aujourd'hui." *Revue française de psychosomatique* 40, no. 2: 43–51. English Translation http://www.kristeva.fr/motherhood.html.

———. 2013. A Tragedy and a Dream: Disability Revisited. *Irish Theological Quarterly* 8, no. 3: 219–30.

———. 2014. "Reliance, or Maternal Eroticism." *Journal of the American Psychoanalytic Association* 62, no. 1: 69–85.

———. 2016. "Interpreting Radical Evil." *Kristeva Circle Address*, Stockholm, Sweden. http://www.kristeva.fr/interpreting-radical-evil.html.

———. 2019. *Passions of Our Time*, edited by Lawrence D. Kritzman, translated by Constance Borde and Sheila Malovany-Chevallier. New York, Columbia University Press.

Kristeva, Julia, and Jean Vanier. 2011. *Leur Regard Perce Nos Ombres.* Paris: Fayard.

Lemma, Jennifer. 2009. "Language Acquisition, Motherhood, and the Perpetual Preservation of Ethical Dialogue: A Model for Ethical Discourse Focusing on Julia Kristeva." *Perspectives International Postgraduate Journal of Philosophy* 2, no. 1: 102–15.

Oliver, Kelly. 2001. *Witnessing: Beyond Recognition.* Minneapolis: University of Minnesota Press.

———. 2003. "Forgiveness and Subjectivity." In *Philosophy Today* 47, no. 3: 280–92.

———. 2013. *Technologies of Life and Death: From Cloning to Capital Punishment.* New York: Fordham University Press.

———. 2014. "Kristeva's Reformation." *Journal of French and Francophone Philosophy* 22, no. 2: 20–25.

———. 2018. *Response Ethics.* Edited by Alison Suen. London: Rowman and Littlefield International.

———. 2020. "The Democracy of Proximity and Kristeva's New Humanism." In *The Library of Living Philosophers, Volume XXXVI: The Philosophy of Julia Kristeva*, edited by Sara G. Beardsworth. Chicago, IL: Open Court.

Trigo, Benigno. 2016. "Lullaby Poetics; Working-Through the Maternal Hold in Puerto Rico (1937)." *Revista de Estudios Hispánicos* 50, no. 3: 653–77.

Chapter 5

Kristeva in a Trans Poetic Frame

Sid Hansen

Introduction: Julia Kristeva and the Transgender Turn

In her introduction to a 2017 special issue of *TSQ: Transgender Studies Quarterly* dedicated to "transpsychoanalytics," Sheila Cavanaugh shares her disappointment in having heard Julia Kristeva "echo the most objectionable element of Catherine Millot's *Horsexe* at the Association for Psychoanalytic Medicine in 2016." According to Cavanaugh, Kristeva stated that "when the difference between men and women is erased lack no longer exists." Her presentation also expressed concern about the "fabrication of gender by overly sympathetic gynecologists and endocrinologists" (2017, 353). While Kristeva has not written about transgender identity explicitly, these comments indicate that she might share in the fraught legacy of psychoanalysts dismissing and pathologizing trans people—from Freud's reduction of female masculinity to "penis envy," to the Lacanian association of transsexuality and psychosis in Millot's *Horsexe*. Subverting this legacy, the *Transpsychoanalytics* volume shows that a "transgender turn" is underway in psychoanalysis, as scholars uncover resources for trans liberation in various psychoanalytic texts, including Kristeva's (326). For instance, Amy Ray Stewart argues that Kristeva's notion of revolt is a trans-affirming account of "renewal, reconfiguration, and regeneration at the level of subjectivity" (351). In her recent book *Revolutionary Time*,

Fanny Söderbäck suggests that Kristeva's understanding of temporality challenges hetero- and cis-normative understandings of time and gender. Notably, Kristeva's term *abjection* is included in an encyclopedic issue of *TSQ* as one of the "key concepts for a twenty-first century transgender studies" (2014, 19–21).

In this chapter, I explore the extent to which Kristeva's account of poetic language can serve as a trans-theoretical resource. I pay particular attention to how poetic language reflects an understanding of sex and gender as entangled. In *Revolution in Poetic Language*, Kristeva refuses dualist distinctions between biology and culture, body and language. Criss-crossing and confounding the gate-kept boundaries of science and art, poetic language is an account of the heterogenous, dynamic, and nonlinear shape of subject formation. In the US, dualist understandings of biological sex and cultural gender undergird many antitrans projects, as coercive social programs of gender normalization attempt to produce and enforce biological sex as a binary natural reality. By contrast, Kristeva affirms the motile imbrication of biology and culture, sex and gender, body and language. Poetic language is one name for this movement; it describes the unique way that heterogenous language can help subjects search for and experiment with new ways of being. This picture of embodied poetics resonates with contemporary trans-affirming attempts to reimagine bodies as diverse and not dichotomous. However, I caution that Kristeva's inattention to the history of racism and colonialism limits the conceptual resourcefulness of *Revolution in Poetic Language* for trans studies. On my reading, poetic language must reckon with the ways that racism shapes the meaning of sex/gender and forms the context of so much psychic struggle today. I argue that such a reckoning must go beyond Kristeva's texts in ways that reimagine not only transpsychoanalytics but also history and poetics more broadly.

Between Sex and Gender: The Empty Violence of Dualism

Kristeva begins *Revolution in Poetic Language* with a "Prolegomenon" that takes aim at the ways that traditional disciplinary approaches to language ignore the role of bodies in signifying processes. According to Kristeva, fields like linguistics confuse the remains or fragments of signification with the whole, treating discourse as "empirical evidence, a systemizable given, and an observable object," yet failing to engage with how it is generated and interrelated (1984, 13). Objectifying language in this way, they amount to "a mere depository of thin linguistic layers, an archive of structures, or the testimony of a withdrawn body" (16). By contrast, Kristeva calls for an analysis of *signifiance* that includes the "unlimited and unbounded generating process," and the "unceasing operation of the drives toward, in, and through language" (17). Against deadened and deadening discourses, *Revolution* aims to bring the speaking body back into the analysis of language. While her critique of disciplinary thinking is sharply worded, the speaking body she mobilizes is not a reactionary theorization of materiality. Instead, it is shot through with heterogeneity that unsettles any dualism between semiotic and symbolic, sex and gender.

The distinction between the semiotic and symbolic lies at the heart of Kristeva's project in *Revolution in Poetic Language*. According to Kristeva, bodily drives make their way into language through a semiotic dimension that she calls the semiotic *chōra*. Based on the bodily signals involved in early development, the semiotic refers to the rhythms, tones, music, and sounds that compose psychic space. An essential support, this early bio-social activity helps encourage the child's acquisition of language and, in adult life, it works to sustain and nourish social ties. Without the semiotic, the subjectivation process is perilous, speech is empty and disconnected, and the psychically wounded lash out, against themselves, others, or both. For Kristeva, poetic language is revolutionary because the materiality of words and the rhythms and tones of poetry can heal and renew frayed social ties. In the music of poetry, semiotic drives find a place in language and a mode of transfer and discharge. Many of Kristeva's readers focus on this subversive role of the semiotic, and the possibility that semiotic drives in language might transform empty, rigid symbolic systems. But it is important to observe that heterogeneity of the semiotic and symbolic cuts both ways. The semiotic is heterogenous, shaped by early events and patterns of communication, and the symbolic is heterogeneous, in being traversed by bodily drives. Instead of a dualism, the semiotic and symbolic compose heterogenous language via "dialectical oscillation" (1993, 97).

Despite Kristeva's emphases, Anglophone readers have widely criticized the notion of the semiotic as essentialist and as more likely to produce stasis than revolution. For instance, in an influential, widely read section of *Gender Trouble*, Judith Butler argues that Kristeva "locates the source of subversion to a site outside of culture itself, [appearing] to foreclose the possibility of subversion as an effective or realizable cultural practice" (2019, 222). For Butler, Kristeva's semiotic *chōra* is the spacetime of embodied drives and nonlinguistic femininity, and the symbolic is the structure of language and disembodied masculinity. On this conservative, dualist picture, the traversal of semiotic drives in language only serves to repeat and reproduce the association of women and minorities with mute stasis. Instead of a dialectical oscillation that is defined by its generation of difference, Butler casts the semiotic *chōra* as the anchor for a patriarchal teleology in which the semiotic is ever subsumed and overtaken by the symbolic. In another widely read essay, Nancy Fraser echoes Butler, arguing that Kristeva offers a psychologized subject "split into two halves, neither of which is a potential political subject" (1992, 51–71).

In *Revolutionary Time*, Fanny Söderbäck undertakes a decisive correction to Butler's misinterpretation of the *chōra*, emphasizing the ways that it is not outside of time or culture, nor is it prone to stasis. Kristeva's notion of the *chōra* is inspired by the term's function in Plato's *Timaeus*, a dialogue that narrates the creation of the cosmos (2019, 202). As Söderbäck emphasizes, the *Timaeus* does not describe a Judeo-Christian act of creation *ex nihilo*. Instead, when the demiurge forms the cosmos in his own image, it is a kind of ordering of differently ordered matter. While Plato describes the *chōra*'s role as that of a receptacle, this does not require that it is passive or static. Instead, "it is the locus of birth and new beginnings. Marked by motility and ever-changing in nature." For Plato, "*chōra* names the expanse, the opening implied in the act of creation or generation, of beings coming into being. In the thrust of origination, the origin is no longer self-contained; it overflows beyond itself" (207). Kristeva's *chōra* shares in these characteristics. A "time-space of primary drives and processes" that supports the development of language, her *chōra* is not "brute matter waiting to be penetrated and impregnated" by the symbolic. Instead, it is a sign of the continuity between semiotic and symbolic. As Maria Margaroni summarizes Kristeva's borrowing of Plato's *chōra*, "the beginning itself is reinscribed as a process" (214, 214). Or as Söderbäck puts it, it is a "beginning that points to yet another beginning" (4). While Butler critiques the semiotic *chōra* as an essentialist outside, a position from which no effective revolution can be launched, Söderbäck's reading shows that the *chōra* is not "outside" or timeless but rather continuous and differently material and temporal.

Given the influence of *Gender Trouble* around the time of the English translation of Kristeva's early works, Butler's misreading of the semiotic *chōra* is consequential. Interestingly, the Kristeva section of

Gender Trouble is followed by a very similar, almost analogous misreading of Michel Foucault's text *Herculine Barbin: Being the Recently Discovered Memoirs of a Nineteenth-Century French Hermaphrodite*. There, Butler claims that Foucault treats Barbin's atypical body as an outside that resists modern rationalities of sexuate intelligibility. On Butler's reading, Foucault makes the same mistake as Kristeva—locating the sources of embodied subversion beyond culture and power—while Butler's own account of embodied gender performativity is historical, cultural, and entangled with power relations. But this foil is too tidy. In Kristeva's texts, the heterogenous body is affirmed as an historical opening, and not in the sense of an origin à la metaphysical history. The rhythms and music of early psychic development are not hardwired givens; they reflect the tangle of specific intimate relationships and intimate histories, from changing cultural caretaking practices to the ways that the body is "molded by a great many distinct regimes," "broken down by the rhythms of work, rest, and holidays; [. . .] poisoned by food or values, through eating habits or moral laws," as Foucault described the interplay in "Nietzsche, Genealogy, History" (1977, 153).

As these Foucauldian resonances suggest, the heterogenous rather than dualist characteristics of the semiotic and symbolic challenge dualist versions of the sex/gender distinction. In its common application, the sex/gender distinction describes sex as passive, material, and static, while gender is active, cultural, and subject to change. In addition to its problematic association of femininity with materiality and masculinity with agency, the distinction disavows the ambiguities of embodiment and relationality, the ways that culture and bodies are entangled from the start, since "every beginning points to another beginning." By contrast, Kristeva's notions of the semiotic and symbolic engage this ambiguity and imbrication. As Tina Chanter observes, it is "unclear where sex stops and culture starts since our very definition of sex is always already bound up in cultural assumptions—just as the semiotic expression is always already bound up with the symbolic order" (1993, 186). On this issue, Kristeva is far from a foil to Butler's historical and social account of sex as materialization. Compared to Butler, however, her project is more engaged with reimagining the meaning of nature, materiality, and sex. Chanter continues on to argue that Kristeva questions "received ideas about the difference between nature and culture that often underlie mistaken notions about the ease with which gender can be siphoned off from sex" (189). Kristeva's text challenges the contemporary social constructionist tendency to speak exclusively of gender or to treat gender as the active term to the blank, passive materiality of sex. In doing so, Kristeva is more attuned to bodies and embodiment, an attention that she insists is crucial to understanding *signifiance*.

Those working from a dualist approach might argue that Kristeva's effort to reimagine nature risks or invites essentialism even if it does not engage in it. However, it should be acknowledged that embracing "received ideas about the difference between nature and culture" carries its own risks and dangers. When sex appears as the blank page on which gender is written, it can link easily with dangerous eugenic projects like conversion therapy. Indeed the traditional notion of gender has its roots in this area via the hetero- and cis-normative research of psychiatrists John Money and Robert Stoller in the mid-twentieth century. In an influential series of articles in 1955, John Money sought to replace the notion of "psychological sex," understood as a variable of sex that develops biologically, with the notion of gender, a variable formed via social learning in the early years of life. Money's research focused on intersex conditions and was guided by the goal of securing heterosexuality. Through Money's influence on Robert Stoller, this normalizing rationale came to shape emerging medical discourses of transsexuality as well. Where Money had worked from a behaviorist method that focused on disciplining the social performance of gender, Stoller's psychoanalytic approach delved into the psychic dynamics of patients' emotional lives. Still, Stoller's therapeutic goals focused on securing the sex binary and achieving normalized results among his patients. In *The Biopolitics of Gender*, Jemima Repo argues that Stoller's protocols for trans patients also reflected racialized postwar discourses of happiness. In the aftermath of the Depression and the Second World War, during a time when "nuclear war was a genuine possibility," the pursuit of individual, materialistic happiness was an organizing aspiration of US social life. The "subtle violence" of Stoller's psychoanalytic notion of gender identity lies in the flexible ways that it coerces people to assimilate into the demand to be happy, institutionalizing "white, bourgeois standards of the healthy mind" (2016, 59).

Despite the historical connection between sex/gender dualism and racial normalization, many theorists tend to assume that gender is an inherently progressive discourse separable from more risky, questionable terrain of sex. The risk of this approach is that it ignores and emboldens reductionist understandings of sex, bodies, and materiality. In the United States, for instance, the notion of biological sex has become more and more invested with fixed, dichotomous, antitrans meanings. In 2021 and 2022, state legislatures across the US have introduced a record number of antitransgender bills, banning healthcare for transgender youth, excluding trans students from k–12 athletics, and shaming businesses for trans-inclusive restroom policies. Funded by right-wing organizations like Alliance Defending Freedom (ADF), many of these bills deploy a reductive binary notion of biological sex. In their dualist view, the sexual binary is a simple and objective fact under attack by the ideology of gender identity (Dobbs 2022). Viewing trans people as an internal danger to US society, the ADF engages in nostalgia for the same mid-century postwar period during which Money and Stoller institutionalized "body and behavior where the middle-class housewife was placed at the root of the path to democracy" (2016, 59). Like the therapeutic violence of Money and Stoller, organizations like Alliance Defending Freedom deploy dualist sex-gender thinking toward an antitrans project of social and psychological control.

Kristeva's account of the semiotic and symbolic can illuminate the psychic and social risks of this intolerant, dualist way of thinking. Antitrans forces attempt to reduce trans people to bodies and to organize symbolic life according to the putative forms of hetero- and cis-normativity. Against the life-supporting oscillation of the semiotic and symbolic, they seek to empty the semiotic of symbolic form and evacuate the symbolic of semiotic drives, leaving both fragile and frayed. When disconnected and emptied, the semiotic and symbolic devolve, and "life becomes a life of death, a life of physical and moral violence, barbarity," especially but not exclusively for those at the "lower echelons of the social edifice" whose exclusions are renewed and repeated (2000, 23). In a later series of writings, Kristeva will describe this phenomenon as "soft totalitarianism," the proliferation of norms aiming to destroy life after having devalued the question of its meaning. Antitrans organizers devalue the question of life's meaning by, at the very least, devaluing the question of the meaning of biological sex; for these organizations, sex is a fixed binary and when it is questioned, it is under threat. Triggered by the ambiguities that accompany any real exploration of sexual life, transphobic acts of rejection and exclusion attempt to secure the binary sexual order. As Robert Philips describes it, "Transgendered bodies [. . .] especially when viewed as physical bodies in transition, defy the borders of systemic order by refusing to adhere to clear definitions of sex and gender. The abject serves as a cleaving point of abstruseness and unease—separating, pathologizing, and psychologizing trans subjectivity. The anxiety at the root of this unease with transgender subjectivity can be traced back to a fear of the ambiguous" (2014, 20). In search of a distinctly white sense of stability, certainty, normalcy, and happiness, antitrans forces reject trans self-making and attack the very ambiguities and entanglements that give life meaning, more broadly.

Instead of totalitarian certainties and fixities, Kristeva's theory of the semiotic and symbolic can be read as reveling in the spirit of questioning and change. Indeed, in *Revolution in Poetic Language*, Kristeva is careful to theorize the transition from semiotic to symbolic as nonoppositional, as taking the form of a question. Of this transition Kristeva argues that "its value lies not in being a brutal cut [. . .] What psychoanalysis calls symbolic castration is a question [. . .] The question opens the *infans* to discourse and allows speech to be taken toward an endless horizon" (Kristeva 2001, 146). Söderbäck's account of the *chōra* is another illustration of the nonbinary, nonlinear, dynamic resources of Kristeva's text. Foregrounding concerns about time and temporality, Söderbäck suggests that Kristeva might help think about "trans embodiment without appealing to dualist and essentializing conceptions of sexuate identity and embodiment" because she "render[s] flexible and open to transformation not only conceptions of 'culture' and 'gender,' but equally so 'nature' and 'sex'" (Söderbäck 2019, 244). Quite simply, "bodies change and that change is embodied [. . .] Any account of that separates 'culture' from 'nature' by positing one as stable and the other as being in constant flux is unable to properly think the complex relationship between [the] two" (227). Beyond the *somatophobia* of sex/gender dualism and the transphobia of soft totalitarianism, Kristeva's account of the semiotic and symbolic seems to invite a more expansive, dynamic, and questioning reimagining of nature.

Poetic Revolt and Trans Resistance

Amy Ray Stewart's "Transgender Subjectivity in Revolt: Kristevan Psychoanalysis and the Intimate Politics of Rebirth" is the first and most extended analysis of Kristeva's relevance to trans studies (579). Inspired by Laura Jane Grace's dramatic performance of burning her birth certificate on stage in 2016, Stewart looks to Kristeva's account of intimate revolt as a "psychical experience of regeneration" that resonates with "subjectivities that exist in-between and beyond established binaries" (579). Kristeva's notion of revolt is rooted in her early account of revolutionary language and elaborated in her later series on the powers and limits of psychoanalysis—*The Sense and Non-sense of Revolt, Intimate Revolt*, and *Hatred and Forgiveness*. In these texts, revolt has three meanings. First, it is a perpetual return to the conditions of subjectivity, an "intimate process of 'turning back' upon ourselves and the buried meanings of our experience" (587). Second, revolt is the rebellious confrontation and displacement of authority in the imagination; a creative process that returns to and renews the authorization by which the individual belongs to the world of meaning. Finally, revolt is "what is most alive and promising about our culture" (Kristeva 2017, 18). The three senses of revolt reflect the heterogeneity of the semiotic and symbolic. When one turns back on oneself to question the buried meanings of experience, the activity of retrospective return is at once affective and reflective. In rebelling against the rules of gender normalization, meanings shift and change through experience not abstract proof. The resuscitation of semiotic drives in language is an event of reconnection that promotes psychic and social survival. In destroying her birth certificate, Laura Jane Grace questions her past and shifts its embodied meaning, opening up a new way to live.

For Stewart, Kristevan revolt is trans affirming because it encourages people to "search for possible new identities and new ways of talking about ourselves" (Stewart 590, quoted). It describes meaningful rebirth in ways that unravel dualisms and resonate with diverse trans lives. Careful to emphasize that trans identity is not monolithic, Stewart argues that that trans subjectivities are generally constituted via a questioning or displacement of the past, whether it be a birth name, a marker of sex, or a social position (593). Trans identities involve transformative experiences of rebirth that make different meaning of one's past, present, and future as openings for change and questioning. This is not necessarily a break or rupture, nor must it cohere in a linear story. It is this same dimension of trans identity that leads Söderbäck to describe queer and trans temporalities as those that "swerve and interrupt, stretch and bend, wrinkle and fold, halt and diverge, redeploy and twist" (2019, 19). As so many trans people attest, these movements are, like revolt, life-saving and life-sustaining.

While Kristeva celebrates revolt, she also recognizes its peril in contemporary US and European culture. With its empty, frayed dualisms, the conditions of "soft totalitarianism" do not support or encourage psychic rebirth. They challenge and exhaust its condition of possibility.

Stewart helpfully turns to Judith Butler's writing on precarity to describe the heightened vulnerabilities and disparities associated with soft totalitarianism, or what Kristeva also calls "the power vacuum." For Butler, "precarity names the largely irreversible and inescapable effects of modern forms of socioeconomic, biopolitical, and psychical crises and unacknowledged suffering experiences by trans and queer communities, among so many other marginalized populations viewed as disposable" (Stewart, 594). Impoverished by brutal economic forces and failed by weak systems of social support, precarity describes the extreme vulnerability that queer and trans people experience in their pathologizing marginalization. It is hard to find the psychic and social resources to revolt when "ours is a consensus society; a regime of the spectacular; a normalizing order" (2019, 93). And yet, revolt is "what is most alive and promising about our culture" (2017, 18).

Although it is associated with her earlier work, poetic language seems to resonate with Stewart's vision of the trans-affirming directions of intimate revolt. In *Revolution*, Kristeva argues that poetic language is distinctive in the way that it carries the semiotic aspects of signification. In its rhythm, music, tone, and grammar, poetry attends to the materiality of words. While all symbolic language must have a semiotic dimension in order to have meaning, poetic language exemplifies this to a greater degree. In this sense, poetry is not a subversion of language as much as it "stands in for [its] infinite possibilities" (Roudiez, 2). According to Kristeva, poetic language reactivates the semiotic by discharging drives and evoking the dialectical oscillation that is necessary for symbolic functioning. "This heterogenous process, neither anarchic, fragmented foundation nor schizophrenic blockage, is a structuring and de-structuring *practice*, a passage to the outer *boundaries* of the subject and society. Then—and only then—can it be jouissance and revolution" (1984, 17). Poetry's revolt unfolds as it recalls the heterogenous conditions of language, as it transgresses and restructures the life-sustaining boundaries of subjectivity. While antitrans forces attempt to dehistoricize bodies and forestall the activity of retrospective return, poetic language can be understood as testifying to the heterogeneity of language and the fact that the subject is in process. The practice of poetry involves an unsettling and empowering traversal of one's personal history, and the conditions of one's coming into being. By poetically traversing the imbrication of body and language, nature and culture, sex, and gender, one experiences the disorienting shattering of a subjectivity that is never wholly present. At the same time, there is the pleasurable drive release of meaning making and the social ties that it promises. It is not surprising that Kristeva uses the language of life and vitality to describe poetic language. In the imbrication and traversal of its rhythms and tones, there is more than just survival, persistence, or automation. Poetry can be life-giving, imaginative, and creative.

"Transgender Subjectivity in Revolt" does not explore poetic language, but Stewart does evoke it. Reflecting on the Latin prefix, Stewart describes *trans-* as a kind of rebirth of the subject-in-process, a poetic practice of "search[ing] for possible new identities and new ways of talking about ourselves" (Stewart, 590, quoted). Moreover, when emphasizing its etymological associations as "across," "over," beyond," breaking off, and refashioning, Stewart cites Susan Stryker, Paisely Currah, and Lisa Moore's account of trans as poetic practice (599). According to Stryker, Currah, and Moore "the movement between territorializing and deterritorializing 'trans-' and its suffixes as well as the movements between temporalizing and spatializing them, is *an improvisational, creative, and essentially poetic practice* through which radically new possibilities for being in the world can start to emerge" (2008, 14, emphasis added). For Stewart, trans- is understood as a transformative poetic movement of revolt. By suspending its suffixes, Stewart affirms the plurality of trans subjectiv*ities*—its "interminable capacities for renewal" beyond even the logics of sex and gender (599).

Conclusion: Questioning Abstraction, Questioning Revolt

In the "Prolegomenon" to *Revolution in Poetic Language*, Kristeva criticizes dead and deadening sciences and theories of language. Abstracted from the speaking body and the signifying process, these "archivist, archaeological, and necrophilic" methods "stratify language into idiolects and divide it into self-contained, isolated islands"; as fields, they amount to "reflections on moments" that are "nevertheless fragments, remains; their individual articulation is often examined but rarely their interdependence or inception" (1984, 13–14). *Revolution* forges a way to explore that interdependence via the heterogeneous oscillation of the semiotic and symbolic. But not all psychoanalytic texts follow suit. Catherine Millot's *Horsexe* concerns itself with a particular isolated fragment of transsexual experience, abstracted from interdependence—the demand for surgery. The focus of the text is the question of how psychoanalysts are to determine which trans patients would benefit from reassignment surgery and which would not (Shepherdson 86). According to Millot, some patients' interest in surgery reflects their identification with a different sex and their pursuit of a different position within systems of sexual difference. By contrast, other patients desire an anatomical change that would amount to an "exit" from sexual difference. While the former group would benefit from surgery, Millot argues that, for the latter, it would precipitate a psychotic break. Here, in a psychiatric and psychoanalytic lineage that includes the work of John Money and Robert Stoller, the transphobia of Millot's *Horsexe* is made more deadly by its institutional power to withhold medical care.

Millot's myopic equation of transsexuality with the demand for surgery is not only an indication of her fragmentary analysis, it also betrays the dualist frame of her clinical question. As Gayle Salamon argues, "Reading the demand for sex change as the 'irrefutable sign' of transsexual identity and understanding that identity to be formed by the narratives that transsexuals offer to their doctors" transforms transness into a linguistic phenomenon (2010, 86). Defined by the "demand," Millot readily describes trans patients as out of touch with the reality of sexual difference and science. From her view, "such a subject does not reside in the social world as create a fully formed one around herself" (87). Despite Millot's obsession with this fragment of discourse, trans people are not defined by the desire for surgery nor are trans "demands" in healthcare contexts necessarily intimate or "irrefutable." Like the objectified, "systemizable" discourse that Kristeva critiques in the "Prolegomenon," the "histories that [trans people] report to their doctors [are] highly scripted and compelled, a set of necessary fictions into which they fit their experiences in order to be recognized as transsexual" (86). Reducing trans people to "the demand" is an abstraction; it betrays the very disconnection that it pretends to discover outside itself. As Kristeva excoriates in *Revolution in Poetic Language*, these kinds of abstractions are the "product of leisurely cogitation removed from historical turmoil, persisting in seeking the truth of language by formalizing utterances that hang in midair" (1984, 13).

Do Kristeva's own comments, reported by Sheila Cavanaugh and referenced at the beginning of this chapter, hang in midair as well? Her complaints regarding the "fabrication of gender by overly sympathetic gynecologists and endocrinologists"? If so, what of heterogeneity, the embodied trans poetic experience of "searching for possible new identities and new ways of talking about ourselves" (Stewart, 590)?

Since access to transition-related care today follows in the tradition of Money and Stoller's model of gender, many trans people would not describe their health-care experiences as "overly sympathetic." For the most part, to be approved for surgery or hormone replacement therapy, patients must be diagnosed with gender dysphoria and must perform their gender identity in accordance with normalized understandings of masculinity and femininity. Gender's plasticity and malleability is limited to its coherence with a developmental arc that ends in the gender binary. Jules Gill-Peterson's *Histories of the Transgender Child* elucidates this aspect of the history of the dualist sex-gender distinction. According to Gill-Peterson, Money and Stoller's sexological understanding of gender emerged during a time when sex became more alterable, and more and more trans people also sought out the clinic in hopes of accessing the resources of medical transition. Gill-Peterson argues that during the 1940s and 1950s, it was increasingly possible that human life "might not be binary, that intersex and trans embodiment were but two facets of life's natural variation" (2018, 97). In this historical moment, the emergence of gender worked to stave off the collapse of the sex binary, providing a developmental justification for normalizing interventions and anchoring assignment and transition to the gender binary. Therefore, it is not just sex-gender dualism that participates in the racial project that Jemima Repo describes in *The Biopolitics of Gender*. In the postwar period, the institutionalization of "white, bourgeois standards of the healthy mind" made use of a dualist sex-gender distinction that was also plastic within a binary, developmental schema. The universalization of this understanding of sex and gender worked to marginalize those patients whose dysphoria or gender performance did not cohere with dominant understandings, especially patients of color whose gender identity expression is often perceived as nonnormative. Understandings of trans that engage with histories of people of color, including trans people of color, are likely to encounter more diverse understandings of sex/gender and more diverse trajectories of transformation and experimentation.

Amy Ray Stewart celebrates the ways that intimate revolt can serve as a poetic practice of "search[ing] for possible new identities and new ways of talking about ourselves" (Stewart, 590, quoted). Underlying this life-invigorating vision of self-experimentation and self-transformation is a notion of trans-affirming dynamism and plasticity. But the history of the sex gender distinction reminds us that, while Kristeva's dynamic account of the semiotic and symbolic departs from dualism to reimagine nature, plasticity is not in itself trans inclusive and affirming, as understandings of change can remain limited by racialized understandings of gender's developmental arc. The key to mobilizing Kristeva's texts for analyses of trans subjectivity lies in motivating her spirit of endless questioning of the past toward encounters that generate rather than limit multiplicity and change. This means reckoning with histories of sex and gender that include the perspectives of rebellious trans people engaged in poetic meaning-making rather than histories that privilege the narrow perspectives of clinicians. Attention to this "historical turmoil" is less likely to abstract trans people from their embodied experiences, reducing trans lives to linguistic phenomena and underacknowledging the cis-normative dimensions of precarity today. Alongside the uniqueness of revolt vis-à-vis individual histories, trans-embodied poetics involves a revolt against broader histories of sex and gender. It rejects racialized narratives of sex and gender that privilege the speech and theoretical models of clinicians, while rendering trans people to mute victims or villains of history. The generativity of Kristeva's understanding of poetic language and revolt hinges on its treatment of history as a question mark, as the opportunity to explore how "the beginning itself is reinscribed as a process" and how a "beginning that points to yet another beginning," as Margaroni and Söderbäck put it (213, 214). Such questioning is substantial and heterogenous, it does not hang in midair, captured by limited understandings of what was and what can be. Instead of being reduced to a linguistic phenomenon that clashes with reality or being bounded by the racist logics of sex or gender, trans-poetics rebelliously challenges the past to open up different possibilities of self-making in the past, present, and future. Given escalating threats to trans communities, especially for trans people of color and especially in the area of healthcare, it is important to support poetic practices that resist empty dualism and to reject psychoanalysis's limited cis-normative visions of self-transformation.

References

Butler, Judith. 1999. *Gender Trouble*. New York: Routledge.
Cavanaugh, Sheila. 2017. "Transpsychoanalytics." *TSQ: Transgender Studies Quarterly* 4, no. 3–4 (November): 326–57.
Chanter, Tina. 1993. "Kristeva and the Politics of Change: Tracking Essentialism with the Help of a Sex/Gender Map." In *Ethics, Politics and Difference in Julia Kristeva's Writing*, edited by Kelly Oliver. New York: Routledge: 179–95.

Dobbs, Jared. "The Demands of Gender Theory." *Alliance Defending Freedom*, https://adflegal.org/blog/demands-gender-theory. Accessed: January 20, 2022.
Foucault, Michel. 1977. "Nietzsche, Genealogy, History." In *Language, Counter-Memory, Practice: Selected Essays and Interviews*, edited by D. F. Bouchard, 139–64. Ithaca, NY: Cornell University Press.
Fraser, Nancy. 1992. "The Uses and Abuses of French Discourse Theories for Feminist Politics." *Theory, Culture, & Society* 9: 51–71.
Gill-Peterson, Jules. 2018. *Histories of the Transgender Child*. Minneapolis: University of Minnesota Press.
Grosz, Elizabeth. 1994. *Volatile Bodies: Towards a Corporeal Feminism*. Bloomington: Indiana University Press.
Kristeva, Julia. 2002. *Intimate Revolt: The Powers and Limits of Psychoanalysis, Volume Two*. New York: Columbia University Press.
———. 2017. "New Forms of Revolt." In *New Forms of Revolt: Essays on Kristeva's Intimate Politics*, edited by S. K. Hansen and Rebecca Tuvel. Albany: State University of New York Press.
———. 1984. *Revolution in Poetic Language*. New York: Columbia University Press.
———. 2000. *The Sense and Non-sense of Revolt*. New York: Columbia University Press.
Lane, Riki. 2009. "Trans as Bodily Becoming: Rethinking the Biological as Diversity, not Dichotomy." *Hypatia* 24, no. 3 (Summer): 136–57.
Millot, Catherine. 1990. *Horsexe: An Essay on Transsexuality*. Brooklyn, NY: Autonomedia.
Oliver, Kelly. 1993. *Reading Kristeva: Unraveling the Double Bind*. Bloomington: Indiana University Press.
Repo, Jemima. 2016. *The Biopolitics of Gender*. Oxford, UK: Oxford University Press.
Phillips, Robert. 2014. "Abjection." *TSQ: Transgender Studies Quarterly* 1, no. 1–2 (May): 19–21.
Roudiez, Leon. 1984. "Introduction." In Julia Kristeva, *Revolution in Poetic Language*. New York: Columbia University Press, 1–10.
Salamon, Gayle. 2010. *Assuming a Body: Transgender and Rhetorics of Materiality*. New York: Columbia University Press.
Shepherdson, Charles. 2000. *Vital Signs: Nature, Culture, Psychoanalysis*. New York: Routledge.
Söderbäck, Fanny. 2019. *Revolutionary Time: On Time and Difference in Kristeva and Irigaray*. Albany: State University of New York Press.
Spelman, Elizabeth V. 1988. *Inessential Woman: Problems of Exclusion in Feminist Thought*. Boston, MA: Beacon Press.
Stewart, Amy Ray. 2017. "Transgender Subjectivity in Revolt: Kristevan Psychoanalysis and the Intimate Politics of Rebirth." *TSQ: Transgender Studies Quarterly* 4, no. 3–4 (November): 577–607.

Stryker, Currah, Moore. 2008. "Introduction: Trans-, Trans, or Transgender?" *Women's Studies Quarterly* 36, no. 3/4 (Fall–Winter): 11–22.

Chapter 6

Stranger than Other Strangers

On the Crossroads between Subjectivity
and Language in Kristeva and Anzaldúa

Fanny Söderbäck

Introduction

In the speech that she gave as she received the Holberg Prize in 2004, Julia Kristeva announced: "The distinction that I have established between the semiotic and the symbolic has no political or feminist connotation" (2010, 11).[1] She made this remark as she was seeking to redress some of the most common misconceptions about her work, especially as they arise in Anglo-American interpretations and engagements. The distinction between semiotic and symbolic that she speaks of here is developed most explicitly in the first part of *Revolution in Poetic Language*. But in that text she declares that "the signifying process joins social revolution" (1984, 61), and that "the text is a practice that could be compared to political revolution" (17). So, how do we make sense of these seemingly contradictory remarks? On the one hand, the claim that the distinction between semiotic and symbolic has *no political or feminist connotations whatsoever*, and on the other, the insistence that the signifying process joins *social revolution* and that the text is a practice that can be compared to *political revolution*? How are we to understand the "revolution" in the title of her doctoral dissertation, if not in political terms?

In what follows, I first trace what I see as the feminist-political potential of Kristeva's discussion of the semiotic and symbolic in *Revolution in Poetic Language*, identifying the avenues her magnum opus opens for a radical thinking and praxis of the deepest political import—despite her own assertion that it not be understood in such terms. Second, I will examine some of her later, we might say "properly political" works (especially those that focus on questions of strangeness and foreignness, such as *Strangers to Ourselves* and *Nations without Nationalism*), reflecting on the ways in which they might betray the revolutionary power of her earlier text. Finally, I will stage something like a dialogue between Kristeva and Chicana feminist Gloria Anzaldúa, whose groundbreaking *Borderlands/La Frontera* appeared in 1987, only three years after the English translation of *Revolution in Poetic Language*. While there is no evidence that the two of them ever read one another's work, and little has been done to stage such a dialogue, the conceptual, stylistic, and thematic kinship of their bodies of work is striking, even as there are also important differences.[2] It is my contention that much can be gained from staging such a dialogue, both in terms of highlighting the revolutionary potential of Kristeva's work, and in terms of further illuminating the blind spots that haunt her work on strangeness and nationalism. While my own attempt here to examine the overlap and divergences between their bodies of work is bound to be all too brief and schematic, it is my hope that putting them into conversation in this context might spark an interest in further exploring the manner in which their respective thinking might converge.[3]

In the spirit of my own concept of *revolutionary time*, which was developed in close dialogue with Kristeva's work (Söderbäck 2019), I will thus argue for the need—fifty years after its publication in French—to *return* to her dissertation so as to better understand but also critically assess her more recent work. In so doing, I hope to join my colleagues in this volume in celebrating and recognizing the monumental importance of *Revolution in Poetic Language*, while also naming and putting some critical pressure on the political avenues that Kristeva's work has since taken.

Revolution in Poetic Language Revisited: A Liminal Politics of Polyphony

In the theoretical portion of *Revolution in Poetic Language* that was translated into English, Kristeva is first and foremost concerned with the relationship between subjectivity and language, stressing the need to view them both as *heterogeneous processes*. She fundamentally challenges the stability of the transcendental ego in favor of what she names *le sujét-en-procès*—the subject in process or the subject on trial that many have come to associate with her work (1984, 37). Simultaneously, she puts into question the study of language as static codification, arguing instead for the need to view processes of signification as constitutively heterogeneous. She characterizes traditional philosophies of language as "nothing more than the thoughts of archivists, archeologists, and necrophiliacs," in that they render language stultified to the point of death—an object of scrutiny and possession (13). In offering a more dynamic account of language, then, Kristeva insists on the need to attend to the "materialist foundation" that brings signification to life in that it makes language sing. It is in this context that she makes the famous distinction between semiotic and symbolic, the former of which "consists of drive-related and affected *meaning* organized according to primary processes whose sensory aspects are often nonverbal," whereas the latter "is manifested in linguistic signs and their logico-syntactic organization" (1995, 104).

Drawing from Sigmund Freud's conception of the unconscious, Kristeva develops "a theory of signification based on the subject, his formation, and his corporeal, linguistic, and social dialectic" (1984, 15). At stake, as Sara Beardsworth succinctly puts it, is our capacity to "return to the crossroads of idealism and materialism" (2005, 40), or what Kristeva herself identifies as the intersection between the "biological and social," or the "heterogeneous functioning" that marks human experience and signification (1984, 41). In other words, the theory of subjectivity and that of signification that Kristeva develops in *Revolution in Poetic Language* are both framed in terms of their heterogeneity and dynamism—the fact that the speaking subject is a crossroads being, marked by contradiction, ambiguity, instability, and affective polyvalence. Such a model of subjectivity makes possible a more dynamic (indeed, revolutionary) model of meaning-making—a heterogeneous practice constituted by both structuring and destructuring (17).

It is this tension and liminality that has inspired many who have read Kristeva's work and found in it tools and resources for political subversion and feminist critique—despite her own insistence that she should not be read in this way. Her rejection of the transcendental ego and its rational rigidity has opened avenues for rethinking subjectivity—as well as political consciousness—otherwise: as embodied, affective, and constitutively relational. And her analysis of signification and her subsequent development of the semiotic-symbolic dynamic has inspired critical engagement with one-dimensional approaches to language and culture, ones that hollow out and abstract at the expense of material-maternal registers and modes of signification.

Elsewhere, I have stressed the importance of reading the semiotic and the symbolic as interdependent and coconstitutive, contra some accounts that have tended to render them as separate entities and then painted Kristeva as an essentialist who posits the semiotic as chronologically prior to, and logically outside of, the symbolic order (Söderbäck 2011, 2019, 201–32). Kristeva's work offers far more complex ways of thinking the relation between the two, and thus for thinking relationality more generally. As she herself puts it: "In opposition to such dichotomies, whether 'materialist' or 'metaphysical,' the text offers itself as the dialectic of two heterogeneous operations that are, reciprocally and inseparably, preconditions for each other" (1984, 66). Sid Hansen and Rebecca Tuvel describe this succinctly: "Just as the semiotic is already and not yet symbolic, the Symbolic is still but no longer semiotic," such that "amid logical and grammatical structures, there is the insistent presence of drives" (2017, 3). Indeed, already in her Prolegomenon to *Revolution in Poetic Language*, Kristeva motivates the need for positing an "outside" that is always already an "inside," and a "before" that is always already an "after," so as to "decenter the closed set and elaborate the dialectic of a process within plural and heterogeneous universes" (1984, 14).

Her work on language, and the elaboration that she offers as she develops the semiotic-symbolic-dynamic, thus gives us a model for thinking otherwise the very nature of difference and differentiation—alterity and alteration—concepts at the heart of much political discourse. That the symbolic order is always subject to an influx of the semiotic and vice versa is what makes both dynamic—what makes transformation in the sense of revolution possible in the first place. I take it that this is why Kristeva herself ultimately describes literary practice and *signifiance* as "inseparable" from political horizons in that they transform and revolutionize, by both "structuring and de-structuring . . . the subject and society" (17). The semiotic, in other words, serves as a precondition for the symbolic, while at the same time also destroying it, tearing at it, transgressing it, remodeling it (50, 62).

If our capacity for political action, renewal, and change has oftentimes been depicted as our emancipation from bodily contingencies, Kristeva's ethical-political subject is instead steeped in affective drives, and it draws from such registers in order to bring life and aliveness to an otherwise deadening discursive apparatus.[4] Put differently, the transformation of social structures depends on semiotic undercurrents. A politics of change must be situated at the crossroads between semiotic and symbolic—a liminal-generative space of transgression and contradiction. Only then can political subjectivity avoid dogmatism, and only then can it be said to engage in practices of revolt-as-renewal. The power of such a "materialist foundation" for language is, in other words, that it has the capacity to pluralize meaning, to open linguistic structures up to heterogeneity and transformation, without ever reducing them to some sort of essential or brute materiality.

In an autobiographical essay from 1983, Kristeva notes: "The psychoanalytic experience struck me as the only one in which the wildness of the speaking being, and of language, can be heard" (2002b, 19). Her works from the 1980s thus set out to more explicitly examine the relationship between subjectivity and language in the context of the analytic practice. In *Powers of Horror*, where she extends and deepens her articulation of the semiotic and the symbolic as well as her examination of the relationship between subjectivity and (poetic) language, Kristeva introduces the idea of the abject: that which is neither subject nor object; which "draws me toward the place where meaning collapses" (1982, 2); and which "disturbs identity, system, order" (4).

Her discussion of abjection is her contribution to one of the most important debates of psychoanalytic theory, namely, how a subject—an "I"—comes into being as someone distinct from others. Kristeva's examination of this process begins at the brink of subjectivity, in the symbiotic relationship between mother and infant. Echoing Freud, she describes this early relationship as marked by an oceanic feeling of plenitude and wholeness on the part of an infant who has yet to distinguish inside from outside, self from other, me from mother. As the process of separation begins, it is far from clear-cut, but rather marked by ambivalence, loathing, and continuously diffuse boundaries. Since the infant feels like it is "one" with its mother, the very process of separating from her inevitably involves a sort of self-separation. As Noëlle McAfee puts it, the infant "must renounce a part of itself . . . in order to become a self" (2004, 48). This process can be violent, painful, and messy: "During that course in which 'I' become," Kristeva writes, "I give birth to myself amid the violence of sobs, of vomit" (1982, 3).

This turn to psychoanalysis should by no means be understood as a turn away from politics—even when Kristeva herself sometimes describes it as such. McAfee, again, explains as follows:

> When in the 1970s Kristeva turned away from the politics of the Left Bank intellectuals to "the only continent we had never left: internal experience," she did not in fact leave politics behind. Rather, she began an inquiry into the way subjectivity is formed, including our subjectivity as political agents in the world. Her work on revolt suggests that the internal experience of every speaking being profoundly shapes the political. Revolt against both external constraints and internalized and unreflected norms allows for the flourishing of an inner domain of freedom. (2020, 760)

Such an inner domain of freedom—our capacity not only to question the world around us but to put *ourselves* on trial—has been the condition of possibility for renewal (political or otherwise) in all of Kristeva's work. We can thus draw an arc from *Revolution in Poetic Language*, via the trilogy of the 1980s (*Powers of Horror*, *Tales of Love*, and *Black Sun*), to the trilogy of the 1990s and beyond (*The Sense and Non-Sense of Revolt, Intimate Revolt*, and *Hatred and Forgiveness*), to trace Kristeva's revolutionary politics, always profoundly grounded in the internal-intimate experience of the speaking subject.[5] As I have put it elsewhere, her revolution "is fought neither in the courtrooms nor in the streets. It unfolds in singular intersubjective encounters, in artistic practice as well as philosophical reflection, through personal transformation, and sometimes in mystical revelations" (Söderbäck 2016, 133). Revolt, for Kristeva, is the active embrace of a great question mark, and as such, it forces us to grapple with the ambivalences and contradictions that condition us as speaking subjects.

Indeed, few thinkers have provided an account of liminality as rigorous and as nuanced as Kristeva has. At the heart of her work—from *Revolution in Poetic Language* to her most recent work on new humanism, vulnerability, and singularity (2018)—stands a commitment to the speaking subject as straddling the crossroads between biology and meaning, affect and language, *soma* and *psuche*. This also renders her work useful for thinking liminality in a range of registers and contexts. For those of us who are invested in examining that which provokes ambivalence in our culture, and that which itself is marked by ambiguity—the fleshy, the fluid, the messy, the nonbinary, the feminine, the sexually devious, the disabled, the rejected, the queer, the racially other, the exiled, that which defies systems and crosses borders—Kristeva undeniably offers a helpful toolbox.

Particularly since the publication of *Powers of Horror*, her articulation of the *abject* as that which "disturbs identity, system, order," "does not respect borders, positions, rules," and confronts us with the "in-between, the ambiguous, the composite" (1982, 4) has been mobilized by thinkers, artists, and activists alike, precisely to evoke and grapple with ambivalence, ambiguity, and liminality. I would argue that this interest in heterogeneity and liminality—the insistence that we are crossroads beings—motivated Kristeva's thinking already in the dissertation, from the opening claims about the need for a more dynamic account of both subjectivity and language, via the elaboration of the *sujet-en-procès* and the peculiar dialectic between semiotic and symbolic that she envisions in the first half of that book, to the engagement in its latter half with negativity, rejection, and expulsion.[6] The revolutionary power of poetic language has to do with its capacity to reach "the very foundation of the social—that which is exploited by sociality but which elaborates and can go beyond it, either destroying or transforming it" (1984, 67).

Kristeva's revolutionary project is thus one concerned with both transformation and destruction. In *Revolution in Poetic Language*, she laid the foundation for both. In her later work on intimate revolt (2000b, 2002a, 2002c), she is most obviously concerned with our decreased aptitude for revolt in the face of a neoliberal society of the spectacle, where we are so numbed by images that we have lost our capacity to imagine. Here, the emphasis is therefore on the urgent need to re-create the conditions of possibility for *transformation*—revolt here is understood first and foremost as a movement of return that makes possible rebirth and renewal.[7] In *Powers of Horror*, she was more immediately concerned with how the very birth of the self always already involved *destruction* in the form of abjection, and how revolt then is premised on an initial tendency for revulsion and expulsion. For Kristeva, transformation and destruction are flip sides of the same revolutionary coin, just like life for Freud must be accompanied by both Eros and Thanatos.

Feminist thinkers as well as others who are attuned to structures of exclusion have often borrowed Kristeva's notion of abjection, or the abject, to make sense of such structures. Whether it be undocumented immigrants crammed together in cargo ships, cultural minorities threatened by genocide, or women and girls who are sexually trafficked, the "abject" has been a useful category for framing the conditions under which these people live, or struggle to survive (Söderbäck 2016, 131). Abjection is about boundaries: the making of boundaries, and the inevitable transgression of boundaries (a transgression that does not stop just because we become full-fledged speaking subjects). Mary Douglas, whose 1966 work *Purity and Danger* provides the backdrop on which Kristeva developed her notion of abjection, knew to connect the taboos imposed on the body to larger normative demarcations: "The body is a model which can stand for any bounded system. Its boundaries can represent any boundaries which are threatened or precarious. . . . We cannot possibly interpret rituals concerning excreta, breast milk, saliva and the rest unless we are prepared to see in the body a symbol of society, and to see the powers and dangers credited to social structure reproduced in small on the human body" (2002, 142). Or, as she puts it elsewhere: "If there is no concern to preserve social boundaries, I would not expect to find concern with bodily boundaries. . . . Consequently I now advance the hypothesis that bodily control is an expression of social control" (2003, 79).

The female body has long been the battleground on which social anxieties about all things ambivalent run their course. With Douglas, we can add that "the mistake is to treat bodily margins in isolation from all other margins" (2002, 150). She explains that "wherever the lines are precarious we find pollution ideas come to their support. Physical crossing of the social barrier is treated as a dangerous pollution. . . . The polluter becomes a doubly wicked object of reprobation, first because he crossed the line and second because he endangered others" (172). And this brings us more specifically to the issue of our fear of border crossers, and the violence with which we tend to respond to those perceived as foreign, or out of place, whether they be immigrants, racialized others, queer and trans folks, or people who otherwise embody mixture or ambiguity.

Stranger than Other Strangers

I want to move now to a reflection on Kristeva's engagement with the role and place of the foreigner or stranger—*l'étranger*. Strangeness and revolution are a conceptual pair throughout Kristeva's corpus. The "strangeness" of language is what gives it life, the "strangeness" of the psyche is what makes it dynamic. It is because we are "estranged" (from ourselves, from our past, from our beginnings) that we must engage in perpetual return,

return as revolt, as renewal, as the recognition of heterogeneity. In *Strangers to Ourselves*, which was first published in French in 1988, about fifteen years after the publication of *Revolution in Poetic Language*, and which provides a sort of genealogy of the category of the foreigner from Ancient Greece to modern cosmopolitanism, Kristeva speaks of the stranger that inhabits each of us. In the final chapter of that book, she draws from Freud's theory of the unconscious and the fact that the self, in the wake of Freudian psychoanalysis, is opaque and internally divided, insofar as the unconscious remains largely hidden yet formative of who we are. In his 1919 essay "The Uncanny," Freud describes the uncanny (*unheimlich*) as familiar (*heimlich* as homely, also related to *heimich* as native) and unfamiliar (*heimlich* as secret or concealed) both at once, such that that which is closest and most familiar to us always also remains farthest away, even estranged (Freud 1978, 219–26). For Freud, a discussion of the uncanny helps us understand the logic of repression-repetition, since, as he points out with reference to Friedrich Wilhelm Joseph von Schelling, "Everything is *unheimlich* that ought to have remained secret and hidden but has come to light" (225), and therefore, the uncanny belongs to the class of frightening things "in which the frightening element can be shown to be something repressed which *recurs*" (241).

On Kristeva's reading of this text, we must recognize that our self is a universe, that we are inhabited by multiplicity and heterogeneity. That "I" am many. And such internal dividedness and multiplicity (a mode of subjectivity that we were introduced to already in *Revolution in Poetic Language*) ultimately make us foreign, or strange. Kristeva goes on to emphasize the ethical implications of becoming aware of our own strangeness: "Henceforth, we know that we are foreigners to ourselves, and it is with the help of that sole support that we can attempt to live with others" (1991, 170). Such ethics has political implications: it suggests a cosmopolitanism "whose solidarity is founded on the consciousness of its unconscious" (192). By recognizing the foreigner within ourselves, "we are spared detesting him in himself" (1). And our confrontation with the foreigner is equally a confrontation with our own unconscious, "that 'improper' facet of our impossible 'own and proper,'" of which Kristeva, echoing Freud, speaks (191). It is, in other words, only in relation to the other that we can come to know ourselves in our fundamental strangeness.

We might say that if Kristeva is seeking to articulate what Kelly Oliver has called a democracy of proximity (2020), the first step in achieving such democracy is, precisely, to grapple with the fact that we are not in full proximity with ourselves, that we are always already at a distance from ourselves, and that therefore we need others in order to achieve that proximity. What is at stake for Kristeva is something other than simply "acceptance" or "tolerance" for those who are different from us. "Living with the other, with the foreigner," she writes, "confronts us with the possibility or not of *being an other*" (1991, 13). It forces us to imagine and confront our very own strangeness. Her own universalism is therefore firmly grounded in an affirmation of difference—indeed her claim is that if there is anything we all have in common, universally, it is that we are all other, all in a certain sense strange: "The foreigner is within me, hence we are all foreigners" (192).

But as Sara Ahmed strives to show in her essay "The Skin of the Community: Affect and Boundary Formation," which is an explicit engagement with Kristeva's work on these issues, "the deconstruction of the host/stranger opposition requires not that we distribute strangeness to everyone (we are all strangers with an equal duty to recognize others as strangers), but that we recognize how strangeness is already *unevenly distributed*" (2005, 96). Or, as she puts it in the conclusion of her essay: "A politics of opening up the community cannot be achieved simply by saying 'we are all strangers,' or by the good will of the national subject. We must acknowledge how others have already been recognized as *stranger than other others*, as border objects that have been incorporated and then expelled from the ideal of the community" (109; emphasis mine).

Our capacity to enter into relations of proximity with others—and especially so if those relations are marked by radical forms of difference—depends on our being able and willing to recognize and respond to the specificity of the other's situatedness *as* a stranger. For Ahmed, this can only be done through an *affective* orientation, and here she finds Kristeva's earlier work on abjection to be useful in that it helps us see "the role of affects (such as disgust) in boundary formation" (96). In the remainder of this section, I will first examine how Kristeva's work on nationalism runs the risk of neglecting the specificity of the stranger, through her calls for assimilation to an allegedly "neutral" universality that she comes to associate with the French nation and Enlightenment ideals. I will then suggest that such an account is at odds with key insights from her earlier work—especially the liminal-polyphonic logics that she had developed in *Revolution in Poetic Language*. I ultimately want to argue that the assimilationist views that Kristeva gives expression to in works such as *Nations without Nationalism*, and in some of her most recent essays and speeches in which she engages issues related to the French Muslim population and hot-button issues such as the veil, religious fundamentalism, and radicalization, depart from some of the most promising ideas and ideals of her earliest work.

In "What of Tomorrow's Nation?"—an essay that was specifically written for an English-speaking audience and which opens *Nations without Nationalism*—Kristeva infamously speaks of "an influx of humiliated and demanding Arabian masses" (1993, 38), wondering why French citizens should "accept [that daughters of Maghrebin immigrants wear] the Muslim scarf [to school]" (36) or why the French should feel compelled to "change spelling" (36). And she proposes that "the 'abstract' advantages of French universalism may prove to be superior to the 'concrete' benefits of a Muslim scarf" (47). It is hard not to read Kristeva's engagement with the "foreigner" in these passages as driven by a desire for assimilation, integration, the leveling of differences (despite her own insistence, in *Strangers to Ourselves*, that our living with others must avoid not only ostracism but also leveling). And what remains unspoken in these troubling passages is precisely the *unequal distribution of strangeness* that Ahmed invites us to reflect upon. As Hanan M. Ibrahim notes: "The cosmopolitanism [Kristeva] calls for is a chimera, for it is based on denying the other her cultural and religious specificity" (2018, 10).

Kristeva wants to insist that "we" can all—if only we are committed enough to the community that is the French nation—become a part of the *esprit général* (she borrows from Montesquieu here) that will guarantee private rights while assuring that immigrants assimilate and learn to embody the "French" lifestyle (1993, 30–34). But while this vision is premised on the notion that we are *all* foreigners (as well as on the fantasy that the *esprit général*—rooted firmly in the French Enlightenment view of secularism—is neutral in the sense of unmarked, seen as rising above cultural or religious specificity), it seems obvious that our place in the *esprit général* will be marked from the start, depending on whether we are "truly" French or just "aspiring" to be so: "For recognition of otherness is a right and a duty for everyone, *French people as well as foreigners*, and it is reasonable to ask *foreigners* to recognize and respect the strangeness of those who welcome them—*French people* in this instance" (31; emphasis mine). As Ahmed puts it: "some others are recognized as stranger than others and as already not belonging to the nation in the concreteness of their difference. The idea that we are all strangers forgets the politics of this differentiation, at the same time as it exercises it, in the prior construction of the French as hosts" (2005, 99). What exactly is it that makes some, in this instance, "French," while others remain "foreign"—especially given that many of the Muslims that Kristeva is speaking of here and elsewhere were not only born in France but have lived there for generations, and that others were born and raised in the North African nations that France annexed under the rule of colonial imperialism (a historical context of which Kristeva, curiously, remains mostly silent)?

For Kristeva, the answer ultimately lies in culture, literature, and language, but it is quite apparent that the *arrondissements* are more "French" than the *banlieus*, that Voltaire and Monnet are more "French" than Memmi and Fatmi, and that Metropolitan French is more "French" than Maghreb patois—which is why Ibrahim insists that Kristeva's cosmopolitanism is a chimera. If we are going to maintain such divisions, does this not entail that we are not all quite "foreign" in the same way, as Kristeva wants to insist? If her own utopian aspirations amount to "a world without foreigners" (1991, 36), then what does it mean to still insist on the importance of the nation-state? Is not the nation, and its *esprit général* in this case, always already premised on positing a "we" and a "them" (a boundary that Ahmed describes as the skin of the community)—a conceptual distinction with enormous practical import, and one that seems so very far from the liminal-heterogeneous landscape that marked Kristeva's earliest (supposedly nonpolitical) work?

Kristeva's remarks in *Nations without Nationalism* (and in some of her more recent speeches and essays) are a reminder that while irreducible difference is a characteristic that we are quite well equipped to ascribe to intimate others with whom we can identify or whom we hold near and dear (in Kristeva's case, her commitment to—indeed her affective as well as political investment in—her adult disabled son), it is much more challenging to extend the same *attentive regard* (Kristeva & Vanier 2011) to those who we experience as being at a greater distance from us, even as we share the same city or call the same nation "home." Interestingly, in broaching the complexities of the lived experience of disability, Kristeva proposes a "democracy of proximity and solidarity" (2013, 223) that would precisely *not* be founded on the notion that we are all strange or all disabled, but would realize, instead, that "the *respect of rights* requires firstly and before anything else *the recognition and the respect for the singular person*" (223). In this context, Kristeva vocalizes a view that seems to oppose to the letter her earlier claims about our shared strangeness: "I reject 'portmanteau words,' 'a holdall,' such as 'we are all different,' all 'others,' all 'vulnerable,' or all 'fragile.' No, we are not 'all disabled.' And this is perhaps even less so than us not 'all' being 'gay' or 'German Jews' " (224).

If Kristeva is well equipped to extend such attentive regard to those who, like her son, navigate the situation of disability (with all of the painful and unjust structures of exclusion that it involves in our ableist world), I worry that, in her work on the nation, she tends to be far more quick to disregard the tangible (and again often painful) experience of exclusion that "others" (in the sense of oppressed or silenced others, racialized others, or colonized others) in our society, after all, share. As she reflects on the challenges involved in incorporating France into a larger Europe—a topic that is often centered in her more recent work—she does this without any mention of the historical fact of colonialism, and the effects it has had on European, and specifically French, identity.[8] When, with Montesquieu, she prompts us to move from the personal to the local, from the local to the national, and from the national to the international (in the context of articulating her own cosmopolitan politics), the arc always takes her from France via Europe to the world. But as Norma Claire Moruzzi has pointed out,

> For the young students from francophone Morocco and Algiers, the European community is not necessarily the most accessible context in which to frame national identity. For a francophone North African immigrant, for instance, the reservation of European over French interests is a further estrangement. Montesquieu's motto presumes a (French) national identity that is implicitly European, rather than, for instance, Maghrebian. Placing the motto on the wall of every French classroom would only emphasize the insistent exclusivity of French nation-state identity, and the social estrangement, not of (European) nationals and citizens, but of (other) foreigners. (1993, 141–42)

Kristeva, in other words, tends to address one side of the problem—the work of recognizing and affirming our own internal strangeness—but she fails to fully acknowledge the lived effects of structural and hierarchical divisions that are the hallmark of our neoliberal-colonial-patriarchal world. For how could the "stranger" that we carry within not always already be shaped by (albeit by no means reducible to) our position within the power structures that we navigate—differently and on a daily basis—vis-à-vis our perceived "strangeness"?

Coloniality, which Kristeva rarely mentions, is one of many such structures, and coloniality is of course wrapped up with issues of racial difference; with the construction of the West as "civilized" vis-à-vis barbarian or backward cultures; as well as with complex gender dynamics—a point that becomes particularly apparent in Kristeva's repeated claims about the need to "liberate" Muslim women from the oppressive practices of their culture. Such views became apparent as early as in her intervention, in the wake of the *affaire du foulard* in 1989 (when three Arab teenagers were refused entry to their public college because they were wearing a *hijab*), in her open letter to Harlem Désir (the founder of *SOS Racisme* and a proponent of the girls' right to wear their headscarves to school—a view not shared by Kristeva), published in *Nations without Nationalism*, in which she again appeals to Montesquieu, *l'esprit général*, and language that privileges "French" culture over its Arab-Muslim counterpart (1993, 49–64).[9] They surface again in later texts such as *This Incredible Need to Believe*, where Islam is depicted as lacking the theological-psychological infrastructure to support critical thinking, and therefore produces a "barbarism founded on the denial of malaise" (2011, 97).

Not only does Kristeva fail to attend to the ways in which some strangers are marked as stranger than others due to the very colonial dynamics that go unmentioned in her work, but what is more (and perhaps also more surprising given the general tenet of her work), while in *Strangers to Ourselves* she encouraged "us" to recognize "our own" strangeness, in *Nations without Nationalism* her appeal to *l'esprit général* and Enlightenment ideals renders that same "we" all but strange, depicting it instead as a kind of blank slate of indifference—the neutrality-universality of European secularism and humanism. But of course, such a move, which characterizes the "French" or perhaps even "European" subject as unmarked or "indifferent" by default, inevitably contributes to the marking of all others as, precisely, "different." What is more, "their difference" becomes construed as a threat to "our indifference," and as such, reveals "our indifference" as being all but indifferent. Ahmed explains,

> The Muslim woman must give up her concrete difference in the interests of the national ideal, in which freedom takes the form of a particular kind of body (*a particularity that is given value insofar as it is represented as abstract-able or detach-able from particular bodies*). . . . In Kristeva's text, moving towards the abstract of the nation as *esprit general* requires moving away

from the veiled woman, as a sign of a difference that cannot be inhabited by those who already inhabit the national ideal. This limitation shows how *the ideal is not empty*, but is already an effect of the privilege for some bodies to inhabit spaces as hosts (bodies-at-home), and hence to decide who gets let into the body of the nation. (2005, 98, 108–9; emphasis mine)

If Kristeva tends to define revolt as an active embrace of the great question mark, and if the praxis of revolt is an intimate praxis requiring that we put ourselves into question, on trial, and in process (remember the politics of solidarity that Kristeva "founded on the consciousness of [our own] unconscious" [1991, 192]), then it seems the *least* revolutionary of all stances is the French-European "non-stance" that she appeals to in *Nations without Nationalism*. The "neutrality" of the French-as-host is nothing but a thinly veiled fantasy of abstraction (just as French freedom and equality were always *brotherly* freedom and equality, not *human* ones as we tend to assume). Elsewhere, Kristeva is careful to remind us that the greatest threat to a dynamic culture of revolt is a "nihilistic suspension of questioning in favor of so-called new values which, precisely as 'values,' have forgotten to question themselves, and as a result, have essentially betrayed the meaning of the re-volt" (2014, 5). Would this not require of us that we similarly question the old "French" or "Enlightenment" values (including that of *l'esprit général*), rather than uncritically embracing them as neutral and universally desirable? As Kristeva herself puts it, such rendering invisible of values *as* values "turns out to be deadly and totalitarian" (5).

McAfee, who identifies in Kristeva's earliest work the political power of attending to the speaking being as "split and on trial," worries that these later "political" texts have evacuated that political potential and radicality, in the name of forms of universality that reinscribe French colonial power as a political ideal: "her writings and addresses on politics tend to begin with assumptions about the superiority of enlightenment universal values embodied in the French Republic and culminate with applying them to issues such as disability, immigration, and the veil" (2020, 753). It is indeed difficult to square such enlightenment ideals with the split, heterogenous, ambivalent subject that appeared on the pages of *Revolution in Poetic Language*, and with the political promise that it offered. If anything, such ideals inaugurate the very fantasy of a transparent-rational-autonomous-unified subject that the Freudian revolution had sought to unravel.

Ahmed finds in *Powers of Horror* a useful toolbox for challenging the assimilationist logics that haunt some of Kristeva's later work. We might add to that toolbox both her earliest work on the revolutionary potential of the liminal-polyphonic dynamics of subjectivity and language, and her later work on intimate revolt understood as perpetual self-interrogation and a critical wrestling with oneself and one's standpoint to make possible new beginnings, rebirth, and new avenues for self-examination. Much of my own work has focused on Kristeva's notion of revolt understood as return and renewal—a psychoanalytically inflicted model of revolt as anamnesis and rebirth (Söderbäck 2012, 2019). Such revolutionary politics of renewal is what Ahmed calls for in the closing lines of her essay, perhaps without even realizing the degree to which they echo central themes in Kristeva's work: "Opening the community to others means turning back, turning around. . . . It means starting again. This promise of new beginnings is the hope of postcoloniality, the hope that coloniality could be posted as we find another way of living with others. Such a hope is one that may require the pain of shedding dead skin—which means recognizing that old skins will have affects and effects—and the itchiness of the emergence of new skins" (2005, 109). It is hard not to hear echoes from Frantz Fanon here. In the closing lines of *The Wretched of the Earth*, he had announced the need to "turn over a new leaf" and birth a "new man" (2005, 316)—his own vision for the hope of postcoloniality. The French original reads: "Pour l'Europe, pour nous-mêmes et pour l'humanité, camarades, *il faut faire peau neuve*, développer une pensée neuve, tenter de mettre sur pied un homme neuf" (2016, 230; emphasis mine). The French expression that has been translated as "turning a new leaf" thus also, more literally, means "making new skin," which of course requires a shedding of old skin—skin, as Ahmed points out, that "will have affects and effects," which is why, on her account (and here she comes close to Kristeva's concept of revolt), we must return, turn back, in order to reenvision and be reborn.[10] Revolt as shedding and growing new skin, a painful process, yet one that carries hope for new beginnings, new forms of subjectivity, perhaps new modes of expression, too.

As others have pointed out before me, it is curious that Kristeva never engages Fanon in her elaboration of revolt as return and rebirth, given her insistence that such work involves our grappling with the stranger that we ourselves have become—a central theme in Fanon's revolutionary project. Jean-Paul Sartre suggested that Fanon's great insight was "that we are estranged from ourselves" (Sartre cited in Gratton 2007,

9)—although, of course, Fanon was acutely aware not only of the unequal distribution of such estrangement, but also of how our response to it (the manner in which we might work through our estrangement and even turn it into political ammunition) is all but symmetrical and has everything to do with colonial dynamics of racialization. Peter Gratton has noted that, as much as Kristeva offers multiple readings of Sartre in her volumes on revolt (Kristeva 2000b, 2002a), she "resists" his preface to *The Wretched of the Earth*, in which he famously urged his fellow Europeans to engage in an act of self-examination: "Let us look at ourselves, if we can bear to see what is becoming of us" (Sartre cited in Gratton 2007, 9). It is this exercise of introspection—one requiring Europeans to grapple with their own implications in past and present colonial logics—that is curiously missing from Kristeva's discussion of the French nation. Its absence haunts her "properly political" texts and marks them as stilted by the kind of stubborn repression that she has devoted her work elsewhere to scrutinizing.

But rather than staging a more robust encounter here between Kristeva and Fanon—which others have done before me (Gratton 2007, Hansen 2020, Ziarek 2004)—I want instead to put Kristeva into conversation with Gloria Anzaldúa, another revolutionary for whom questions of return as renewal, liminality, heterogeneity, polyphony, and strangeness are key. It is my hope that such staged encounter might help us shed new light on the power and limits of Kristeva's revolutionary project.

Monsters of the Crossroads: Heterogeneity and Strangeness in the Borderlands

Anzaldúa, who was born just one year after Kristeva, but who passed away prematurely from complications related to diabetes in 2004, grew up in the Rio Grande Valley in southern Texas, near the border of Mexico—an area lending its name to the title of her most celebrated work: *Borderlands/La Frontera*. To date, little has been done to read Anzaldúa's work alongside that of continental feminists. It might be worth noting that Anzaldúa herself was wary of making such connections. In an essay where she reflects on the process of writing *Borderlands/La Frontera*, she gives voice to a growing frustration with the demand that she cite "Foucault, Lacan, Derrida, or the French feminists" (2009c, 192). She views these "master writers" as lacking experience with the context she engages in her work, and she worries that their writing is all too "disembodied," as well as prone to talking about people of color as "the quintessential example of the postmodern condition," while at the same time failing to actually engage writers of color as voices worthy of full theoretical attention (192–93). Kristeva has similarly expressed frustration with being expected to cite certain thinkers whose work she herself does not take up in her writing. In her response to Hansen's contribution to the *Library of Living Philosophers* volume devoted to her work—in which Hansen raises some of the same concerns I have raised here regarding Kristeva's tendency to reproduce colonial logics by skirting them, and in which they critically examine her silence on Fanon—Kristeva remarks: "Why should I ask myself about the admirable Fanon whose trajectory, like many others, did not cross mine?" (2020, 602).

So why would I nevertheless stage such a dialogue? I do so in the spirit of Anzaldúa's explicit commitment to alliance building (especially in her later work), Kristeva's commitment to intertextuality and polyphony, and both of their commitments to liminal-generative spaces of transgression and contradiction, where unexpected encounters can happen. It is my contention that tracing the connections between their works might serve as a bridge-building effort of sorts—despite the undeniable differences between them and the fact that the dialogue must remain imaginary.

As we have seen, Kristeva draws from the psychoanalytic notion of the unconscious and a model of subjectivity that views us as opaque and internally divided. She insists that each self is a universe, that we are internally heterogeneous, and such internal dividedness and multiplicity ultimately make us foreign, or strange. Anzaldúa similarly develops a theory of subjectivity grounded in liminality and hybridity—the new mestiza consciousness that is made possible in and through the Borderlands. Looking at her own image in the mirror, she sees multiple faces that reflect the different parts of her life, each marked by a different set of relations and social constellations, each situated, each with a lifeworld of its own. She sees "a stranger's face," and notes: "*tenía un caracter multíplice*" (2012, 66). Being a stranger to herself, she has multiple selves, identities, faces staring back at her.[11] Her conception of selfhood, as María Lugones puts it in a commentary on Anzaldúa's work, is one marked by perpetual "germination" (1992, 32).

Kristeva and Anzaldúa are thus both deeply invested in a dynamic conception of selfhood that stresses multiplicity, heterogeneity, ambiguity, and strangeness.[12] The *sujet-en-procès* that we first encountered in *Revolution in Poetic Language* and that appeared in Kristeva's later work as constitutively uncanny and strange takes multiple shapes in Anzaldúa's body of work: the shadow beast, the new mestiza, the nepantla—these are all figures meant to evoke a multiplicitous self that refuses stability, universality, and homogeneity. Such a self is always situated, "caught between worlds" (Anzaldúa 2012, 61), and has a tolerance for ambiguity and contradiction. "These numerous possibilities leave *la mestiza* floundering in uncharted seas . . . subjected to a swamping of her psychological borders" (101). Identity is a process-in-the-making, a shape-shifting activity, always in flux. As Ortega puts it, Anzaldúa's account "serves as an inspiration for those who wish to move beyond traditional understandings of the subject or of selfhood that do not take into consideration the importance of situatedness, liminality, ambiguity, and plurality" (2016, 29).

For Anzaldúa, as for Kristeva, this dynamic notion of subjectivity depends on a conception of the self as constitutively linguistic. The subject is a *speaking subject*, and the question of language stands at the heart of their respective elaborations of heterogeneous-liminal selfhood at the crossroads. *Borderlands/La Frontera* is half poetry and half theoretical essay, and it is written in both Spanish and English, as well as the many dialects and mixtures of these two languages that are spoken in the Chicana community. Using Kristeva's vocabulary, we might say that it is not just a multilingual but a truly polyphonic text. As such, it is also a deeply self-conscious and self-affirming text. It performs a kind of resistance to a monolingual culture that does not allow for "accents," and that privileges "male discourse" (Anzaldúa 2012, 76). For Anzaldúa, the very process of writing amounts to overcoming a tradition of silence that has served to repress the "border tongue," the "living language," and the "forked tongue" (77) that constitutes a homeland, a motherland, a Borderland, for those whose voices cannot be expressed in the monolingual (Kristeva might say monotonous) discourse of the "mainland."

The speaking subject is, for both Kristeva and Anzaldúa, also a writing subject. And as we have seen, for Kristeva, (poetic) writing is a revolutionary practice. To be sure, Anzaldúa's poetic-theoretical writing is revolutionary, and it insists on the vital importance of overcoming various forms of repression and silences. If Kristeva's revolutionary project was one concerned with the "wildness of the speaking being" (2002b, 19), Anzaldúa famously asserts the vital necessity for such wildness to be spoken and heard: "Wild tongues can't be tamed, they can only be cut out" (2012, 76). The border crosser is thus an agent of linguistic terrorism: "We are your linguistic nightmare, your linguistic aberration, your linguistic *mestizaje*," Anzaldúa exclaims (80). Elsewhere, she has described this revolution as the attempt to write left-handed in a right-handed world (2009d, 28). Her writing is a powerful revolt against the white imperative of right-handed reason. And of course, for both our border crossers, the power of (poetic) language and writing is its capacity to give voice to the embodied, the semiotic, to affective drive. Anzaldúa describes her own process as *organic writing*: "It's not on paper that you create but in your innards, in the gut and out of living tissue" (2009d, 33).

Kristeva and Anzaldúa share an acute sense of foreignness in their lived realities, and they have both centered this experience in their writing. Yet situatedness matters, and these two thinkers are clearly differently situated. Paying careful attention to these differences, I want to take seriously Ahmed's suggestion that strangeness is in fact unevenly distributed and that some others have already been recognized as stranger than others. What is more, I want to take seriously Anzaldúa's insistence on the epistemic privilege of the oppressed: "Those who are pounced on the most have it [awareness] the strongest—the females, the homosexuals of all races, the darkskinned, the outcast, the persecuted, the marginalized, the foreign" (2012, 60).

Kristeva describes herself as "a European citizen of Bulgarian origin with French Nationality and American by adoption" (2018, 311), and nowhere, she declares, "is one *more* a foreigner than in France" (1993, 30). She explicitly identifies as a cosmopolitan, elaborating that this means that "against origins and starting from them," she has "chosen a transnational or international position situated at the crossing of boundaries" (1993, 16). Throughout her work, she stresses the importance of multilingualism, hybridity, mixing, and crossing: "At the intersection of two languages," amid "hybridization," she identifies with the "men and women of the borderlands" (2000a, 167–78). She claims liminality as a dwelling for thinking and living, while recognizing that such abode is one that marks her as different to the point of anomaly. Identifying as an alien in a space in-between, she confesses to speaking a "strange language," embodying a "monstrous intimacy," all of which makes her, Kristeva, "a monster of the crossroads" (167).

Anzaldúa shares this sense of inhabiting a monstrous state of liminality. An exile who belongs nowhere and everywhere, and whose very existence is defined by ambiguity and contradiction, the new mestiza that she births in her work resists rigid boundaries and binary thinking. She "copes by developing a tolerance for contradictions, a tolerance for ambiguity" (2012, 101). This psychic restlessness can be disorienting and displacing, and can lead to the dissociation of identity, much like abjection did for Kristeva. As Ortega notes in *In-Between*, Anzaldúa "describes a self that lives on the borders but that can cross them and facilitate passages across worlds" (2016, 19). Herself an outcast living in "a constant state of transition," Anzaldúa identifies with *los atravesados*: "the squint-eyed, the perverse, the queer, the troublesome, the mongrel, the mulatto, the half-breed, the half dead; in short, those who cross over, pass over, or go through the confines of the 'normal'" (2012, 25). The abject, abjection. Stranger than other strangers. "I felt alien," Anzaldúa notes, "I knew I was alien. I was the mutant stoned out of the herd, something deformed with evil inside" (65).

Diasporic, yet no migrants, Chicanas never quite crossed the border, but the border crossed them, as the United States annexed parts of Mexico and incorporated that body of land into its geopolitical territory (28). And now, the border runs through their very bodies and communities, a scab that keeps hemorrhaging (25), a dividing line that marks them as subjects who, like corn, are the product of crossbreeding: "designed for preservation under a variety of conditions" (103). Mestiza, mestizaje, "the officiating priestess at the crossroads" (102), transcending dualisms, blending the two sides into a third, the Borderland, a space of unbound potential and of imagining otherwise.

Anzaldúa describes herself as a border dweller, as an inhabitant of the *herida abierta*, or open wound, "where the Third World grates against the first and bleeds" (25). As a woman, she poses a particular kind of threat to male binary culture: "Woman is the stranger, the other. She is man's recognized nightmarish pieces, his Shadow-Beast. The sight of her sends him into a frenzy of anger and fear" (39). But this female strangeness is also a source of identification and solidarity. Identifying with no nation yet claiming all nations as her own—an eternal exile and cosmopolite—Anzaldúa's strongest kinship is that with fellow women: "As a *mestiza* I have no country, my homeland cast me out; yet all countries are mine because I am every woman's sister or potential lover" (102). Kristeva is far more wary of womanhood as a shared category of identification and thus as a potential source of coalition building or solidarity, since she worries that it runs the risk of totalizing.[13]

Yet, both Kristeva and Anzaldúa tend to insist in their work that women are uniquely situated when it comes to issues of exile and border crossing. As Sandra Regina Goulart Almeida notes in her analysis of bodily encounters in *Borderlands/La Frontera*, Anzaldúa "works out this theory of the borderlands, of hybridization, in terms of female imaginary, figures, and roles," and Almeida pauses to reflect briefly on the fact that "these female figures evoke Julia Kristeva's notion of women as boundary-subjects" (2008, 117). She quotes Kristeva from *Nations without Nationalism*: "Women have the luck and the responsibility of being boundary-subjects: body and thought, biology and language, personal identity and dissemination during childhood, origin and judgment, nation and world" (Kristeva 1993, 35). The very ambiguity that has caused women to be marginalized and devalued in our culture also marks them as more adept border crossers. Anzaldúa's *nepantlera* (the bridge-builder) or her *nagual* (the shapeshifter) are feminine figures of strangeness; ever-expanding figures that stretch and transform, that make possible growth and transformation, or new births. In Kristeva, such flexibility is ascribed to the maternal, which (contrary to what a slew of feminist critics of her work might suggest as they situate the mother as confined by the moors of essentialism) is a force of gestation and transformation, the ultimate border crossing subject, the paradigmatic figure of new beginnings.

For Anzaldúa, the ambivalent-ambiguous serves as a focal point for a new consciousness that refuses boundaries-as-separation, insisting instead on the Borderland as an opening, a transformative space of mixing and mingling. If borders limit and constraint (materially and metaphorically), the Borderland is an in-between space of possibilities and creation. What was once a "nightmare" can become a "numinous experience" (2012, 95). This ambiguous characteristic of the Borderland—it being a source of suffering (an open wound) but also the uniquely hybrid, mutable, malleable space out of which can arise "a new *mestiza* consciousness, *una consciencia de mujer* . . . a consciousness of the Borderlands," as Anzaldúa famously puts it (99)—is echoed in Kristeva's work, and in her reflections on her own journey from Bulgaria to France. To be sure, Eastern Europe can be seen as a liminal space, a Borderland, and as such, it is a place of pain and suffering but also one where intellectual and creative work has the capacity to bend open new worlds, new horizons, and thus serve as a site of resistance and revolt against the powers that be.

We should add here that for Kristeva, loss, perpetual mourning, and linguistic displacement are not *only* features in the lives of those who have left their birth country behind like she herself did, but also more generally for a speaking subject "guilty" of matricide, for whom individuation depends on abjection and separation, which is to say, for all of us. Or, as

Miglena Nikolchina puts it in an essay on parables of exile in Kristeva's work: "The speaking being dwells in language as an exile. With Kristeva, language is the homelessness of being" (1991, 235). Exile is a constitutive feature of the speaking subject. We have all in some sense lost our mother tongue. We are all foreigners, hence there are no foreigners. Yet, I maintain with Ahmed that some foreigners are more foreign than others. And some speakers are more homeless than others. As Anzaldúa puts it, the border crosser speaks an "orphan tongue . . . it is illegitimate, a bastard language" (2012, 80). As a woman of color, for Anzaldúa the very process of writing is a quest for "making soul," for overcoming the "internalized exile" that haunts her and demands of her that she "reconcile" the other within herself: "We came to see the alien within us and too often, as a result, we split apart from ourselves and each other" (2009d, 30).

While the Kristeva of *Nations without Nationalism* by and large masks her own foreignness, speaking instead from the vantage point of the French nation, French Enlightenment ideals, *l'esprit général* (and we have seen the limits this puts on her outlook), elsewhere she centers her personal experience with foreignness, and this typically results in far more subtle reflections on liminality, bilingualism, border crossing, bridge building, incomplete mourning, remembering, as well as *re-membering*. It matters, of course, that Kristeva left her native Bulgaria for Paris—and established herself there as one of France's leading intellectuals and psychoanalysts, a powerhouse of cultural capital—whereas Anzaldúa insisted on claiming and reclaiming her native Borderlands as a privileged territory for thought and action. This difference in situatedness is undeniable, and I would argue that it gives Anzaldúa epistemic privilege on matters pertaining to the marginalization that results from being stranger than other strangers (we might add, here, her being queer, Chicana, a woman of color, chronically ill, and so on).

Echoing Kristeva's own words, Ortega described her interpretive trajectory during her keynote lecture at the 2018 meeting of the Kristeva Circle as follows: "I travel with Kristeva, and away from her." And as I engage a similar journey in this text—a journey with and away from Kristeva, as well as a journey *back* to the Kristeva of *Revolution in Poetic Language*—I am particularly interested in how she speaks of *her* own journey: *Je me voyage*, "I travel myself" (Kristeva & Dock 2016)—an expression that highlights her commitment to a multiplicitous self, a subject in process that is always already also a subject on trial, whose becoming is tied to self-reflection *as* acknowledgment of our constitutive ambivalence—

insofar as we are precariously situated *between* biology and meaning, corporeality and language, semiotic and symbolic, affect and thought . . .

An obvious difference between Kristeva and Anzaldúa has to do with the former's lifelong engagement with and contributions to psychoanalysis, which the latter does not share. This difference is significant, and it has tangible consequences on their respective projects and the theoretical toolbox they draw from to develop their thought. But it seems worth noting, in this context, that while Anzaldúa does not tend to reference Freud in her work, she repeatedly uses the language of the unconscious to describe her own shadow, and she is certainly concerned with psychic suffering, with the need for psychic flexibility, and with the possibility for psychic transformation as a revolutionary tool—what she calls, in her later work, spiritual activism, and what follows the seven stages of *conocimiento* (2015b, 117–59).[14] As we have seen, "the *mestiza*'s dual or multiple personality is plagued by psychic restlessness" (2012, 100). Being situated in the Borderlands can, again, cause suffering and confusion, but it also equips us to engage in transformative practices of resistance: "The struggle is inner" (109), it is "work that the soul performs," and it "takes place underground—subconsciously" (101), in "the dark, chthonic (underworld)" (61). Kristeva consistently identifies such "underground" work as revolutionary. Indeed, she cites Freud, who in a 1936 letter to fellow psychoanalyst Ludwig Binswanger wrote: "I have always dwelt only in the ground floor and basement of the building. [. . .] In that you are the conservative, I am the revolutionary" (Freud cited in Kristeva 2000b, 15). For Kristeva, Freud's revolutionary power "signifies the possibility that psychoanalysis has to access the archaic, to overturn conscious meaning" (2000b, 15).

Both Kristeva and Anzaldúa thus locate the work of social and political transformation in the psychic space of intimate revolt. For both, the individual and the social are linked in the voyage of resistance and transformation. As Anzaldúa puts it, "awareness of our situation must come before inner changes, which in turn come before changes in society. Nothing happens in the 'real' world unless it first happens in the images in our heads" (2012, 109).[15] Lugones thematizes this link between the intimate and the social in Anzaldúa's work: "As I understand the liberatory project, the inner and the collective struggles are not separable; they are 'moments' or 'sides' of the liberatory process. [. . .] Anzaldúa's *desafío* [challenge] is about the creation of a new culture, an intimate and also and inseparably, a collective struggle" (2006, 96).

Our greatest enemy, then, is psychic stagnation and dogmatism, and change, for Kristeva, always depends on a dynamic psychic life.[16] Anzaldúa shares this view and inscribes it into her conceptualization of a new mestiza consciousness: "Rigidity means death. Only by remaining flexible is she able to stretch the psyche horizontally and vertically. *La mestiza* constantly has to shift out of habitual formations; from convergent thinking, analytic reasoning that tends to use rationality to move toward a single goal (a Western mode), to divergent thinking, characterized by movement away from set patterns and goals and toward a more whole perspective, one that includes rather than excludes" (2012, 101).

Revolt as psychic transgression-transformation and renewal. The shedding of skin and the growth of new skin (for Anzaldúa, quite literally, since she envisions this journey as one of entering into the serpent). Intimacy as the privileged locus for a kind of dissent that can result in the shattering of the self and of worlds. This work of transformation depends on a kind of consciousness-raising that puts consciousness aside, that "tears the fabric of our everyday mode of consciousness" (61), or what Anzaldúa names *la faculdad*. She describes it as "the capacity to see in surface phenomena the meaning of deeper realities, to see the deep structure below the surface" (60). A form of perception that is irreducible to conscious reasoning, *la faculdad* arises from "the part of the psyche that does not speak, that communicates in images and symbols which are the faces of feelings" (60). It is hard not to hear the resemblance here with Kristeva's semiotic, that affective register that grounds symbolic expression while simultaneously tearing it apart. And if Kristeva insisted that the semiotic brings life and music to otherwise stilted and fixed realities, Anzaldúa associates *la faculdad* with profound vitality too: "The one possessing this sensitivity is *excruciatingly alive* to the world" (60; emphasis mine).

For Kristeva, the work of memory and of bringing together or gathering that which has been dis-membered—a meaning-making activity—is not just a practice of sublimation, but also of revolt. *Re-membering, re-volter*. The return to and of the body, a return that is always also a rebirth, a new beginning, an act of creation and creativity. Shedding and growing skin. And such a return *does* involve our recognizing our internal strangeness. But it also must involve our grappling with the way in which that strangeness is situated and how it is inflicted with external matters such as power and privilege, as well as social/historical/collective modes of repression and exclusion. As Anzaldúa notes (and here we hear echoes from Sartre urging his fellow Europeans to engage in an act of self-examination): "Gringo, accept the doppelganger in your psyche. By taking back your collective shadow the intracultural split will heal" (2012, 108).

Building off of what I said in the previous section, this seems to me precisely where Kristeva would have important lessons to learn from Anzaldúa. If the talking cure is to be truly transformative—and if our awareness of our unconscious (the stranger within) is to have robust ethical and political implications for the lived realities of those who are perceived as "more strange" than "the rest of us"—it seems that our repeated returns ought to move beyond our own Oedipal beginnings, so as to include awareness of how Oedipus the exile always remained firmly situated within a European lifeworld. Perhaps it is no coincidence that the monster of the crossroads of that story—the Sphinx—produced a riddle that ultimately framed the human in universal-masculine terms (that the answer to her riddle was Man).[17] When Anzaldúa returns us to different imaginaries—to *Coatlicue*, to *Yemayá*, to *la Llorona*—these already indicate a strangeness more deeply embedded in an otherwise and otherwhen, vis-à-vis hegemonic European heritages and horizons.[18] A strangeness more strange, perhaps, than the one born out of a European mythos and consciousness. But as such, it may also have more transformative and unsettling—indeed *revolutionary*—potential.

Notes

I would like to thank Emilia Angelova for inviting me to contribute to this volume, and for being immensely patient with me through difficult times. My first attempt to sketch a dialogue between Kristeva and Anzaldúa took place at the 2018 Kristeva Circle Conference at Cal State Northridge. Thanks to Sid Hansen for inviting me to give the plenary address there, and to all the participants of that session, who asked just the right questions to help me frame this project. As a 2020 recipient of the DePaul University Center for Latino Studies Faculty Fellowship, I was able to spend some focused time examining the intersection between these two thinkers. Thanks to the other fellows in that program who offered helpful feedback on an early draft of this essay. I presented a later draft to members of the Södertörn University Philosophy Department, who offered invaluable comments and suggestions. I would like to acknowledge and thank the students who took my two graduate seminars at DePaul University where the details of this essay were fleshed out: *Stranger than Other Strangers: Anzaldúa, Kristeva, Ahmed* (Winter 2021); and *French Feminism II: Julia Kristeva* (Winter

2022). Students in the former seminar offered insightful comments on how we might read these bodies of work together, and students in the latter joined me for a close reading of Kristeva's work on revolution and revolt, including *Revolution in Poetic Language*. I am lucky to have such amazing students and am always indebted to their great insights and the many wonderful questions they ask along the way. I am especially indebted to Paula Landerreche Cardillo, who served as my research assistant, and who helped me dig up resources and identify important passages. Her work was impeccable and invaluable, as always. Generous funding for this project has been provided by the DePaul University Center for Latino Studies.

1. See also Kristeva (2002a, 258). In an autobiographical essay, Kristeva has remarked more generally, that upon her return from China, notably in 1974 (the same year as when *Revolution in Poetic Language* was first published), she bid her "farewell to politics, including feminism" (Kristeva 2002b, 19).

2. Some prior attempts have been made to put Kristeva and Anzaldúa into conversation: Kelly Oliver and Benigno Trigo were among the first to do so, in the context of their own analysis of Orson Welles's film *Touch of Evil* (Oliver and Trigo 2003, 130–34); Sandra Regina Goulart Almeida subsequently noted in passing that both Kristeva and Anzaldúa characterize women as boundary-subjects (Almeida 2008, 117); and Jorgelina Corbatta has offered a two-page "imaginary dialogue" between Kristeva and Anzaldúa, which sketches some of the shared ground of their thinking (Corbatta 2014, 362–63). As much as my own tracings of the intersection between their work in the final section of this chapter is bound to be tentative and schematic, these prior engagements are even more brief. To be sure, a lot could be done to stage a more systematic encounter between them.

3. Anzaldúa's work has been hugely influential in a range of disciplines for decades already, but it is only more recently that it has been taken up more systematically in philosophical circles. Mariana Ortega's *In-Between: Latina Feminist Phenomenology, Multiplicity, and the Self* (2016) was groundbreaking in this regard, in that it reads Anzaldúa's work as properly phenomenological, and therefore as contributing in significant ways to discussions of fundamental concepts such as time, space, and subjectivity, as these are taken up by thinkers such as Martin Heidegger. Nancy Tuana and Charles Scott's *Beyond Philosophy: Nietzsche, Foucault, Anzaldúa* (2020) is similarly important for situating Anzaldúa in a philosophical landscape. Andrea J. Pitts's *Nos/Otras: Gloria E. Anzaldúa, Multiplicitous Agency, and Resistance* (2021) brings to the fore philosophical themes such as subjectivity and agency in Anzaldúa's work, and reads it in relation to existentialist phenomenology, relational ontology, as well as recent work in critical disability studies and trans feminisms. These works have inspired and shaped the reading I offer here, although none of them reference Kristeva explicitly in their analysis.

4. For a careful and systematic account of Kristeva's materialism, and its effects on ethics, see Ziarek (2020). Elsewhere, Beardsworth has noted that poetic language "is the site of transformation of meaning and the subject," and she goes on to note that this renders poetic language as "equivalent to, if not more than, ethics" (2004, 51). In *Revolution in Poetic Language*, Kristeva herself defines ethics as "the negativizing of narcissism within a *practice*," which is to say that "a practice is ethical when it dissolves those narcissistic fixations (ones that are narrowly confined to the subject) to which the signifying process succumbs in its socio-symbolic realization" (1984, 233).

5. Emilia Angelova speaks of a "turn" in Kristeva's work "from revolution as seeking to overturn symbolic orders to revolt as disrupting symbolization altogether," and her own work is meant to "reveal how the sort of negativity at work in revolt is very different than in revolution" (Angelova 2020, 556). For discussions of the trajectory from revolution to revolt in Kristeva's work, see Beardsworth (2005) and Hansen and Tuvel (2017). Note that whereas these thinkers argue for a "turn" from her early elaboration of revolution to her later conception of revolt, I want to stress that there is continuity and overlap between the two (and that both, moreover, ought to be viewed as political in kind and scope).

6. In this chapter, I focus primarily on the parts from *Revolution in Poetic Language* where Kristeva examines and explains the relationship between the semiotic and the symbolic. For a succinct reading of the sections of the book that deal more explicitly with negation-expulsion—including the political implications of those terms—see Kramer (2013).

7. As Oliver has noted: "The prefix 're-' forms a central axis of Julia Kristeva's writing and thinking. She emphasizes *rebirth, revolt, return, re-pulsion, representation, rejection,* among other renegotiations and repetitions of the past" (Oliver 2014, 20). For analyses of Kristeva's concept of revolt as temporal return, see Sjöholm (2005) and Söderbäck (2012; 2019).

8. Expressing concerns that Kristeva "did not even mention or seemingly consider the legacy of French colonialism in Africa in her discussion of the 'suburban troubles' in France," Elaine P. Miller is dismayed that Kristeva has "turned away from the abject history of her own adopted nation" (2014, 43). For similar concerns, see Gratton (2007) and Hansen (2020).

9. See also Moruzzi (1993, 141) and Ibrahim (2018, 4–5) for helpful contextualizations of the *affaire du foulard* and more generally on the fraught discussions about the use of *hijab* in France.

10. I would like to thank James Walker for bringing my attention to the French expression in the closing lines of Fanon's text.

11. In "Geographies of Selves," Anzaldúa examines the self as a universe at more length, as she elaborates an expansive model of interconnectedness that

centers the strangeness of the self (2015a). It would be interesting to develop a close reading of her notion of *Nos/Otras* in that context in relation to Kristeva's stranger, but I will not be able to do so here. See Pitts (2021) for a rich elaboration of this dimension of Anzaldúa's work.

12. Anzaldúa's conception of selfhood arguably develops over the course of her work. For the purposes of this essay, I will focus primarily on her earlier work, although as Martina Koegeler-Abdi has pointed out, with Ortega, even if we follow the shift from *mestiza consciousness* to *nepantlera* in her work, we find that in both cases, Anzaldúa "develops alternative subjectivities that dismantle the Western philosophical and political tradition of unitary, rational subjects that base subjectivity on the exclusion of the other" (Koegeler-Abdi 2013, 72).

13. Kristeva has repeatedly expressed worry that feminism runs the risk of totalitarianism, in the sense that it reduces all individual women to the category of Woman. In "Women's Time," for example, she raises this concern: "Is feminism not about to become a sort of religion? Or will it manage to rid itself of its belief in Woman, Her power, and Her writing and support instead the singularity of each woman, her complexities, her many languages, at the cost of a single horizon, of a single perspective, or faith?" (1995, 221). In her most recent work, she has begun to identify as a "Scotus feminist," with reference to Duns Scotus's conception of *l'ecceitas*, or singularity. See, for example, Kristeva (2018, 80). Anzaldúa is of course also aware of the risks of a universalizing conception of womanhood, one that would ignore important differences of class, race, and sexuality, among others. In the 1990 essay "Bridge, Drawbridge, Sandbar, or Island," she notes: "Sisterhood in the singular was a utopian fantasy invented by whitewomen" (2009a, 149). In her later work, she was more optimistic about bridging such differences to achieve transnational feminist coalitions and alliances.

14. AnaLouise Keating describes spiritual activism as locating "authority within each individual by synergistically linking self-change with social transformation" (2016, 13).

15. In "La Prieta"—one of her earliest essays—Anzaldúa elaborates on this claim: "I believe that by changing ourselves we change the world, that traveling El Mundo Zurdo path is the path of a two-way movement—a going deep into the self and an expanding out into the world, a simultaneous creation of the self and a reconstruction of society. And yet, I am confused as to how to accomplish this" (2009b, 49).

16. See, especially, Kristeva's trilogy on *The Powers and Limits of Psychoanalysis*: *The Sense and Non-Sense of Revolt* (2000b), *Intimate Revolt* (2002a), and *Hatred and Forgiveness* (2010).

17. For a fascinating reading of the myth of Oedipus as a founding text for the Western-philosophical obsession with (abstract) universality at the expense of (embodied) singularity, see Cavarero (2000, 7–16).

18. As Anzaldúa herself puts it: "Let's all stop importing Greek myths and the Western Cartesian split point of view and root ourselves in the mythological soil and soul of this continent" (2012, 90).

References

Ahmed, Sara. 2005. "The Skin of the Community: Affect and Boundary Formation." In *Revolt, Affect, Collectivity: The Unstable Boundaries of Kristeva's Polis*, edited by Tina Chanter and Ewa Płonowska Ziarek. Albany: State University of New York Press.

Almeida, Sandra Regina Goulart. 2008. "Bodily Encounters: Gloria Anzaldúa's Borderlands/La Frontera." *Ilha do Desterro* 39: 113–23.

Angelova, Emilia. 2020. "Abjection and the Maternal Semiotic in Kristeva's Intimate Revolt." In *The Library of Living Philosophers Volume XXXVI: The Philosophy of Julia Kristeva*, edited by Sara G. Beardsworth. Chicago, IL: Open Court.

Anzaldúa, Gloria. 2015a. "Geographies of Selves: Reimagining Identity." In *Light in the Dark/Luz en lo Oscuro: Rewriting Identity, Spirituality, Reality*, edited by AnaLouise Keating. Durham, NC: Duke University Press.

———. 2015b. "Now Let Us Shift . . . Conocimiento . . . Inner Work, Public Acts." In *Light in the Dark/Luz en lo Oscuro: Rewriting Identity, Spirituality, Reality*, edited by AnaLouise Keating. Durham, NC: Duke University Press.

———. 2012. *Borderlands/La Frontera: The New Mestiza*. 25th Anniversary Edition. San Francisco, CA: Aunt Lute Books.

———. 2009a. "Bridge, Drawbridge, Sandbar, or Island." In *The Gloria Anzaldúa Reader*, edited by AnaLouise Keating. Durham, NC: Duke University Press.

———. 2009b. "La Prieta." In *The Gloria Anzaldúa Reader*, edited by AnaLouise Keating. Durham, NC: Duke University Press.

———. 2009c. "On Writing Borderlands/La Frontera." In *The Gloria Anzaldúa Reader*, edited by Ana Louise Keating. Durham, NC: Duke University Press.

———. 2009d. "Speaking in Tongues: A Letter to Third World Women Writers." In *The Gloria Anzaldúa Reader*, edited by Ana Louise Keating. Durham, NC: Duke University Press.

Beardsworth, Sara G. 2005. "From Revolution to Revolt Culture." In *Revolt, Affect, Collectivity: The Unstable Boundaries of Kristeva's Polis*, edited by Tina Chanter and Ewa Płonowska Ziarek. Albany: State University of New York Press.

———. 2004. *Julia Kristeva: Psychoanalysis and Modernity*. Albany: State University of New York Press.

Cavarero, Adriana. 2000. *Relating Narratives: Storytelling and Selfhood*, translated by Paul A. Kottman. London and New York: Routledge.

Corbatta, Jorgelina. 2014. "An *Imaginary* Dialogue between Gloria Anzaldúa and Julia Kristeva." *Hispania* 97, no. 3: 362–63.

Douglas, Mary. 2003. *Natural Symbols: Explorations in Cosmology*. London and New York: Routledge Classics.

———. 2002. *Purity and Danger: An Analysis of the Concept of Pollution and Taboo*. London and New York: Routledge Classics.

Fanon, Frantz. 2016. *Les damnés de la terre*. Montréal, QC: Kiyikaat Éditions.

———. 2005. *The Wretched of the Earth*. Translated by Richard Philcox. New York: Grove Press.

Freud, Sigmund. 1978. "The Uncanny." In *The Standard Edition of the Complete Psychological Works of Sigmund Freud*, vol. XVII (1917–1919), translated by James Strachey. London: Hogarth Press.

Gratton, Peter. 2007. "What Are Psychoanalysts for in a Destitute Time? Kristeva and the Community of Revolt." *Journal for Cultural Research* 11, no. 1: 1–13.

Hansen, S. K. 2020. "Intimate Revolt at the Margins of Community and the Hope of Postcoloniality." In *The Library of Living Philosophers, Volume XXXVI: The Philosophy of Julia Kristeva*, edited by Sara G. Beardsworth. Chicago, IL: Open Court.

Hansen, S. K. and Rebecca Tuvel. 2017. "Introduction: Twenty Years of Revolt." In *New Forms of Revolt: Essays on Kristeva's Intimate Politics*, edited by S. K. Hansen and Rebecca Tuvel. Albany: State University of New York Press.

Ibrahim, Hanan M. 2018. "Foreigners to Kristeva: Refashioning Orientalism and the Limits of Love." *Journal of Commonwealth Literature*: 1–12.

Keating, AnaLouise. 2016. "Gloria Anzaldúa." In *Fifty-One Key Feminist Thinkers: The Key Concepts*, edited by Lori Marso. London: Routledge.

Koegeler-Abdi, Martina. 2013. "Shifting Subjectivities: Mestizas, Nepantleras, and Gloria Anzaldúa's Legacy." *MELUS: The Society for the Study of the Multi-Ethnic Literature of the United States* 38, no. 29: 71–88.

Kramer, Sina. 2013. "On Negativity in *Revolution in Poetic Language*." *Continental Philosophy Review* 46, no. 1: 465–79.

Kristeva, Julia. 2020. "Reply to Emilia Angelova, Sarah K. Hansen, and Daniel Cohn-Bendit." In *The Library of Living Philosophers, Volume XXXVI: The Philosophy of Julia Kristeva*, edited by Sara G. Beardsworth. Chicago, IL: Open Court.

———. 2018. *Passions of Our Time*. Edited by Lawrence D. Kritzman, translated by Constance Borde and Sheila Malovany-Chevallier. New York: Columbia University Press.

———. 2014. "New Forms of Revolt." *Journal of French and Francophone Philosophy* 22, no. 2: 1–19.

———. 2013. "A Tragedy and a Dream: Disability Revisited." *Irish Theological Quarterly* 78, no. 3: 219–30.

———. 2011. *This Incredible Need to Believe*. Translated by Beverly Bie Brahic. New York: Columbia University Press.

———. 2010. *Hatred and Forgiveness*. Translated by Jeanine Herman. New York: Columbia University Press.

———. 2002a. *Intimate Revolt: The Powers and Limits of Psychoanalysis*. Translated by Jeanine Herman. New York: Columbia University Press.

———. 2002b. "My Memory's Hyperbole." In *The Portable Kristeva*, edited by Kelly Oliver, translated by Athena Viscusi. New York: Columbia University Press.

———. 2002c. *Revolt, She Said*. Edited by Sylvère Lotringer, translated by Brian O'Keeffe. Los Angeles, CA and New York: Semiotext(e).

———. 2000a. "Bulgaria, My Suffering." In *Crisis of the European Subject*, translated by Susan Fairfield. New York: Other Press.

———. 2000b. *The Sense and Non-Sense of Revolt: The Powers and Limits of Psychoanalysis*. Translated by Jeanine Herman. New York: Columbia University Press.

———. 1995. *New Maladies of the Soul*. Translated by Ross Guberman. New York: Columbia University Press.

———. 1993. *Nations without Nationalism*. Translated by Leon S. Roudiez. New York: Columbia University Press.

———. 1991. *Strangers to Ourselves*. Translated by Leon S. Roudiez. New York: Columbia University Press.

———. 1984. *Revolution in Poetic Language*. Translated by Margaret Waller. New York: Columbia University Press.

———. 1982. *Powers of Horror: An Essay on Abjection*. Translated by Leon S. Roudiez. New York: Columbia University Press.

Kristeva, Julia, & Samuel Dock. 2016. *Je me voyage: Mémoires*. Paris: Fayard.

Kristeva, Julia, and Jean Vanier. 2011. *Leur regard perce nos ombres*. Paris: Fayard.

Lugones, María. 2006. "From Within Germinative Stasis: Creating Active Subjectivity, Resistant Agency." In *Entre Mundos/Among Worlds: New Perspectives on Gloria E. Anzaldúa*, edited by AnaLouise Keating. London and New York: Palgrave Macmillan.

———. 1992. "On *Borderlands/La Frontera*: An Interpretive Essay." *Hypatia: A Journal of Feminist Philosophy* 7, no. 4: 31–37.

McAfee, Noëlle. 2020. "Kristeva's Latent Political Theory." In *The Library of Living Philosophers, Volume XXXVI: The Philosophy of Julia Kristeva*, edited by Sara G. Beardsworth. Chicago, IL: Open Court.

———. 2004. *Julia Kristeva*. New York and London: Routledge.

Miller, Elaine P. 2014. "Investing in a Third: Colonization, Religious Fundamentalism, and Adolescence." *Journal of French and Francophone Philosophy* 22, no. 2: 36–45.

Moruzzi, Norma Claire. 1993. "National Abjects: Julia Kristeva on the Process of Political Self-Identification." In *Ethics, Politics, and Difference in Julia Kristeva's Writings*, edited by Kelly Oliver. London and New York: Routledge.

Nikolchina, Miglena. 1991. "The Lost Territory: Parables of Exile in Julia Kristeva." *Semiotica* 86, no. 3/4: 231–46.
Oliver, Kelly. 2020. "The Democracy of Proximity and Kristeva's New Humanism." In *The Library of Living Philosophers, Volume XXXVI: The Philosophy of Julia Kristeva*, edited by Sara G. Beardsworth. Chicago, IL: Open Court.
———. 2014. "Kristeva's Reformation." *Journal of French and Francophone Philosophy* 22, no. 2: 20–25.
Oliver, Kelly, and Benigno Trigo. 2003. *Noir Anxiety*. Minneapolis: University of Minnesota Press.
Ortega, Mariana. 2018. "The Incandenscence of Abjection: Horror, Borders, Subjectivity." Unpublished keynote lecture at *The Kristeva Circle*, Cal State Northridge.
———. 2016. *In-Between: Latina Feminist Phenomenology, Multiplicity, and the Self*. Albany, State University of New York Press.
Pitts, Andrea J. 2021. *Nos/Otras: Gloria E. Anzaldúa, Multiplicitous Agency, and Resistance*. Albany: State University of New York Press.
Sjöholm, Cecilia. 2005. "Revolutions of Our Time: Revolt as Return." In *Kristeva and the Political*. London and New York: Routledge.
Söderbäck, Fanny. 2019. *Revolutionary Time: On Time and Difference in Kristeva and Irigaray*. Albany: State University of New York Press.
———. 2016. "Julia Kristeva." In *Fifty-One Key Feminist Thinkers: The Key Concepts*, edited by Lori Marso. London: Routledge.
———. 2012. "Revolutionary Time: Revolt as Temporal Return." *Signs: Journal of Women in Culture and Society* 37, no. 2: 301–24.
———. 2011. "Motherhood According to Kristeva: On Time and Matter in Plato and Kristeva." *philoSOPHIA: A Journal of Continental Feminism* 1, no. 1: 65–87.
Tuana, Nancy, and Charles Scott. 2020. *Beyond Philosophy: Nietzsche, Foucault, Anzaldúa*. Bloomington: Indiana University Press.
Ziarek, Ewa Płonowska. 2020. "A Materialist Ethics of Psychoanalysis? Reflections on Matter, Forgiveness, and Vulnerability." In *The Library of Living Philosophers, Volume XXXVI: The Philosophy of Julia Kristeva*, edited by Sara G. Beardsworth. Chicago, IL: Open Court.
———. 2004. "Kristeva and Fanon: The Future of the Revolt or the Future of an Illusion?" *Southern Journal of Philosophy* 42: 25–41.

Chapter 7

Theories of Poetic Resistance

Julia Kristeva and Sylvia Wynter

ELISABETH PAQUETTE

Introduction

The focus of this paper is the function of poetry within theories of resistance, exploring primarily the works of Julia Kristeva and Sylvia Wynter. Through a comparative analysis, I demonstrate the extent to which Kristeva and Wynter can be understood as engaged in common projects. What these projects have in common is evident in Wynter's various references to Kristeva. That said, in this paper I also demonstrate the ways in which Wynter's decolonial project at times strains or disrupts the limits of Kristeva's work.

What I aim to develop below are the political implications of Kristeva's and Wynter's respective articulations of the poetic. For instance, for Kristeva, I articulate the kinds of opening that the poetic enacts, as well as the kinds of possibilities that arise as a result of such openings. Similarly, for Wynter, I address the kinds of experiences that become expressible as a result of the poetic. In both instances, I turn my attention to the *operation* of poetry and the poetic, as located in text, but also as a mode for, or being for the purpose of, revolution.

Building upon various scholars past and present, I argue that a point of contention between Kristeva and Wynter is located within a conceptualization of sociogeny that is absent from Kristeva's project. As such, in this paper I also offer an analysis of sociogeny, its foundation in the writings of Frantz Fanon, and the role it plays for Wynter's theory of the poetic.[1] I argue that Wynter's attention to processes of dehumanization, humanism, and race by way of this conception of sociogeny transgresses, exceeds, and ruptures the limits of Kristeva's articulation of the poetic. I begin this paper with Kristeva's articulation of the poetic.

Julia Kristeva and the Poetic

Often, when I think of the relation between the semiotic and the symbolic in Kristeva's work, I think of two of Audre Lorde's essays, namely, "The Master's Tools Will Never Dismantle the Master's House" and "Poetry is not a Luxury." In the latter essay, Lorde describes the role of poetry for providing new words or modes of expression for experiences that previously felt unnameable and inexpressible. She states, "This is poetry as illumination, for it is through poetry that we give name to those ideas which are—until the poem—nameless and formless, about to be birthed, but already felt. The distillation of experience from which true poetry springs births thought as dream births concept, as feeling births ideas, as knowledge births (precedes) understanding" (Lorde 1984b, 36). The unnameability of these experiences is due to the social structures that seek to keep them invisible, such as racism and sexism, as well as the way these forms of systemic oppression overlap. In a similar manner, the themes in Lorde's "The Master's Tools" emphasize the importance of developing tools that exceed dominant social structures, such as white supremacy, in order to disrupt and dismantle these structures. It is for this reason that Lorde turns to poetry in order to invent new words.

While Julia Kristeva employs the framework of psychoanalysis, her discussion of poetic resistance is in some ways harmonious with Lorde's discussion of poetry in the essays described above. That said, Kristeva formulates her conception of the poetic through her discussion of the semiotic and the symbolic. In *Revolution in Poetic Language* in particular, she states that "the semiotic . . . constantly tears [the symbolic] open, and this transgression brings about all the various transformations of the signifying practice that are called 'creation.' Whether in the realm of metalanguage (mathematics, for example) or literature, what remodels the symbolic order is always the influx of the semiotic" (62). The symbolic denotes systems of signification, of which language or linguistic signs are just one. A subject who "means" makes meaning and attempts to convey meaning to others through various relations (23). The symbolic provides the conditions for such conveyance, again invoking not only language but also networks of relations, such as culture or other institutions that allow for the conveyance of meaning, often made evident when one moves between spaces wherein the conveyance of meaning is easier or more difficult. The semiotic is also situated alongside meaning production, albeit in a manner not already constrained by a logic whereby meaning becomes clear. To that end, the semiotic can be understood as what comes before a structured system of language comes about, and what is not (or has not yet) been codified into the system of meaning.

The semiotic provides the conditions through which something new can come about, but for this to be possible the semiotic must also be named; the subject must enunciate that which does not already exist within the expression of the law, social practices, or already established language. Therein lies the paradox at the heart of the semiotic operation: while we might understand the way the semiotic is operative in art, poetry, and music, we cannot name it and stay within the operation of the semiotic. To name these modalities of the semiotic is to reinscribe them into the symbolic structure.

This relation between the semiotic and the symbolic is one of continuous tension. The semiotic is both prior to and outside the symbolic, and yet internal to the symbolic as well. Never does one (either one) fully incorporate the other, and this is because they are necessary for each other. Meaning itself (as both creative and existent) depends upon the maintenance of this tension.

Considering this tension, the semiotic is allusive. It exists as a trace that is barely visible or as a murmur that one cannot quite make out; and yet it is because its meaning cannot be discerned through the symbolic order, and likewise it is because the poetic cannot be limited to linguistic practices, that the revolution of the symbolic order is possible.

It is in this way that Kristeva describes revolutionary practice: "the political activity whose aim is the radical transformation of social structures" (1984b, 104). For Kristeva, the poetic language is not what is colloquially referred to as poetry, that writing that adheres to a certain style and/or structure. Rather, the conception of poetic language that Kristeva invokes here is conceived of as that writing that seeks to disrupt social structures, that pushes one to discomfort and even to hate the poetic being written given its effect of turning social orders on their heads, whereby social orders are what provide many (or for Kristeva, us) safety and security. Poetry's eternal function is "to introduce through the symbolic that which works on, moves through, and threatens it" (81).

As such, "Poetic language covers that wide body of texts where the signifying process can be seen at work—provided one uses the proper tools of analysis" (Roudiez 1980, 7). Kristeva frequently engages with art and music as forms of poetic language.[2] The essential feature of poetry becomes, through Kristeva's self-defined method of analysis called "Sémanalyse," defined as a 'critique of meaning, of its elements and its laws'" (Roudiez 1980, 4). The revolutionary practice of poetic language is thus located in the analysis of the foundations of social orders.

Furthermore, poetic language, or this revolutionary process, holds a particular importance for the construction of the subject position. For Kristeva, the subject emerges through the thetic phase that begins with the mirror stage and is completed by the Oedipus complex. It is through the thetic phase that signifying practices are developed, and as such a subject-object relation comes into view (Kristeva 1984b, 62–63). Regarding poetic language, however, for Kristeva the subject is threatened, disrupted by that operation in terms of its relation to the social realm.[3] However, at the same time, "the irruption of the semiotic within the symbolic is only relative. Though permeable, the thetic continues to ensure the position of the subject put in process/on trial" (Kristeva 1984b, 63). As such, her articulation of the semiotic and the symbolic allows for a new conception of the subject, no longer simply unified through language.

Kristeva's *Revolution in Poetic Language* has had a significant impact on psychoanalysis because of the development of a new conception of the subject. As noted by Sina Kramer, "She seeks to uncover a notion of the subject as a sort of fragile process through its symptoms in art, poetic language, and theoretical texts," which she calls the subject-in-process/on-trial (Kramer 2013, 465). Kristeva's critique of the unified subject is dependent upon her articulation of the semiotic because the semiotic is "the time or space which both produces and disrupts subjectivity" (468). Against Sigmund Freud and Jacques Lacan for whom the relation of the symbolic and the semiotic is an absolute break, Kristeva frames the relation as one of continuous tension and relation, as a "porous and traversable" boundary between the two (467). Kristeva's articulation of the semiotic as in continuous tension with the symbolic is what provides the condition for a revolution in poetic language, and also a subject not fully formed but in process.

The resonances between Lorde's writing and Kristeva's are certainly prominent whereby the poetic provides the conditions to name what was unnameable given the symbolic organizing structure. However, my central concern for this paper is a critical interrogation of the role Kristeva's project can play for, or alongside, decolonial theory. In order to engage in this critical interrogation, in the following section I develop Sylvia Wynter's account of the poetic for the purpose of revolution.

Sylvia Wynter and the Poetic

Within a large majority of Wynter's work on the poetic, there is an inherent tension between what she names discourse and episteme. Here, we might think of discourse, often referred to as everyday discourse, as a replication of social orders that determine how sameness and difference are signified. Epistemes, on the other hand, are the foundations upon which these social orders or everyday discourses are based. There is nothing inherent or necessary about any particular episteme, and as such they can be changed and thus provide the conditions for revolutionary change, without being itself revolutionary. Epistemes are pretheoretical, self-organizing, and make "routine knowledge possible" (Henry 2006, 263).

Both epistemes and discourses are kept in place by a process Wynter calls "autopoiesis." In "Wynter and the Transcendental Spaces of Caribbean Thought," foremost Wynter scholar, Paget Henry, notes two different modes of autopoiesis. The first mode pertains to social orders, which "is the process by which human self-organization has been able to establish and maintain internally coded social orders while at the same time adapting to changes in its surrounding environment" (Henry 2006, 261). Here, poetic discourse can be used to "lessen opaqueness" (261). However, "we will never really transcend this mode of coded inscription" (261). With this in mind, Henry turns to the epistemic, wherein we can find the second mode of autopoiesis.

Autopoiesis (in the epistemic mode) is a mode of self-constitution, but which happens through exclusion. Operating alongside or under social orders, epistemes are marked by what they exclude. The primary example that Wynter is concerned with is the episteme that constitutes what it means to be human, which changes depending on the geopolitical and historical context.[4] This mode of exclusion produces the material existence that is both coded as present (to the extent that it serves to mark inclusion through exclusion) and absent (through the mode of exclusion). Wynter calls this position the liminal, wherein "liminal categories are marked by problems of systemic devaluation and minimalization in representation" (Henry 2006, 265).

Epistemes are thus developed autopoietically through a system of binaries (inclusion and exclusion). In order to bring about change at this epistemic level, "an individual or a group substantially transforms or moves beyond the episteme of its day by changing the binary oppositional ordering of its governing template and thus is able to think new thoughts in new discourse" (Henry 2006, 267). In other words, transformation (or revolution) requires that an individual or a group address the system of valuation that operates on the basis of inclusion through exclusion.

Contradictions and Interventions

Inherent to this epistemic transformation is the introduction of contradiction. For instance, the assertion of Black peoples as human within a social and epistemic order that presumes their unhumanness invokes a contradiction with the social and epistemic order. Similarly, the assertion of Black peoples in the US as both Black and American (or African American), against the presupposition (socially and epistemically) of Americanness tied to whiteness in the US, similarly makes evident contradictions at play. Furthermore, the self-determination of Black- and African American–identified populations (in the previous examples) exceeds the social and epistemic preconditions ordering relations and provides the conditions (is the condition) for new thoughts and new discourses.

This twofold move is particularly important to Wynter, as evidenced by Henry as well: "The liminal other will persistently say, do, or achieve things that challenge and contradict its representation within the episteme. Such challenges create crises of credibility for the episteme and confront it with the need for change" (Henry 2006, 268). These contradictions are lived by marginalized communities in the everyday, and thus consistently and constantly interrupt the everyday discourse and underlying epistemes that are premised on white supremacy. A striking example of this kind of intervention as contradiction comes from the 1968 sanitation strike in Memphis, Tennessee, whereby striking sanitation workers carried signs, draped over their bodies, which stated, I Am a Man." In this instance, one can see not only the performative of asserting one's humanity, but that this assertion comes in the face of their dehumanization thus making explicit the lived contradiction.

According to Henry, Wynter's approach "demands of us a well developed poetics. In particular, an interventionist poetics that is capable of rewriting the governing codes and templates that inscribe the a priori condition of epistemic and social orders," in order to change the "epistemic motion in the interest of reclaiming the humanity of the condemned" (2006, 270). As such, this poetics opens up revolutionary possibilities for social change at the same time that it challenges us to explore more deeply the repairing of liminal and other tendencies to systemic error that still continue to plague our sociological and epistemic creativity" (270). Transformation (or revolution) for Wynter, thus, is located neither in everyday discourse, nor in epistemes, but in an interventionist poetics. As such, we know that Wynter's poetics must exceed the foundations of the epistemic order (270).

Wynter's poetics has this transformational capacity because poetry signals the ability to create, to invent new signs, and most importantly to reconceive of relations. The poetic is not an object for thought; it is the means through which new thought and new meaning becomes possible. Perhaps most importantly for Wynter, the poetic is a process that is inherently human, and, as such, through engaging in the activity of reconception and naming, poetry is itself humanizing. In other words, it is through poetry that processes of dehumanization can be engaged and disrupted.[5] In "Unsettling the Coloniality of Being," for instance, she states that "one cannot 'unsettle' the 'coloniality of power' without a redescription of the human *outside* the terms of our present descriptive statement of the human, Man" (Wynter 2003, 268, my emphasis). Poetry thus provides the conditions for a redescription of what it means to be human through the deployment, or creative potentiality, of poetry as a process.

For Wynter poetry is, first, a mode of self-determination that is determined outside of the terms of the present description of what it means to be human, and thus outside of the present epistemes that determine everyday discourse. It is a new self-founding concept that exists independent of the current order of existence, and only in this way does poetry allow for the creation of new ground, upon which "new objects of knowledge can find their efficient criterion/condition of truth" (Wynter 2003, 207–8).

Returning to Kristeva

Kristeva is similarly moved by the role of contradictions for seeking out or opening up the possibility of systemic change. According to Kristeva, "Out of these objective contradictions, drive rejection will bring forth the new object whose determinations exist objectively in material externality, which means that this moment of practice is not simply an 'apparition,' within which the presence of consciousness, of the law of 'being'" (Kristeva 1984b, 203–4). In other words, it is out of contradiction that the new object of language comes into being. Furthermore, recalling *Revolution in Poetic Language*, Kristeva states, "The appearance of the new object, the new thesis, is the result of this conflict. The new object is a moment of the process whose conflict constitutes the most intense moment of rupture and renewal" (204).

The overlap between the projects of Wynter and Kristeva is thus significant. Whereby Wynter is concerned with discourse and epistemes, Kristeva is concerned with the symbolic. Their concerns are the processes through which social logics are structured and reconstructed. Furthermore, they both maintain these logical structures can be altered or changed, and as such there is nothing necessary about a particular structure or logic. The mode or process of this change is located in the tension between the symbolic and the semiotic for Kristeva, and in the contradictions that become evident in epistemes for Wynter. Finally, both Kristeva and Wynter engage with the poetic as central to the process of this kind of radical change, whereby the poetic provides the condition for introducing something new into a system of order or logic.

Importantly, both Kristeva and Wynter are concerned with addressing the violence of dominant orders. For instance, Kristeva states, "The problem, then, was one of finding practices of expenditure capable of confronting the machine, colonial expansion, banks, science, Parliament—those positions of mastery that conceal their violence and pretend to be mere neutral legality" (Kristeva 1984b, 83). Presumably for Kristeva, then, there is a desire to address colonial expansion as a form of violence.

That said, a central difference that I wish to make evident in this paper is the modality through which such poetic revolutionary movement becomes possible. Or perhaps, for whom such revolution becomes possible. This differentiation is in what I am calling Wynter's attention to multiplicity, and her engagement with Frantz Fanon's conception of sociogeny.

Multiplicity

In "Beyond Liberal and Marxist Leninist Feminisms: Towards and Autonomous Frame of Reference," Sylvia Wynter engages in an analysis of European feminist movements. Herein she invokes a discussion of Catharine MacKinnon and the relation between universality and particularity. In essence, Wynter is concerned with whether feminist movements (of liberal and Marxist-Leninist leanings) call into question the structure of universal (or natural) categories that it seeks to subvert, or whether they perpetuate the dominant structure or what she calls the major referent (heterosexuality or colonialism, for instance). Wynter argues that MacKinnon seeks to "relativize the Referent, to deconstruct its conditionality" (Wynter 1982, 27) a process that "unfixes and relativizes both heterosexuality as the general Equivalent of Sexuality, and at a more complex level, . . . deconstructs and relativizes all General equivalents of identity; relativizes all referents" (28). In other words, heterosexuality is a system that represents what sexuality must be, thus marginalizing nonheterosexuality. Addressing such marginalization requires an unfixing of heterosexuality as the norm, and furthermore a refusal of complicity in this system of heteronormativity. Furthermore, for Wynter it is insufficient to refuse or relativize heterosexuality as a referent alone; rather, all referents must be addressed. This is another way of saying that it is insufficient to address heteronormativity alone, rather, one must also address other normative and marginalizing systems and their referents such as racism and colonialism.

In her description of MacKinnon, Wynter invokes the writing of Julia Kristeva. She states: "In this context her [MacKinnon's] formulation of the interrelation between systems of power and systems of representation realizes Kristeva's call for a feminism able to call in question the very apparatus of order" (Wynter 1982, 29).[6] Wynter cites Alice Jardine's English translation of Kristeva's "Women's Time," published in 1981, noting Kristeva's desire to develop a feminism that refuses a role in representation, and seeks to make representation the object of inquiry—a move that is consistent with Kristeva's *Revolution in Poetic Language*.

Wynter also cites Kristeva in conversation with Alice Jardine: "That this rupture can be in complicity with the Law, or, rather, that it can constitute a point of departure for even deeper changes . . . that is the major problem" (Wynter 1982, 13).[7] The question for Wynter thus becomes whether a rupture, for feminism in this instance, "functions as an autonomized particularity, rather than as a particularity constitutive of a new non-middle class mode of universality" (14). Seeking to refute the binary between universality and particularity, Wynter eschews an amorphous universal that assumes that there is a sole response to systems of oppression by subsuming all difference under the same, and rejects a narrow particularity that is presumed to only address one form of oppression (2).[8] Instead, she calls for a new kind of particularity. In essence, what Wynter is putting forward is a conception of feminism that seeks a universal filled with particularity from which to address multiple forms of oppression, not by subsuming all difference into the same (amorphous universality) but by addressing the different ways that different forms of oppression operate. She states, "Where there is power, there is resistance, and multiplicity of power relationships lead to a multiplicity of points of resistance, present 'everywhere in the power network'" (34). A feminist project that is too amorphous will further marginalize particular groups, and one that it too closed or narrow will likewise serve to reinforce or perpetuate the oppressive system it seeks to upend.

Given Wynter's call for multiplicity above, her description of the liminal is purposefully ambiguous, or perhaps more appropriately, is open given that this position in some sense will depend upon geopolitical and historical contexts (for instance). Within this vein, it is for this reason that Wynter's project of interventionist poetics is not based upon a dichotomy, or a binary system: "In short, we all have transcendental work to do, for which we are going to need a poeisis of a poetics that will empower us and supply us with the ceremonies by which our current local concepts of the human and their liminal others can be de-instituted and reincorporated in new and more inclusive epistemes" (Henry 2006, 281).

Wynter, invoking the writings of C. L. R. James, thoroughly develops her own conception of poeisis: "by this she means the discursive strategies through which James was able to reach the foundations of both Marxism and liberalism in order to restructure them" at a subtextual level that is pluri-conceptual (i.e., multiplicitous) rather than mono-conceptual (Henry 2006, 275). As Henry notes, synthesis (in the Marxist tradition) is not a suitable framework for this project because it is grounded in a fixed center (282).[9] Invoking here a Hegelian or Marxist framework, synthesis is the resolution of a contradiction into something new. For Henry and Wynter, however, synthesis does not provide the conditions for thinking through multiple forms of oppression, and the multiple solutions that they require. A pluri-conceptual framework, however, seeks to exceed a binary framework and emphasize multiplicity (Wynter 1982, 33–34).[10] As a result, for Wynter, "there can be no one revolutionary subject or no single correct line. Rather there must be multiple revolutionary subjects and multiple lines" (Henry 2006, 277). The value of this project is that it is neither constrained to one particular form of oppression, nor so ambiguous that it presumes a position from nowhere that fails to address oppression at all.

According to Henry, Wynter's projects means "developing the ability to displace gender as an exclusive founding category of knowledge production and self-troping, and to reincorporate it into a more inclusive epistemic foundation. However, this expansion must be secured by making its process of auto-instituting the feminine an integral part of its concept of the human" (Henry 2006, 281). Furthermore, refusing complicity in oppressive systems requires that one be attentive to multiple forms of oppression operating simultaneously and/or separately.

Wynter names the dilemma the prioritizing one form of oppression over another wherein one form of oppression stands in for them all. For instance, when feminism marginalizes racism, it "logically ignores the special position of Black women in a sexist, racist and class society" (Wynter 1982, 30). The dilemma thus becomes that if one marginalizes racism when engaging in such critical feminism (for instance), then one becomes complicit in the law that maintains racism, rather than its refusal.

Sociogeny

Part and parcel to Wynter's emphasis on interventionist poetic operation as multiplicitous is her conceptual engagement with Frantz Fanon's sociogeny. Originally published in 1952, in *Black Skin, White Masks* Frantz Fanon notes the limitation of psychoanalysis for addressing the kinds of affective implications of being a Black man living in an anti-Black world. As noted by Romy Opperman:[11] "sociogeny is the study of the social environments in which pathologies emerge. Sociogeny overcame what were then the dominant tendencies in both psychiatry and psychoanalysis; countering both psychiatry's focus on organic and inherited constitution (phylogeny) and psychoanalysis's focus on the individual (ontogeny)" (2019, 64). As noted by Pitts, Fanon locates ontogeny in the writings of Sigmund Freud. They state, "This ontogenetic approach considers experience, desire, and psychopathology as locatable within an individual developmental trajectory, albeit a trajectory that is shaped by general features of sexual and appetitive desires, and kinship relations" (Pitts 2022). Regarding phylogeny, Pitts notes "Other psychiatrists of the era, including notably Carl Jung, held views about the inheritance of collective consciousness and memories, which framed the human psyche in, as Fanon describes it, phylogenetic terms" (Pitts 2022). Fanon doesn't reject phylogeny and ontogeny as practices, rather, he notes that they are limited in their attempts to address particular sociogenic and political contexts, namely, colonialism.

While by no means the only example, Fanon's critique of psychologist Octave Mannoni's *Prospero and Caliban: The Psychology of Colonization*, written in 1948, in Madagascar following a revolt, is particularly striking. Fanon devotes chapter 4 of *Black Skin, White Masks*—titled "The So-called Dependency Complex of the Colonized"—to critiquing Mannoni's *Prospero and Caliban*, as a failure to "grasp the true coordinates" of the colonial situation (Fanon 2008, 65). In part, Fanon notes that Mannoni's attempt to deal with colonialism does not consider that through colonization, the Malagasy peoples have been *produced* in relation to the Europeans as colonial subjects and, furthermore, that Mannoni's attention to psychology fails to address the economic consequences of colonization (Fanon 2008, 77). As stated by Fanon, "Monsieur Malagasy seems to us to lack the slightest basis on which to ground any conclusion concerning the situation, the problems, or the potential of the Malagasy in the present time" (88). Here again, we see that Fanon is critiquing Mannoni's attempt to address colonialism, while failing to address the processes through which colonialism was established, thinking here specifically of affective, subject formation and economic structures. Instead, Mannoni stresses a desire for dependence on behalf of colonized subjects (Mannoni 1990, 86).

The context in which Fanon develops an account of sociogeny is not only his experience of French colonialism in Martinique, the anti-Black racism he experienced in Paris, France, as well as his participation in the anticolonial movements in Algeria. But also, Fanon was a trained psychologist and philosopher. As noted by Pitts, "Fanon's writings in psychiatry . . . demonstrate a careful attunement to the sociogenic origins of pathology, alienation, and bodily comportment among racialized populations" (Pitts 2022). Such attunement takes the form of addressing the process through which colonization takes place at both the structural or external level (i.e., the material conditions) but also the internalized level (i.e., the internalization of stereotypes, or what Pitts names as pathology and alienation). Sociogeny is the method that Fanon develops to be able to do this work. Finally, "Fanon appears to consider the alienation experienced by colonized subjects as pointing to an existential condition *not shared* by all, and dependent on different forms of material positioning vis-à-vis the extant relations given in a racist society" (Pitts, 2022). In other words, the colonial context requires a particular methodology that is not applicable to all contexts or all persons.

Finally, as Fanon noted in 1952, "We shall see that the alienation of the black man is *not* an individual question" (2008, xv, emphasis mine). As such, phylogeny and ontogeny are limited to the extent that they focus on the individual. Furthermore, addressing colonialism for Fanon requires that we develop a sociogenic method which recognizes there are oppressive structures that impact groups of people differently. In other words, addressing colonialism requires that one understand the ways in which colonized peoples as a people are produced through colonization.

Returning to Kristeva

My question, and thus the goal of this chapter, is to consider the extent to which Kristeva's poetic project is capable of thinking through multiplicity and sociogeny for a decolonial project.

Regarding multiplicity, we might turn to the writings of Trinh T. Minh-ha. In *Woman, Native, Other*, Trinh T. Minh-ha has already articulated a concern about Kristeva's project on the basis of addressing multiplicity, looking specifically at Kristeva's discussion of Chinese women as indistinguishable from Chinese men. Such a statement problematizes how an Asian-identified, woman-identified person might "fit" into Kristeva's project. As noted by Trinh, "there is simply no point outside Kristeva's 'sexual difference' from which to take up a position" that is both ethnic *and* feminine (Trinh 1989, 104).[12] Specifically invoking the writing of

Kristeva in this instance, Trinh is here emphasizing what seems to be a strain at the heart of Kristeva's writing about women; namely, a tension between antisexist movements and antiracist movements.

The question of "fit" made explicit by Trinh can be extended to a structural issue within Kristeva's project. As such, what follows serves as both a critique of Kristeva's *Revolution in Poetic Language*, or perhaps more pointedly, the role the poetic can have within and for revolution, but also an invitation to Kristeva (and Kristeva scholars) to address the limitation of her project. Stated otherwise, I propose that one refuse a kind of complicity that forecloses the possibility of a poetic resistance that maintains space for a multiplicity. Specifically, as I seek to make evident below, it is Kristeva's reluctance to include sociogeny that proves to limit the revolutionary impact of her project.

Regarding sociogeny, there is a limited amount of scholarship in English that addresses the relation between Fanon and Kristeva. One reason why this might be the case is Kristeva's refusal to herself engage with Fanon's writing on psychoanalysis. In the essay titled "Kristeva and Freud," Ewa Plonowska Ziarek begins with the following statement by Kristeva about Fanon: "I have often heard people speak of him, but I have never read anything by him. He isn't part of the mainstream Psychoanalytic Studies" (2004, 25).[13] Fanon's continued marginalization with psychoanalysis scholarship is perhaps testimony to his attempts to expand or disrupt mainstream psychoanalytic theory. Regardless, his work continues to be of foremost importance to understanding the limitations of this field.

Furthermore, while there is limited scholarship on the topic of Kristeva and Fanon, various engagements have served to resituate Kristeva's project without engaging with the critiques offered by Fanon. For instance, in "Kristeva and Fanon," Ziarek's attempt to draw Fanon and Kristeva alongside one another through the respective engagements with feminist logic is firmly situated for Kristeva in the "development of female subjectivity" (Ziarek 2004, 35). In a similar manner, Peter Gratton states that "psychoanalysis . . . offers ways of disengaging the individual from a normalizing and disciplining society" (Gratton 2007, 4). Therein, Kristeva is cited as stating the following: "I [Kristeva] consider that my work as an analyst is political work, to take it in a microscopic and individual sense" (Gratton 2004, 4).[14] Kristeva's turn to the individual is well documented, and central even to texts, like Gratton's, that seek to reconcile the political projects of Kristeva and Fanon. But again, what these texts fail to recognize is Fanon's explicit critique of psychoanalysis because it overemphasizes the individual. For decades, scholars have written about how psychoanalysis needs to exceed a kind of individual framework if it is to address multiple forms of oppression and be applicable to a decolonial framework.

To what extent, then, can Kristeva's theory of poetic revolution address colonialism if it does not move beyond what Kristeva names as the microscopic, or from this individual framework? To what extent can it grasp the true coordinates of colonialism? And by marginalizing discussions of coloniality that are central to Fanon's work, does she remain complicit in colonialism?

In "Investing in a Third: Colonization, Religious Fundamentalism, and Adolescence," Elaine P. Miller offers a comprehensive account of what Kristeva names "the culture of religious fundamentalism as 'adolescent' . . . [in] their capacity to hold on to a static fantasy that is passionately and protractedly believed to be true" (Miller 2014, 36). While the position of the adolescent is not linked to immaturity—"We are all adolescents when we are in love" (36)—it does, however, map onto a developmental or progressive narrative wherein the adolescent fixates on an " 'ideal object' in place of the parental figures and what they represent" (38). In her description of "suburban troubles" in France, an explicit reference to neighborhoods where many people from the French colonies in Africa have immigrated to (many of whom are citizens and/or children of immigrants), she names the ideal object as religious fundamentalism.

Miller's critique in this essay pertains to Kristeva's invocation of religion, or religious fundamentalism, and the source (or site) of the troubles, and as the ideal object. However, as Miller states, "It is not religious concerns that cause most unrest in these 'suburban troubles,' but rather unemployment and discrimination and a de facto second class citizen status" (Miller 2014, 41). Furthermore, "News reports indicate that anger over poor housing conditions, racial profiling by the police, inadequate basic public services . . . were the primary reasons for dissatisfaction among residents of this and other suburbs" (41).[15]

Miller's attention to the history of French colonialism and its ongoing manifestations through de facto second-class citizenship, poor housing, and racial profiling as a cause of social unrest (and perhaps the overpolicing of particular neighborhoods, is an important point that ought not go unnoticed) is of foremost importance. That said, I would like to take this analysis one step further. We see that Kristeva's analysis of what she names religious fundamentalism is based on a particular psychoanalytic framing of childhood development (ontogeny) and a failure to "grasp the true coordinates" of colonialism.

Again, as noted by Pitts, "Fanon seeks to examine the colonial situation as the sociogenic origins of the pathological behaviors and tendencies named within psychiatry, a situation that is *produced* via a set of material conditions" (Pitts 2022). Furthermore, Fanon states that "the criminality of the Algerian ... [is] not, therefore, the consequence of how his nervous system is organized or his specific character traits, but the direct result of the colonial situation" (2004, 233).

Return to Wynter

Importantly, for Fanon, revolution requires moving beyond the individual by itself. Likewise, citing Foucault, Wynter states the following: "The subjectivity that psychoanalysts deal with ... we must be liberated from that type of singularity" (1982, 36). Focusing on the individual alone fails to address anti-Black racism.

Similarly, clarifying her remarks on feminist theory, Wynter states, "So when I wrote—in a 1997 essay—about feminist thought and Western thought in general as being *a-cultural*, I meant to underscore that they are *a-sociogenic* or *a-autopoietic*" (Wynter & McKittrick 2015, 30, 53, 64). Including sociogeny is thus a necessity for feminist thought for Wynter. Wynter maintain that poetic resistance must include a notion of the sociogenic principle.[16] On this point, in "The Pope must Be Drunk," Wynter states the following: "Faced with the regularity of the autophobic and reflexly aversive responses displayed by his black patients to themselves, their physiognomy, together with their equally reflex preference for 'whiteness,' Fanon proposed that such an 'aberration of affect' could not be an individual problem to be dealt with by psychoanalysis. Fanon set in motion the disenchanting of our present understanding and conception of being human" (1995, 31). Alongside Fanon, Wynter argues for the importance of including the sociogenic principle for addressing forms of oppression, and for her theory of poetic revolution. As noted by Michael Monahan, for Wynter, "The Sociogenic principle, put simply, claims that we are the kinds of things that we are (both as individuals and as a species) as a result not only of the biological processes that produce us, but also as a result of the *social* processes and conditions in which that biology function and through which we are produced" (Monahan, forthcoming).

For Wynter, a feminism in its own name must not only unfix a single major referent or law such as patriarchy or sexism, but must unfix all referents (1982, 28). In other words, if feminism is to be successful, it must not only address sexism, but it must also address other forms of oppression, such as racism and classism. Of course, we can expand Wynter's analysis to include a multitude of forms of oppressions, such as ableism and settler colonialism, and indeed her project calls for such interventions or interruptions. Therein, multiplicity and interruption are a calling of oneself and one's critical system of analysis into question, something that feminism in its own name ought to be able to do.

My invocation of sociogeny is a call to psychoanalysis at this time. The model that Kristeva offers for addressing systemic oppression, for instance, is situated between poetic revolution and psychoanalysis. Importantly, psychoanalysis and poetic revolution are inherently bound up for Kristeva, to the extent that she utilizes poetic language to call into question the apparatus of the ordering of psychoanalysis for a feminist project. However, Kristeva's critical analysis does not go far enough because it continues to maintain the ontogenetic project of psychoanalysis, failing to account for sociogeny, and thus marginalizing racism within her revolutionary project.

Conclusion

Sylvia Wynter is reader of Julia Kristeva's work and demonstrates the ways in which Kristeva's work can be amenable to a form of feminism that calls into question the apparatus of order (Wynter 1982, 29). And certainly Kristeva's work on the poetic is one attempt to do so, not only in her "Women's Time" essay published in English in 1981, which Wynter cites in her 1982 essay titled "Beyond Liberal and Marxist Leninist Feminism."

At the same time, however, there is reason to hold the projects of Wynter and Kristeva in tension. Notably, Kristeva's insistence on the politicality of psychoanalysis for critically analyzing the colonial situation falls short. It assumes an apparatus or order that marginalizes racism because it prioritizes the individual (or ontogeny) and excludes sociogeny. Despite the interesting work that the poetic as revolution offers, reinforcing the centrality of the binary of subject and society to the exclusion of a sociogenic framework does not succeed in achieving the plural and heterogenous, nontotalizing outside that Kristeva seeks in *Revolution in Poetic Language* (1984b, 14).

At the same time, however, there is much work left to be done to unpack Kristeva's project through a decolonial lens. For instance, Kristeva herself might consider engaging with the writings of Sylvia Wynter and Frantz Fanon, and their discussions of sociogeny. Decentering the individual for psychoanalysis and reconceiving of the subject-in-process with this in mind could allow for sociogeny to have a prominent place in her theory of revolutionary poetic language.[17]

That said, and for the time being, I hope to have adequately expressed my concern about the extent to which Kristeva's articulation of poetry and revolt cannot account for decolonial struggles. Returning to the words of Trinh T. Minh-ha, we might also ask about the extent to which this self-determination is possible given Kristeva's reluctance, or concealing of multiple forms of oppression and resistance, and the importance of addressing the particularity of one's social and political position in order to do so.

Notes

1. In various ways, this paper seeks to note the limitations of various authors who have sought to bring Kristeva and Fanon into conversation, based on Kristeva's and Fanon's shared engagement with psychoanalysis—which is true—but which omit Fanon's critique of psychoanalysis in *Black Skin, White Masks*. See Gratton 2007, Weltman-Aron 2004, and Ziarek 2004.

2. Throughout her work, Kristeva extends this point to music and to art as well. See Kristeva *Revolution in Poetic Language* (1984b), 63, 80.

3. Kristeva states, "The irruption of the motility threatening the unity of the social realm and the subject" (1984b, 80).

4. Wynter's description of what it means to be human is dependent upon the organizing forces of a particular era. For a robust description, see McKittrick 2006 or Paquette 2020.

5. The poetic is not chaotic, nor is it dependent upon the current worldview.

6. Here, Wynter is invoking Kristeva's "Women's Time" (1981).

7. Wynter is citing an epigraph in Jardine's "Introduction to Julia Kristeva's 'Women's Time.'" Jardine's epigraph is from Kristeva's *La Révolution du langage*

poétique (1974), 494. This is several years before the publication of the English translation titled *Revolution in Poetic Language* (1984b).

8. Wynter's reference to a narrow particularity and an amorphous universal is very likely an invocation of Aimé Césaire's "Letter to Maurice Thorez," delivered in 1956, and his concepts of "narrow particularism" and "emaciated universalism" (152). Therein, Césaire resigns from the Communist Party because of its failure to address race in addition to class.

9. Henry calls for a "tidalection" that is grounded in "multiple centers that are mutually displacing and reincorporating of each other" (Henry 2006, 284).

10. For a more detailed elaboration of Wynter's pluri-conceptual model, see Paquette 2020.

11. As noted by Romy Opperman, while Wynter's use of sociogeny "arguably departs from Fanon's original use . . . her turn to the 'sociogenic principle' [is] a response to the demands of climate change" (2019, 75).

12. Furthermore, according to Trinh, "identity as points of re-departure of the critical processes by which I have come to understand how the personal—the ethnic me, the female me—is political" (1984, 104).

13. Ziarek is citing Kristeva, *Revolt, She Said* (2002), 110.

14. Gratton is citing Julia Kristeva in *Julia Kristeva, Interviews*, edited by Ross Mitchell (New York: Columbia University Press, 1996), 24, 42. Gratton also references Kristeva, Julia "Kristeva in Conversation with Rosalind Coward," *Desire* (London: ICA Documents, 1984a), 27.

15. Miller concludes by stating that "While Kristeva's analysis focuses on the individual unmoored from recognition, she might have also turned to the imaginary 'father,' who in this case is unloving" (2014, 43).

16. In *Red Skin, White Masks* (2014), Glen Sean Coulthard makes explicit that addressing settler colonialism requires transformations on both the subjective and the objective level. Coulthard is drawing explicitly from Fanon's *Black Skin*.

17. The critique that I have offered in this paper could be expanded through Wynter's discussion of Man 2, the conception of what it means to be human that is currently dominant and maintained through the marking of the damned, the poor, the jobless, as firmly located in an individualistic conception of the human. Drawing a connection between Man 2 and the subject of psychoanalysis is one way to expand this analysis.

References

Césaire, Aimé. 2010. "Letter to Maurice Thorez." Translated by Chike Jeffers. *Social Text* 10328, no. 2: 145–52.

Coulthard, Glen Sean. 2014. *Red Skin, White Masks*. Minneapolis: University of Minnesota Press.

Fanon, Frantz. 2008. *Black Skin, White Masks*. Translated by Richard Philcox. New York: Grove Press.

———. 2004. *The Wretched of the Earth*. Translated by Richard Philcox. New York: Grove Press.

Gratton, Peter. 2007. "What are Psychoanalysts for in a Destitute Time? Kristeva and the Community of Revolt." *Journal for Cultural Research* 11, no. 1: 1–13.

Henry, Paget. 2006. "Wynter and the Transcendental Spaces of Caribbean Thought." *Caribbean Reasonings: After Man, Towards the Human: Critical Essays on Sylvia Wynter*. Edited by Anthony Bogues, 258–89. Kingston, Jamaica: Ian Randle.

Jardine, Alice. 1981. "Introduction to Julia Kristeva's 'Women's Time.'" *Signs: Journal of Women in Culture and Society* 7, no. 1: 13–35.

Kramer, Sina. 2013. "On negativity in *Revolution in Poetic Language*." *Continental Philosophy Review* 46, no. 3: 465–79.

Kristeva, Julia. 1984a. "Julia Kristeva in Conversation with Rosalind Coward." In *Desire*. London: ICA Documents, 22–27.

———. 1996. *Julia Kristeva, Interviews*. Edited by Ross Mitchell. New York: Columbia University Press.

———. 2002. *Revolt, She Said*. Translated by Brian O'Keeffe. New York: Semiotext(e).

———. 1984b. *Revolution in Poetic Language*. Translated by Margaret Walker. New York: Columbia University Press.

———. 1981. "Women's Time." Translated by Alice Jardine and Harry Blake. *Signs* 7, no. 1: 13–35.

Lorde, Audre. 1984a. "The Master's Tools Will Never Dismantle the Master's House." In *Sister Outsider: Essays and Speeches*, 110–13. Freedom: Crossing Press.

———. 1984b. "Poetry Is Not a Luxury." In *Sister Outsider: Essays and Speeches*, 36–39. Freedom: Crossing Press.

Mannoni, Octave. 1990. *Prospero and Caliban: The Psychology of Colonization*. Translated by Pamela Powesland. Ann Arbor: University of Michigan Press.

McKittrick, Katherine. 2006. *Demonic Grounds: Black Women and the Cartographies of Struggle*. Minneapolis: University of Minnesota Press.

Miller, Elaine P. 2014. "Investing in a Third: Colonization, Religious Fundamentalism, and Adolescence." *Journal of French and Francophone Philosophy* XXI, no. 2: 36–45.

Monahan, Michael. Forthcoming. "Reason, Race, and 'The Human Project': Sylvia Wynter, Sociogenesis, and the Philosophy of the Americas." In *Philosophizing the Americas: An Inter-American Discourse*, edited by Jacoby Adeshei Carter and Hernando A. Estévez. New York: Fordham University Press.

Opperman, Romy. 2019. "A Permanent Struggle against an Omnipresent Death: Revisiting Environmental Racism with Frantz Fanon." *Critical Philosophy of Race* 7, no. 1: 57–80.
Paquette, Elisabeth. 2020. *Universal Emancipation: Race Beyond Badiou*. Minneapolis University of Minnesota Press.
Pitts, Andrea J. 2022. "An 'Extension of the Occupier's Hold': Frantz Fanon on Psychiatry, Carcerality, and Etiology." *Chiasmi International* 24: 293–310.
Roudiez, Leon S. 1980. "Introduction." In *Desire in Language: A Semiotic Approach to Literature and Art*, edited by Leon S. Roudiez, translated by Thomas Gora, Alice Jardine, and Leon S. Roudiez, 1–22. New York: Columbia University Press.
Trinh T. Minh-ha. 1989. *Woman, Native, Other: Writing Postcoloniality and Feminism*. Bloomington: Indiana University Press.
Weltman-Aron, Brigitte. 2004. "The Politics of Irony in Fanon and Kristeva." *Southern Journal of Philosophy* 42, no. 1: 42–47.
Wynter, Sylvia. 1982. "Beyond Liberal and Marxist Leninist Feminisms: Towards and Autonomous Frame of Reference." *Feminist Theory at the Crossroads*, Annual Conference of the American Sociological Association, San Francisco.
———. 1987. "On Disenchanting Discourse: 'Minority' Literary Criticism." *Cultural Critique* 7: 207–44.
———. 1995. "The Pope Must Have Been Drunk, The King of Castile a Madman Culture as Actuality, and the Caribbean Rethinking Modernity." In *The Reordering of Culture: Latin America, the Caribbean and Canada in the Hood*, edited by Alvina Ruprecht, 17–42. Ottawa, ON: Carlton University Press.
———. 2003. "Unsettling the Coloniality of Being/Power/Truth/Freedom: Towards the Human, after Man, Its Overrepresentation: an Argument." *CR: The New Centennial Review* 3, no. 3: 257–337.
Wynter, Sylvia, and Katherine McKittrick. 2015. "Unparalleled Catastrophe for Our Species? Or to Give Humanness a Different Future: Conversations." In *Sylvia Wynter: One Being Human as Praxis*. Edited by Katherine McKittrick, 9–89. Durham, NC: Duke University Press.
Ziarek, Ewa Plonowska. 2004. "Kristeva and Fanon: The Future of Revolt of the Future of an Illusion?" *Southern Journal of Philosophy* XLII: 25–41.

Chapter 8

Proust among the Patients

Kristeva on Proust, Psychoanalysis, and Politics

ELAINE P. MILLER

In *Proust among the Nations*, Jacqueline Rose (2011) writes that, at moments, it is almost impossible to tell Proust and Freud apart (9). Rose uses Proust's discussion of the late nineteenth century "Dreyfus Affair" to frame her own analysis of the Israeli/Palestinian conflict. The book interrogates the ways in which humans "countenance, and then take responsibility for, the most disturbing versions of our own histories" (18). While Rose primarily considers the specifically political ramifications of humans taking stock in this way (in our capacity as citizens of nation-states), Julia Kristeva, whose work Rose draws on in the book, focuses for the most part on the individual dimension of this kind of history. Rose and Kristeva believe that the psyche and the polis share a dimension of unpredictability in their development, and that the attempt to control this equivocation—and subsequent inevitable failure to do so—is a common problem of both individuals and nation-states. Both Rose and Kristeva also invoke Proust (among others) in the service of explicitly psychoanalytical investigations of their respective subjects. Both believe that art has the capacity to impel humans to take responsibility for personal and political trauma. However, whereas Kristeva believes this project must be undertaken on a one-on-one basis that resembles the psychoanalytic session, Rose argues that countenancing the entire historical and political context of trauma can and must form part of the "treatment." For Rose, the dire situation of Palestine in the wake of Israeli occupation of the West Bank and construction of a barrier wall within it is a pressing contemporary crisis to which psychoanalytic insights can be productively applied. Kristeva is concerned with Islamic activism and terrorism in France, a crisis that she attributes to globalism and a need to believe rather than to any historical-political context out of which it emerges.

In this chapter, I will consider these two approaches that use Proust to analyze Middle Eastern/European relations in addressing what one might overly broadly term a cultural conflict, explaining why a psychoanalytic reading of Proust's literature seems relevant to both Rose and Kristeva in this context. I will argue that in contrast to Rose's work, Kristeva's interpretation is misplaced in the context of political struggle. Kristeva's earliest published writing in *Revolution in Poetic Language* held much more promise as a political analysis than her current efforts at addressing Islamic fundamentalism in France.

I will examine Kristeva's shift from an emphasis on the childhood development of linguistic ability in the child and the reemergence of proto-linguistic psychic forces in poetic language (in *Revolution in Poetic Language*), to her focus on the adolescent, and in particular, the ways in which this shift may go awry. I will argue that although Kristeva's interest in the revolutionary capacity of poetic language and other forms of art endures today, she now perceives a danger in poetry's capacity to unleash semiotic forces, and this caution has shifted her focus from a political to an economic lens, from the collective to the individual, and from revolution to reinvestment in the symbolic. Kristeva argues that immigrant youth in Europe suffering from a lack of recognition from the social order may turn to fixation on an idealized object that demands extreme and often violent allegiance. It is in the literary form of Proust's writing in particular that Kristeva finds a way of addressing the perceived rupture, which threatens the integrity of the subject. The second part of this chapter will question what it is that brings Kristeva and Rose together in thinking of the conflict between Islam and Christianized Europe alongside the writing of Proust.

Rose follows Proust's account of the *l'affair Dreyfus*, the controversy surrounding the trial of Alfred Dreyfus, a captain in the French army of Jewish descent who was accused of treason and found guilty primarily because of the influence of anti-Semitic groups. What happened in France at the turn of the century, Rose (2011) writes, "was in many ways the forerunner of Vichy" (61). The clear wrong of the Dreyfus affair lent support among some Europeans to the idea that Jews needed to find a nation of their own where such injustice would not take place. Although Proust was a Dreyfusard, supporting those who sought to exonerate Dreyfus when it became clear that evidence supported the guilt of another person, he nonetheless, as Rose puts it, "did not go there" in thinking the solution to European anti-Semitism lay in the formation of a separate state. As Rose writes: "Partition is not a solution, not anywhere. For Proust, group identity is always defensive—like homosexuals huddling together against the hatreds of the world. It would, writes Proust at the end of the exordium to *Sodome et Gomorrhe*, be a 'deadly mistake' to propose 'just as people have encouraged a Zionist movement, the creation of Sodomist movement'" (87). Rose warns against understanding the Dreyfus affair as justification for a Zionist state: "A different version of the story would instead take from Dreyfus a warning—against an over-fervent nationalism, against infallible armies raised to the level of theocratic principle, against an ethnic exclusivity that blinds a people to the other peoples of the world, and against governments that try to cover up their own crimes" (61). In Rose's mind, Kristeva would agree with her argument, which draws on Proust. She cites what Kristeva terms the "perverse underside of all collective identities" to argue that Kristeva, like Rose, believes in the dangers of nationalism, and would espouse instead a "world of permeable boundaries, seedlings crossing over borders, the souls of the dead caught in an animal or plant, calling out to us for release, but only if we happen to pass by" (88–89). She cites Kristeva's allegiance to Freud, who wanted a world "accessible to the free play of other associations," including, in the minds of the earliest Jewish critics of political Zionism, such as Martin Buber and Ahad Ha'am, free association between Jew and Arab (90). And it is true that this allegiance seems likely given Kristeva's early work.

Kristeva is well known for her conviction that the political follows the logic of the psyche, including the claim that we are all "foreigners to ourselves" by virtue of the presence of an unconscious within each of us. In *Strangers to Ourselves, Nations without Nationalism*, and other writings, she argues that no homogeneous unified identity, group or individual, is possible or desirable. However, her recent comments about the role of Europe vis-à-vis "Africa and Syria" (2017a, 48), and about immigrant protests and terrorist actions in Paris and Marseille (2014a) seem to completely overlook the legacy of France's colonial history as a contributing cause to its current "suburban troubles," especially when put side by side with Rose's robustly political approach to the equally fraught question of Palestinian political autonomy. Kristeva proposes a solution to political and economic protests in France that addresses the individual rather than structural or historical issues.[1] Kristeva's analysis deplores the symptoms of political unrest in France but only diagnoses the cause in terms of individual trauma. By contrast, Rose more productively points out the political roots of the problem, arguing that an intellectual analysis alone cannot provide a solution to problems too large and complicated to fully address.

As Rose outlines, the UN resolution 181 of November 1947 proposed the partition of Palestine into two entities, Jewish (56%) and Palestinian (44%), effectively creating an identity for the Palestinian as an enemy or foreign body in the midst of the land in which they had lived for hundreds of years. Rose (2011) writes that this plan "vitiated the Zionist concept of Jewish statehood," which had been described by one of the foremost prestate Zionist thinkers, Ahad Ha'am as the "divine gift of memory," the "living force of sentiment in common," and the "foundation of national consciousness" (86). Rose also cites Bernard Lazare, a Jewish secular thinker of whom Proust knew and thought of favorably, to the effect that a nationalist wants freedom above all, and not necessarily to reconquer Jerusalem (61). These thinkers argued for a spiritual and cultural Zionism, not a particular geographical site. The subsequent reinterpretation of Zionism as requiring above all a land, and furthermore a land that was already occupied, followed the logic of European colonization, and turned the Palestinian into an unwanted entity in a manner that Rose compares to the futile attempt to get rid of an unwanted part of the mind. Freudian psychoanalysis began with two fundamental insights: the mind is divided, "but the boundaries between one part of the mind and another are strangely porous" (67). We cannot simply get rid of the foreign aspects of our psyche, even through therapeutic analysis. "We are all," she writes, "the failed ethnic cleansers of our own souls" (67). And this is equally true for cultures that clash; the mind and contemporary political life are torn apart by the question of the stranger and their desire (69–70). In Rose's mind, the significance of both Proust and Freud, and of Kristeva, is their emphasis on border crossing, allowing us to glimpse possibilities "where worlds and minds can escape their self-inflicted boundaries, where peoples do not have to entrench their borders and shut down, and where no national group has to subordinate its identity as a citizen completely to the reason of state" (92).

In the past ten years, Kristeva been involved in an "intercultural and interdisciplinary" team effort, in conjunction with caregivers from the *Hôpital Cochin*, which aims to address, through psychoanalysis, play, and exposure to literature, philosophy, and Western culture, the suffering of Muslim youth in France attracted to radicalization. Although there is only a tangential connection, on the surface, between the suffering of Palestinians under occupation and the frustrations of immigrants who apparently "freely choose" to move to a country that formerly colonized them, Kristeva also turns to Proust for insight into how to approach this problem. Rather than a public solution that would address laws and institutions in France that disadvantage these young people both economically and socially, the effort she describes uses literature, both European and non-European, to "invent" countless specific, individual versions of "loving intelligence" to replace a perceived authoritarian demand stemming from (Islamic) religion (2014b, 406). Exposing the young people to texts by Cervantes, Proust, St. Teresa, and "Sufi poets" aims to affect them at the level of the prereligious "need to believe."

According to *Revolution in Poetic Language*, Kristeva's first book, published in French in 1974, art's revolutionary role is not to address the individual directly in the way a psychoanalytic session might. However, in an analogous manner, it may awaken something within the observer or listener of which they were not at all previously aware, namely, an "underneath" of language corresponding to a prelinguistic set of desires that requires the positing of the artwork to come to light, although they cannot be reduced to it. This process, while it is only intelligible through language, nonetheless can have the effect of "exploding the subject and his ideological limits" by uncovering psychic drives and desires and showing them to be criss-crossed with political and economic forces that exceed the individual (1984, 15). Here Kristeva links the formalizing tendency in linguistic symbolism and philosophy to an "activity encouraged and privileged by (capitalist) society," which "represses the *process* pervading the body and the subject" (13).

In the section "Negativity: Rejection," Kristeva devotes a subsection to the concept of "independent and subjugated force" in Hegel. Kristeva's account of Hegel's "Force and the Understanding" opens up a way to understanding the relationship between the semiotic and symbolic dimensions of language. In an earlier section, Kristeva (1984) relates Hegelian "force" to Husserlian *hyle* and the Platonic *chōra* in that it is "apprehended through difficult reasoning" and "lost as soon as it is posited," yet "nonexistent without this positing" (32). The symbolic and semiotic aspects of language relate to each other in the manner of a force and its outward expression. To underline this point, Kristeva quotes from Hegel's diary of 1831, where he refers to a "logic behind consciousness," which "further determine[s] [the] object for itself" (19).

The semiotic aspect of language can be understood developmentally in terms of an infant's acquisition of language, as a "preverbal functional state that governs the connections between the body [. . .], objects, and the protagonists of family structure," that is, as a "logic behind consciousness" (1984, 27). In contrast, the symbolic is constituted by language as a preexisting formal, conscious, system of signs. In the process of poetic language, this formal system of signs is "dismantled" but not rendered incoherent, for "no text, no matter how 'musicalized,' is devoid of meaning or signification," and, indeed, signification is pluralized by the eruption of the semiotic within the symbolic (65).

In "Force and Understanding," Hegel recounts the experience of natural consciousness as it attempts to understand and theorize what it takes to be an external world over and against itself. Here, consciousness initially conceptualizes nature as mechanical, devoid of subjectivity, and thus external to itself, but as the account develops, the reader experiences the genesis of a reflective concept of nature in which thought is intertwined with being in the same way the symbolic is intertwined with the semiotic; this movement implicitly effects the emergence of self-consciousness. The mutual involvement and indeed identity-in-difference of consciousness and its object becomes apparent by the end of the section. From a purely formal, mechanical, or physical understanding of being, consciousness transitions to an account of the interdependence of the living forces of nature and of subjectivity, or body and mind.

Hegel uses the concept of "force" to embody consciousness' shift of attention away from static objects toward a dynamic world of continuously self-dirempting forces, a configuration identical to its own activity. As Hegel writes in the *Encyclopedia Logic*, this "reflection-into-another of what exists" cannot be thought independently of its own reflection (Hegel 1991, §124, 193). Force connects subject and object; its effects, including, for example, electricity or magnetism, are perceptible in the objects that we sense (Hegel 2018, §134). This "relation to self as other" can be attributed to all of living nature as an autonomous, reciprocally conditioning whole, and to the structure of self-consciousness, which relates to itself in self-differing.

The expansiveness of Hegel's approach is reflected in Kristeva's account of revolutionary language in *Revolution in Poetic Language*. Kristeva's account of the complex imbrication of semiotic forces with conceptual language spans Hegelian phenomenology, Freudian psychoanalysis, Marxist economics, and twentieth-century linguistic theory, including a description of the organismic structure of the "genotext" and "phenotext" of a poetic text. The genotext includes the semiotic processes: transfers of drive energy detectable in nonsignifying aspects of poetic language, such as timbre and rhythm, organizing a space "in which the subject is not *yet* a split unity that will become blurred, giving rise to the symbolic" (1984, 86). The genotext is "language's underlying foundation," while the phenotext is language that communicates, which presupposes a subject who enunciates and an addressee (87). At the same time the book is fundamentally political.

We can see this political nature in the very articulation of what Kristeva calls the "thetic phase" or "thetic break," in which subject and object are identified and separated from each other. All enunciation, Kristeva (1984) writes, is thetic in that it connects two separate positions, "redistributing them in an open combinatorial system" (43). Structural anthropology draws an equivalence between this system of language, also known as the symbolic, and the social order (79). In the thetic, social positions and their relations, such as kinship structure but also the state, are set up. All of these "neither question nor challenge the thetic, but rather function as a result of it" (74).

Drawing on the anthropological account of Claude Lévi-Strauss, as well as the Freudian psychoanalytic account of the band of brothers, Kristeva identifies sacrifice at the origin of symbolism and the social order. In order to put an end to semiotic or presymbolic violence, sacrifice sets up the symbol, transforming bodily into linguistic being. This "theologization of the thetic" (1984, 78) "confines violence to a single place," for example, the sacrifice of an animal involves "killing substance to make it signify" (75). Sacrifice can be viewed as the "imposition of social coherence," confining future violence through a symbolic act (75). Nevertheless, the dance and music and theater that accompany sacrificial rituals allow semiotic violence to break through the symbolic border, allowing for, Kristeva writes, a "flow of jouissance into language" (79). Thus, sacrifice and art complement each other as two sides of the thetic function. Religion seizes hold of the symbolic side, and art points to the opposite pole of trans-symbolic jouissance while nonetheless respecting the thetic limit

(80). Poetry becomes "a permanent struggle to show the facilitation of drives within the linguistic order itself" (81).

Later in *Revolution and Poetic Language*, Kristeva (1984) argues that modern poetic language "realize[d] a subtle, fragile, and mobile equilibrium" between "two poles of heterogenous contradiction," the pole of explaining and knowing the world, on the one hand, oriented toward establishing stable institutional and linguistic structures; and the pole of transforming and changing the real through cogitation, oriented toward process and struggle, on the other (178–79). Language in these kinds of text "attacks what it itself has produced [. . .] in order to check and subdue it," and in doing so, radically realizes the productive contradiction between structure and process, symbolization and semiotization (179). Kristeva writes that art's function as a signifying practice is to re-introduce into language, "through binding and through vital and symbolic differentiation," the heterogeneous rupturing of a drive excitation which "could not be grasped by the various symbolizing structures" that the subject has at its disposal, such as family or state or language as a whole, because it was left out at "first symbolization" (180).

However, this aesthetic nature of poetic language did not always exist. During the time of the Renaissance up to and during the French Revolution, Kristeva (1984) argues, poetry had become nothing more than a "fetishization, a surrogate for the thetic," or position of the subject, which challenged nothing. For revolutionary poetic language,

> The problem, then, was one of finding practices of expenditure capable of confronting the machine, colonial expansion, banks, science, Parliament—those positions of mastery that conceal their violence and pretend to a mere neutral legality. Recovering the subject's vehemence required a descent into the most archaic stage of his positing, one contemporaneous with the positing of social order; it required a descent into the structural positing of the thetic in language so that violence, surging up through the phonetic, syntactic, and logical orders, could reach the symbolic order and the technocratic ideologies that had been built over this violence to ignore or repress it. (83)

The key to measuring the significance of this revolutionary poetic praxis is Freud's psychoanalytic inquiry, "which looks for the process of the subject through the positing of language" and identifies sexuality as the nexus between language and society (84). Kristeva explicitly relates Freud's work to Marx's belief that capitalism had produced its own gravedigger. Colonial imperialism, she writes, "produces its true gravedigger in the non-subjected man, the man-process who sets ablaze and transforms all laws, including—and perhaps especially—those of signifying structures" (105). The productive process of the modern text belongs "to this social change that is inseparable from instinctual and linguistic change" (105). Falling outside of the sphere of material production, the signifying process "transforms the opaque and impenetrable subject of social relations and struggles into a subject in process/on trial," one who can join into the "process of capitalism's subversion" (105). Work, she writes, when it is not reified into the specific exchange structures of a given society (under global capitalism this would be the whole world), "shares something with this signifying process" (104). Revolutionary practice takes place at the level of the text when political resistance to material and social obstacles is stymied. As a result, "the signifying process comes to the fore" and only subsequently "radiates toward the other components of the space of production" (105).

Given this explicitly political charge identified in revolutionary poetic language, including a resistance to colonial expansion and global capitalism, what has happened to Kristeva's account of the power of language to resist in the years since? In her 1993 collection of essays published as *Nations without Nationalism*, Kristeva addresses the "cult of origins," the tendency in Europe for everyone to trace their roots, and she attributes this trend in part to the "bankruptcy of Marxism," particularly the "humiliation that progressive doctrines have wreaked on national and religious realities" (2). She calls the cult of origins a "hate reaction" that ultimately stems from a mistrust of self and a withdrawal into a "sullen, warm, private world" (3). She identifies a crisis in national identity happening in France as the result of immigration from Africa, Asia, and Central Europe, leading to a hatred of foreigners, a topic also addressed in her *Strangers to Ourselves*. Speaking against the National Front of le Pen, she nonetheless puts France forward as a nation with an exemplarity that is both transitional and cultural. She means "transitional" in a psychoanalytic sense, leading to a cosmopolitan society respecting that nonetheless retains an anchor to a "general spirit" of French secularism and Enlightenment values. The transitional object, theorized by Donald Winnicott, is a "fetish" that allows the child to move away from total dependence on its mother "toward an area of play, freedom, and creation that guarantees our access to speech, desires, and knowledge" (41). There are "motherlands" and "fatherlands" that "prevent the creation of a transitional object," according to Kristeva (41–42).

France, by contrast, Kristeva (1993) argues, is a "transitional nation that offers its identifying (therefore reassuring) space," on condition that individuals accept the *ésprit général* that is French culture (42). Here she asks: "It is time . . . to ask immigrant people what motivated them (beyond economic opportunities and approximate knowledge of the language propagated by colonialism) to choose the French community with is historical memory and traditions as the welcoming lands. The respect for immigrants should not erase the gratitude due the welcoming host" (60). One might ask what else should motivate citizens of a nation rendered dependent on and secondary to a European power for years? In an even more surprising turn, she continues: "Should not foreigners' indispensable right to vote and their access to French nationality go through a pedagogical, mediatized, and political process opening up that question? For, without it, how shall we manage to have the citizens of that historically mobile group known as France today be something else than selfish people withdrawn into their own common denominators, more or less integration-minded or even death-bearing, and become 'confederates' in the *ésprit general*" (61). Transitional phenomena, including babbling and other prelinguistic oral activities (activities Kristeva also foregrounded in considering the nonsignifying aspects of poetic language and the nonrepresentational aspects of visual art), "start each human being off with what will always be important for them, i.e., a neutral area of experience which will not be challenged" (Winnicott 1971, 95).[2] The aim of a transitional object, however, ultimately is to effect the child's transition from a state in which it is wholly dependent on the mother, or first external object, and thus suffers at her absence, to a state where the child successfully transforms her into a symbolic internal object, helping them achieve independence.

In 2002, Kristeva published a series of interviews in *Revolt, She Said*, and in one of them she discusses the protests of France-born Algerians in the suburbs of various French cities. She is looking for, she says (2002), a "liberated form of representation of revolt," one that will require a "new cultural space" to open up "that will not become a space for religious dogma."

> All these young people in French suburbs [France-born Algerians] have a need to express their unhappiness. But if you

allow this unhappiness to enter Islam, people begin adhering to dogmas. An open mind, a mind set on revolt as I understand it, could become a permanent voice on a level of esthetics, literary creation, discussions, art and the communication which has to be established with these young people. It is this type of liberated form of representation of revolt that I am looking for. This implies that a new cultural space will open up that will not become a space for religious dogma, but one that understands the spiritual anxiety driving religious dogma. In this scenario it is via education, culture and creativity that this need for revolt could be expressed, without strangling itself in dogmatism and fundamentalism. (106)

Here, Kristeva implies, the unhappiness resulted in rioting because it was channeled through religious fundamentalism, and she suggests instead art and creativity as solutions to problems of economic depression, lack of upward social mobility, and police brutality. Kristeva's writings that followed focused on what she calls the "incredible need to believe," which can manifest itself as adherence to organized religion, but can more productively be linked to art, literature, and communication.

Two salient themes in Kristeva's reading of Proust apply to her beliefs about the efficacy of art and literature in combating the violence caused by religious fundamentalism, and in particular to her work at the Hopital Cochin. First, Kristeva argues that Proust's *In Search of Lost Time* broke with the literary tradition as well as metaphysical conventions that preceded it in giving expression to a new form of temporality that accords well with the technique of psychoanalysis, which was developing at around the same point in history. Second, and relatedly, Kristeva argues that Proust's technique of literary narration provides a kind of exemplary healing power that mirrors the talking cure in psychoanalysis. It is these elements of Proust's writing among other literary works that, Kristeva believes, allow "radicalized" Muslim youth in France to "reconnect with the French language," "fill a 'symbolic void,'" and "undo" their tendency toward "nihilism" (Kristeva et al., 2018).

Kristeva writes (1996) that human beings "are of the same substance as time because it defines the boundaries of our speech" (167). Literature provides a time of "rapture" that is beyond everyday temporality, and yet does not escape time, or is not opposed to time in the way that eternity functions in religious discourse. What Proust's novelistic style accomplishes is to allow the reader the possibility of experiencing and naming "the irreconcilable fragments of time" that pull us in multiple contradictory directions at every moment in time, more so today than perhaps ever before (168). The fragmented chronology of the present is both attested to and challenged in Proust's writing.

Kristeva (1996) writes that for Proust there are two types of sublimation that accord with two types of time. The first "kills you with pleasure and it is enjoyable to see it die with time" (1993, 183). This would follow the linear temporality of the calendar or clock, the "natural" temporality of a sequence of "nows," the trajectory of a biological life, and aligns with the traditional Freudian account of sublimation. The second "fills you with silence and suspends time . . . causing memory to bounce back and forth between sensed experience and words," and is a new form of sublimation (183).

These two types of sublimation have their counterparts in two temporal dimensions of Proust's text. The first consists of the immediate temporality of the events of the plot, even when the directionality of *In Search of Lost Time* reverses that of ordinary life by starting from a moment of involuntary memory and moving backward into the past. The second temporality is the one that is presented at the end of "Time Regained" and called, simply "Time" (with a capital *T*). This kind of time "transcends measurement, space, and duration by telescoping two events, signs, or sensations in order to present a metaphor as an index of truth," or by layering one character on top of another (Kristeva 1996, 307). Kristeva is quick to emphasize that the two times of time cannot be opposed to each other as "objective" and "subjective." Rather, time in Proust is "hybrid," and it is this hybridity that gives the text its force.

To understand this hybridity, it is helpful to contrast Proust's use of both registers of temporality to the distinction made by Henri Bergson between mathematical (or measurable) time and duration, a division that is sometimes assumed to have influenced Proust. Kristeva cautions the reader against too quickly assimilating Proust's view with that of Bergson. Bergson sought to disentangle time from space, arguing that while a multiplicity within the register of space implies a sequentially juxtaposed series of entities (quantitative multiplicity), a multiplicity within time, or duration, involves an overlapping of heterogeneous qualities that do not negate each other (qualitative multiplicity) (Lawlor & Moulard-Leonard 2013). By contrast, for Proust, time is simultaneously a sequential chain of heterogeneous events that have an identifiable beginning and end, but in the moment of memory, a suspension of this linear temporality allows for the bouncing back and forth of memory between language and sensation. In this regard, Kristeva argues that his ideas on temporality are much closer to those of Arthur Schopenhauer, who described the imbrication of chaotic, contradictory Will, which is not ruled by the principle of sufficient reason or the principle of individuation, with the sequentially ordered sequence of the realm of representation.

For Schopenhauer, art, and, in particular, music, has the capacity to remove humans from the raging of the will and the suffering of quotidian life, allowing them to rest in withdrawal or meditation, while for Proust, art allows humans to experience the interpenetration of the two forms of time, an experience that gives both pain and beauty, death and life. Proust thus engages equally with what Kristeva calls a traditional Western philosophical linkage of temporality and death, and a feminine temporality of natality and beginning.[3] Kristeva notes (1996) that Proust insisted that his work had therapeutic power in the same way that Schopenhauer considered art had this power (262).

As we have seen, Proust's text is not an ordinary linear narrative, but unfolds through what Kristeva (1993) calls a "two-faced 'being,' " stretched between the world of the present and the historical self (54). Rather than a unidirectional temporality, he establishes a world of the imagination populated by a proliferation of metaphors connected to each other "in space," thus integrated into a metonymic structure (63). The narrative structure of *In Search of Lost Time* is not a line, but a kind of Möbius strip, continually curving back in on its own past, in such a way that the present can take it back up into itself.

In *Revolution in Poetic Language*, Kristeva (1984) described narration as a signifying practice in which the life drive and death drive are articulated not as two distinct instinctual forces, but as "poured into the rigid molds of a nondisjunctive structure" in which negation is reduced to correlations between opposites, such as good and bad, small and large, and inside and outside (90). This is because narrative views society through the structure of the patriarchal family.

The subject's first reconstruction of their past history takes the form of the narrative, the most quintessential of which, for psychoanalysis, is the Oedipal narrative. Kristeva (1984) writes that the "matrix of enunciation" in the narrative centers around the axial position called "I," which "is a projection of the paternal role in the family" (91). This position is mobile and can take on all the various possible roles within the inter- and intrafamilial relations. It also presupposes an addressee or respondent who can gather together the multiple "I's" and recognize itself in them. In a narrative, various "masks" or "protagonists" correspond to the way in which parents or other social structures are encountered and resisted. Kristeva writes that the "subjectal structure" is thus an "infinite series," yet one that is anchored by the normativity of the parental and social network (91). Because these social and familial structures remain firmly in place, strictly linguistic structures in the narrative obey grammatical rules. Here, language functions in such a way as to allow no more than a faint trace of the semiotic, the full reintroduction of which would otherwise have disarticulated and pluralized it (91).

In her 2009 *This Incredible Need to Believe* (written at the time of her work at the Hôpital Cochin), Kristeva reflects on the child's transition to independence from its mother specifically in the terms of religion. Looking at Freud's response to Romain Rolland's objection that Freud had not properly recognized the "oceanic feeling" as the origin of religious sentiment, she recalls Freud's speculation that Rolland's account of "an indissoluble bond, of being one with the external world as a whole" (Freud 2010, 25) (which Freud himself claims never to have felt) is a remnant of the time when the child was not fully individuated but remained fused with the mother. For Freud, this feeling is completely explicable through imagining the gradual process of separation between the ego and external objects that gratify or disappoint it. What we call our ego, he writes, is "only a shrunken residue of a much more inclusive—indeed, an all-embracing—feeling which corresponded to a more intimate bond between the ego and the world about it" (Freud 2010, 29). For Kristeva (2011), this allusion evokes the semiotic prehistory of language, dominated by sensation, which also supports belief understood as "the strong sense of an unshakable certainty, sensory plenitude, and ultimate truth" (7). In a sleight of hand, she takes the explanation that Freud had denied was the "*fons et origo* of the whole need for religion" to be the source of an "incredible need to believe" in a nonreligious sense. The focus on the incredible need to believe leads Kristeva to zero in on the relationship of the child to the parents, and to deemphasize the political and economic context that shapes this relationship and everything else. This shift of focus informs her strangely apolitical account of protests by Muslim activists and what she calls potential terrorists.

The infantile feeling of all-embracing plenitude stems from the mother-child relationship. As Freud describes it, the mother's breast is the thing that the infant desires most of all, but it must learn to separate from it, given the fact that the breast comes to elude it from time to time as it grows older. Kristeva follows Melanie Klein in calling the initial or proto-object of the child's fantasy a split "good" or idealized part-object "mother" who provides everything, on the one hand, and a "bad" part-object "mother" who abandons the child for periods of time, on the other.[4] The child's primary identification with an imaginary "father" interrupts what Kristeva (2014a) calls the "horror of the dual interdependence of the mother and the child," and leads, in this later account, to the child's entrance into symbolic language (17). This "father" is not an object per se, but rather a place of separation between ego and object. Through identification with this imaginary one in whom the mother has "invested" the symbolic identity of the child, the semiotic murmuring and stammering of the child is transformed into spoken language and linguistic signs, and the good and bad mothers are unified into one, more complex entity or object. This account is couched in the language of economics. Kristeva calls this investment a kind of extension of credit, based on the Sanskrit *khred*, which is also the root of the Latin *credo*, "I believe" (16). Without recognition from/investment in this other, the subject cannot come fully into being. This "father of individual prehistory," as Freud called the place of "investment" other than the mother, lies between and effects the transition between the nurturing "mother" and the linguistic and law-giving "father," and serves as a guarantor for the child of transition to a more stable, independent, and flexible, intersubjective identity.

The imaginary "father" is aligned with intersubjective values such as trust, support, and opportunity, as a kind of social welfare. One might equally call this imaginary place a "not-mother" rather than a "father"; it manifests the necessary relinquishing of the fused mother-child bond to a third, which is midway between it and full, individual presence in the intersubjective world. This place serves as a guarantor of a belonging in the broader social and economic (and potentially political) context in which one finds oneself.

In linking "credit" to "belief" etymologically, Kristeva (2014a) describes the "incredible need to believe" as grounding an expectation of restitution or repayment: "I set down a good and await my pay" (16).[5] This "expectant believing" implies trust, recognition, and reciprocity, the last both intersubjective and material. For the "investment" to be successful it must, like an economic transaction, provide a return in the form of social recognition and linguistic fluency. Kristeva (2009) describes this moment of investment as fulfilling a "prereligious" need to believe in a truth that sustains and brings the subject into being, a belief in the "God Logos," as Freud called it in *The Future of an Illusion* (3).

The imaginary father appears as a "life raft" on the "horizon of the 'oceanic feeling,' but the oceanic feeling itself remains something to which art sometimes bears witness" (Kristeva 2009, 10). The oceanic feeling reappears in literature and art, particularly in the writing of Proust, as an "exaltation" or "plenitude" manifesting the child's prelinguistic relation to the mother (7).

The transition from mother to "imaginary father" develops over the course of time, but is not fully fixed by the time of adolescence. Kristeva (2009) calls the adolescent one who continues to believe in the object relation, even when it is not extended credit by the imaginary father, and because of this continuing, yet unrequited belief, "suffers cruelly from its impossibility" (15). The object relation in psychoanalysis is a relation to an object of real or fantasized need. In early development, the child builds up object relations in response to an initially inchoate but dawning awareness of its need to eventually separate from the mother or caregiver; in other words, it looks for somewhere to "invest" itself.

The assurance of creditworthiness responds to this prereligious, presocial need for investment. However, when creditworthiness is not firmly established, due to an unreliable Third, rather than receiving credit and being invested indeterminately into an identification with the symbolic order, the child, unmoored, may turn instead to a determinate and fixed object of adherence. Mistrust of parental authority may lead to fixation on a fantasized "ideal object," escaping childhood by declaring unwavering adherence to a religious or a political ideal.[6]

This is Kristeva's account of the "suburban troubles" in France. Kristeva argues in "Adolescence: A Syndrome of Ideality" (2007) that religious fundamentalism (and in particular Islamic religious fundamentalism) is nihilistic and adolescent in the sense that an adolescent may turn to idealization rather than investment in the social, intersubjective bond even after identifying with the Third who is the object of the mother's desire outside of her bond to the child, because the initial investment has only a weak link to the future subject who responds to it.[7] Thereby, the subject's relation to language, rationality, and ethics may be compromised.

The Third is a guarantor for the child of transition to a more stable, independent, and flexible, intersubjective identity who acknowledges and responds to its capacity for meaning (Kristeva 2009, 9). Without full recognition from or investment in this other, who represents all others, the "I" or subject cannot fully come into being and is susceptible to ideology. In such a case, adolescents may turn away from family and society, and at its most extreme, the death drive may be unbound. Kristeva calls this a "triumph of evil," caused by the "ruthlessness of global migration," which results in radical disconnection among people. It results ultimately in "blind destructivity and finally auto-destruction" (2014a, 22–23). The adolescent separates from the parental figures and replaces them with a new model, "rush[ing] toward a new love that will open the doors to new paradises" (19). Because the ideal object is not mortal or in time, it surpasses all others. This allegiance effects a "deep disorganization of the self," an unbinding in which the "I" is replaced by a "drive ready to go to any extreme" (2014a, 17), radicalizing the dismantling of the self that Kristeva found in poetic language.

Kristeva identifies this adolescence at the root of terrorist leanings in young people in France. In an interview with Carmine Donzelli (2009) from 2006, she identifies the "crisis of our 'suburbs' " as neither religious nor aimed at France's enforced secularity or laicity (17).[8] The solution to this crisis, in her view, must focus on the individual and take place in an encounter analogous to the psychoanalytic situation. In the case of one individual, "Souad," who suffered from anorexia and had been radicalized online, Kristeva (2017b) details the work of an intercultural team of psychoanalysts, sociologists, and psychologists who worked with her to "welcome her into a new, recomposed family" without questioning her beliefs.[9]

Kristeva (2017a) calls it, "lacework": delicate, painstaking, slow, finely attuned to the individual. In her writing on belief and her references to the "suburban problems," Kristeva (2014a) addresses what she calls a tendency in adolescence toward "disobjectalization," in which the other may come to have neither meaning nor value, where "the death drive alone, the malignity of evil, triumphs" (22). Adolescent belief "inevitably goes hand in hand with adolescent nihilism" (2009, 16). This dismantling of subjectivity, unlike the one described in her early work on poetic language, is neither revolutionary nor salutary. The way to respond to this adolescent search, according to Kristeva, is through works that will safely take the believer through the undoing, through literature or art, addressing the "need to believe" rather than a specific religion. Reading Proust is part of the project of reconnecting with the French language.

According to Kristeva, the radicalized individual is an adolescent who turns to rigid structures, absolute religious values, and violence, because they had no loving third to safeguard their passage to adulthood. In this case, the heterogenous rupturing could not be bound, leading to a rejection of the old object in order to invest in a new, idealized and all-powerful one, and ultimately dismantling the self.

In a piece published in 2017, Kristeva asks, "Does European Culture Exist?," and answers in the affirmative, although she also argues that Europe in the twenty-first century is undergoing a crisis. Kristeva (2017a) espouses a selective border-crossing identity that would open up trans-Europe, but at the same time, firmly shut out a "Jihadist exaltation ringing at [Europe's] door from Africa and Syria" (47). One of the causes of this crisis, she argues, is the denial of the "need to believe" and the "ideality illness" specific to the adolescent (47). She describes the adolescent as partaking in "Idealism and nihilism—empty drunkenness and martyrdom rewarded by paradise." She argues that "Europe is the place *par excellence* to elucidate a need to believe" (48).

Can we read the reinvestment of the subject into the French language in this way? Or could there be another version of this account, in which the disappointing third was not family but the French state? Achille Mbembe (2009), too, has identified the psychic injury resulting from decades of institutionalized racism in the wake of French colonization of parts of sub-Saharan Africa and the Maghreb starting in the nineteenth century, and the slave trade that preceded it (49). He notes that the public and the media in France prefer to speak of "urban violence" or "suburban problems," avoiding the mention of race, which is a central dimension of the riots (59). Mbembe indicates that the violence of the suburbs is not merely physical, but leaves "deep psychic wounds" (60). Kristeva notes the psychic wounds but identifies the lack of an anchor for the "incredible need to believe" as their source. In this she is perhaps correct, but the missing "father of individual prehistory" needs to be not an individual, "private" one,[10] but a political, intersubjective one.

Mbembe points out that the violence of the 2005 uprisings in Paris and other French cities is a "self-inflicted disaster" stemming from the history of French colonization of parts of sub-Saharan Africa and the Maghreb in the nineteenth century, and the slave trade that preceded it. "The root cause of the crisis in the *banlieues*," Mbembe (2009) writes, "is the way France has historically tried to dodge the question of race even while engaging in multiple practices of 'racialization' at every level of daily life" (55).

Mbembe (2009) compares the situation in the *banlieues* to Palestinian refugee camps. "If we are not careful," he writes, "the structure of power relations [in France], pushed to the limit, may easily lead to a "Palestinization" of the *banlieue*, directly related to the colonial ideology of race wars" (53). The term *Palestinization* refers to the system of repeated identity checks, screening, and expulsion forced on Palestinians in territory occupied by Israel and African would-be immigrants to France, as well as endemic problems such as discriminatory practices in schooling and employment, and housing segregation. Young rioters of African descent speak to an absence of recognition and respect, constant police harassment, and widespread surveillance (60).

Mbembe outlines four stages to the chronology of state-sponsored racism in France. The first era included both the slave trade and anti-Semitism, a time when the other was considered to be either property or something that could be cast off. The second era was that of colonial imperialism, a time when the *Codes de L'Indigénat* specified hierarchical laws similar to those of Jim Crow in the United States. The third era began with the mass emigration of North African colonized subjects to France and other areas around the Mediterranean basin. Mbembe calls this era a period of "invisible racism," which often and especially targets those called "immigrant workers." The fourth and current era, that of globalization, is characterized by Mbembe as the "age of resentment," visible in "LePenism" and other far-right political movements.

We might ask if Kristeva's deficient parent-child relationship might also be read into the relationship between colonizer and colonized, occupier and occupied. Can the "parent's" neglect in this case also lead to the failure of smooth adolescent transition? Rose implies this neglect to be the case in the Israeli-Palestinian situation. But Kristeva is interested in the themes of temporality, language, and time filtered through the consciousness of the author, and not with the implication of Proust for politics.

Although *In Search of Lost Time* is a narrative, its dual temporal structure permits disarticulation and pluralization. To become a "patient of the imaginary" in a Proustian sense is to turn to art to give us a renewed ability to discover the dynamic and fluid sensations within and associated with objects that have become either fixed and frozen or ephemeral and virtual. The psychic temporality of Proust's literature affects the readers' bodies as much as their minds, opening language up to an unsettling but productive sensuality, weaving new signs by "multiplying and unfolding words into perceptions" (Kristeva 1996, 169).

For Rose, by contrast, Proust's narrative is neither therapeutic nor conservative in terms of social structures. Rather, it provides a witnessing and recording of suffering. Samuel Beckett (1931) writes that the creation of the world (in Proust) takes place not once and for all at one time, but in a way that is constantly renewed day by day (8). In Rose's (2011) reading of Beckett reading Proust, suffering allows the mind to reach its full potential (147); in Beckett's (1931) words, playing on a phrase Kant uses to describe the mental activity involved in a judgment of taste, the suffering of being *is* "the free play of every faculty" (20). Unlike habit, which tries to "empty the world of both beauty and threat," suffering in the sense of undergoing—indirectly in our sublimation and vicariously in our reading and aesthetic experience—embraces both (Rose 2011, 148).

Notes

1. In an earlier paper, I (2014) pointed out the limits of Kristeva's analysis of Islamic terrorism in France as a phenomenon of psychic "adolescence," even though her account of the vulnerability of "adolescent" believers who do not have a meaningful "Third" to turn to the call of ideology is convincing. The Third is too often conceived as an individual—a parent or caregiver. What the analysis leaves out is the fact that North African and Arab immigrants have not been recognized as full members of the social contract in France. Religion may be a place to turn in order to feel a sense of recognition and power that is lacking in political life. Of course, terrorist attacks in France cannot be uniquely traced to the Israeli/Palestinian situation or the legacy of French occupation of North Africa. But the truth is that both of these crises stem from the European colonial project, which Kristeva does not address.

2. See also Kristeva (1984).

3. See Kristeva (2010, 90).

4. See Kristeva (2001, 66f).

5. Kristeva also refers (2009) to the linguist Emile Benveniste's insistence on the correspondence between belief and credit, meaning "to give one's heart, one's vital force, in the expectation of a reward" (4).

6. See Kristeva (2007).

7. Kristeva 2007. See also Miller (2014a).

8. In 2005, the first riots in Clichy-sous-bois, a suburban housing project northeast of Paris with a large immigrant population, were set off by the deaths by electrocution of fifteen-year-old Bouna Traoré and his friend, seventeen-year-old Zyed Benna. The subsequent outrage, which included both relatively peaceful mass protests and destructive actions such as setting cars ablaze, clearly reflected perceived class and racial discrimination, but had no clear connection to religion.

Instead, news reports indicate that anger over poor housing conditions, racial profiling by the police, inadequate basic public services, and, in the years since the incident, no prosecution of the police who caused the incident, were the primary reasons for dissatisfaction among residents of this and other suburbs. See Miller (2014) for more on the problematic nature of Kristeva's comments on the "suburban problem" in Paris.

9. J'ai déplacé mon séminaire sur "Le besoin de croire" de l'Université de Paris 7 à la Maison des adolescents, pour le personnel soignant de l'hôpital Cochin. Philosophes, psychologues, sociologues et psychanalystes se joignent à une équipe interculturelle et interdisciplinaire. Souad, appelons-la ainsi, qui avait été suivie pour anorexie il y a deux ans, s'est radicalisée sur Internet. Elle se définit comme un "esprit scientifique," sèche les cours de français et de philo, "langages de colonisateurs," elle se dit "féministe" parce qu'elle "n'aime pas les hommes" et "ne fait confiance qu'à Allah." Elle porte la burqa et se prépare à partir faire le djihad, devenir une épouse prolifique de lionceaux kamikazes. L'équipe interculturelle l'accueille dans une nouvelle famille recomposée et n'interroge pas sa croyance. Souad met du temps à fendre l'armure, à se raconter, à prendre du plaisir à jouer avec les autres, à rire avec ses nouveaux amis et d'elle-même. Elle a enlevé sa burqa, retrouvé ses cours de français, et découvert la poésie arabe des soufistes sensuels . . . Il y a des chemins qui redonnent leur fierté aux identités en souffrance. C'est un travail de dentelle.

For the caretakers at Hôpital Cochin, I moved my seminar on "The Need to Believe" from the University of Paris 7 to the Maison des Adolescents. Philosophers, psychologists, sociologists, and psychoanalysts all took part in an intercultural and interdisciplinary team. Souad (as we'll call her), a patient there for the past two years due to her anorexia, had been radicalized on the Internet. She self-identified as a "scientific spirit," skipped her French and Philosophy "language of the colonizers" courses, called herself "feminist" because she "didn't like men" and "only trusted Allah." She wore a burqa and was preparing for jihad, in order to become the spouse of "lion cub kamikazes." The intercultural team welcomed her into a new, recomposed family, and did not question her beliefs. It took time for Souad's armor to be chipped away, for her to talk about herself, to take pleasure in playing with others, to laugh with her new friends and at herself. She took off her burqa, went back to her French courses, and discovered the Arabic poetry of sensual Sufis. . . . There are ways to give back dignity to suffering identities. It is lacework.

10. Kristeva (2014b), through her alter ego Sylvia Leclerque, declares that religion is a "private matter" (8).

References

Beckett, Samuel. 1931. *Proust*. New York: Grove Press.
Freud, Sigmund. 2010. *Civilization and Its Discontents*. Edited and translated by James Strachey. New York: W. W. Norton.
Hegel, G. W. F. 1991. *The Encyclopedia Logic*. Translated by T. F. Geraets, W. A. Suchting, and H. S. Harris. Indianapolis. IN: Hackett.
———. 2018. *Phenomenology of Spirit*. Translated by Terry Pinkard. Cambridge, UK: Cambridge University Press.
Kristeva, Julia. 1984. *Revolution in Poetic Language*. Translated by Margaret Waller. New York: Columbia University Press.
———. 1993. *Proust and the Sense of Time*. Translated by Stephen Bann. New York: Columbia University Press.
———. 1996. *Time and Sense: Proust and the Experience of Literature*. Translated by Ross Guberman. New York: Columbia University Press.
———. 2009. *This Incredible Need to Believe*. Translated by Beverly Bie Brahic. New York: Columbia University Press.
———. 1993. *Nations without Nationalism*. Translated by Leon S. Roudiez. New York: Columbia University Press.
———. 2001. *Melanie Klein: On Matricide as Pain and Creativity*. Translated by Ross Guberman. New York: Columbia University Press.
———. 2007. "Adolescence, A Syndrome of Ideality." *Psychoanalytic Review* 94, no. 5: 715–25. Accessed at http://www.kristeva.fr/adolescence.html.
———. 2010. *Hatred and Forgiveness*. Translated by Jeanine Herman. New York: Columbia University Press.
———. 2014a. "New Forms of Revolt," *Journal of French and Francophone Philosophy* 22: 2.
———. 2014b. *Teresa, My Love*. Translated by Lorna Scott Fox. New York: Columbia University Press.
———. 2017a. "Homo Europaeus: Does European Culture Exist?" In *The Philosophical Salon: Speculations, Reflections, Interventions*, edited by Michael Marder and Patricia Viera, 45–49. London: Open Humanities Press.
———. 2017b. "N'ayons pas peur du besoin de croire." In *Madame Figaro*. http://www.kristeva.fr/madame-figaro-22-12-2017.html.

Kristeva, Julia, Marie Rose Moro, John Ødemark, and Eivind Engebretsen. 2018. "Cultural Crossings of Care: An Appeal to the Medical Humanities." *Medical Humanities* 44, no. 1: 55–58.

Lawlor, Leonard, and Moulard-Leonard, Valentine. 2013. "Henri Bergson." Last modified May 8. http://plato.stanford.edu/archives/win2013/entries/bergson/.

Miller, Elaine P. 2014. "Investing in a Third: Colonization, Religious Fundamentalism, and Adolescence." *Journal of French and Francophone Philosophy* 22, no. 2: 36–45.

Rose, Jacqueline. 2011. *Proust among the Nations: From Dreyfus to the Middle East*. Chicago, IL: University of Chicago Press.

Winnicott, Donald. 1953. "Transitional Objects and Transitional Phenomena." *International Journal of Psycho-Analysis* 34, no. 2: 89–97.

Part Three

The Evolving Meaning of Ontological Loss

From Revolution to Revolt

Chapter 9

From Praxis to *Chōra*

The Filter of (In)Humanization
in Julia Kristeva's Early Work

MIGLENA NIKOLCHINA

Preliminary Remarks

This essay will explore the dynamic underlying the continuity and transformation of some of Kristeva's major concepts between her first book published in French, *Semeiotike* (1969),[1] and her magnum opus *Revolution in Poetic Language* (1974),[2] while not losing sight of later developments in Kristeva's thought. *Semeiotike* is in many ways the crucible preparing not only *Revolution in Poetic Language* but also all of Kristeva's subsequent work. The essays collected in this youthful *tour de force* (Kristeva was not yet thirty at the time) were conceived and written with remarkable speed immediately after Kristeva's immigration from Bulgaria to France in 1966. They articulate the major theoretical tasks of Kristeva's future inquiries and introduce or prepare the ground for the concepts that Kristeva will continue to explore, elaborate, refine, and sometimes reconceptualize. Kristeva's work in its totality studies artistic practice as the privileged but not unique manifestation of the continuous making and unmaking of both meaning and the subject. The concept of *signifiance*,[3] which provides the most general designation of these processes and remains central to

Kristeva's thought, is already dominant in *Semeiotike*. Kristeva introduces there a considerable number of terms and various perspectives in order to articulate what exactly is taking place in *signifiance*. In this optics ranging from theories of gesture to Leibniz's differential, she takes a critical stance regarding Ferdinand de Saussure's conception of the sign (if it ever were his[4]) and delineates her lasting interest in the frontier between the inhuman and the human, between the inanimate and the biological, and between sensoriality and code. After Kristeva's psychoanalytic turn, this traverse will be compressed to the transversal operation of the drives. The point I want to make here is that this turbulent zone is already regarded as translinguistic in *Semeiotike*, where Kristeva explores the passage from the infinity of all possible signifying combinations to (as Kristeva insists) the infinite generation in (avant-garde) artistic production. A major question emerges from the accretion of perspectives through which she addresses this passage, a Leibnizian question as to the transition from possibility to actuality: how is infinity *filtered*?

The word *filter* does figure in *Semeiotike* without being definitively conceptualized. It appears rather strikingly in an epigraph to the essay "Engendering the Formula." The epigraph is a quotation from the *Rig-Veda* (translation unspecified), which states "By these two things, by the filter and by the engendering (of the formula), clarify me in totality!" (1969, 217). The essay is, hence, about one of the two clarifying "things," the engendering of the formula as its title claims. However, it says almost nothing about the other thing, the filter. Rather parsimoniously, Kristeva tells us that the filter is the particular arrangement of both "seminal" and "phonic" elements that constructs the text; furthermore, it would seem that the filter is situated between the infinite engendering and the formula. It thus appears that the essay fulfills only half of the clarification posed by the *Rig-Veda*: it elaborates the engendering but leaves out the mystery of the filter. The formula is engendered but how is it filtered? This question is, I believe, the driving force behind the conceptual shift from *Semeiotike* to *Revolution in Poetic Language*. It might very well be propelling later shifts in Kristeva's work with the role of psychoanalysis steadily growing in importance. In retrospect, these shifts can be seen as drawing a line of demarcation between inhuman (say, algorithmic) and human processing of the possible—an effect going much deeper than Kristeva's occasional pronouncements against robotization. Hence my suggestion to designate this line of demarcation as "filter of (in)humanization."

The need to explore this filter led to the abandoning of certain early concepts and the emergence of others. Most notably, in *Revolution in*

Poetic Language, the concept of the *chōra* will appear as neither model nor copy, that is, as susceptible to neither constructivist nor mimetic approaches, and as the bafflement of reason from Plato to contemporary A(G)I. Yet there is a continuity between Kristeva's earlier concepts and the later ones, which, I believe, is paramount for a proper appreciation of her systematicity in investigating the blend of the *infans* and the artist up and against a miraculous phenomenon: the extraction of the speaking being—before it can address another or even express itself–from the cosmic fabric (Kristeva [1977] says "the corporeal-ecological continuum" [440]). Thus, while the later concepts might be regarded as limiting *Semeiotike*'s Leibnizian understanding of creativity by confining this understanding to the psychoanalytical framework of subject formation, it could also be argued that, on the contrary, the (in)human filter expands the earlier perspective with the infinite appearing on the side of the subject.

There is another aspect to be remembered when considering these developments in Kristeva's thought. In performing their preparatory work, which has not lost its own groundbreaking significance, the essays in *Semeiotike* incorporate the crossing point and overlap of, as one might say in Yuri Lotman's terms (1990), two seething semiospheres: the one Kristeva imports from her precocious and very active involvement in Bulgarian intellectual debates (including the priorities and clandestine strategies vis-à-vis an authoritarian regime) and the one she encounters on her arrival in the then-free country of France, which happens to be the amazing French philosophical moment of the 1960s. The very tensions that this encounter produces seem to require a language that can make the two sides intelligible to each other and, furthermore, allow an external viewpoint to their own blind spots. Kristeva responds to this challenge by widening the reach of her early work to encompass a remarkable range of disciplines and discourses. Ostensibly, this widening is carried still further in *Revolution in Poetic Language*; yet at the same time, the later book also inaugurates a methodological tightening of Kristeva's focus, which channels her future theoretical development. Certain terms elaborated in *Semeiotike* are no longer used in *Revolution in Poetic Language*; others, like *semanalysis*, will be abandoned later on. The very widening might, in fact be seen as the means for achieving the later compression.

Tracking all the changes involved in this double-edged process is a demanding task. In what follows, I will limit myself to the cases of two conceptual hybrids or doubles, so to speak. I call them hybrids or doubles because in certain cases they tend to fuse into a compound and, in other cases, to function separately. The first case, already present in *Semeiotike* and carried over in *Revolution in Poetic Language*, is the fusion of Kristeva's master term *signifiance* and the Marxian term *praxis* into signifying practice.[5] The second case is the osmosis of two of Kristeva's major terms, which are not yet present in *Semeiotike* but become central in *Revolution in Poetic Language*, the semiotic and the *chōra*. This second case involves the disappearance—which I will examine in the second half of my analysis—of two of the most interesting terms in *Semeiotike*, *nombre* and *nombrant* (in view of the specificity of Kristeva's usage I will keep these terms in French). *Signifiance*/praxis and semiotic/*chōra* regularly collapse into each other, with one of them acting as a qualifier of the other. There is the signifying practice as the manifest form of *signifiance*, and there is the semiotic *chōra*, manifested and perceived as the semiotic. Before I try to unravel this doppelgänger effect, I will present a few more observations on Kristeva's Bulgarian political and theoretical prehistory.

Politics of the Avant-garde: Always Dissident

The censorship of artistic experimentation became a major symptom of the transformation of East European revolutions into repressive regimes and, consequently, modernism and the avant-garde became an important battleground for opposing dictatorship. Initially, the Russian avant-garde was for the most part strongly supportive of the Bolshevik Revolution. Radical artistic experimentation in all spheres of the aesthetic realm was frequently bound up with no less radical utopian ideas like (bio)cosmism[6] and *Zaum*.[7] When Stalin came to power, he decided he would tolerate no such nonsense and a range of measures from bullying into submission to forced relocation, incarceration, murder, and a wave of more or less suspicious suicides drove the avant-garde underground. A crude notion of mimesis and realism became the norm for politically correct art: as Bulgarian-born literary theoretician Tzvetan Todorov (1973), an ex-pat in France like Kristeva, would comment at approximately the time of the appearance of *Semeiotike*, "A common and simplistic view presents literature (and language too) as an image of 'reality,' as a tracing of what is not itself, a kind of parallel and analogous series" (175).

Bulgaria was out of luck since one of the most dogmatic proponents of the realist dogma and a staunch Stalinist aesthetics hardliner was Bulgarian philosopher Todor Pavlov (1890–1977). His major treatise *Theory of Reflection* was initially published under a pseudonym in Moscow in

1936.[8] There are still mysteries and unexplored aspects of Todor Pavlov's biography, which includes his professorship in Moscow and, when the Soviet army entered not-yet-communist Bulgaria, becoming regent to the underage Bulgarian prince Simeon before the Bulgarian monarchy was ultimately abolished. After the communists consolidated their power in 1947, he was at various times president of the Bulgarian Academy of Sciences, director of the Institute of Philosophy, honorary president of the Union of Bulgarian Writers, and so on, while also taking high ranking positions in the Bulgarian Communist Party.[9] Pavlov was probably a Soviet agent, and his protégés were always quick to look for Soviet backup in their battles against what they saw as deviations from the correct party line. All this allowed Pavlov considerable although incessantly contested control over various areas of Bulgarian cultural and intellectual life. His staunch ideas of realism as a reflection of reality, his vehement insistence on "partisanship" as a mandatory aspect of any intellectual activity, and his militant rejection of modernism in literature and the arts made the struggle for emancipation of the humanities from their role of "handmaidens of politics" (as was the habitual expression at the time) more difficult in Bulgaria than what we find in most other countries in the Soviet bloc.[10]

Art historian and theoretician Dimitar Avramov evokes a telling anecdote. At a Moscow Art Exhibition of the Socialist Countries Poland had the nerve to include abstract paintings and, on top of everything, to defend theoretically this choice both in the exhibition catalog, and at the follow-up international discussion on "Socialist Art and Reality," held in Moscow in March 1959. It was imperative, Avramov (2015) ironically comments, that this crime against the politically correct aesthetics be publicly condemned. The mystery is, he goes on to say, "why was the "dirty work" of prosecutor always assigned to us, the Bulgarians? Was it, perhaps, self-imposed?" (196–97). Avramov abstains from answering his own questions sticking to the fact: the Bulgarian participants did do the dirty work at this discussion.

I make this detour because I believe there is an aspect of Kristeva's lifelong theoretical interest in the avant-garde, which has been insufficiently understood. Against the background of revolutions quickly metamorphosing into tyranny, the question that Kristeva's early work asks is, what is it in revolutions that survives the revolutions? What is their vital, indispensable part? At the time when the essays in *Semeiotike* were written and published, a number of important works appeared in Bulgaria, which, in direct challenge to the Pavlovian dogma, treated artistic creativity in general and modernist art in particular as irrepressible reservoirs of freedom (Nikolchina 2021). Seen in this perspective, Kristeva's early work belongs to Bulgarian theoretical trends as much as it participates in shaping the currents in 1960s French thought.

The Case of Praxis

Praxis (more commonly rendered in English as practice, in French *pratique*) is a Marxian term with a complicated rhizomatic history. Transformation as a process dissolving the subject/object division is its central characteristic. It usually points toward the first of Marx's *Theses on Feuerbach* stating that "The chief defect of all hitherto existing materialism—that of Feuerbach included—is that the thing, reality, sensuousness, is conceived only in the form of the *object or of contemplation*, but not as *sensuous human activity, practice* [*praxis* in the German original], not subjectively."[11] Praxis, then, is human activity that cuts across the dichotomy of subject and object. A major figure in bringing the notion of praxis center stage was Hungarian born philosopher Georg Lukács. His influential work *History and Class Consciousness*, initially published in German in 1923, appeared in French translation in 1960. In it, Lukács translates Marx's concept "commodity fetishism" as "reification" and opposes it to praxis conceived as the process whereby human beings transform themselves by transforming the world. In the 1930s, in his prison notebooks, Italian philosopher Antonio Gramsci refers to Marxism in general and to his own "radical historicism" as "philosophy of praxis." Representatives of the Frankfurt school like Theodor Adorno and Herbert Marcuse, as well as existentialist Jean-Paul Sartre, took different stances in this discussion which, in fact, involved controversies and disagreements. Praxis became inscribed in the clash of "humanist" and "antihumanist" interpretations of Marx, and in disputes surrounding the continuity or discontinuity between the "young" and the "mature" Marx.[12]

In 1965, the year before Kristeva arrived in Paris, Althusser's famous seminar on "Reading Capital" took place, delineating, not without reference to Mao Zedong, various modes of praxis as processes of production and transformation (economic, political, ideological, and theoretical).[13] In the same year, in Croatia, then part of Yugoslavia, the journal *Praxis* was launched with the professed goal to promote "a really Marxist, nondogmatic and revolutionary approach to the open issues of our time" (Petrović 1965). As Predrag Vranicki put it,

> Following Marx, we see man as par excellence a being of practice, a being who freely and consciously transforms his own life. Practice is an *eo ipso*, polyvalent category for it embraces all sides of man's being. We do not need here to repeat what has been said so many times since Marx, and what it is the precondition of all speculation: that man exists and develops only by transforming his natural and social reality and that in this way he transforms himself also. (Vranicki 1965)

The journal's emphasis on Marx's humanism can be directly related to the currents that brought about the 1968 Prague spring (in what was then Czechoslovakia) with its slogan for "socialism with a human face." Sartre's status in the Eastern bloc was more ambiguous for a number of reasons I cannot pursue here, but Gramsci, the Frankfurt philosophers, and the Yugoslavian *Praxis* group, no matter how much the individual thinkers differed, were all perceived as unacceptable "revisionists" by the dogmatic Marxism of Eastern bloc regimes, and the Czechoslovakian attempt to reform socialism was crushed by a Soviet-led invasion.

Now, of all the "revisionists," Lukács was possibly the most heavily censored in the Bulgarian context. Todor Pavlov deemed Lukács his most reviled theoretical rival for unknown reasons, which might be ideological, and which might also include the temporal overlap of their sojourn in Moscow where they belonged to disparate institutions and philosophical circles.[14] Whatever the case, which, to my knowledge, has not been properly researched, Lukács was unpublishable and practically unmentionable in print in Bulgaria until the 1980s. Nevertheless, possibly in the wake of the French edition of *History and Class Consciousness*, but also with regard to Lukács's earlier work, his theory of the novel and his conceptualization of alienation, the influence of Lukács in the 1960s was as pervasive as it was unacknowledged. Lukács and especially his notion of alienation, more or less loosely treated, produced cross-disciplinary reverberations. The one modernist Lukács appreciated, Thomas Mann, became the one modernist abundantly translated and explored. Literary scholar, writer, and Kristeva's close friend Tzvetan Stoyanov (1930–1971) succeeded in publishing the first part of a study, in which he planned to survey the history of literature and philosophy from the Enlightenment to modernism through the prism of tragic, ever-increasing alienation. The prism of alienation thus smuggled Lukács without ever referring to him. This reticence makes discerning his influence difficult especially since it overlaps with attempts: on the one hand, to introduce Martin Heidegger in philosophical discussions of alienation (one such attempt fared disastrously,[15] though in the long run Heidegger did better than Lukács); and, on the other, to promote the open and enthusiastic reception of Mikhail Bakhtin, Bulgaria being probably the first country outside of Russia where Bakhtin became immensely popular. In fact, there is proximity between Lukács and Bakhtin in certain key aspects which have been studied by Galin Tihanov (2000) and which have undoubtedly facilitated Lukács's convoluted Bulgarian reception. The whole conceptual bundle of alienation and reification, on the one hand, and praxis, on the other, resonated with Bakhtin's ideas and had, in the East European context, the surreptitious agenda of opposing ideological dogma.

It is hence not surprising that, upon arrival in France, Kristeva would choose to write her first thesis in a Bakhtinian perspective under the supervision of Lucien Goldmann, one of the finest followers of Lukács. Her choice was dictated by, in her own words (2016), the fact that Goldmann's "rereading of Hegel in the light of Georg Lukács, the famous Hungarian philosopher and innovator of Marxism, was closer to my philosophical training in Bulgaria" (64). However, by the time of the defense, a dramatic reversal had taken place. As Kristeva puts it, "In my frenzied Sixty-Eight drive, which I now find grotesque, I indulged in a veritable act of parricide, calling Professor Goldmann a 'naphthalene Marxist,' he was 'overtaken by History,' did not understand anything about the Freudian revolution, wanted to impose his own repression on us, and so on" (65).

Kristeva does not expound on the theoretical details of this parricidal drama yet one point of contention between her and Goldmann is obvious: it is psychoanalysis, the "Freudian revolution." This difference is connected to another one that can be deduced from Goldmann's lectures on Lukács and Heidegger—delivered in 1967–1968, that is, at the time Kristeva was writing her thesis under his supervision. Goldmann (2009) points out there that Lukács, unlike Heidegger, insists on the collective character of praxis: "according to the dialectical thought of Lukács . . . praxis is not individual" (38).[16] Praxis has a plural subject; it is related to proletarian class consciousness. Now in the Bulgarian context, class consciousness was a concept heavily weaponized by the likes of Todor Pavlov for the persecutions of intellectuals and we will find it not once in *The Text of the Novel* (Kristeva 1970), the book which came out of Kristeva's work with Lucien Goldmann; nor does it appear in *Semeiotike*. In *The Text of the Novel*, there are multiple references to Lukács's theory of the novel; none to *History and Class Consciousness*. Nevertheless, the drama with Goldmann, and the general intellectual atmosphere that somehow presupposed everybody should clarify their stance on these issues, must have had their say. In *Revolution in Poetic Language*, Kristeva provides a systematic elaboration of her understanding of the concept of practice and—finally—turns to the notion of class consciousness via Lukács. Outside of *Revolution in Poetic Language*, praxis as signifying practice (*pratique signifiante*) will be subjected to some further explorations. In *Polylogue*, there is an essay on Georges Bataille with the title "Experience and Practice," which is contemporaneous with *Revolution in Poetic Language* and expounds in more detail the place of Bataille in Kristeva's own perspective. In the collective endeavor of *La Traversée des Signes*, Kristeva sets herself the task to find out whether different modes of production are bound up with different types of subject formations and signifying practices. The project is abandoned in her later work in a simultaneous movement away from Marxian debates and toward deeper involvement with psychoanalysis. Signifying practice settles as the phenomenal aspect of the process of *signifiance*: *signifiance* as the process of engendering and shattering the subject *appears* as signifying practice.

From One Practice to Another

What can this bonding of *signifiance* and practice tell us? Kristeva profusely uses *practice* as a term in her early work and, in fact, throughout all her work. Practice can be qualified as social, aesthetic, artistic, symbolic, and so forth. In *The Text of the Novel*, it is most frequently qualified as "semiotic" and never as signifying; signifying practice and *signifiance* appear in *Semeiotike* as, I believe, a later development that will crystallize in *Revolution in Poetic Language*. The notion of praxis, in short, precedes *signifiance*. The latter emerges from Kristeva's search for a term that transposes those aspects of praxis that matter to her onto the understanding of language—especially the language of literature, but also of arts in general, of the avant-garde in particular—and ultimately of the formation and de-formation of the subject that these practices reveal. In fact, the program is already formulated in the essay "The Bounded Text," which is included in *Semeiotike*, and which repeats verbatim a statement from *The Text of the Novel*, defining the object of semiotics as "*several (plusieurs) semiotic practices* which it considers as *translinguistic*: that is, they operate through and across language. . . . The text is defined as a translinguistic apparatus that redistributes the order of language" (Kristeva 1980, 36). This redistribution shakes the communicative aspect of language by relating it to other things; what things exactly, how they operate through and across language, will become questions pertaining to signifying practice and *signifiance*. Semiotics will be initially replaced by Kristeva's neologism *semanalysis*, a term she later abandons, while *the* semiotic, as is well known, and as will be discussed further below, becomes Kristeva's term describing an ordering that precedes meaning and the subject, and as such becomes one of two modes involved in *signifiance*, the other one being the symbolic as meaning, syntax, logic, and the stabilized "thetic" point of subjectivity.

Signifiance as a term, then, emerges from the transposition of praxis onto the (trans)linguistic register. It is a translation of praxis into the process of production and destruction of meaning and the subject. The mark of praxis on *signifiance* involves process and transformation; praxis also transmits the Marxian concern with social change. Yet there are also dramatic differences ensuing from the transposition of praxis in the space where signs are generated and pulverized; that is, from praxis being, precisely, a signifying practice. These differences are already operating in *Semeiotike* without being explicitly addressed. Kristeva makes up for this lack in two separate sections of *Revolution in Poetic Language*: "Practice" and "The State and Mystery" (the latter is not included in the English translation of the book). There, on the basis of a rereading of Hegelian dialectic and negativity, Kristeva takes issue with the Marxist idea of the subject as an atomistic, that is, individualist subject (against her own idea of the subject-in-process). In "The State and Mystery," with Lukács's *History and Class Consciousness* as her major reference, she confronts her disagreements with Goldmann (never mentioned) and the dogma prevalent in her country of origin (never evoked) arguing that proletarian class consciousness, a totalization of atomic subjects, can become truly transformative—putting it into Lukácsian terms, can resist reification and function as praxis—only by infiltrating the socio-symbolic structures with "the negativity that changes the production of totality into the infinity of process" (Kristeva 1974, 388). Class consciousness has to become signifying practice and open itself to the infinity of process: in sum, it has to relinquish both class and consciousness. Poetic language is the true revolution. Kristeva's treatise is possibly the most massive philosophical vindication of the revolutionary avant-garde, which was stifled by the totalitarian turn of revolutions in the East and by commodification and the society of the spectacle in the West.

Praxis, in sum, has this effect on *signifiance*—it keeps the link with the various Marxian approaches to transformation, including Lukács and Goldmann, alive, yet in coupling with *signifiance*, it is transfigured: signifying practice is, precisely, signifying, and *therefore* resisting reification. Practice dissolves the subject's compactness and self-presence: a far cry from the *Praxis* group's vision of a "being who freely and consciously transforms his own life"; or from Lukács's plural subject of class consciousness. Practice in Kristeva's (1984) perspective demands the pulverization of the unity of consciousness by a translinguistic outside: "The *subject* is only the *signifying process* and he [sic] appears only as a *signifying practice*, that is, only when he is absent *within the position* out of which social, historical, and signifying activity unfolds" (215).

This stance will undergo an inversion toward the notion of revolt (rather than revolution) in Kristeva's later work, which supplements it without canceling it: a development that will not concern us here.[17] The question that arises at this point is what the translinguistic outside is, and—as I formulated it from the start—how it gets *filtered*. This question takes Kristeva to the concepts of *chōra* and semiotic, but not immediately. There were some intermediary steps in *Semeiotike*, with the couple *nombre/nombrant* among the most remarkable of them.

The Semiotic, the *Chōra*: Why Two Terms?

To begin with, why do we need *two* terms, the *semiotic and* the *chōra*? Kristeva presents the semiotic and the *chōra* in *The Revolution in Poetic Language* as very similar terms, without really explaining why we need them both. Always present in her later works, and universally taken up by commentators, the semiotic has been progressively refined to designate rhythm, alliteration, gesture, color, and all sorts of abstract sensory arrangements that are prior to meaning but are always present in varying degrees in different types of discourse. Julia Kristeva links the charms of the semiotic, but also its corrosive aspects (from the point of view of meaning), to the prelinguistic exchanges (echolalia, rhythmic movement, laughter) between the young child and the "maternal receptacle": everything begins in this immemorial embrace, in this auto-erotic dyad of two fusional skins.

It is here that Kristeva introduces the *chōra*. The term is taken from Plato's *Timaeus* as one of those concepts apprehended by means of difficult reasoning: lost from their articulation but nonexistent without it. Supporting her definition of the *chōra* with quotations from Plato's dialogue, Julia Kristeva describes it as a dynamic space defying all representation, unstable, uncertain, seething and, though named, unnameable. The semiotic has thus been retained to designate the material, observable, tangible, phenomenal aspects of this prelinguistic ordering as it appears in subsequent symbolic structures, in a more or less rebellious way, as the case might be. As such, the semiotic, somewhat trivialized, belongs to the field of literary or media studies and constitutes a phenomenon that belongs to aesthetics and rhetoric. The *chōra*, on the other hand, seems to be there to remind us of the logical and chronological positioning of the semiotic beyond time, in the timelessness of the maternal embrace.

However, questions remain. Is a second term really necessary for understanding the semiotic? How do they differ? Is it not a reduplication, a repetition? The *chōra* is sometimes described as semiotic, sometimes as semiotizable. The question is whether there is a *chōra* outside of semiotization, a *chōra* that is not yet semiotized. The very strong implication of *Revolution in Poetic Language* is that the *chōra* comes into being by being semiotic; its ontologization as prior, pre-existing and foundational can only be a secondary, a posteriori effect. On the one hand, it is unnameable but made tangible by semiosis; on the other hand, it is lost as soon as it is made tangible. So, if it is lost at the moment when it is not semiotized—that is, at the moment when it does not coincide with the semiotic—why introduce this doubling of the semiotic?

The *Nombre*

Some answers may emerge if we go back to *Semeiotike*. As already pointed out, Kristeva's interest in modernism and the avant-garde had as its background developments that had transformed art, and especially modernist art, into an area of ideological surveillance and control, and, consequently, into a reservoir of resistance in communist countries. In the 1960s French "philosophical moment," Kristeva's inquiry into modernism takes the form of a theoretical question: what exactly gives the avant-garde its transformative potential? What makes it a force that resists stagnation, a force for change? The crossing of a Marxian concept, praxis, and Kristeva's critique of the Saussurian sign coalesces into the notions of *signifiance* and signifying practice as involving a zone of perpetual agitation where meaning and subject are continually produced and dissolved. This gives rise to further questions. What is this thing that is not a sign and operates in avant-garde writing; are there *units* of *signifiance* that deploy their revolutionary action as translinguistic processes traversing meaning and representation?

Each of the essays in *Semeiotike* offers a different perspective and experiments with different concepts in order to capture the transformative nature of the avant-garde and, beyond that, change in general. In "Engendering the Formula," this other articulation of the materiality of the text, this articulation that is not constrained by the sign, is called *nombre*. The *nombre* is constituted by the "graphic or phonic units" of the "minimal signifying set" that can be isolated in the text; "the *nombre* is the first movement of organization, that is to say of demarcation and ordering. A movement that differs from the simple 'signify' and, shall we say, covers a wider space where 'signify' can be understood and find its place" (Kristeva 1969, 233). *Signifiance* such as it is manifested in the writing of avant-garde, "while showing itself in language does not enunciate anything about anything, but is produced in its own trace where words are notations of applied sets. Without exteriority, but in the always re-launched germination of its differences, the domain thus described is equal to the inhuman of the formal sciences—of mathematics" (263). Like numbers in mathematics, these textual *nombres* can signify—count or account for—one thing or another or, indeed, for an indefinite quantity of things.

"Engendering of the Formula" is a response to Sollers's (1968) novel *Nombres (Numbers)*. In Sollers's novel, the use of "numbers" evokes, among other things, the number symbolism of Dante, who incorporated numbers into his poetic language and transposed his beloved Beatrice into the numbers three, nine, and their products. In *Logiques*, a collection of essays that appeared the same year as *Nombres*, Sollers (1968) quotes Dante as saying that "Beatrice is a 9." Julia Kristeva alludes to this essay in "Engendering the formula" to remind us that, in much of Dante's writing, Beatrice is dead.

Nombres is dedicated to Юлия, Julia's name in Cyrillic script. Written shortly after Kristeva and Sollers's wedding, this novel is indeed as much about numbers as it is about *She*. While the word *woman* never appears (if I am not mistaken) in *Nombres* (1968), *She* is presented in a questioning regarding whether *She* would not be "more inaccessible now that she was at once entirely here, only here, like a corpse with its head severed [. . .] Yet if I stretched out my arm to reach her, I knew that I would be able to verify nothing; that during my sleep she would have become her own bloody and deaf sleep" (57).

Unlike Beatrice who is present by never being here, *She* becomes inaccessible by her very presence. If Beatrice reaches a new life by being dead, *She* achieves the transcendence of a headless corpse by being alive. As Kristeva (2000) will comment much later in *The Sense and Nonsense of Revolt*, to the medieval and Dantesque tradition, the French avant-garde adds its "erotic excitation with this decapitated feminine" (122). *She* of *Nombres* joins this tradition of an "unhinged," beheaded and beheading femininity that, Kristeva reminds us, includes Villiers de L'Isle-Adam's fantasy of making love with a headless woman, the fin de siècle fascination for Salome, André Breton's Nadja, as well as "other chimeras, constructing the image of an intractable and entrancing femininity" through an encounter with "the aceph alous, wounded, decapitated feminine" (122–23). In short, the corpse with the severed head probably did not go unnoticed by the young bride; still, it took decades for Kristeva to confront decapitation as a theorist, novelist, and even, at one point, a curator.[18]

"Engendering the formula" hence marks the beginning of Kristeva's long-lasting project to understand what avant-garde artists in general, but also this avant-garde writer in particular, were doing. I would like to emphasize Kristeva's lucidity in discovering herself as Юлия, the foreigner, in the avant-garde phantasmatic of femininity—and in the phantasmatic of femininity *tout court*. Both too close and too far away, a stranger and a headless corpse, and yet, perhaps, a dreamer of unfathomable bloody dreams, her reiterated response to the risk of being trapped in this chimera was to keep her head: responding to the avant-garde erotica with a relentless passion for understanding. "Engendering the Formula" is the first example of a long series of explorations of masculine artists of the avant-garde akin to Louis Aragon who, as Kristeva (2000) puts it, "identifies with a feminine hypostasis, he absorbs it, he is she: he . . . writes the impossible of femininity, assimilates it, sucks its blood" (145). In short, while the poet claims that She is a number, the theorist wonders how the number becomes She.

The *Nombrant*

Hence the *nombrant*. *Nombrant* according to Kristeva is what germinates into the *nombres* as the smallest graphic or phonic units of the text. Kristeva's use of *nombrant* is rather unique. Sollers does not use *nombrant* in *Nombres*, nor does Derrida in "Dissemination," which he also wrote in response to Sollers's novel. Nor, for that matter, does Badiou in "Infinitesimal Subversion" (1969), to which Julia Kristeva refers in her early text (1969, 234, 236) but which she also evokes much later, as we shall soon see. Leibniz is an important point of reference for "Engendering the Formula," but the term *nombrant* does not appear in *The System of Leibniz and Its Mathematical Models* by Michel Serres, which was published in 1968, and to which Kristeva also refers.[19] In Jules Vuillemin's *Philosophy of Algebra*, which she quotes, *nombrant* does not seem to be an important term: Vuillemin only notes that *nombres nombrants* are ordinals, that they indicate the position of something (first, second, etc.), while cardinals (*nombres nombrés*), tell us the number of things.[20]

In fact, this somewhat archaic term tends to appear today mostly in the discussions of Plato, Aristotle, and Plotinus. With these authors in the background, however, *nombrant* seems to have played an important role in the discussions of seventeenth-century French philosophy. There is, for example, Malebranche's concept of "intelligible extension" (*l'étendue intelligible*), which implies that "*nombres nombrants* [are] to concrete numbers [*nombres concrets*] exactly what intelligible extension is to sensible extension" (Laporte 1951, 170). Malebranche's idea of intelligible extension may be a complicated question, but it seems clear that it encompasses infinity and potentiality: intelligible extension is "the archetype of an infinity of possible worlds" (163n4). However likely or unlikely this connection to Malebranche may be in a discussion of Kristeva (she refers several times to Descartes but never to Malebranche), I will emphasize here that the relation between *nombrant* and *nombre* seems to be a relation between, on the one hand, intelligibility as infinite possibility and, on the other, sensibility, or even sensoriality.

In any case, the *nombrant* is defined by Julia Kristeva as the "signifying infinity" composed of all possible linguistic combinations, already actualized, or to come; composed, that is, of the limitless resources of the signifier that different languages and different signifying practices have used or will use. It is inexhaustible. It is "white" (like white light or white noise?). It is spatial and eternal. It infuses infinity into the *nombre* as a graphic and phonic unit and gives it back its function of "infinite point"

(Kristeva 1969, 232–36 et passim). Sooner or later, it will be flattened to integrate the Saussurian plane of the two-dimensional sign as signifier/signified and the linearity of enunciation: even avant-garde writing cannot escape this fate. Formulas will be generated. Avant-garde writing, however, as Sollers illustrates it in *Nombres*, proves to be the practice that, by sabotaging the sign, which it nevertheless includes in its deployment, bears witness to the infinity of the *nombrant* as infinite engendering. In his text (deceptively called novel), Sollers draws on the *nombrant*, the ordinal, to order his *Nombres*, these infinitesimal units of subversion. The *nombrant*, the ordinal, orders *nombres*, the cardinal. As has been rightly noted, this model of textual germination evokes Leibniz's theory of the compossibles, according to which the entity that comes into being "must by necessity bear marks of the virtual entities which have not been realized in its place, but which could have been" (Johnson 1988, 81).

The F(eminine) Boson

The mystery remains as to what exactly is generated in the formula or, to evoke the case of Sollers's novel, how the white *nombrant* is filtered into *She*. Why Beatrice and not just a nine? The total overhaul of the conceptualization of engendering in *Revolution in Poetic Language* could be seen as the product of this questioning, with the effect that the *nombrant* and the infinite points of its *nombres* seem to have completely disappeared, opening the way to the maternal *chōra* accompanied by the semiotic.

The first obvious aspect of this transformation is the emphasis on the sensory aspects that is already a characteristic of *nombres*. In "Engendering the Formula," Kristeva, as quoted above, compares the deployment of the avant-garde writing to "the inhuman of the formal sciences—of mathematics" (263). In fact, I am tempted to say, mathematics should be the purest form of the semiotic. If Kristeva abandons her mathematical analogies and elevates music to this supreme purity, it is, I presume, because this art, notoriously attracted to mathematics, is a sensory phenomenon, while mathematics, for all its beauty, not that obviously so. And, *stricto sensu*, they both mean nothing. The semiotic, in short, emphasizes sensoriality.

The most important aspect of the conceptual transformation, however, springs from linking the material and sensorial nature of the minimal units of ordering to the maternal body with all the complexities that

Kristeva will discover in this link and this "reliance." The recasting of the conceptualization of engendering thus opens the way for Kristeva's search for the "Higgs boson" of the feminine (2021) or of, so to speak, the boson of (P)h, F, Φ . . . I put forward the word filter to name this apparatus that she will continue to elaborate in all her future work: the filter that seems to have remained ignored in the *nombrant-nombre* dynamic. As I already pointed out, "filter" is never really conceptualized. Yet, in the collection *Polylogue*, a couple of years after *Revolution in Poetic Language*, the word *filter* emerges in a rather curious way in another essay by Kristeva that treats another novel by Ph(ilippe) Sollers: the essay "Polylogue" devoted to *H*. Notably, *H* opens by a kind of revisiting the "bloody sleep" that the narrator of *Nombres* suspects *She* might be dreaming: in the beginning of *H*, *She* dreams that the narrator throws a ball high up, and the ball falls back like a bomb. . . . Kristeva remarks (1980) about this dream that it is "an ironic comment on Surrealist automatism's *cadavre exquis*, or 'exquisite corpse' " and that it evokes "the magic 'filter' or 'philtre,' structuring and regenerating the intoxication of a shattered, but not lost, identity . . . 'this *phi* floating on my lips' " (171). In the same collection, the essay titled "Motherhood according to Giovanni Bellini" links this structuring and regenerating filter to the maternal body as "more of a *filter* than anyone else—a thoroughfare, a threshold where 'nature' confronts 'culture' " (238).

Or, as Kristeva will put it decades later via Diderot's daughter, "You make soul by making flesh."[21] Making soul by making flesh in the place where the subject is constantly made and unmade is the filter that Kristeva inserts between the infinity of the *nombrant* and the *nombres*: this flesh-and-soul is what leads her to abandon these concepts and replace them with the *chōra* and the semiotic. Within the infinity of digital production, she opens up the space for the embodied subject. If the word *filter* is never conceptualized, it is for a good reason: its function of carnal and sensorial threshold and place of passage is absorbed and distributed in the new conceptual couple, the maternal *chōra* and the semiotic. And yet, the links are still there. On the one hand, the questions that guide Kristeva in "Engendering the Formula," but also in the other essays of *Semeiotike*, are already questions concerning the translinguistic (sensory, but also social) aspects of *signifiance*. On the other hand, like *nombres* in "Engendering the Formula," the semiotic is devoid of exteriority; it produces differentiation without enunciating or addressing anything. The resurgence of the semiotic in the practice of modernist artists is hence something that is not exactly an aspect of their psychological insight: it is, on the contrary, something that leads beyond subjectivity, beyond psychology, beyond biology, into vibrations, pulsations, currents, and quanta of energies. Looking at the semiotic via "Engendering the Formula" makes this inhuman aspect more visible: the human floats like a fragile knot in a restless transhuman fabric. Even in technical terms, the semiotic concerns mainly those aspects of art that seem the easiest to translate into frequencies (sound), wavelengths (color), kinesis, and so on. It is what they are, a border between the human and the inhuman, the precarious insistence of the biological and the inanimate in the human. Traversing this place—through what I have called a filter of (in)humanization—pulverizes the subject (Kristeva studies it as revolution, poetic language) or regenerates the subject (Kristeva studies it as revolt, fiction).[22]

The question raised by the persistence of *nombre* in the semiotic is hence: has the *nombrant* really disappeared? Or perhaps it is still there, holding the key to understanding why the semiotic needs to be accompanied by the *chōra*: semiotizable but perhaps, at some level, not yet semiotized, infinite, eternal, "white"? The comparatively recent reemergence of the conceptual set of "Engendering the Formula" in the "Letter to Denis Diderot on the Infinitesimal Subversion of a Nun," is telling. Echoing in its title the title of Badiou's youthful essay, this letter is an invocation to imagine the subject as "the infinitesimal, giving back to the number its infinity-point" (2014, 589). "Teresa's extraordinary innovation," says Kristeva—adding a strikingly modern sixteenth-century saint to her trilogy of female geniuses—" consists in this incorporation of the infinite, which, working backward, against the grain, returns the body to the infinite web of bonds" (588). The mystical nun seems to have found a means of (dis)incorporation directly in the *nombrant*.

Kristeva defines this exploit of the feminine as "fiction." Her other term for this fiction, which she studies in Proust and Colette and pursues in her own novels, is transubstantiation. With fiction, of course, the enormous apparatus of the embodied filter of the (in)human, of signifying practice, of revolution and revolt, is again brought into play. The question remains, nevertheless, whether signifying practice *needs* a filter? Is it possible to subtract the filter from an automated germination of the *nombrant* into *nombres*? do without the process that "makes soul by making flesh"? subtract the subject that "gives back to the number its infinite point"? Can the sheer growth of input data (say, "all possible linguistic combinations, already actualized, or to come; composed, that is, of the limitless resources of the signifier that different languages and different signifying practices have used or will use" [Kristeva 1977, 232]) join or, according to another school, produce—the formula (the algorithm)—of the singularity making soul without the need for any flesh? Make the human without the human? *Subtract the human in computation*? While solving this task seems to be more difficult than the media tries to assure us, what seems beyond doubt is the opposite effort to subtract the human from the human: reduce our five senses to only the two that can be rendered remotely by new technologies and transfer our sociality to the planes of algorithmic surveillance. The promise of an augmented human has taken the form of a reduced human. The transformative feminine elaborated in Kristeva's work is mobilized today as preparation for the replacement of sexual reproduction by biotechnological production. What revolt today? asks Kristeva. But also: What *chōra* today? What filter of (in)humanization? In the context of her work, these are, perhaps, identical questions.

Notes

1. Kristeva's (1965) very first book is in Bulgarian.

2. Part of this work appeared in English as *Revolution in Poetic Language* (1984).

3. In the various translations, there have been various solutions for rendering Kristeva's term. I will stick to its original form, which, in English, aptly conveys its novelty as well as its relatedness to signifying practice, that is, signifying as process, which will concern me here. I deal more extensively with the development of signifiance in relation to Kristeva's psychoanalytic turn in Nikolchina (2020).

4. On this problematic issue, see Stawarska's (2015) insightful study.

5. I will use both *praxis* when the meaning is closer to a generalized Marxist understanding and *practice* when more specific meanings are implied.

6. Cf. Boris (2018).

7. *Zaum* is Russian avant-garde poet Velimir Khlebnikov's neologism, which has been translated as "transrationalist." See Cooke (1987).

8. Pavlov (1936).

9. For a typically vague and unreliable account, see Tsenkov (1973).

10. I deal in greater detail with the 1960s battles with Pavlov in Bulgarian academia in Nikolchina (2021).

11. https://www.marxists.org/archive/marx/works/1845/theses/theses.htm.

12. It has been claimed that Lukács draws from *The Capital* corollaries that are in tune with the early writings, although they were yet not published at the time, thus illustrating the continuity of Marx's work (see Feenberg [2014]).

13. See Althusser, et al. (2016).

14. Pavlov lived in Moscow for only four years (1932–1936), during which time he was dean in the Institute for Red Professorship. His work is not the worst that the regime produced but the ideologically motivated persecution of intellectuals, which he imposed after the communists took power in Bulgaria, has condemned it to oblivion. Lukács had a much longer and more turbulent stay in the Soviet Union: he was part of important intellectual circles and, it seems, had trouble in fitting the dogmatic mainstream. Cf. Saxena (2018).

15. See Znepolski (2020).

16. Goldmann's lectures were published posthumously.

17. For later developments in Kristeva's understanding of *signifiance*, see Nikolchina (2020).

18. Theoretically (Kristeva 2000); as fiction (1998); there is also the study (2012), which grew out of a 1998 exhibition curated by Kristeva at the Louvre.

19. Cf. Kristeva (1969, 237).

20. Kristeva (1969) refers to an earlier edition of this book in *Semeiotike* (235n4 and 26).

21. Letter to Sophie Volland, August 10, 1769. *Correspondance de Diderot*, ed. R. Versini (Paris: Laffont, 1999), 960. Quoted by Kristeva (2014, 588).

22. I address Kristeva's arc between poetry and fiction in Nikolchina (2020).

References

Althusser, Louis, Etienne Balibar, Roger Establet, Pierre Macherey, and Jacques Rancière. 2016. *Reading Capital: The Complete Edition*. Translated by Ben Brewster and David Fernbach. New York: Verso.

Avramov, Dimitar. 2015. *Letopis na edno dramatichno desetiletie (Chronicle of a Dramatic Decade)*. Sofia, Bulgaria: Dobrev.

Badiou, Alain. 1969. "La subversion infintésimale." *Cahiers pour l'Analyse* 9, no. 8: 118–37.

Cooke, Raymond. 1987. *Velimir Khlebnikov: A Critical study*. Cambridge, UK: Cambridge University Press.

Feenberg, Andrew. 2014. *The Philosophy of Praxis: Marx, Lukács and the Frankfurt School*. New York: Verso.

Goldmann, Lucien. 2009. *Lukacs and Heidegger: Towards a New Philosophy*. Translated by William Q. Boelhower. New York: Routledge.

Groys, Boris (ed.). 2018. "Intertextuality and the Psychical Model." In *Russian Cosmism*. Cambridge, MA: MIT Press.

Johnson, Christopher M. 1988. "Intertextuality and the Psychical Model." *Paragraph* 11, no. 1: 71–89.

Kristeva, Julia. 1969. *Semeiotike: recherches pour une sémanalyse*. Paris: Seuil.

———. 1970. *Le Texte du roman*. Berlin: Walter de Gruyter.

———. 1965. *Harakterni tendencii v zapadnata literatura ot XX vek (Characteristic Tendencies in 20th Century Western Literature)*. Sofia, Bulgaria: DKMS.
———. 1974. *La Révolution du langage poétique: L'avant-garde à la fin du XIXE siècle, Lautréamont et Mallarmé*. Paris: Seuil.
———. 1977. *Polylogue*. Paris: Seuil.
———. 1980. *Desire in Language: A Semiotic Approach to Literature and Art*. Translated by T. Gora, A. Jardine, and L. S. Roudiez. New York: Columbia University Press.
———. 1984. *Revolution in Poetic Language*. Translated by M. Waller. New York: Columbia University Press.
———. 1998. *Possessions: A Novel*. Translated by Barbara Bray. New York: Columbia University Press.
———. 2000. *The Sense and Nonsense of Revolt: The Powers and Limits of Psychoanalysis*. Translated by Jeanine Herman. New York: Columbia University Press.
———. 2012. *The Severed Head: Capital Visions*. Translated by Jody Gladding. New York: Columbia University Press.
———. *Teresa, My Love*. 2014. Translated by Lorna Scott-Fox. New York: Columbia University Press.
———. Forthcoming. "Prelude à une Ethique du Féminin." June 30, 2021 Cerisy Lecture, http://www.kristeva.fr/cerisy-prelude-a-une-ethique-du-feminin.html.
Kristeva, Julia, and Samuel Dock. 2016. *Je me voyage*. Paris: Fayard.
Laporte, Jean. 1951. *Études d'histoire de la philosphie française au XVIIIe siècle*. Paris: J. Vrin.
Lotman, Yuri. 1990. *Universe of the Mind: A Semiotic Theory of Culture*. Translated by A. Shukman. London: Tauris.
Lukács, Georg. 1960. *Histoire et conscience de classe*. Translated by Kostas Axelos and Jacqueiline Bois. Paris: Les Éditions de Minuit.
Nikolchina, Miglena. 2014. "Inverted Forms and Heterotopian Homonymy: Althusser, Mamardashvili, and the Problem of 'Man.'" *boundary 2* 41, no. 1 (Spring): 79 100.
———. 2020. "Signifiance and Transubstantiation: The Returns of the Avant Garde in Kristeva's Philosophy of Literature." In *The Philosophy of Julia Kristeva*. Edited by Sara Beardsworth. Chicago, IL: Open Court: 265–82.
———. 2021. "Breaking the Code: Political Control and the Humanities in 1960s Bulgaria." *Berichte zur Wissenschaftsgeschichte* 44, no. 4: 373–90.
Pavlov, Todor. 1936. *Teoriya otrazheniya: Ocherki po teorii poznaniya dialektichskovo myshleniya* [*Theory of reflection: Essays on the theory of knowledge in dialectical thinking*]. Moscow, Russia: Gosudarstvennoe sotsial'no ekonomicheskoe izdatel'stvo.
Petrović, Gajo. 1965. "Why Praxis?" *Praxis* 1. Retrieved from: https://www.marxists.org/subject/praxis/issue-01/why-praxis.htm.

Saxena, Ranjana. 2018. "György Lukács and the Russian Soviet Factor." *Social Scientist* 46, no. 1–2 (January–February): 65–90.
Serres, Michel. 1968. *Le système de Leibniz et ses modèles mathématiques*. Paris: Presses Universitaires de France.
Sollers, Philippe. 1968a. *Nombres*. Paris: Seuil.
———. 1968b. *Logiques*. Paris: Éditions du Seuil.
Stawarska, Beata. 2015. *Saussure's Philosophy of Language as Phenomenology: Undoing the Doctrine of the Course in General Linguistics*. Oxford, UK: Oxford University Press.
Tihanov, Galin. 2000. *The Master and the Slave: Lukacs, Bakhtin, and the Ideas of Their Time* Oxford, UK: Clarendon Press.
Todorov, Tzvetan. 1973. *The Fantastic: A Structural Approach to a Literary Genre*. Translated by R. Howard. Ithaca, New York: Cornell University Press.
———. 1970. *Introduction à la littérature fantastique*. Paris: Seuil.
Tsenkov, Boris. 1973. *Todor Pavlov: teoretik na izkustvoto i literature kritik* [*Todor Pavlov As Theoretician of Art and a Literary Critic*]. Sofia, Bulgaria: BAN.
Vuillemin, Jules. 1993. *La Philosophie de l'algèbre*. Paris: Presses Universitaires de France.
Vranicki, Predrag. 1965. "On the Problem of Practice." *Praxis*, no. 1. Retrieved from: https://www.marxists.org/subject/praxis/issue-01/vranicki.htm.
Znepolski, Ivaylo. 2020. *Communism, Science and the University: Towards a Theory of Detotalitarianisation*. Oxon, UK: Routledge: 132–77.

Chapter 10

The Mental Image and the Spectacular Imaginary

Kristeva with Lacan and Sartre

Surti Singh

Introduction

Julia Kristeva's work is often periodized as undergoing a shift from her conception of politics as transgression against the law in her 1974 text *Revolution in Poetic Language,* to an acknowledgment in her work of the 1990s that this model of revolution can no longer account for a political situation in which power is more diffuse.[1] Central to the shifting operation of power from a centralized source to its decentralized effects was the growing presence of the image in contemporary Western societies, a phenomenon that Kristeva saw as endemic to societies of the spectacle, "where an increasingly virtual imaginary reigns" (Kristeva 2003, 123). It was Kristeva's contention that the growing power of the commercial image created psychic deficits that plagued individuals at the end of the twentieth century: it precipitated a loss of the imaginary, or the faculty by which individuals produce fantasies.[2] With the diminishment of the imaginative faculty, individuals were beholden to commercial images that induced the passive consumption of fantasy. In response to this dismal situation, where individuals were "barely free enough" to use a remote control, Kristeva turned to art, cinema, religion, and literature in search of alternative models to the robotizing spectacular imaginary (4).

Although her understanding of politics changed, what Kristeva sought in these alternative imaginaries maintained a continuity with her early concerns in *Revolution in Poetic Language*. In this text, Kristeva both affirmed and radically reinvented central tenants of Lacan's theory that placed the imaginary at the heart of subject formation, which he described in the theory of the mirror stage. In the short but crucial chapter devoted to Lacan's theory of the mirror stage and castration, Kristeva articulated her own radical view of the semiotic in subject formation, which challenged Lacan's imaginary/symbolic distinction. The ideas that she developed here were important not only for understanding Kristeva's view of subject formation, but also because they formed an enduring, methodological concern that continued into her later work, particularly in her discussions of the fate of the imaginary in the society of the spectacle. That is, Kristeva's drive to discover what is *anterior* to the Lacanian model of the imaginary, which she situated in the semiotic *chōra*, provides the model for how she later seeks an alternative imaginary to the society of the spectacle.

Kristeva's search for an alternative imaginary includes theoretical forays into the works of Saint Ignatius, Aragon, and Barthes, among others. But in *Intimate Revolt*, Jean-Paul Sartre's work, to which she devotes three chapters, takes center stage. As I demonstrate, Kristeva's turn to "old Sartre" forms a vital hinge in her analysis of the imaginary in the society of the spectacle. Kristeva argues that Sartre's phenomenology opened the horizon in which psychoanalysis—hers and Lacan's—could develop. Her turn to Sartre, then, is also a return to what is theoretically anterior to Lacanian psychoanalysis. As such, Kristeva believes that returning to Sartre's notion of the imaginary affords certain avenues for resistance to the society of the spectacle closed off by the purely Lacanian schema. At the same time, Kristeva does not see a stark opposition between Lacanian psychoanalysis and Sartrean phenomenology; rather, she views Lacan's and Sartre's works to be complementary. For Kristeva, Sartre poses questions about the imaginary that ultimately could only be broached by the psychoanalytic notion of the unconscious. In this sense, Kristeva's turn to Sartre's phenomenology against the backdrop of Lacanian psychoanalysis allows her to present a view of the imaginary in the society of the spectacle that demonstrates its connection to both repression and resistance.

The Mental Image and the Spectacular Imaginary | 213

The first section of this chapter examines Kristeva's reading of Lacan's mirror stage and theory of castration in *Revolution in Poetic Language*. Focusing on the connection between the specular image and the world of objects, I situate this discussion in the contrast between Lacan's notions of the imaginary and the symbolic, and Kristeva's notions of the semiotic and the symbolic. While this section covers terrain that has been discussed by others, it sets the stage for the second section, which turns to Kristeva's reading of Sartre and his phenomenological conception of the image and the imaginary, which she argues underlines the psychoanalytic conception of the imaginary. In doing so, I demonstrate that Kristeva posits a continuity between the work of Lacan and Sartre. Although she criticizes Sartre for ultimately ignoring the unconscious determinants of the image, she views the centrality of negativity to his account of the mental image and the imagination as providing the basis for a possible freedom from the suffocating development of the spectacular imaginary. In the concluding third section, I explore how Kristeva's attention to the mental image and imaginary in Sartre provides a framework for understanding the link between the mental image and the spectacular imaginary. Thus, through these three sections, I argue that Kristeva's early engagement with the Lacanian theory of subject formation in *Revolution in Poetic Language* has a significant impact on her turn to Sartre in her later works in the context of her investigation of subject formation in the society of the spectacle.

The Mirror Stage, Castration, and Subject Formation

Lacan's Mirror Stage and Castration

With the theory of the mirror stage, Lacan famously described the event of jubilant recognition when an infant (6–18 months) encounters their image in the mirror, an event of imaginary identification that precipitates the subsequent development of the symbolic "I."[3] Lacan situated his understanding of the formation of the ego (*moi*), which begins with this process, in opposition to the ego psychology of his time: the infant's identification with the specular image depends on a gestalt experience, an experience opposed to the traditional philosophical view of self-reflection inaugurated by Descartes's *cogito* (2007, 75). On Lacan's view, the subject does not come to certainty about itself through an internal process of thinking, but rather, through a visual identification with something external that relies on an *Aha-Erlebnis* or gestalt experience (75). In contrast with the kind of illumination that flows from reason, Lacan notes that this recognition is precipitated by an illuminative mimicry. Lacan focuses on the experience of motility that the child undergoes after the moment of recognition. The mirror stage inaugurates the playful assimilation of oneself to the image via gesture or the body. At the same time, expanding beyond the inner confines of the Cartesian subject of doubt, Lacan describes the infant as being captivated by "the virtual complex and the reality it duplicates—namely, the child's own body, and the persons and even the things around him" (75). The child's fascination, then, also arises from its situatedness within the reflected environment—the mirror duplicates the child in relation to others and objects.

While Lacan describes the assumption of the specular image on the path to subject formation as a joyous experience, it is also a contradictory process that remains unresolved for the rest of the child's life. On the one hand, Lacan describes this process as *identification*, an experience that transpires when the infant recognizes its image in the mirror. On the other hand, this moment of identification is accompanied by alienation, one that arises from the relationship between the unified image in the mirror and the infant's fragmented image of the body. Lacan notes that the infant who assumes the specular image is "still trapped in his motor impotence and nursling dependence," and that there is a discord between how the mirror image appears to the infant and the experience of the turbulent movements that animate it (2007, 76). Thus, the ego that develops during the mirror stage is deeply alienated, it is an imaginary construct that Lacan describes as having features of "paranoiac knowledge" (76). Mimetic identification, then, paradoxically precipitates disidentification, a separation from the image that does not logically correspond to the inner experience of the infant, that is, it produces a disconnect between the inner motility of the infant and the static external visual image. For Lacan, this alienation is constitutive of subject formation.

In addition to the spatial capture involved in the mirror stage, there is a temporal dialectic that arises from the subject's formation.

> The mirror stage is a drama whose internal pressure pushes precipitously from insufficiency to anticipation—and, for the subject caught up in the lure of spatial identification, turns out

fantasies that proceed from a fragmented image of the body to what I will call an "orthopedic" form of its totality—and to the finally donned armor of an alienating identity that will mark his entire mental development with its rigid structure. Thus, the shattering of the *Innenwelt* to *Umwelt* circle gives rise to an inexhaustible squaring of the ego's audits. (Lacan 2007, 78)

The assumption of the specular image designates a stage prior to the subject's identification with another and prior to language. It is a primordial form or "ideal-I," that is, a form that is the "root-stock of secondary identifications" (76). The subject is thus set in a "fictional direction" that will never coincide with the subject's becoming, or with the subject's attempt to resolve its alienation from its own reality, between *Innenwelt* and *Umwelt* (76). Indeed, this relationship is not a linear, causal connection between the inner world and the outer world, but rather, it is *extimate*, one in which the exterior is already within the interior of the subject as an alienating core that can never be completely known (1992, 139). Instead of "out-there," the symbolic is already present in the imaginary; it is precisely the place of the "Other."

Lacan describes the coming to the end of the mirror stage—through the infant's identification with its imago and the drama of primordial jealousy—as inaugurating a dialectic that links the I to "socially elaborated situations" (2007, 79). Lacan describes this moment as one that "tips the whole of human knowledge [*savoir*] into being mediated by the other's desire, constitutes its objects in an abstract equivalence due to competition from other people, and turns the *I* into an apparatus to which every instinctual pressure constitutes a danger, even if it corresponds to a natural maturation process" (79). Importantly, the normalization of this maturation process is brought about through cultural intervention, and Lacan points to the Oedipal phase, for example, as inaugurating sexual object choice, which is precisely when castration comes to have a core bearing for the infant's development.

Finally, and looking ahead to Kristeva's discussion, the mirror stage is infused with negativity or aggressivity, and Lacan explicitly distances the negativity that transpires in this process from the existential/phenomenological understanding of the term, which is precisely the understanding that Kristeva will recuperate, and which will be addressed further on.[4] In the next section, I address Kristeva's elaboration of Lacan's theory, insofar as she attends to a developmental phase prior to the mirror stage originating in the infant's relationship to the mother. This will set the stage for the implicit return of the mirror stage in *Intimate Revolt*. In this text, the society of the spectacle stunts the function of the imaginary endemic to subject formation and, therefore, decimates this faculty in the individual. In turn, by showing that the psyche shelters certain semiotic processes—precisely as a form of negativity—that transpire before entry into the mirror stage, Kristeva suggests that their disruptive qualities can intervene in the otherwise suffocating society of the spectacle.

Kristeva on Lacan's Mirror Stage and Castration

In chapter 6, "The Mirror and Castration: Positing the Subject as Absent from the Signifier," Kristeva situates her own thinking about subject formation in relation to Lacan. She attributes to Lacan's mirror stage and his theory of castration two points of "the thetic phase of the signifying process, around which signification is organized" (1984, 46). The thetic phase, as Kristeva explains in the preceding chapter, designates identification between the subject and its image, on the one hand, and the subject and its objects, on the other hand. Thus, the two points that Kristeva identifies—the mirror stage and castration—facilitate two separations (between the subject and its image, and between the subject and its objects) that allow the sign to emerge. First, as discussed above, the mirror stage precipitates the infant's spatial capture of its image, but it requires at the same time that the infant remains separate from the image. Its lack of motor coordination and physiological immaturity—what Kristeva calls the infant's "semiotic motility"—produce a sense of fragmentation rather than unification.[5] Kristeva agrees with Lacan that it is the human being's premature birth that makes it possible to posit its image as something separate. Second, the spatial capture of the image paves the way for the subject's relationship to objects, and here, Kristeva also follows Lacan: "the specular image is the 'prototype' for the 'world of objects.' Positing the imaged ego leads to the positing of the object, which is, likewise, separate and signifiable" (46). Kristeva sees a vital link between the specular image internal to the subject—the imaged ego—and the world of objects. That is, with the mirror stage, Kristeva acknowledges that Lacan established the centrality of the image to the relationship between the subject's inner world and the outer world.

Nevertheless, while acknowledging the crucial place of the imaginary in subject formation, Kristeva maintains that the child's experience prior to the mirror stage, its semiotic motility, is primarily marked by drives and is not fully captured by the Lacanian concept of the imaginary.[6] Kristeva describes this fluid state of the semiotic [*le sémiotique*] by taking as her guide Melanie Klein's elaboration of the Freudian theory of the drives.

> Drives involve pre-Oedipal semiotic functions and energy discharges that connect and orient the body to the mother. We must emphasize that "drives" are always already ambiguous, simultaneously assimilating and destructive; this dualism . . . makes the semiotized body a place of permanent scission. The oral and anal drives, both of which are oriented and structured around the mother's body, dominate this sensorimotor organization. The mother's body is therefore what mediates the symbolic law organizing social relations and becomes the ordering principle of the semiotic *chōra*, which is on the path of destruction, aggressivity, and death. (1984, 27–28)[7]

Kristeva's reworking of the Freudian notion of the drive involves a rethinking of his distinction between drive and meaning, and an elaboration of the drive beyond its usual understanding as "energetic, biological or electrical . . . as something neuronal," and specifically, differently from Lacan for whom the drive is bound up with language and the symbolic realm (145).[8] For Kristeva, the drive operates outside of the symbolic and may not necessarily be encapsulated by it, and it is also something that operates prior to language.[9] In this way, Kristeva accords a different modality of meaning in the semiotic other than that found in the symbolic.

Kristeva's notion of the *chōra*, which she adopts from Plato's *Timaeus*, designates this modality, one that emerges in the relationship between the infant and the mother's body, and that transpires through sound and movement.[10] For Kristeva, the *chōra* designates a state that is prior to representation and lacks the kind of spatial and temporal coordinates precipitated by the imaginary dimension of the mirror stage (1984, 26). Kristeva notes that the *chōra*: "precedes evidence, verisimilitude, spatiality, and temporality. Our discourse—all discourse—moves with and against the *chōra* in the sense that it simultaneously depends upon and refuses it. Although the *chōra* can be designated and regulated, it can never be definitively posited; as a result, one can situate the *chōra* and, if necessary, lend it a topology, but one can never give it axiomatic form" (26). One of the primary differences between the *chōra* and the imaginary phase of the mirror stage is that the latter is oriented almost solely by vision and the capacity to demarcate form. Even though in the mirror stage the infant precedes through a gestalt experience rather than self-reflection, the centrality of this experience revolves around the infant's capacity to visually capture its unified form in the mirror, which creates the specular ego. In contrast, the *chōra* precedes specularization, and its drives are ordered not through the symbolic law but through the mother's body.

The two separations—the infant from its own image and from objects—makes possible the appearance of the sign, which is the voice that emerges from the semiotic *chōra*: "The sign can be conceived as the voice that is projected from the agitated body (from the semiotic *chōra*) onto the facing *imago* or onto the object, which simultaneously detach from the surrounding continuity" (1984, 46–47). For Kristeva, the formation of the sign during the mirror stage only becomes possible through vocalization, which brings into conflict the infant's primary motility in the semiotic *chōra* and the experience of "positing-separating-identifying." It inaugurates the speaking subject, a subject that is always constituted in and through language.

The mother's body, which acts as a receptacle for every utterance or vocalization (demand), up until now occupies the place of the other. In this role, the mother is the phallus, but the discovery of castration detaches the infant from the mother, and the discovery of lack makes the phallus a symbolic function. Thus, for Kristeva, castration puts the "finishing touches" on the process of separation. Kristeva describes this as such: "This is a decisive moment fraught with consequences: the subject, finding his identity in the symbolic, *separates* from his fusion with the mother, *confines* his jouissance to the genital, and transfers semiotic motility onto the symbolic order. Thus ends the formation of the thetic phase, which posits the gap between the signifier and signified as an opening up toward every desire but also every act, including the very jouissance that exceeds them" (1984, 47). Signification emerges from the gap between the drive or semiotic motility of the infant and its imaged ego, between the mother and the demands that are directed toward her. This gap is the place of the signifier that is the "Other."

The thetic phase, then, is a "threshold" between the semiotic and the symbolic, between what Kristeva describes as two heterogeneous realms. However, Kristeva does not view a neat separation between them, rather, she notes that while the symbolic includes part of the semiotic, their "scission" is precipitated by this break between signifier and signified. In this regard, Kristeva describes the symbolic as a split unification, something that can be envisioned in the way that an eyelid brings together "two edges of a fissure" (1984, 49).[11]

On Kristeva's view, the transition through the mirror stage is never definitively complete. In the speaking subject, the one inaugurated by this process, fantasies "articulate this irruption of drives within the realm of the signifier; they disrupt the signifier and shift the metonymy of desire, which acts within the place of the Other, onto a jouissance that divests the object and turns back toward the autoerotic body" (1984, 49). Kristeva views language to be a defense construction against the semiotic drives—their destructiveness and aggressivity, essentially against the death drive. Language, then, which is symbolic, has a protective function against "drive attacks" by making the body into something that can take a position and signify. It is thus fantasy, as it appears in art or in psychosis, that reminds us of these drives. Castration, then, is necessary precisely because it posits a stable subject that is shielded from the "drive attacks." Rather than giving way to fantasy or to psychosis, the drive attacks can thus lead the subject to a "'second-degree thetic,' that is, a resumption of the functioning characteristic of the semiotic *chōra* within the signifying device of language. This is precisely what artistic practices, and notably poetic language, demonstrate" (1984, 50). Kristeva's thetic is thus a permeable boundary and different from Lacan's view of castration that once imposed, perpetuates the well-ordered signifier.

Lacan's notion of the imaginary, then, seems to occlude the separation from the mother that the child undergoes, what Kristeva describes in *Powers of Horror* as a "a violent, clumsy breaking away, with the constant risk of falling back," that the child experiences in relation to the mother's body, what Kristeva terms the process of abjection (1980, 13).[12] In this sense, Kristeva's discovery of what is anterior to the mirror stage—logically and chronologically—designates a different kind of temporal and spatial experience that cannot be captured by Lacan's conception of the imaginary. Kristeva presents a topology of mental space rooted in the child's relationship to the mother that defies a linear temporality—the semiotic both precedes and succeeds the Lacanian symbolic. Furthermore, Kristeva decenters the primacy of the visual in identification and instead emphasizes the infant's bodily gestures and vocalization as already ushering in the infant's entry into the symbolic, prior to the mirror stage.

The Mirror Stage of the Spectacle

FROM LACAN TO SARTRE

In *Intimate Revolt*, Kristeva illustrates the way in which the spectacle powerfully substitutes the developmental phase of the mirror stage with its own reflective surface. In such a society, subjects who are weaned on the images of the spectacle no longer go through an active construction of subject formation but, rather, passively identify with a given schema of representation. If for Lacan, the subject's identificatory processes only emerge with the imaginary, then for Kristeva, within these parameters, the subject becomes vulnerable to total cooption by images that *perform* the function of the imaginary for the subject. The subject no longer actively constructs its own self, as in Lacan's mirror stage, but instead, passively consumes it. The major question for Kristeva, then, is: "what happens when the imaginary is reified in the society of the spectacle . . . when this universe of the real image becomes the only reality . . . evacuating the singular fantasies of the independent mental act, imposing a stereotype of representation that kills individual phantasmatic creation in favor of a standardized imaginary?" (2003, 128). It is in the face of both the decline of verbal culture in favor of a standardized imagery, but also in the face of the diminishment of the imaginary capacity itself, that Kristeva takes on a broader investigation of the image and the imaginary. But rather than Lacan, one of the central figures in her investigation is Jean-Paul Sartre, to whom she devotes three chapters of this book. His early work on the imagination and the imaginary, Kristeva contends, provides an avenue of resistance to the otherwise all-encompassing and suffocating spectacle.[13]

Given the framing of this chapter with Lacan's essay on the mirror stage, it is worth returning to his brief remarks at the very end, which do not mention Sartre by name but signal his work, *Being and Nothingness*. For Lacan, existentialism/phenomenology is unable to fully develop the crucial role of negativity in subject formation because it fundamentally misunderstands it. That is, existentialism abides by the very Cartesianism that Lacan rejects, and thus understands negativity only within the parameters of the self-sufficient consciousness of the cogito. Within this framework, existentialism cannot account for the fundamental misrecognition that characterizes the ego, described in the mirror stage. Thus, Lacan's direct point of critique is that Sartre's phenomenology is overly beholden to the Cartesian cogito, as it posits an ego based in perception-consciousness, whereas Lacan posits an ego that is inherently dissonant, that proceeds from a misrecognition rather than recognition, and is fundamentally motivated by the unconscious.

Kristeva provides a more generous reading of Sartre's concept of negativity and positions it as offering resources to counter the deadening effects of the society of the spectacle, which functions like a global mirror, endlessly seducing subjects and capturing them in the lure of identification. Kristeva too underscores the fact that Sartre did not account for the unconscious in his analysis of the imaginary, but this does not prove as great of a detriment for Kristeva as it is for Lacan. Even though Sartre begins with the Cartesian subject of consciousness, his understanding of this consciousness has parallels with the psychoanalytic understanding of consciousness. For Kristeva, from a psychoanalytic point of view, "consciousness is continually traversed by the unconscious and therefore continually nihilates and questions itself," and she sees something similar in Sartre since he also defines consciousness as something that is "nihilating and interrogating, a process, in conflict and in flux" (2003, 124). On one hand, this conception of consciousness allowed Sartre to avoid the unconscious, but on the other hand, Kristeva sees that his formulation also worked as a corrective against a certain reception of Freudian psychoanalysis that sanitizes it of the negativity that he accorded to the unconscious.

Furthermore, Kristeva does not see a stark opposition between Lacan's development of psychoanalysis and Sartre's phenomenology, rather she poses the question of whether Lacan's distinction between the specular "ego" from the symbolic "I" does not echo Sartre's "transcendence of the ego."[14] If the specular ego preserves a false or illusory identity, as was discussed earlier in connection with the mirror stage, then the symbolic I is "an infinite process of perpetual questioning." For Lacan, "all ego formation that is specular and imaginary . . . is false at the outset" (2003, 129). For Kristeva, it is on the postphenomenological terrain, and particularly on the terrain set by Sartre, that Lacan was able to "formulate such a conception of a subject that is not the ego" (130). Kristeva locates her own notion of the subject-in-process as posing the same challenge to the "ipseity of the ego." With this framework in place, Kristeva goes on to elucidate Sartre's conception of the in-itself and the for-itself as it emerges in his theory of the transcendence of the ego. Kristeva locates a fundamental negativity that emerges in the dialectic between these positions, which allows Kristeva to delineate a phenomenological dimension that she sees underlining the Lacanian formation of the ego and her own understanding of the subject-in-process.

For Kristeva, the spectacle erases this negativity, and this has a profound effect on subject formation. Indeed, on Lacan's and Kristeva's accounts the ego is not a self-same entity, but rather takes on temporary spatial and temporal coordinates, a process that on Sartre's account also relies on a certain notion of freedom that Kristeva finds attractive. Yet, the spectacle enforces a collapse of the for-itself into the in-itself, of the real into the imaginary. Individuals become identified with the ego, which is an imaginary construction—it is taken as real, and therefore, subjectivity proceeds solely through an alienating formation produced by the spectacle, rather than through one's active construction and confrontation with negativity.

Kristeva on Sartre's Mental Image and the Imaginary

Although Kristeva acknowledges Sartre's mistake in not accounting for the unconscious, she avoids endorsing a binary between the ego consciousness of phenomenology and the unconscious subject of psychoanalysis.[15] Rather, Kristeva focuses on the principle of negativity, which she views as continually traversing the two realms. Indeed, Kristeva introduced this model in *Revolution in Poetic Language*, a model that accounts for the Freudian unconscious: "We view the subject in language as decentering the transcendental ego, cutting through it, and opening it up to a dialectic in which its syntactic and categorical understanding is merely the liminary moment of the process, which is itself always acted upon by the relation to the other dominated by the death drive and its productive reiteration of the 'signifier'" (1984, 30). Kristeva demonstrates a similar model in Sartre, particularly in his account of the mental image. The imaginative consciousness, which is thetic and involves a positional act, is continually traversed by the nonthetic; that is, although the imaginative consciousness posits an object, that object doesn't exist or is unreal, it is essentially a nothingness. For Kristeva, as for Sartre, the nothingness inherent to the imaginative consciousness is a quality endemic to consciousness in general, even though it is more apparent when it comes to the mental image. In this sense, images are not opposed to concepts but, rather, concepts and images are two forms that thought in general can take. Generally, images are integrated into conceptual knowing but the reverse can also take place, where conceptual knowing is "debased" into imaginative consciousness.

For Kristeva, this "debasement" is suggestive for what occurs in the society of the spectacle, insofar as consciousness begins to take the image as a thing or object. In what follows, I will address Kristeva's discussion of the Sartrean mental image, before moving on to how this analysis sheds light on the problems and possible solutions to the impact of the society of the spectacle on psychic life.

Kristeva discusses Sartre's view of the mental image in chapter 11 of *Intimate Revolt*, where she begins by noting its four determinants or characteristics. First, for Sartre, the image is primarily a consciousness, an understanding that she believes erroneously neglects the unconscious determinants of the image, even though he veers close to them in his theory. Nevertheless, putting the neglect of the unconscious aside, Kristeva highlights that Sartre's formulation of the image as a consciousness allows him to importantly dissociate the image from objecthood. The image is not a thing or an object, but rather, as consciousness, it is a *relationship* to the object (2003, 165). In other words, the imagining consciousness denotes a structure with certain laws that produces a relationship to the object.

However, the relationship to the object is peculiar, insofar as the imaginative consciousness involves, second, a quasi-observation. Sartre contrasts imagining with the acts of perceiving and conceiving an object. While perceiving and conceiving produce a certain kind of knowledge about the object, the image, conversely, does not reveal anything new about the object. Objects appear in the image exactly as they are already known, such as, for example, when Sartre describes imagining a cube: if one imagines a cube and turns the image of the cube over in one's head, something new will not be learned beyond what has been put into that image. Since there is nothing new to be learned in the image, Sartre designates an "essential poverty" to it (2004, 10). For Sartre, then, the imaginative consciousness is a quasi-observation since there is an attitude of an observation, but this attitude does not reveal anything new about the object.

Third, Kristeva notes that "the imaginative consciousness posits its object as nothingness" (2003, 165). While all consciousness is thetic (here Kristeva instructs the reader to return to "The Semiotic and the Symbolic" in *Revolution in Poetic Language*), that is, all consciousness is defined by a positional act, there is a difference in the way that the imaginative consciousness posits its object when compared with perception. Perception "posits its object as existing," whereas in the image, the posited object is not there. As Sartre clarifies, this nothingness can take four forms: the imaginative consciousness "can posit the object as nonexistent, absent, or as existing elsewhere; it can also 'neutralize' itself, which is to say not posit its object as existent" (2004, 12). In this sense, Sartre characterizes the imaginative consciousness as "intuitive-absent," it is an image of something that is "given as absent to intuition . . . the image has wrapped within itself a certain nothingness. Its object is not a simple portrait, it asserts itself: but in asserting itself it destroys itself. However lively, appealing, strong the image, it gives its object as not being" (14). Kristeva here begins to open the question about the implications of this feature of the mental image—is this "virtual nonbelief" a source of freedom or simply a source of illusion? As will be discussed further on in the context of the society of the spectacle, Kristeva will maintain a certain ambivalence, suggesting that the outcome can be both.

Kristeva turns finally to the fourth feature of Sartre's description, the spontaneity of the mental image. Kristeva notes, importantly, that the imaginative consciousness, in and through its thetic character, involves, " 'a non-thetic consciousness of itself': a sort of transversal consciousness that has no object, proposes nothing, is not knowledge of an external realty" (2003, 165–66).[16] Sartre describes it as "a diffuse light that consciousness emits for itself . . . an indefinable quality that attaches itself to every consciousness" (2004, 14). This quality gives the imagination a vivid creativity unlike perceptual consciousness, which appears to itself as passive. The imagination grasps itself as an imaginative consciousness, "a spontaneity that produces and conserves the object as imaged" (14). Kristeva's description of this aspect of the imaginative consciousness converges with Lacan's insistence that the mirror phase produces paranoiac knowledge. Kristeva notes that "the all-powerful and paranoid latencies of the imaginative consciousness are put into perspective here as an 'indefinable counterpart of the fact that the object occurs as a nothingness' " (2003, 166). Given the parallel that emerges here between the paranoiac structure of knowledge in the mirror stage and Kristeva's view of the fourth determinant of the imaginative consciousness, it is worthwhile to parse this connection further, particularly as it maps onto Kristeva's understanding of the society of the spectacle.

Sartre's remarks on hallucination are particularly relevant, where he returns to the idea that the "irreality of the imaged object is correlative to an immediate intuition of spontaneity. Consciousness has a *nonthetic* consciousness of itself as a creative activity," precisely what Sartre described in the fourth determinant of the image discussed above (2004, 149). Sartre here reiterates that this consciousness of spontaneity appears as a traversal consciousness, and he raises questions that are pertinent for Kristeva's analysis of the spectacular imaginary: in the phenomenon of hallucination, "how do we abandon our consciousness of spontaneity, how do we feel ourselves passive before the images that we in fact form; is it true that we confer *reality*, which is to say a presence in flesh, on these objects that are given to a healthy consciousness as absent?" (149). Sartre will answer these questions by arguing that in hallucination, it is not that we take the unreal to be real, but that our attitude toward reality changes, we do not approach reality through perception.

Indeed, turning to Sartre's remarks on acoustic hallucination, Kristeva notes there is no correspondence between imagination and perception but, rather, hallucination "coincides with a brusque annihilation of the reality perceived" (2003, 175). Importantly, this should not be viewed as an obliteration of reality. Rather, hallucination does not occur in the real world, it excludes it. As a form of imaginative consciousness, hallucination involves an unreal space and time. In this sense, visual or auditory hallucination involves a temporary loss of perception, but once the hallucination is over, the real world reappears. It designates an attitude toward the real that involves something like a double consciousness: "In hallucination, the production of an unreal object persists at the same time as the consciousness of its unreality (its nonthetic consciousness). It is the attitude toward the real that is changed in hallucination and not the real itself: the unreal appears as an impairment of the sense of the real" (2003, 175). In other words, the imagination does not replace perceptions, but rather, perceptions are in a sense dulled—they "are blunted but not abolished" (175).

Although Sartre does not distinguish between consciousness and the unconscious, Kristeva suggests that, here, such a distinction can be mapped onto Sartre's description, particularly since he refers to the "the 'interrupted unity' of consciousness" (2003, 175). To make her case, Kristeva quotes Sartre: " 'These two worlds have collapsed: we are dealing here with a third type of existence which no words can describe. Perhaps the simplest thing to do would be to call them unreal lateral apparitions, the correlatives of an impersonal consciousness' " (175). These unreal lateral apparitions can only be described, put into language, after the fact. For Kristeva, there is a lot of effort here on Sartre's part to avoid the unconscious, but she sees it as the notion that is undeniably suited to this phenomenon. Drawing on a theory of the unconscious, Kristeva explains hallucination psychoanalytically as "a return to sensations in words under the pressure of unconscious drives, a return provoking the splitting of the subject between an observant consciousness, on the one hand, and a constellations of words/sensations with the value of reified images, relics of the incorporated object, on the other," which leads Kristeva to ask a pertinent question: "But what is the object at issue here?" (176).

For Kristeva, Sartre's work opens onto the psychoanalytic point of view, that is, this object is the mother, and here, her analysis links up with what she described in *Revolution in Poetic Language* as occurring prior to the mirror stage—precisely the infant's relationship to and separation from the mother. Now from the perspective of Sartre's phenomenology, Kristeva describes this separation from the mother by employing his terms: "the representation of the mother is the primary and fundamental existence in regard to which the speaking being must precisely 'transcend' and 'nihilate' himself" (2003, 176). In the process of separation—which proceeds through incorporation, identification, and symbolization—what the subject incorporates are "conglomerations: sensations, drives, semiotic traces of the maternal presence" (176). Kristeva's description recalls her discussion of the *chōra*, which is precisely characterized by this motility. The incorporation-conglomerations have an acoustic primacy, which is also what Kristeva pointed to in her discussion of what is anterior to the mirror stage, and what emerges from the *chōra* and is projected onto the image in the mirror: "acoustic signifiers, that is, the sensibility of words, the music of babbling, the rhythms of thought" (176). Kristeva affirms Sartre's view that hallucination constitutes the imaginary, which is part of thought or the symbolic: "it is made of this patchwork that initiates the capacity to represent-imagine-think" (176). Thus, in the case of secondary hallucination, it can be understood in the adult "when the psychical apparatus is invaded by incorporations-conglomerations under the pressure of the drive and desire and when the pure consciousness that the paternal function guaranteed does not resist this assault: consciousness then finds itself in revolt, to the point of collapse" (176). Kristeva points to artists who have sustained the risk and danger of encountering the primordial maternal object in the imaginary of art—figures such as Picasso, Bacon, and Aragon. In this way, Sartre's work offers Kristeva a way to approach the possibility of freeing oneself from the primordial object such that one can become capable of imagining it, a capacity that she views to be integral to the possibility of freedom itself.

Conclusion: The Spectacular Imaginary

One of the most pernicious features of the spectacle is that it functions like a global mirror, substituting the interior mental processes that Lacan described, which were facilitated by the imaginary, with an identifying function that essentially destroys the imaginary. As Kristeva notes, the spectacle collapses the real and the imaginary. In the spectacle, the image loses its relation to its referent, to the object that is not present, in essence, the spectacular image is severed from the nothingness that Sartre locates as the object of the imaginative consciousness. The spectacle thus presents itself and aims to become the "Only Objective Reality," and the individual remains captivated by and merely consumes imaginary constructions instead of producing them or being transformed by them (2003, 173).

Sartre's early theory provides Kristeva with the tools to rethink the negativity endemic to Lacan's mirror stage and annihilated by the society of the spectacle. Sartre's conception of the imaginative consciousness as a nihilating consciousness, which makes present what is unreal, offers a way for her to recoup a certain form of negativity that is tied to freedom. In this sense, hallucination is a pertinent example, because it brings to the forefront the problem generated by the spectacular imaginary, where the image is taken as a thing or an object. Yet, as Sartre's remarks on hallucination also indicated, it is not that reality is abolished, but rather, our perspective toward reality changes. The image is always a nihilation of the thing, and thus there is a dimension of identification and alienation, or presence and absence, that is endemic to the image itself and to the imaginative consciousness. For this reason, Kristeva sees promise in Sartre's account of this nihilating character of the image, given the role of phantasm or the society of the spectacle in psychical life.

In this light, Kristeva's rethinking of the Lacanian imaginary is facilitated by the resources of phenomenology, particularly Sartre's views of the image and the imaginary. Kristeva's attention to Sartre's remarks on hallucination recalls the fragmented body of the mirror stage, but she demonstrates that this body is infiltrated by semiotic drives. Kristeva introduces the subject's relationship to the mother and abjection, in line with both her reading of the *chōra* and the process of separation that she delineated in her reading that occurs prior to the mirror stage. Finally, this emphasis on the primordial object leads to Kristeva's insistence on the sensible intimacy of certain aesthetic productions in contrast with the robotizing imaginary of the spectacle, in order to consider the possibility of resistance to the otherwise all-encompassing reign of the image (2014, 4). While Lacan would go on to formulate Freud's analytic theory through the notion of extimacy, as Cecilia Sjöholm has argued, Kristeva's critique of extimacy leads her to posit intimacy, a concept that implies a certain femininity that is under erasure in the Lacanian notion of extimacy (2005, 91–92).

Kristeva thus introduces an important phenomenological dimension to the question of the relationship between the mental and the social, or between the reification of the mental image and the reification precipitated by the spectacular imaginary. Her reading of Sartre, from within a broader psychoanalytic framework, insists on a greater autonomy to the subject that is always in process, one that is both seduced and fascinated by the spectacle, but on her view, not mechanistically determined by it. Sartre's analysis of the mental image opens the door to a conception of the imaginary that is riven with the nonthetic, precisely what Kristeva designated as the semiotic in *Revolution in Poetic Language*. The subject preserves something of the semiotic, a process anterior to the subject's formation in and through the images of the spectacle, that resists the logic of both Lacan's imaginary and the spectacular imaginary. In the context of the spectacular imaginary, the question thus arises as to whether these unconscious processes could challenge the self-subsistent appearance of the spectacle itself, and whether it would thus be liable to be undone by the very processes that allowed for its formation—the separation from and occlusion of material (and for Kristeva—maternal/feminine) reality.

Notes

1. See, for example, Sara Beardsworth, "From Revolution to Revolt Culture," in *Revolt, Affect, Collectivity: The Unstable Boundaries of Kristeva's Polis*, ed. Tina Chanter and Ewa Plonowska Ziarek (Albany: SUNY Press, 2005).

2. In 2014, Kristeva reinforced this picture of a society that deracinated individuals from their own fundamental capacity central to subject formation in "New Forms of Revolt," *Journal of French and Francophone Philosophy* 23, no. 2 (2014): 1–19.

3. Jacques Lacan, "The Mirror Stage as Formative of the I Function as revealed in Psychoanalytic Experience," in *Écrits: The First Complete Edition in English*, trans. Bruce Fink (New York: Norton, 2007). For an in-depth discussion of Lacan's concept of the Imaginary, particularly with respect to the mirror stage, see Anthony Wilden, "Lacan and the Discourse of the Other," in *The Language*

of the Self: The Function of Language in Psychoanalysis, trans. Anthony Wilden (Baltimore. MD and London: Johns Hopkins University Press, 1981).

4. See also "Aggressivity in Psychoanalysis," in *Écrits: The First Complete Edition in English*, trans. Bruce Fink (New York: Norton, 2007) for Lacan's discussion of how aggressivity originates in the mirror stage.

5. For an explication of Kristeva's conceptions of the semiotic and the symbolic, see Noëlle McAfee, *Julia Kristeva* (New York: Routledge, 2004). There is controversy over Kristeva's use of the terms, with some commentators viewing the more revolutionary possibilities of the semiotic being lost in her work of the 1980s, where the semiotic is forsaken for the symbolic. For a defense of this concept, particularly as it appears in Kristeva's work of the 1980s, see Kelly Oliver's discussion in *Reading Kristeva: Unraveling the Double-Bind* (Bloomington: Indiana University Press, 1993). Oliver's strategy is to emphasize the dialectical oscillation between the semiotic and the symbolic in Kristeva's work.

6. For a defense of Lacan against Kristeva's criticism, see Gavin Rae, "Maternal and Paternal Functions in the Formation of Subjectivity: Kristeva and Lacan," *Philosophy and Social Criticism* 46, no. 4 (2020): 412–30.

7. For a discussion of Melanie Klein's view of negativity, see Jacqueline Rose, "Negativity in Melanie Klein," in *Reading Melanie Klein*, ed. Lyndsey Stonebridge and John Phillips (London and New York: Routledge, 1998).

8. "Interview: Sharing Singularity," in *Kristeva: Live Theory*, ed. John Lechte and Maria Margaroni (London and New York: Continuum, 2004).

9. For further discussion of this point, see Sara Beardsworth, *Psychoanalysis and Modernity* (Albany: SUNY Press, 2004).

10. Kristeva's use of the *chōra* waned after *Revolution in Poetic Language*, perhaps because, as Maria Magaroni discusses, it came under attack for its essentialist implications. " 'The Lost Foundation': Kristeva's Semiotic Chōra and Its Ambiguous Legacy," *Hypatia* 20, no. 1 (Winter 2005): 78–98. For a defense of the *chōra* in Kristeva's work against the charges of essentialism, See Fanny Söderbäck, *Revolutionary Time: Time and Difference in Kristeva and Irigaray* (Albany: SUNY Press, 2019). For an overview of the reception of Plato's *chōra* in French philosophy more generally, see Emanuela Bianchi, "Receptacle/Chōra: Figuring the Errant Feminine in Plato's Timaeus." *Hypatia* 21, no. 4 (Autumn 2006): 124–46.

11. Kelly Oliver helpfully distinguishes between two ways in which Kristeva uses the symbolic, one in the same sense as Lacan's symbolic, but in another sense as a moment with the semiotic in *Unraveling the Double-Bind*, 10.

12. There is controversy over the extent to which Lacan neglects the mother in his theory of the mirror stage. See Shuli Barzilai, who argues for a radical absence of the mother in Lacan's mirror stage in "On Chimpanzees and Children," in *Lacan and the Matter of Origins* (Stanford, CA: Stanford University Press, 1999), as opposed to Elizabeth Grosz, who reads into Lacan's theory, a "(m)other-mirror image" in *Jacques Lacan: A Feminist Introduction* (Routledge, 1990), 32.

13. In this chapter, I limit my remarks to Kristeva's engagement with Sartre's notion of the imaginary, and do not address the imaginary in Kristeva's wider corpus. For such a discussion, see John Lechte, "The Imaginary and the Spectacle: Kristeva's View" in *Kristeva: Live Theory*, ed. John Lechte and Maria Margaroni (London and New York: Continuum, 2004).

14. For an attempt to demonstrate the influence of Sartre's *Imagination* on Lacan, see Marie-Andrée Charbonneau, "An Encounter between Sartre and Lacan," *Sartre Studies International* 5, no. 2 (1999). Charbonneau writes that "although there is no direct evidence, I maintain that Lacan could never have written "Au-delà du principe de réalité" in its particular form without having had beforehand consulted Sartre's *Imagination*," 34. See also Diego Tolini and Felipe Muller, "Sartre and Lacan: Considerations on the Concepts of the Subject and of Consciousness," *Psychoanalysis and History* 17, no. 1 (2015): 87–105, who argue that "the Lacanian concept of the subject seemed to be based on categories related to the notion of unreflective consciousness that Sartre developed in the 1930s, especially in his book, *The Transcendence of the Ego*," 89.

15. Frederic Jameson argues that "Sartre's 'Cartesianism' is not properly understood unless the attendant stress on the impersonality of the consciousness is also grasped, on its utter lack of quality of individuating attributes, its 'nature' as a mere speck or point without substance or consistency." "Imaginary and Symbolic in Lacan: Marxism, Psychoanalytic Criticism, and the Problem of the Subject," *Yale French Studies* 55/56 (1977): 343.

16. On John Lechte's reading, perception is thetic and the image is nonthetic, presented in "Julia Kristeva and the Trajectory of the Image," in *Psychoanalysis, Aesthetics, and Politics in the Work of Julia Kristeva*, ed. Kelly Oliver and S. K. Keltner (Albany: SUNY, 2009), 85. This reading misconstrues Kristeva (and Sartre's) point that the image is both thetic (it posits something, it is a relationship to an object) and it is nonthetic (its object is nothingness). The traversal of the nonthetic through the thetic is precisely what makes Sartre's description of the mental image captivating for Kristeva, it posits a certain structural affinity between phenomenology and psychoanalysis, that is, the nonthetic traversing the thetic is a certain model of the unconscious without naming it as such.

References

Kristeva, Julia. 1980. *Powers of Horror: An Essay on Abjection*. Translated by Leon S. Roudiez. New York: Columbia University Press.

———. 2003. *Intimate Revolt: The Powers and Limits of Psychoanalysis*. Translated by Jeanine Herman. Columbia University Press.

———. 2014. "New Forms of Revolt." *Journal of French and Francophone Philosophy* 23, no. 2: 1–19.

Lacan, Jacques. 1992. *The Ethics of Psychoanalysis: The Seminar of Jacques Lacan*, vol. 7. Edited by Jacques Alain-Miller, translated by Dennis Porte. New York: Norton.

———. 2007. "The Mirror Stage as Formative of the I Function as revealed in Psychoanalytic Experience." In *Écrits: The First Complete Edition in English*, translated by Bruce Fink. New York: Norton.

Sartre, Jean-Paul. 2004. *The Imaginary: A Phenomenological Psychology of the Imagination*. Translated by Jonathan Webber. London and New York: Routledge.

Sjöholm, Cecilia. 2005. *Kristeva and the Political*. London and New York: Routledge.

Chapter 11

Rhythm and the Semiotic in Revolution in Poetic Language

JOHN MONTANI

> Following the same instinct for rhythm that chose him, the poet doesn't forbid himself from seeing a lack of proportion between the means unleashed and the result.
>
> —Mallarmé, "The Mystery in Letters"

Introduction

This essay is a study of the role rhythm plays in some of Kristeva's writings on the semiotic. Drawing from Kristeva's *Revolution in Poetic Language* and *Desire in Language*, I argue that rhythm is what traverses the boundary between the semiotic and the symbolic order. I show how, for Kristeva, rhythm engenders sense in poetic language and awakens insight by acting as an intermediary between unconscious drives and thetic consciousness. Kristeva's writings on the semiotic are replete with references to rhythm and the notion of rhythm often occurs at critical moments within her texts. However, Kristeva withholds any thoroughgoing exposition of rhythm in her work and provides little thematic treatment of its formative role in the semiotic.[1] This essay seeks to retrieve rhythm in Kristeva's work as an attempt to show its critical importance for her understanding of the semiotic. I argue that rhythm is essential to the process of transposition that underlies her notion of intertextuality. Then, I explore the role rhythm plays in her understanding of the text as a practice. Next, I provide a structural account of her notion of semiotic rhythm from a phenomenological and psychoanalytic perspective. Finally, I consider how rhythm and the semiotic are integral not just to practices of experimental art and poetry but to philosophical thinking as well.

Rhythm between the Semiotic and the Symbolic

An initial challenge one faces in comprehending Kristeva's notion of the semiotic is grasping the relationship between the semiotic and the symbolic. One is confronted with this problem when reading part 1 of *Revolution in Poetic Language*, where the relationship between the semiotic and symbolic is first introduced. Rather than conceiving these two realms to be dichotomous, one is faced with the task of grasping them in a dynamic exchange within the *signifying process*. To avoid the tendency to take these two realms to be dichotomous, a formal and generative notion is needed to account for their reciprocal influence. We first catch sight of such a notion in Kristeva's discussion of the semiotic *chōra*.

For Kristeva, the *chōra* is an originary semiotic process. She situates this process within the primary processes of the unconscious uncovered by Freud. However, for Kristeva, the semiotic *chōra* is not completely inaccessible to consciousness, nor is the semiotic *chōra* an amorphous biological chaos continuously warded off and repressed. The semiotic *chōra* exerts a latent order on the symbolic and constantly infringes on thetic consciousness. She (2006a) writes, "Though deprived of unity, identity, or deity, the *chōra* is nevertheless subject to a regulating process, which is different from that of the symbolic law but nevertheless effectuates discontinuities by temporarily articulating them and then starting over, again and again" (26). The incessant toil of the *chōra* regulates and articulates a semiotic process that underlies and interrupts speech and writing. What is important to recognize here is that the *chōra* serves a formal and generative function as a process of articulation and regulation. However, the *chōra* is not something posited by consciousness, nor can it be fully represented in the symbolic order. Instead, it is a dynamic process that intercedes enunciation and transmutes signification.

Toward the end of her analysis of the semiotic *chōra*, Kristeva (2006a) alludes to a preverbal semiotic rhythm inspired by the work of Stéphane Mallarmé (29). Here, rhythm shows up as a semiotic process analogous to the regulation and articulation of the *chōra* (26).[2] Rhythm is a semiotic movement that guides speech and writing as well as a mode of articulation that churns out preverbal impulses that result in linguistic expression. She writes, "This space underlying the written is rhythmic, unfettered, irreducible to its intelligible verbal translation" (26). Rhythm is initially shown to be a preverbal mode of articulation and a semiotic momentum. Beneath the symbolic order of the written text, Kristeva locates this semiotic rhythm that orchestrates and instigates poetic invention. Rhythm is thus a *via regia* to the semiotic *chōra*; it is both a way the semiotic becomes inscribed in the symbolic and a way the semiotic gets read in the symbol. As a formal and generative process, rhythm is a dynamic preverbal power that interweaves the semiotic and symbolic within the signifying process.[3] Whether through experimental practices in art and literature or the involuntary release of irrepressible drives, rhythm is a semiotic movement that comes to structure and disrupt syntax, expressing bodily and unconscious forces. Thus, we can say that rhythm is a latent and instinctual language of the semiotic *chōra*. However, we will see how rhythm is not bound exclusively to the semiotic, and I will show how it breaches the symbolic by passing through thetic consciousness, invoking the drives, and producing new forms of sense in novel linguistic expression.

Kristeva gives an account of thetic consciousness in chapters 5 and 8 of *Revolution in Poetic Language*. Departing from Husserl, she describes thetic consciousness as a porous boundary, rather than a strictly noetic or transcendental structure. For Kristeva, the thetic plane of speech and writing is constantly interrupted by sighs, stutters, slips of the tongue, and the like. Thetic consciousness is conceived not as a transcendental condition for thought but as a psychic production that marks an initial phase and breaks into the signifying process. The thetic phase, she (2006a) writes, "constitutes the subject without being reduced to his process precisely because it is the threshold of language" (45). We see how, for Kristeva, the conscious speaking subject is not at the origin of the signifying process but speaks and emerges at the threshold of language through its instinctual drives. Therefore, thetic consciousness does not ground or constitute itself, nor does the symbolic guarantee the fulfillment of signification or exhaust the semiotic in the signifying process. Drawing on psychoanalytic theory, Kristeva understands thetic consciousness to be a traversable boundary susceptible to unconscious impulses whose intrusion produce literary devices like metaphor, anaphora, and metonymy. In short, she writes, "The thetic phase marks a threshold between two heterogenous realms: the semiotic and the symbolic" (48). I noted earlier how the semiotic *chōra* was said to effectuate discontinuities in the symbolic by releasing unconscious drives and regulating forces rising up from the body. In *Revolution in Poetic Language*, the question of how these two heterogenous realms communicate and become coordinated is of critical importance.

Thus far, we have seen how the *chōra* is not bereft of order nor is it kept firmly within the recesses of the unconscious. The *chōra* is a rhythmic locus that set loose semiotic movements that compose undercurrents in language and provoke instinctual articulations that break and restore syntax. We will come to see how the discontinuities effectuated within the symbolic are held together and launched by the rhythms of the semiotic *chōra*. Rhythm will be shown to be an intermediary process through which the two heterogeneous realms of the semiotic and symbolic cross, coalesce, or communicate.

Rhythm is by no means the only possible intermediary process between the semiotic and the symbolic, but it is one of the most compelling candidates presented in *Revolution in Poetic Language*.[4] Since Kristeva so often characterizes thetic consciousness as a boundary, limit, or threshold, reading *Revolution in Poetic Language* leads to the question of just how this boundary gets traversed. This question is equally a question of how we as readers are able to enter the semiotic dimension of a text and how we as writers are able to draw out the semiotic and inscribe it on the page. In keeping with the political themes of *Revolution in Poetic Language*, I suggest that rhythm is not a purely theoretical concept in Kristeva's work but is more importantly a *practice*. In art, writing, and politics the struggle against oppression and efforts to produce radical breaks in the social order come up against limit situations where the risk of defeat, delirium, or death loom large. Rhythm becomes a practice insofar as it provides an intermediary path through which ideology can be dislodged by instinct, cliché broken by invention, and absolute knowing replaced with jouissance.

Habits, work weeks, and collective struggles are held together by rhythms that take root in the body and whose transformation depend on the overturning of forces that perpetuate the status quo and lie beneath the threshold of language. Rhythms help maintain forms of social domination and thus contain the germs of their subversion.[5] Rhythms are sites of practice insofar as they help secure the knots and contradictions within oppression and hence hold in reserve the possibility of their undoing. For Kristeva, semiotic rhythms are not specific to individual bodies, nor do they serve solely to structure the predilections of personal life. Rhythms are carried out through us but are not wholly carried out by us. To assume that a revolutionary potential in language is bound by the limits of subjectivity is to overlook how for Kristeva, the semiotic is not just a subjective stratum but part of a wider social and political continuum. In her essay, "The Speaking Subject" Kristeva (2006c) writes, "The present renewal of semiology considers sense as a signifying process and a heterogeneous dynamic, and challenges the logical imprisonment of the subject in order to open the subject towards the body and society" (288). The thetic boundary is not reducible to the personal threshold of internal monologue but is a site of the subject's corporeal and discursive convergence with society and history. Whether or not one avows the theses presented in *Revolution in Poetic Language* about the revolutionary potential of poetic language, to view Kristeva's conception of language as bound to subjectivity is to miss the complex relationship between the psyche and the world in her work. As we saw earlier, thetic consciousness is not a transcendental condition of subjectivity but a phase of psychic production that cannot be divorced from the social, historical, and ecological world. Rhythm becomes a sociopolitical practice insofar as its descent through the thetic threshold brings one into closer contact not only with unconscious drives in language but to the larger libidinal economy of the social and historical world.

Rhythm and Transposition

In her chapter "Breaching the Thetic: Mimesis," Kristeva (2006a) writes, "all transgressions of the thetic are a crossing of a boundary between the true and the false—maintained, inevitably, whenever signification is maintained, and shaken, irremediably, by the flow of the semiotic into the symbolic" (48). The effraction of the thetic by the flow of semiotic articulation is a condition and dynamic process at the heart of Kristeva's notion *transposition*. Adding a third process to the primary processes of the unconscious, Kristeva shows how the thetic is not only permeated by involuntary semiotic pulsations, but also how the semiotic comes to alter the thetic position within the signifying process. Not only are linguistic devices like metaphor, anaphora, and metonymy referable to the primary processes of displacement and condensation, but entire structural shifts within writing and dreams are the result of another psycholinguistic process: transposition, whereby the "passage of one signifying system to another demands a new articulation of the thetic—of enunciative and denotative positionality" (2006a, 60). The polyvocality of literary experiments and the shifts of tone and style in writing are attributable to these passages of signifying systems into one another, which enact a cross channeling or transposition of signifying structures into one another. Rhythm can be seen as a formal and generative process that effectuates the passage of signifying systems into each other, transposing them into novel linguistic expression.

The transposition of signifying structures in the psyche can be linked to the transposition of sensations in the body. Merleau-Ponty (2014) once spoke of the body as a "ready-made system of equivalences and inter-sensory transpositions" (243–44). We can understand Kristeva's notion of intertextuality phenomenologically and psychoanalytically as a transposition of sensations in the lived body and a transposition of significations within the signifying process. The notion of transposition helps us understand how one moves from the lived body to the written body or "from a carnival scene to a written text" (Kristeva 2006a, 59). However, the question concerning this conversion must be raised. What effectuates the passage between systems and what guarantees not only the movement of sensation and signification among one another but also what enacts their formal shift in thetic position? Once again, a formal and generative process is required. Even though the chapter where transposition is introduced concentrates primarily on the psychic process of mimesis, elsewhere in Kristeva's writing, there is evidence that suggests rhythm is equally responsible for the transposition underlying her notion of intertextuality.

A few chapters after her introduction to the process of transposition, Kristeva invokes an operation she calls "instinctual rhythm." She (2006a) writes, "As a provocation for the subject, instinctual rhythm simultaneously posits and passes through the object" (99). Rhythm's instinctual power to both pass through and posit objects in thetic consciousness make it a compelling candidate for the semiotic process underlying Kristeva's notion of transposition. Elsewhere, when criticizing linguistics' attempt to assume a metalinguistic position of analysis, Kristeva (2006b) writes, "The speech practice that should be its object is one in which signified structure (sign, syntax, signification) is defined within boundaries that can be shifted by the advent of a semiotic rhythm that no system of linguistic communication has yet been able to assimilate" (24). This statement suggests that a semiotic rhythm is what shifts and transposes signifying structures into one another; a process metalinguistic approaches fails to account for due to their neglect of the immanent dynamics at work within the signifying process. Since these processes take place within the genesis of language, they cannot be gleaned by attempts to analyze them from a theoretical position purportedly outside of language.

Transposition is characterized by a unique form of creative passage within the signifying process. As a passage through signifying systems and a new articulation of the thetic from out of its passage, transposition preserves the economy of the thetic while creatively disrupting it. Kristeva (2006a) writes, "Mimesis and poetic language do not therefore disavow the thetic, instead they go through it (signification, denotation) to tell the 'truth' about it" (60).[6] This truth is a "second truth" that reveals an underside to the "first truth" of the symbolic by superseding it through a semiotic impetus which in turn transforms it.

Thinking transposition in terms of rhythm sheds light on the "instinctual intermediary" Kristeva identifies between signifying systems that become transposed. She (2006a) writes, "Transposition plays an essential role here inasmuch as it implies the abandonment of a former sign system, the passage to a second via an instinctual intermediary common to the two systems, and the articulation of the new system with its new representability" (60). The "instinctual rhythm" brought forth a few chapters later suggests that rhythm is a peculiar kind of passage through sign systems and their common instinctual intermediary.[7] Thinking of rhythm as the instinctual intermediary between signifying systems shows how signification is permeated with and permutated by rhythms that exceed signification but nonetheless come to revive and reorganize the signifying process. As a dynamism proper to the semiotic *chōra*, rhythm traverses psyche and soma by opening signification onto powers harbored in the body, which alter its power to signify.

The body's intersensory transpositions and synesthetic encounters are woven together by the intimate rhythms it builds with the sensible world. Moreover, the psyche follows the senses and is drafted by each rhythmic entanglement, which ensnares the body in its affective relations to the world. The advent of a semiotic rhythm shifts discursive registers and forges connections in signification within the psyche. Rhythm effectuates the passage of sensation and signification by corresponding the senses and altering the thetic position of signification. In this way, rhythm gives rise to novel forms of sense within the signifying process by transposing implicit messages of intersensory correspondences into poetic fabulations. As a simultaneous passage through and trans-positing of thetic consciousness, rhythm can be seen as a dormant power of innovation and integration underlying Kristeva's notion of transposition.

Rhythm and the Effraction of the Thetic

Images of shattering, tearing, and pulverizing are scattered throughout *Revolution in Poetic Language*. While attempting to follow the text's own semiotic currents, one stumbles on upheavals in its exposition that mark entries of the semiotic into its own signification. Earlier, we noted how the effraction of the thetic by the semiotic serves as a condition for the process of transposition. This effraction is at once an institution of the symbolic and a possibility for its renewal. Kristeva cautions against understanding the relation of the semiotic to the symbolic as foundational or transcendental. She (2006a) explains that "Although originally a precondition of the symbolic, the semiotic functions within signifying practices as a result of the transgression of the symbolic. Therefore, the semiotic that 'precedes' the symbolic is only a *theoretical supposition*" (68).

The effraction of the thetic retroactively discloses the semiotic as a coterminous dynamic enfolded within the symbolic. Thus, the semiotic does not "precede" the symbolic in practice but exceeds it by hearkening on the powers that institute its break into the signifying process. She (2006a) affirms that "the semiotic we find in signifying practices always comes to us after the symbolic thesis, after the symbolic break" (68). The semiotic thus only appears après-coup as a result and condition of signifying practice in its spontaneous generation. For Kristeva, the poetic language of writers like Mallarmé, Lautréamont, and Artaud enact a violence endemic to the symbolic order. However, this enactment is not accomplished by fiat and does not arise out of decisions made by these authors. Instead, the shattering of the symbolic that takes place in poetic language happen through rhythms that do not simply repeat the symbolic order but renew it by dismantling that order, exporting semiotic impulses across its attempts to signify.

At work in Kristeva's notion of rejection is an energetic "logic of renewal" that she opposes to the logic of repetition.[8] Rejection, she (2006a) writes, "constitutes the key moment shattering unity, yet it is unthinkable outside of unity, for rejection presupposes thetic unity as its precondition and horizon, one to be always superseded and exceeded" (147). The logic of renewal she elucidates is irremediably tied to a violence that shatters the unity of comprehension but is nonetheless unthinkable without such unity. As the semiotic presupposes the symbolic break for its irruption into the symbolic, so does rejection presuppose thetic unity as a precondition for its shattering. In other words, only that which is first unified can be shattered and only that which comes after the thetic break can renew its possibility. Kristeva is equally vigilant about not positing rejection as an origin of the thetic, as she is about not conceiving the semiotic as an original precondition for the symbolic. In lieu of an origin, she describes the law of rejection as "one of returning, as opposed to one of becoming; it returns only to separate again immediately" (147). The law of return and the logic of renewal that belong to rejection are neither a return to unity nor a repetition of the self-identical. Instead, the rejection that shatters the unity of thetic consciousness and renews the thetic break happens according to expenditures carried about by rhythms. Rhythm is neither a return to origin nor a repetition of identity but an expenditure that passes through the thetic and reveals its anarchic break into signification, providing a chance for its renewal.[9]

In poetic language, the anarchy of signification comes into expression. The kind of poetic expression that has the power to renew language exceeds the constraints that allow it to be a vehicle of communication. Apart from communication, poetry seeks invention. Poetry pierces through the limits of signification, not by arresting them and retreating into nonsense, but by detonating the means of communication and unleashing their semiotic elements. Kristeva notes that poetic language is not "immobilized in an unthinking inertia; instead, it shatters conceptual unity into rhythms, logical distortions (Lautréamont), paragrams, and syntactic inventions (Mallarmé)" (2006a, 186). The effraction of the thetic is wrought by the rhythms that come to destabilize its unity. Nevertheless, the function of rhythm in poetic texts is not only to disrupt the symbolic but to reactivate a violence proper to it and to break open its unforeseen capability. Rhythm comes to renew the static dictates of conceptual unity by opening it onto its genesis, which it must repress in order to stabilize thetic consciousness.

Rather than repeat the symbolic, rhythm provides a means of surpassing its limits in order to renew its possibility. Kristeva (2006a) notes that the unbounded release of energy in rejection "obeys a certain regulating process, which we have called the *semiotic*" (172). After the semiotic breach of the thetic, not only does rhythm offer regulation but a response to the demand for a new articulation of the thetic in poetic language. By entering the rhythm of poetic language, we are put in touch with its semiotic insurrection and open ourselves to a birth of sense that happens at the limits of signification. Rhythm facilitates the practice and experience of "the text." The text, Kristeva writes, "is a trans-subjective and trans-phenomenal experience. In other words, the text shatters, and rebinds experience in the process" (187). Putting experience to the test, rhythm takes one into the text as an experience of limits, which confront us with struggles deposited in language and afflictions that lurk at the borders of its articulation.

Rhythm and the Text as a Practice

We emphasized how rhythm is not a purely theoretical concept in Kristeva's work but is more importantly a practice. To further clarify this practice, rhythm must be situated in the practice Kristeva calls "the text." As the fourth and final signifying practice she outlines, the text is first described as an "endless rhythm" that passes beyond implicit laws in the signifying process while questioning and transforming its boundaries from within (2006a, 99–101). Kristeva distinguishes the text from narrative, metalinguistic analysis, and theory. However, the practice of the text cannot be divorced from these other discursive practices but instead acts on them by suffusing their symbolic order with drives that disrupt their continuity. Kristeva explains that "The drive process cannot be released and carried out in narrative, much less in metalanguage or theoretical drifting. It needs a text" (103). The drive process needs a text to be released in practice, but the text must be able to infiltrate and transmogrify these other discursive practices in its execution. The text usurps the other three signifying practices in the following manner: "The text must move through them; it cannot remain unaware of them but must instead seep into them, its violent rhythm unleashing them by alternating rejection and imposition" (103). The text invades discursive practices by casting them into rhythms that awaken a violence dormant beneath their symbolic valence. The theoretical attitude, the metalinguistic position, and the schema of grand narratives are thrown into question through a text practice that sets the symbolic aflame by exposing it to a semiotic paroxysm.

Practicing texts involves undergoing a turmoil that removes the protections lent by the symbolic order. Leading into furies compressed within discourse, the text exposes the symbolic to its semiotic premonitions, which animate its development but cannot be appropriated by its signifying order. For this reason, the text cannot be grasped, surveyed, or subsumed under stories or statements made about it but must be practiced and carried out according to a decree that emerges in the course of its own unfolding. This kind of practice poses a threat to ordinary habits of theoretical discourse. Kristeva (2006a) suggests that as theorists "We read signifiers, weave traces, reproduce narratives, systems, and driftings, but never the dangerous and violent crucible of which these texts are only the evidence" (103–4). To experience the danger and violence of a text, the intellectual tendency to decipher and capture its signification must be renounced. This is not merely a matter of letting one's guard down but of becoming displaced by and vanishing into a text. Through the rhythm of a text, we displace ourselves by means of a vertigo that brings forth latent powers in language that resist signification but nonetheless provoke its transfiguration.

A text involves its writer and reader in a drama that exceeds them. In order to enter the "violent crucible" of the text, Kristeva calls upon rhythm as the very means through which writer and reader become plunged into it. She (2006a) writes, "Going through the experience of this crucible exposes the subject to impossible dangers: relinquishing his identity in rhythm, dissolving the buffer of reality in a mobile discontinuity, leaving the shelter of the family, the state, or religion" (104). One's identity is relinquished through a rhythm that carries them into the text and carries the text out through them. We can see how rhythm accomplishes a dissolution of identity and dismantles the shelter afforded by the symbolic. The paradox of the subject in the text is that the subject appears only when it disappears; that is, the subject is revealed as the absence through which the text appears. In order for the text to appear, writer and reader must disappear into the text. Rhythm is a way the subject disappears into the text, thereby allowing the practice of the text to appear. In other words, rhythm is a way for the text as a practice to take place. But for Kristeva, the text *is* the place of its own taking place; a place where "nothing shall have taken place, except the place" (210).[10] Rhythm lets the place of the text take place by passing the subject into its autonomous organization.

In order for the text to take place, the focal addressee to which the signifying process is directed must be abolished. Kristeva understands this dative relation to be a relation of transference. When the signifying process is no longer addressed *to* someone, it becomes able to encounter signifying structures themselves. She (2006a) writes, "To hamper transference, the text's analysis must produce the certainty that the analysts place is empty, that 'he' is dead, and that rejection can only attack signifying structures" (209). Rejection is able to transgress and transform the boundaries within the signifying process once that process is redirected toward its own matrix of enunciation. Then, the practice of the text becomes a form of revolt that calls the symbolic order into question. The text becomes an active form of delirium, absent not only of an addressee but also of an addresser. However, by dissolving its writer and reader into a semiotic rhythm, the text breaks open the subject's narcissistic imprisonment and frees its signifying process from the forces that command the directions of its discourse. The text seeks to ignite a stimulus of revolution latent in language, it attempts to break the social order by shattering the symbolic order, enduring a madness that might undo the logic of its oppression. For Kristeva, the text is a way for theoretical discourse to open its conceptual unity onto a madness that exceeds it and thus has the power to transform it. The semiotic rhythm set forth in the text practice provides a medium through which poetic language attempts its revolution.

A Structural Sketch of Semiotic Rhythm

The final chapter of part 1 in *Revolution in Poetic Language* titled "Four Signifying Practices" provides a reference to rhythm's semiotic structure that I wish to bring into view. I will attempt to provide a phenomenological and psychoanalytic account of rhythm's semiotic structure, even though Kristeva bases this structure on the literary device the *anaphora*. The etymological roots of the word *anaphora* suggest a process of "carrying back," as the literary device is one where the initial utterance of a phrase is carried back over to begin the next, creating a rhythm and momentum within its full expression. One memorable anaphoric expression of the twentieth century occurs in Martin Luther King's "I Have a Dream" speech, where King echoes the phrase "let freedom ring"; "*So let freedom ring* from the prodigious hilltops of New Hampshire. *Let freedom ring* from the mighty mountains of New York. *Let freedom ring* from the heightening Alleghenies of Pennsylvania." The deeply rhythmic character of the anaphora is what makes it such a powerful and memorable literary device. Kristeva first highlights the important semiotic dimension of the anaphora in the last chapter of part 1 in *Revolution in Poetic Language*, when she writes: "The text's semiotic distribution is set out in the following manner: when instinctual rhythm passes through ephemeral but specific theses, meaning is constituted but is then immediately exceeded by what seems outside meaning: materiality, the discontinuity of real objects. The process' matrix of enunciation is in fact *anaphoric* since it designates an elsewhere: the *chōra* that generates what signifies" (2006a, 100). From this excerpt, we can see how the passage of rhythm through the thetic threshold signals a return into the semiotic *chōra* from which that rhythm emerged. Rhythm carries the semiotic sense into the symbolic and designates an "elsewhere" which is none other than the semiotic *chōra* from which it arose. The semiotic distribution Kristeva alludes to is a rhythmic distribution wherein the semiotic and the symbolic enter a dynamic exchange by virtue of a rhythmic efficacy accomplished by the anaphora. One does not merely "read" the anaphora but is *carried* into the semiotic rhythm from which the anaphora arose and through which its sense was generated. This passage gives us a first clue to a potential semiotic structure of rhythm in *Revolution in Poetic Language*. A few chapters later, a discussion of the anaphora reappears, but this time in an even more suggestive way which sheds light on rhythm's semiotic structure.

In the concluding paragraph of her chapter on "Negativity as Transversal to Thetic Judgment," Kristeva describes a creative procedure within those practices of experimental writing that she is dedicated to and so keenly aware of. Here, she provides not only a propaedeutic for a semiotic practice but gives an indirect structural account of how the semiotic subject immerses itself in the symbolic order and how the symbolic becomes reworked in semiotic practice. She (2006a) writes: "The subject moves through the linguistic network and uses it to indicate—as in anaphora or in a hieroglyph—that the linguistic does not represent something real posited in advance and forever detached from instinctual process, but rather that it experiments with or practices the objective process by submerging in it and emerging from it through the drives" (126). We can see how, for Kristeva, linguistics is not something that can be separated from the body's instinctual drives, nor can it be fully accounted for by metalinguistic theories. Thus, practicing the "objective process" of the linguistic network involves a submersion into the instinctual drives in order to provoke an emergence from the semiotic *chōra* in the symbolic. The semiotic practice of art and literature thus provide a concrete practical knowledge of the conditions and corporeal genesis of language.

Once again, we should caution here and not reduce Kristeva's understanding of the semiotic to a "subjectivist" theory, which would ground the practices of art and literature in personal values. To view art or literature as irreducibly subjective is to miss the trans-subjective character of instinctual drives which circulate within sociolinguistic milieus as much as they do within subjectivity. Such a view ignores Kristeva's original revision of Hegelian negativity through the Freudian death drive in her notion of rejection. In the chapter "Negativity as Transversal to Thetic Judgment," Kristeva (2006a) writes, "*The sole function of our use of the term "negativity" is to designate the process that exceeds the signifying subject, binding him to the laws of objective struggles in nature and society*" (119).[11] Kristeva's italicization of this sentence and stress on "objective laws" shows an awareness of a potential misreading that would reduce her theory of the semiotic to the subject. Thus, the rhythmic submersion into the instincts underlying language is not merely a retreat into a solely subjective consciousness but is a fall into the unconscious and social struggles that plague history. Poetic practice and its experiments in sense are not theoretical objects but expenditures of forces that reconfigure the signifying process and resuscitate thetic consciousness. Rhythm is not a theoretical insight made about the unconscious sources of poetry but a manifestation of unconscious forces latent in the signifying processes. Kristeva writes, "Poetic rhythm, does not constitute the acknowledgment of the unconscious but is instead its expenditure and implementation" (164). Similarly, she describes the process of rejection as one that "pulsates through the drives in a body that is caught within the network of nature and society" (122). Viewed from an understanding of Kristeva's notion of rejection, we can see how the structure of semiotic rhythm exceeds the subject by plunging it into trans-subjective forces that govern language and economize desire.

Kristeva's description of experimental art and writing practices cited above bring to light a semiotic structure at work in the rhythm that underlies the anaphora. In recasting thetic consciousness as a permeable boundary, she brings phenomenology and psychoanalysis into conversation, transposing them into one another. From her description of the semiotic practice of experimental writing as a submersion of thetic consciousness into the semiotic *chōra* and an emergence from the semiotic back into the symbolic, one can take notice of how this relies on an essential rise-fall structure. Expressions like "raising consciousness," "gives rise to," "arises from" and conversely "falling in love," "falling apart," or "falling asleep" attest to such a rise-fall structure. Phenomenologically speaking, this structure exhibits *anathetic* and *catathetic* phases of consciousness.[12] The anathetic phase is the emergent semiotic articulation as it rises up and passes through the thetic phase. The catathetic phase issues a fall wherein the thetic suffers a gravitation pull toward the unconscious and fades from thetic consciousness.

Following Kristeva, we can map these phenomenological phases onto the semiotic practice she describes in terms of a submersion into the semiotic and an emergence from the semiotic. The thetic submersion undergoes a "catagenetic" spiral into the semiotic drives whereas the semiotic emergence unfolds in anathetic pulsations whereby semiotic articulations take shape as they turn into more discrete significations. This rise-fall structure within consciousness is best understood in terms of Kristeva's notion of rejection. For Kristeva, rejection is both a psychoanalytic and phenomenological concept. She (2006) writes: "Our conception of rejection will oscillate between the two poles of drives and consciousness, and this ambiguity will reveal the ambiguity of process itself, which is both divided and unitary. But to the extent that these two threads (drives and consciousness) intersect and interweave, the *unity of reason* which consciousness sketches out will always be shattered by the *rhythm* suggested by drives" (148). Situating the semiotic structure of rhythm within Kristeva's notion of rejection underscores its intermediary status as that which traverses the conscious-unconscious threshold in semiotic practice. We see how rhythm's semiotic weight has the power to shatter not only the linguistic chain but the unity and organizing principle of reason itself. Elsewhere, Kristeva speaks of rhythm as "trans-logical."[13] The theme of rhythm's *transversal function* is highlighted at the end of the chapter on "Negativity as Transversal to Thetic Judgment." There, she describes the subject of enunciation not as a fixed point but as a process of expenditure. In the full thrall of a poetic rhythm, one passes through the instinctual organs of a text that inscribe the semiotic *chōra* into symbolic figurations. Kristeva (2006a) concludes the chapter by noting that "The best metaphor for this transversal rhythmicity would not be the grammatical categories it redistributes, but rather a piece of music or a work of architecture" (126). Rhythm's transversal function takes advantage of the rise-fall structure of consciousness in order to break through restrictions in discourse and shatter the unity of reason.

Psychoanalytically speaking, this rise-fall structure can be linked to Freud's theory of unbound and bound cathexis. Following Breuer, Freud (1989) notes that "charges of energy occur in two forms; so that we have to distinguish between two kinds of cathexis . . . a freely flowing cathexis that presses on towards discharge and a quiescent cathexis" (35). The irruption of a semiotic rhythm into speech or writing is unleashed as a form of unbound energy cathexis that takes shape in anathetic phases of consciousness as a rhythm passes through the thetic boundary, giving rise to signification. Conversely, the disintegrations of signification and the decay of verbal articulation mark catathetic phases that draw the signifying process back into the unconscious economy of bound cathexis. To use Aristotelian language, we can say that the unbound-bound cathexis economy is the material cause of rhythm's transversal function, whereas the rise-fall structure of the anathetic-catathetic phases is the formal cause. These are a few preliminary sketches intended to help clarify the semiotic structure of rhythm in Kristeva's work. By understanding this structure more fully, we might gain better access to the semiotic in texts understood as practices rather than a better concept of the semiotic in texts understood as a theory.

Rhythm and Philosophical Practice

To conclude, I would like to suggest that rhythm's transversal function and semiotic structure are at work not only in the practices of art and literature, but additionally within philosophical thinking as well. A close review of Hegel's account of speculative logic in the Preface to the *Phenomenology of Spirt* and Gadamer's hermeneutic logic of question and answer in part 3 of *Truth and Method* suggest not only a latent rhythmic structure within each logic, but also a semiotic element that comes to characterize the event of philosophical insight. Without reviewing each in extensive detail, I suggest that rhythm's transversal or trans-logical function in Kristeva can be read as central to Hegel's speculative logic and Gadamer's hermeneutic logic. In *Desire in Language*, Kristeva (2006b) draws attention to rhythm's capacity to produce "instinctual breakthroughs" that she finds "situated at the most intense place of naming" (167). We have already noted how, for Kristeva, instinctual rhythm is what passes through objects of thetic consciousness and trans-posits those objects into one another. In *Desire in Language*, Kristeva offers another telling formulation regarding rhythm, consciousness, and instinct. She writes, "Consciousness in rhythm and instinctual drive, instinctual drive and rhythm in consciousness: they are the repossession and representation of delirium and the loosening of this repossession and representation" (180).[14] Rhythm thus rattles and repossesses representational thinking and provokes the delirious breakthroughs of nonrepresentational sense. We find a similar process at work in Hegel's speculative logic.

When first explaining his speculative logic in paragraphs 56–62 of the *Phenomenology*, Hegel speaks of a peculiar "counterpunch" that representational thinking suffers when encountering the speculative proposition. Representational thinking, Hegel (2019) writes, "is impeded in its course by what in the proposition has the form of a predicate being the substance itself. It suffers, to picture it in this way, from a counter-punch" (38). For Hegel, speculative propositions come as a blow or punch to one's thought as the speculative predicate violates the predicate-subject structure of representational thinking. This "blow" or "counterpunch" of the speculative proposition can be seen as a semiotic upsurge within the speculative insights of the *Phenomenology*. Speculative propositions do not ensure easy and effortless insight. Instead, they arise as a violence or counterpunch to normal habits of thinking. The baffling propositions that occur throughout Hegel's writings produce pauses or caesuras where the reader suffers the force of a speculative sense. This semiotic counterpunch of speculative predication and the sublation of the subject into the predicate is, Hegel tells us in paragraph 61, held together by *rhythm* (39). Rhythm is thus what gives rise to the speculative breakthrough and sublates that breakthrough into the knowing element of the whole. This accounts for the provocative statement Hegel makes in paragraph 56 of the Preface to the *Phenomenology*, that "This alone is the rational, the rhythm of the organic whole" (35). We find analogous statements made by Kristeva in *Desire in Language* that concern an affinity between rhythm and rationality. She (2006b) notes how the Hegelian *Aufhebung* necessitates an intensification of the signifying process which push it beyond the limits of the subject-predicate structure, concluding that in the *Aufhebung*, "instinctual rhythm becomes logical rhythm" (173).

Indebted to Hegel's speculative logic, Gadamer's hermeneutic logic of question and answer also suggests a semiotic dimension to philosophical thought. In particular, the semiotic mode of insight takes place in what he calls "the hermeneutic priority of the question" and the "sudden idea." Gadamer (2011) writes, "A question occurs to us that breaks through into the open and thereby makes an answer possible. Every sudden idea has the structure of a question. But the sudden occurrence of the question is already a breach in the smooth front of popular opinion" (366). Following Kristeva, we can understand this breach in terms of a semiotic rhythm and irruption into thetic consciousness. Questions that pose themselves and ideas that suddenly occur to us arise as a semiotic impetus that begins a process of philosophical reflection. Moments of insight and profound breakthroughs rupture the organization of consciousness in ways that are not purely intellectual but are patently semiotic. Thus, I suggest there is revolutionary potential just as much in philosophical thinking as there is in poetic language. Both Hegel and Gadamer's logic rely on an underlying rhythmic structure that helps bring confusion to clarity within the whole of thinking, which necessarily includes the unthought element of thinking. The event of thinking and its reception as thought are enveloped by rhythms that express the full experience of philosophical insight. We find not only a semiotic dimension within the "logic" of philosophical thought outlined by Hegel and Gadamer, but also a rhythmic structure that traverses the boundary between philosophical insight and common opinion.

Conclusion

This essay has attempted to provide a preliminary sketch of the structure of semiotic rhythm in Kristeva's work and to show the vital role rhythm plays in *Revolution in Poetic Language*. Furthermore, it has sought to explicate Kristeva's notion of transposition in terms of rhythm and show how rhythm is essential to her understanding of the text as a practice. After this study of rhythm and the semiotic in Kristeva's work, I hope new avenues for further research in phenomenology, psychoanalysis, and semiotics become available. The aim of this project has been to retrieve rhythm in Kristeva's work so as to gain greater clarity into her understanding of

Rhythm and the Semiotic in Revolution in Poetic Language | 251

the semiotic. The task ahead involves bringing these insights into a deeper conversation with phenomenology and psychoanalysis to generate a more thorough intertextual engagement dedicated to the question of rhythm.

Notes

1. There is one scant section titled "Rhythm and Death" in her essay "The Ethics of Linguistics." This section occupies a mere page of this short essay and is far from a comprehensive treatment of rhythm as a whole.

2. Kristeva (2006a) writes, "the *chōra* precedes and underlies figuration and thus specularization, and is analogous only to vocal or kinetic rhythm" (26).

3. Benveniste (1997) has shown that "ῥυθμός, according to the contexts in which it is given, designates the form in the instant that it is assumed by what is moving, mobile and fluid, the form of that which does not have organic consistency; it fits the pattern of a fluid element, of a letter arbitrarily shaped, of a robe which one arranges at one's will, of a particular state of character or mood." Benveniste concludes that "We can now understand how ρυθμός meaning literally "the particular manner of flowing" could have been the most proper term for describing "dispositions" or "configurations" without fixity" (285–86).

4. Kristeva often speaks of rhythm and "intonation" in the same breath. Glossolalia, echolalia, and murmurs within texts are equally compelling candidates for this function but are given far less treatment by Kristeva.

5. This is the central theme of Marxist and social critic Henri Lefebvre's late work *Rhythmanalysis*.

6. Kristeva describes this truth as a "second truth" that is cleared by a "first truth" of signification or *Bedeutung* in order to produce a confrontation with signification. Later, Kristeva (2006a) notes that a text's independence from the transference relation "deprives the text of immediate truth criteria" (cf. 209). The question of truth in poetry finds some relief in her statement that as "neither true nor false, their truth consists in the ability to participate in the process of contradiction which, logically and historically, both includes and goes beyond them" (222).

7. See pages 96–104 in *Revolution in Poetic Language* for Kristeva's treatment of "instinctual rhythm."

8. Cf. 172 in *Revolution in Poetic Language* for Kristeva's account of rejection's logic of renewal.

9. Kristeva connects the emergence of the symbolic to sacrifice and art. She (2006a) writes, "Sacrifice reminds us that the symbolic emerges out of material continuity through a violent and unmotivated leap" (78). Bracketing the anthropological thesis regarding sacrifice, I lay emphasis on the violent character of this emergence and interpret its "unmotivated leap" as an anarchic break.

Such a break not only provides a chance but *is* chance, which sets "a throw of the dice." As a second function of the thetic, poetic language is an "opening onto semiotic vehemence and its capacity for letting jouissance come through" (2006a, 80). Poetry thus becomes "an explicit confrontation between jouissance and the thetic" (2006a, 81); cf. 74–84 on the two events that institute the symbolic order.

10. This phrase of Mallarmé's is repeated in section IV, "Practice." Cf. Kristeva (2006a, 210–15).

11. Further, on page 124 she (2006a) writes, "True negativity is a dialectical notion specific to the signifying process, on the crossroads between the biological and social order on the one hand, and the thetic and signifying phase of the social order on the other."

12. I have invented these terms with the aim of providing more detailed and focused research in phenomenology and semiotics. I believe that what they illuminate, and their application might shed light on more nuanced and liminal experiences of consciousness as well as pave the way for understanding the genesis of semiotic expression more thoroughly.

13. She (2006b) writes, "Poetry is a practice of the speaking subject consequently implying a dialectic between limits, both signified and signifying, and the setting of a pre- and trans-logical rhythm solely within this limit" (27).

14. Hegel once referred to a "logical instinct" in his *Science of Logic*, one which he thought guided the speculative spirit of the German language.

References

Benviniste, Émile. 1997. *Problems in General Linguistics*. Translated by M. E. Meek. Coral Gables, FL: University of Miami Press.

Freud, Sigmund, and James Strachey. 1989. *Beyond the Pleasure Principle*. New York: Norton.

Gadamer, Hans-Georg. 2011. *Truth and Method*. New York: Continuum.

Hegel, Georg Wilhelm Friedrich, et al. 2019. *The Phenomenology of Spirit*. New York: Cambridge University Press.

Kristeva, Julia. 2006a. *Revolution in Poetic Language*. New York: Columbia University Press.

———. 2006b. *Desire in Language: A Semiotic Approach to Literature and Art*. New York: Columbia University Press.

———. 2006c. "The Speaking Subject." In *Structuralism: Critical Concepts in Literary and Cultural Studies*, edited by Jonathan D. Culler, 282–92. New York: Routledge.

Lefebvre, Henri, Stuart Elden, and Gerald Moore. 2013. *Rhythmanalysis: Space, Time and Everyday Life*. London: Bloomsbury.

Merleau-Ponty, Maurice. 2014. *Phenomenology of Perception*. New York: Routledge.

Chapter 12

Excription and the Negativity of the Speaking Subject

Reading Kristeva with Heidegger

EMILIA ANGELOVA

Julia Kristeva recovers the speaking subject at a time when theories of language and subjectivity in the 1970s linguistic turn ignored the role of the body and insufficiently attended to the event of speaking. As Kelly Oliver recognized, Kristeva attempts to "bring the speaking body back into discourse" (1991, 6). To do this, Kristeva argues that in the newborn infant the logic of language is already operating at the material level of bodily processes; in addition, bodily drives continually and relentlessly make their way into language anew. That is, signifying practices are at once the origin and the result of material bodily processes at work, in a continuous memory of the present.

I will attempt to show that from *Revolution in Poetic Language* (1974) to her later work, *Hatred and Forgiveness* (2005), Kristeva develops an ethics of aesthetics, a temporal constitution, an ethics of the ontology of the body—of the speaking body—through her "signifying practices" (1984, 123). Negativity or genuine negation—what she calls Hegel's "fourth negation" (109, 125)—which underlies the idea of signifying practice, introduces the construction of a subject whose foundation is creative and productive of meaning since it is premised on the possibility of sublimation. I understand this theory of sublimation as introducing a futurity, which is in turn premised on a theory of excription (Jean-Luc Nancy 1986, 20), signifying the exteriority of freedom. While Kristeva does not use the word *excription*, she speaks in a similar way of the inscription of exteriority (110–13), to argue that exteriority is where meaning comes from.

The first half of this chapter takes up the possibility of the symbolic as founded on the premise of temporality—and the death drive—introduced since Freud, through Heidegger, and in Derrida's *Archive Fever*, which Kristeva theorizes as a dual foundation of the retrieval of meaning. Signifying practices are conduits of a dual authority of signification. Desire and its temporalization are structured on the same model, as is the death drive and temporalization. In the second half, I examine how Kristeva motivates her position of "the perversion of the mother-child link" and show that it is inclusive of the theory of signifying practices. Through the semiotic and its indebtedness to the fourth negation, she reappropriates the thought of *verwandelt*, "perversion"—from *The Phenomenology of Spirit*, Hegel's chapter "Force and Understanding," to reconnect negativity with alienation theory or idealization (*verwandelte Formen*) theory. This more radicalized praxis, which is never limited to the individual, is the foundation of the subject as constructed on the theory of sublimation.

Temporal Latency of Grief and the Nonphenomenological Moment in Kristeva

Sara Beardsworth makes a major contribution in exploring the negativity of the speaking subject. In four main points, set up against Freud, she argues that inscription in Kristeva is indebted to incomplete mourning, not melancholia. First, there has to be mimetic identification of the narcissistic double if there is to be a "history of language" (Beardsworth 2005, 67).[1] This emphasizes that the Lacanian or Freudian paternal metaphor (vs. the hallucinatory metaphor in Kristeva's *Powers of Horror*) does not, in some arbitrary way, break the subject who arrives as a latecomer, as slave to its values—to the social taboos, tradition, normativity. Second, Beardsworth urges that without a "pre-historical corporeal responsiveness" of the maternal, there would be "no inscription (mark) of the substrate" (67). This emphasizes the embeddedness of speech acts in the dynamic of the mother-infant dyad, not in the object as a random external signified.

Third, Beardsworth argues that Kristeva embeds unorthodox psychoanalytic practice to engage Modernity, the experience of a sense of loss, totalitarian structures taking over the social life of community in the 1970s, for example, similar to theorizing the sovereign in Foucault's *Society Must Be Defended*. Fourth, Beardsworth identifies this as theorizing the idealization (*verwandelte Formen* of alienation, the question of "materialism or idealism") of the complex, a perversion of the mother-child link and sublimation—for, Kristeva adds a pre-Oedipal neurosis, as Beardsworth explains (66),[2] a revival of hysteria, a "double reversal of desire" (Kristeva 1993, 88–89, 70–71).

Kristeva and Arendt, in Beardsworth, form a couple (Beardsworth 2017). Given the work on Arendt in Kristeva, it is worth reviewing. The above, on negativity, as I want to generalize this term for the moment, is to the effect that linguistic matricide is a psychic violence, a fantastical act of thinking that fails the authority of evaluation, and is in turn socially and symbolically sanctioned—but also is foreclosed for proper mourning under the code of social life of the bourgeois family. Beardsworth writes that Arendt did want to understand the form, intuition or knowledge, and passage to action (revolutions) as a question of ethics, that is, of morality. In Kristeva, the form of this passage to action need not take the form of an action in the world. Maternal reliance corresponds to unconditional love as a never-ending, limitless promise, as the inseparable duality of physical presence of the other (our complete dependency on the caregiver at the earliest stages) bound up with a certain abjecting of the maternal body (our complete reliance on the love that the mother will give to us). From this, Beardsworth puts forth the idea for a systematic reading of the latency of grief, which she understands as the "turn" informing the works of 1974 through 1997.[3] This is, "the unconscious inscribes semiotic meaning,"[4] which points out that the mode of retrieval of meaning in question is the inscription of the temporal latency of grief. Inscription operates as the middle term of memory of the present, where the past is not something bygone, and the question of the future "itself" presents as what comes and transforms, returns, repeats, haunts.

In sum, since 1974 and onward, in elaborating the structuring of the subject, Kristeva introduces neurosis of the pre-Oedipal kind, where there is loss, and this loss is separation from both nature and the maternal body and, in addition, is a resistance that has not been sublimated. The question of the subject, as Oliver argues, becomes a question about preserving the semiotic as the source of productive internal tension: the productive tension between the abjected mother (matricide that is a psychic violence causing anguish, since triggering relation to the abject) and the evaluating authority of the symbolic (causing anguish, since inflicting a fear of persecution). Internal abjective tension of the semiotic thus structures the subject (of the unconscious), split between two temporalities, which is uniquely Kristevan. I argue that, from the question about *archē*, this structuring is, more specifically, a writing, the future itself as return, and thirdness as return.

In the rest of this section, situating Kristeva on the continuum of the 1970s, I introduce her system of inscription as akin to an ethics of the semiotic aesthetic, as presupposing something intrinsic to the workings of internal tension that pushes phenomenology to its limits. Kristeva assumes that the ethical relation sets itself up within the system and code of language and yet is irreducible to it. So far as the inscription of the semiotic belongs to a dialectic of the mother-infant dyad, which is destined to assume symbolic identity, in recognition of the social role of self and other, Kristeva posits a right to freedom from complete subordination. To refer to this right, I use the term *excription*. An unlikely ally because of his opposition to psychoanalytic interpretation is Levinas—his motivation of the latency of grief, however, is helpful. Levinas, referred to in Kristeva (2018, 230, 233), recalls materiality and need, in the relationality of acts emphasizing the "food, drink, shelter," and "tenderness" that I offer "to" the other (cf. Nelson 2020, 82, 97). Materiality has no representation in the system of language; it is a diacritical form, subjecting the I anterior to the ego's will of self-mastery and self-control over my speech. The idea of ethics as responsibility to and for the Other is the paradox of my subjectivity, where the will is not an attribute that I possess. The paradox of my subjectivity is temporal since, constitutively, it happens "after the fact" of the encounter occurred by the relation of self to oneself. Yet, the recurrence of the self-relation is normative, because articulating the subjectivity of self is a possibility only in the account of realizing the priority of suspending violence against the "stranger" and the "child"—to use two of Levinas's images. This temporal recurrence of the institution of subjectivity (turning me inside out) through the encounter with the Other and all the others, in that "the Other has no Other," draws its motivation, nonetheless, from the ethical relation, and this is of interest to us. Not reducing subjectivity to the repetition of the same, and thus not demoting the other to the same, is a condition of the (im)possibility of this conversion, hence an ethics.

Simon Critchley (1998/2008)[5] comments on latent grief as that upon which the subject-in-process is constituted, likening Kristeva to Levinas, all while distinguishing both from Lacan. Critchley anchors two articles on Levinas on the "rebellion against signification of the Thing" (199). Namely, the rebellion against signification means that the Other has no representation, where the ethical is a prohibition sustained not through the Law as a metaphysical category, but rather through an excess of signification over subjectivity's own mark, an inscription. This prohibition underlying the relation "to" alterity depends on being sustained, as it were, without the Other's solicitude. At the expense of anguish so that the failure of the Other to make an appearance might be ensured, the ethical relation necessarily sets itself up as a loneliness of the witness. That subjectivity is engendered through the witness to and for the absence/presence of the Other—and it cannot be otherwise if ethics is to hold out—will be raised to the status of skepticism, a "pure question mark," as concerns the normativity of the ethical. At its own foundation, such an ethics is itself self-founding instituted by the Other and substituting for the act of intervention, as if provoked through the Other's giving, thus inaugurating a life. In *Black Sun*, Kristeva formulates the successor of abjection into the ego, not as correlate object, but hollowed out like a shadow—it follows me and casts a shadow, and thus, a sadness, and a propensity for melancholia in the person susceptible to the depressive position.

In Kristeva, ever since her early work, the ethical relation traces to Hegel. The fourth negation, as I show later, situates the nonphenomenological alongside ethics. Hegel engages the legacy of the French Revolution ("freedom toward the object," cf. Hegel, 1991, §10) as a republicanism (as does Levinas). Hegel argues that Culture, in the Enlightenment's battle with Faith, does not exhaust the concept. Rather, for Hegel, metaphysics, interpreted not as a Statism, but also not as a closed cultural system, resorts to ideas such as justice and time, which apply to empirical beings through the symbols of language and ties the ground of the relation to the Absolute. The ties map to a quasi-transcendental principle, unifying the subject over these symbols such that neither social institutions nor the individuals in them in a given epoch hold sway. Approached in this manner, in Hegel, there exists no way of overcoming an excess of heteronomy, the schism of substance inhering in itself as subject and never as predicate.

To restate, the objective world-historical movement of what is Hegelian negativity finds the *free* subject as emerging in structured, continuous movement. Kristeva adopts the movement from "comedy inherent in the Greek democracy" (1984, 128) and through the advent of revealed religion (which in the system of Spirit's Laws doubles with the death of aesthetic or "high" art), and through the logical totality traced in the French Revolution. In Hegel, the subject precisely does not strive toward an other in order to reduce it to the same. In fact, it's precisely the opposite.

That is, the dialectic of mark and sign in Kristeva draws from resources in Hegel, and as I will argue, negativity becomes the idea of temporal latency of grief: "But that an accident and such, detached from what circumscribes it, what is bound and is actually only in this context with others, should attain an existence of its own and the separate freedom—this is the tremendous power of the negative; it is the energy (*Energie*) of thought, of the pure 'I'" (1977, M19). The boldness of phenomenological articulation here stems from a negativity: the movement of the pure I is the freedom of excription. The pure I as self-foundation, and what was qualified as ethical relation in Levinas (above), is not posited in a subject anguished by an inaccessible sociality or transcendence. Negativity is "mediation," the objectivity of the movement that does not approach from a transcendent beyond to overtake the static *terms* of pure abstraction as a process. Kristeva adopts dissolving and binding these within a mobile law of thought.

To recap, in Kristeva, the exteriority of freedom is that it comes from the outside—the social community of those who have nothing in common (the "future" community), a community always constituting itself around no longer and not yet a "beyond," one building off a residue after transcending transcendence. Hegel posits that "[T]he consideration of the will's determinacy properly belongs to the Understanding and is in the first instance not speculative" (1991, §8). In that the will is determined in two senses, that is, in both content and form, it derives its determinacy in form from its purpose and the fulfillment of its purpose. But Hegel urges, "My purpose is at first only something inward, something subjective, but it should also become objective and cast aside the defect of mere subjectivity." "If what has a defect does not at the same time stand above its defect, it cannot recognize the defect as a defect" (1991, §8). In this aim of "unification of the unity," the "use" of the will is desire's "double reversal," which is a thematic of the withdrawal, of recession, and the breakup of this negative limit. This negative limit as a possibility of creativity, of agential potentialities, enters through the problematic of discourse—language as a dialectic of speech begins with alienation, *die Bildung* (1977, M594).

While considering her renewed interest in 1987, in contrast, in 1974, Kristeva had not yet revaluated how Heidegger belongs in the thematic of negativity. Passing through Heidegger, her work since 1987 forges a broad alliance between critical social theory, on the one hand, and equivalences in phenomenology and psychoanalysis of "liberating the death drive" (Derrida 1995), on the other. The important connection is that negativity takes on the dialectic of desire and a double reversal—expulsion toward and for the Other, and back to oneself—and overall, the question of the archive.

Below, I review how the 1970s influence from Heidegger directly concerns the fourth negation, Hyppolite's "genuine negation" in Hegel, and emphasizes the possibility of revaluation of the contribution to phenomenology by, and recommencement of her study of, Heidegger.

This particularly implies the bivalent modality of ontic-ontological (vs. subjectivity) attunement, mood, *Stimmung*, and I dwell for a moment on this (cf. Nancy 1993, 185; cf. Kristeva 2018, 265–67). Bringing the speaking body back into discourse begins expressly with Heidegger, specifically in how Kristeva articulates mood.

In *Being and Time*, no sooner than it opens to the ontic-ontological dimension of language (equiprimordiality of discourse, *Sprache*, with the phenomenon of mood, and silence, *Stille*)—being assailed in bad moods, Dasein flees the brute facticity of its being-delivered over to the *Stimmung*, the there, and is pulled into the world in the mode of everyday absorption. Attunement is disclosed in the mode of avoidance, abandon. Being opened out in disclosure, shattered up from within, delivers to the ambiguity of the comportment of Dasein; its "doing" at the same time conceals and unconceals, as in how one busies oneself with errands and tasks after the death of a loved one, or "throws oneself" into work after a breakup. *Jemeinigkeit*, one's own factical thrownness into the openness of Being announces itself as something we must bear; and simultaneously one's own thrownness into everyday-being-absorbed is that which Dasein attempts to avoid, to tranquilize this primary dimension. Kristeva makes a stipulation that we agree with Heidegger, just not with "disclosure." (cf. Kristeva 2018, 53).

Kristeva posits (in *Powers of Horror*) that the "doing" in Heidegger is a liability, an unstable relation to the ethical. Further, she posits Freud over Lacan on the notion of attaining language, privileging the "cry"—*der Nebenmensch schreit* (cf. Critchley 1999, Kristeva 1988). Accession to the word operates in oscillation, if not "echolalia," then at least with heightened "creativity," "bridge," or "affect subtending language." I will return to this in part 4. The bivalence of mood, as Heidegger stipulates, lies with its capacity for internally maintaining a contradiction to its anterior shapes without cutting its losses, more like a recording machine. The "priority" of attunement over the constituted individual announces itself as unforeseeable, occurring from without, in the way that Heidegger plays on the active and passive voice of the German verb *finding, finden*. He writes: "In attunement, Dasein is always-already brought before itself, it has always already found itself, not as perceiving oneself to be there but as one finds one's self in attunement" (Heidegger 2010, 132). Dasein always-already finds itself thrown in a field of meaningful relations. But all the same if Dasein can vanish to itself and to the other, the forgetting of Being and as well, the forgetting of the other, and it is so because what Dasein encounters is never bare life, but its environmental surround (cf. *Innenwelt* and *Umwelt*, above). It so encounters itself and the other in the modes of circumspection and concern outlined in Heidegger's analysis of World and Being-With. But Kristeva, as I show, inserts as precondition of the disruption a variation of bivalence—what she calls the perversion (of idealization, materialism, or idealism) of the mother-child link.

To sum up: Heidegger's attunement has the character of being affected or moved, founding the subject in a mode of circumspection that is other than the embeddedness in the object. The subject forms in the letting, the reversal, as he writes, "Letting something be encountered is primarily *circumspection*, not just as sensation or staring out at something. Letting things be encountered in a circumspectful heedful way has—we can see this now more precisely in terms of attunement—the character of being affected or moved" (133). In other words, for Heidegger, attunement is the existential structure for the *emergence* of "mattering." It is only because we are touched by the world in its mattering to us that things are "freed for" (*Gelassenheit*) their disclosure. The clue to transforming Kristeva's stance on Heidegger is that in 1952 he underscores the aesthetic creativity of the poet, the path "to" language, changing the relation to the word as signifying (yet not embedded in) the object, that is, the path of interpretation, that all linguistic signs are *res interpretans* (Kristeva 2018, 38; Heidegger, 29).

The *Chōra* and the Archive—Sublimation, Where Kristeva's Green Differs from Derrida

Derrida's 1994 *Archive Fever* differentiates between the process of "archiving" and the content actually being "archived." Beginning from the root word *Archē*, Derrida draws attention to its dual meanings: The first is the "physical, historical, or ontological principle" of where things come from (1). The second is the "nomological principle," or that which is concerned with law and authority. The Greek meaning of archive, *arkheion* is "home . . . residence of the superior magistrates, the archons" (2). Historically, the archons of ancient Greece were the "document guardians," wielding enormous power since they were in literal possession of the laws, and therefore they were the ones who could interpret them as they saw fit (2). "Archontic power" is that impulse which "gathers the functions of unification, identification, and classification" (2). This power must at the same time take on the shape of ordering, running through reflexively as the "power of consignation," the coordination of signs into a "single corpus . . . system or a synchrony in which all the elements articulate the unity of an ideal configuration" (3). On the one hand, is the "need" to categorize, to define all aspects of the world, which is felt by certain institutions (science, the state, capitalism, etc.)—the relation to the vertical Other. On the other hand, is this already categorization of political power; for it to be legitimate, it must control the archive since that means it controls, by extension, memory (4)—the question of the future itself as a concern of the horizontal, that is, the excription of the Other from the vertical.

Derrida's approach to writing is shared by Kristeva. This internally conflicted antinomian impulse, creative yet negating, is well known: Freud's "death drive." The key is the split nature of the death drive as such; it is the creator of archive and, simultaneously, its negation—the archive's opposite: *Anankē* or "invincible necessity" (10). This destructive impulse is, to Derrida, co-constitutive of the archive itself, always necessarily present; it is as diabolical evil is to God (12, 13). The death drive for Kristeva, likewise, in its threat to the archival desire, is precisely what sparks the "archive fever," desire itself. By 1974, Kristeva in this way reads Freud's *Beyond the Pleasure Principle* along with Hegel via Bataille, "paroxysmal bursts of death in life."

Kristeva already derives what Derrida calls "archival machines" and the future itself (14). The theoretical underpinnings of Freud's psychoanalytic model of memory, the "mystic pad," follow a sort of internalized instrument for recording (14, 15). Freud's model, the field of psychoanalysis, is valid for Kristeva. More organically than Freud, Kristeva will follow up on the mother-child amorous link (versus what Freud calls female subjectivity [see Kristeva 2012, 88]): "the technical structure of the archiving archive also determines the structure of the archivable content" (17).

Below I begin to demonstrate how sublimation and transference in Kristeva's works from around 2005 form intrinsic parts of the study of the negativity of the speaking subject—what Kristeva means by "liberating the death drive." The continual renewal of hope through creativity forms an intrinsic part of the extended notion of sublimation in Kristeva: "My research (on Proust, Colette, Céline, and others) has led me to believe that this paradigm of perversion might be the foundation for the subject constructed on the model of sublimation. There would be no sublimation creativity without a certain perversity of the mother/child link. Isn't the dead mother the mother of an artist?" (Kristeva 2005, 180). For Kristeva, the perverse mother-child link is a semiotic structure that is a necessary component for the individuation of the speaking subject. It refers to a tripartite foundation of the signifying process—the condition of possibility of puncturing the pure pleasure principle, namely, unconscious or unbounded activity; the splitting of the mother-infant dyad through the incorporation of the intrapsychic violence of rejection (by the mother, e.g., weaning off); and investing the reality principle or ego, awareness of consciousness, or bounded activity. Investment structurally depends on a fourth step, the unbinding accomplished through the advent of speaking, or, entrance into language. The individuation of the subject (that one is subject to language and its norms) is indebted to the work of the death drive, splitting as such. As I claim, the third party (the Name of the father, law of the Father, introjection taking it back in, and liberating the death drive) structurally is comparable to the theme of desire and temporalization, as reviewed above in Heidegger on mood, and Derrida on the archive.

In short, the mode of bringing back before itself is Heidegger's clue to the splitting, and via the negativity of the relation. Being brought back before itself functions as a mode of producing meaning, a delivery over to attunement of Dasein. This is so only if the character of internal modification or rupturing within language is a precondition for being, a capacity (cf. Freud's "A Note Upon the Mystic Writing-Pad," 1924) out of which is enabled the condition of (im)possibility of Being-in and being-with. The mode of Dasein's openness, one's own susceptibility to being delivered over to mood, owes to pure presencing as foundation in a metastable stasis, and Dasein is helpless before this susceptibility to being called back before (total recall) without a warning in advance. Heidegger explains this as a thematic of the schematism (of Imagination), a liability of the *focus imaginarius* in excess of both the transcendental and the empirical, as that standpoint without a visible scar of being, a mark, from out of which without a warning Being, or duty, calls. In Kristeva, this potentiality of Dasein for being brought back-before itself assumes the form of Speech Being (2005, 15–16). Speech Being is the enabling condition of resisting collapse of the freedom of the Other into a thing, reducing the Other to a mode of being-in-itself (vs. being-for-itself), and Kristeva adds if under proper conditions, it will enable reversal of desire, as a freedom, as a question concerning origin, self-beginning.

The prototype of the artist in Kristeva, the poet, is not the surrealist. For Benveniste, the social is a signifying space, like in Heidegger's Speech Being, it is announcing the word's relation to having a world and being in the world with others.[6] That is, the *enoncé* only can ascertain itself as positionality in language at the risk of surpassing limit (surpassing locking-in e.g., of echolalia). Benveniste claims the untranslatability of the *enoncé*, as though it's a closed axiology of value without which social language will have no meaning. When Kristeva insists that the drives "attack" metaphor—by which she means not the metalanguage of an overarching category of meaning in Lacan, but rather the negative drive force—the clash between two drives of opposite charges—life-death, love-hate, beginning-ending, libido-aggression—even as it forewarns, is nevertheless powerless in the face of time lapsing, curbing desire. What specifically relates artistic creativity, insofar as it forms a "word" to the temporal latency of grief, namely, the psychic violence of the fantastic murder of the mother, an act of poetry that is not a murder? Sublimation does.

In "Language, Sublimation, Women," Kristeva summarizes the main contributions to her understanding of the unconscious based on the analyst André Green. Chief among them is Green's reading of Freud's term *sublimation*, a defense mechanism of the ego that protects the conscious mind from thoughts and urges that are not socially acceptable through the production of alternative drives. Sublimation is generally considered a "positive" or mature defense mechanism, as it generates creative drives that are socially acceptable. Green interprets sublimation as having a double orientation: toward the object of the drive and toward itself as the ego.

As a result, sublimation is "a narcissistic [ego-oriented] retention of the life drive over the productions of the ego . . . [it] liberates death drive towards itself and towards others" (180). Sublimation has a productive role in child development, as "the death drive is activated by sublimation, and the paradigm of perversion assuming ego defences favours sublimatory processes" (180).

But Kristeva extends this claim and argues that "There would be no sublimation creativity without a certain perversity of the mother/child link" (180). The mother here is an object for the unconscious mind from which sublimation produces its drives, an object whose role in the Oedipal triangle requires reimagining (phantasm), given the dual character of Green's sublimation. For Kristeva the child is originally "wholly" a part of the mother. The child must suffer a "rejection" from the mother to be individuated, one that is internalized as an absence, and presence-absence: "Mama belongs to papa: I am left to console myself with her absence" (181). This rejection is due to the presence of the father, which is not the "ferocious father of the primitive horde" but "a third party between the child and the mother" (181) (cf. *Tales of Love*, 28).

That is, the mother retains a split function in the child, with eroticization (one has the desire to wholly subsume the object), and simultaneously prohibition (one has the desire to absolutely reject) as its poles. This split function is why the "dead" mother is the mother of the artist, as the prohibition of the mother produces creative drives via sublimation. It is also why the mother is a "perverse" object, as the mother can neither be completely appropriated nor rejected. Kristeva argues that the individuation that results from the rejection of the mother individuates the child specifically as a speaking subject: "We are still within the consequences of the 'double reversal': the ego invests the oedipal couple in the optimal manner, which allows it to invest the investment, that is, its own psychic functioning, and to become a speaking being" (181). This individuation of the subject through the rejection of the mother avoids the "trap" of the Lacanian empty signifier of the paternal metaphor whereby the unconscious is "enclosed" by linguistic science. Instead, the mother-child link is the "primary sublimation" that permits the individuation of the speaking child, its "perversity" a result of the split mother (182).

To summarize, Kristeva's aesthetic theory of investing the investment, becoming a speaking being, is an important part of theory of negativity (ultimately dual semiotic authority of signification). To theorize "perversity" as a result of the split mother, in her discussion on the

Excription and the Negativity of the Speaking Subject | 265

causes and expressions of female hysteria in 2005, Kristeva will introduce a pathological temporality, or atemporality, that is specifically the temporality of the unconscious. Hysteria is rooted in "traumatic memory" (132); this is a fundamentally somatic memory whose cognitive correlate is repressed, severed, or absent (145), whence the emergence of the symptom as an embodied complaint. The four primary "modes" of hysteria, namely, "passivization, the 'scene,' amnesiac dissociation, and somatization" (130) represent the various irruptions of "metapsychological" inscription into "temporal conscious representation" (150) by way of physical or somatic events. These modes are, in nature, indexical and lend themselves to observation and interpretation.

To elaborate on the nature of hysterical time, as founded on a traumatism taking place within unconscious temporality, Kristeva will introduce Bergson's contrasting concepts of "duration" and "abstract time" (135). As a result of the split mother, she finds that hysterical time lends itself to interpreting via Bergson's distinction between time experienced as an embodied, experiential continuity, as in duration; and then, the "succession of immobile sections" constituting abstract time (135). Abstract time refers to time as it is represented in consciousness and in memory, abstracted from the continuous experience of the subject and fixed imagistically. For Kristeva, hysterical time becomes a prototype of genuine negation, in that it is in search of a perverse iteration on the average "everyday" understanding of (inauthentic being) abstraction of cognitive representation. Above, we paid attention to Heidegger's theory of the splitting as such of Being, and the delivery over to mood in Dasein's abstract "doing," as latency of grief, seeking avoidance of fear of absorption. Here, in hysteric time, for Kristeva, the iteration is on the "immobility" proper to a temporal consciousness of sectioning—time "vanishes." It no longer appears in the context of linear succession. Rather, the oppressive immobility of unconscious temporality refers to its location outside (*aux des hors de temps*) the register of conscious representability. Again, in the symptom of embodied somatic complaint, the referral is viable on this condition, only insofar as this encompasses not only the abstraction of language and concepts but also the conscious experience of duration; of moving through time, and of control over memory of the past.

Kristeva's discussion of hysteria pivots to the possibility of the somatic functioning as a site of inscription that is anterior to, and divested from the regime of language and signification—and therefore, outside of "time." However, inscription, even "engraving" (141) insofar as it refers to the use of a system of signs to "mark" a substrate, already gestures to the difficulty in treating the somatic wholly on its own terms. Kristeva insists that the "spatial" region of somatic impact is relentlessly "temporalized," first, by the interruptions of the hysterical symptoms, and, second, by the attempt on the part of the analyst to convert "timelessness" to "the mobility of duration" (135). To sum up: through the analytic therapeutic session, the unconscious, for its part, becomes a place of (love, affective subtending) "passion," that is, where primary excitation is "metabolized" (151), namely, into a representation which is semiotic (the potentiality of rebelliousness of the semiotic), opens out to a suffering subjectivity, however "infralinguistic" (132) the opening may be.

In place of transition to the project of 1974, let me reiterate how the infralinguistic part of subjectivity relates to temporalization. From this perspective, it seems that there may be a benefit to recognize that the "sensoriality outside time" (147), which Kristeva characterizes as spatial and temporally immobile, may be better thought of as ongoing, and having a duration and a prepsychic trace of "memory" that is properly somatic. This is what I approached above through the question about the archive (Derrida) and the embodied complaint of the death drive as symptom of the splitting as such; and in Kristeva, this is furthermore a result of the split mother. Embedded in the statement by Freud, "the unconscious ignores time" (132), is a privileging of conscious time over somatic time. As much as the recurrence of the somatic symptom may disrupt and fracture conscious time, it must properly be thought of as recurrence, as the dynamism and development of somatic duration via Bergson, and Kristeva adds, as a result of the split mother. The analytic and interpretive hermeneutics of Kristeva invests with primarily psychic significations the fact that the "space" of somatic experience has a "timeless"/temporal ephemeral totality, not unlike inscribing the negativity of *chōra*—which bears attending to. Kristeva's infralinguistic part of subjectivity aligns with Green on the primacy of projective identification with the "dead" "unburied" mother.

In the next part, I clarify that repeating from the future—to this remembrance from the future itself—*Zeitlichkeit* in Heidegger of 1929, is a model of the "approach" of the Other in Kristeva, the ethical relation sets itself up in language: as dependency on liberating the death drive. This is simultaneously an iteration on the question about sublimation, as the perversion of the mother-child link. Hegel's *Rückfrage* and the labor of the fourth negation, which I take up in detail, will imply a consequence— namely, that the inversion cannot fully be removed.

Freud, the Speculative Hypothesis of the Death Drive and Hegel in 1974

In *Revolution in Poetic Language*, the rupturing force of heterogeneity is measured by the two strokes of the overthrow of dialectic (202–4). Kristeva verbatim appropriates this language of two overthrows of the dialectic, challenging Hegel. The first overthrow emphasizes that the "signifying subject never is," though its practices are (215). The real mainstay of meaningfulness is *signifiance*, practice, a "text" or "writing," that is, an interest in the object (the *analysandum*) orienting out of the sign as thirdness. The formation of the *analysandum* that sets Kristeva apart from Lacan, we know, is inaugural of the "interaction between," "indebtedness to" one another of semiotic and symbolic, and to the Other. The subject is constituted by the dialectic between the two and is thus "marked by an indebtedness to both" (24). For this move of the transcendental third or mediator, or transcendental signifier as semiotic, Kristeva argues that, if we adopt Hegel, what we are here observing are but effects of a negativity, as is language "itself" (Macdonald 2014, cf. Kristeva, 109). The second overthrow is the breaking up of the sign as this excess. She considers this excess to be a psychic negativity as "separate from the body proper and, *at the very moment of separation*, fixes it in place as absent, as a sign [. . .] as signifiable (which is to say, *already taken on as an object within the signifying system and as subordinate to the subject who posits it through the sign*)" (123, emphasis added).

"Paroxysmal contradiction," as Kristeva proposes in *Black Sun*, is the trace of sign, through the sign, the semiotic heterogeneity of language itself as "text" and semiotic signifying process, which reruns, gathers the trace (55). Semiotic trace as defined in *Revolution in Poetic Language*, is never actually present and yet "never without a remainder," as its composition masters the rule of the sign; "if it is lost, it can be refound," repetitions, iterations (25). Combining these traits as salient objections to the positivism of logico-mathematical and technological tools leads her to argue:

> The theory of meaning now stands at a crossroad: either it will remain an attempt at formalizing meaning systems by increasing sophistication of the logico-mathematical tools which enable it to formulate models on the basis of a conception (already rather dated) of meaning as the act of a transcendental ego, cut off from its body, its unconscious and also its history; or

> else it will attune itself to the theory of the speaking subject as a divided subject (conscious/unconscious) and go on to attempt to specify the types of operation characteristic of the two sides of this split, thereby exposing them to those forces extraneous to the logic of the systematic. (28)

Kristeva recognizes that the theory of meaning ought to turn away from abstract models and turn to the theory of the divided subject, where the two sides of the split conscious/unconscious are exposed to "forces extraneous to the logic of the systematic" (28). The operations are the semiotic and symbolic, and thetic. An overthrow of the dialectic, against Hegel as a backdrop recalls the extraordinarily dense division 1 of *Revolution in Poetic Language*. Throughout this remarkable division, we find Kristeva uniquely equipped for theoretical salient intervention into Hegel: of specific interest to us are formulaic expressions pointing to the "first does not actually take place until after the second is established," said in relation to Force, Hegel (32–33, 48–49). Likewise, in division one, Kristeva's main concern is explaining the "absence of the subject in the sign"—and yet, through putting imprints on the sign, the absence of the subject is posited as relation "to" the absence.

Kristeva's major concept of the fourth negation is that of true negativity or genuine negativity, as opposed to ideal negation, and proceeds from this dialectic in Hegel denoting excess. True negativity—rejection/repetition "constitutes the key moment shattering unity, yet it is unthinkable outside of unity, for rejection presupposes thetic unity as its precondition and horizon, one to be always superseded and exceeded" (147).

My position, in sum, is that Kristeva puts together Freud and Hegel and Heidegger to pursue what a pre-Oedipal formation of the subject would need to presuppose, if it is to be the basis for a more robust "right to intervention" in the social and reclaiming lost foundations, unrestricted solidarity (14, 15). The temporal aspect, *Nachträglichkeit* as overthrow and ontic-ontological force functions as systematic foundation in Kristeva from the very start, in the doctoral work, and it therefore presents itself as broadening to revolution. In Kristeva's coinage, *jouissance* and revolution (16, 17; 116), though, viewed from the perspective of the subject-in-process, like the *chōra*, the latter (revolution) is permanently a protective shield: when it functions without blocking (sexual) experience, a fluid "inside/outside." In *Black Sun*, this will become explicitly the negativity of the affect/structure or subject/outside structure, and "negativity of the speaking subject"—a trajectory outlined as follows: "Signs are arbitrary because language starts with a negation (*Verneinung*) of loss, along with the depression occasioned by mourning. 'I have lost an essential object that happens to be, in the final analysis, my mother,' is what the speaking being seems to be saying. 'But no, I have found her again in signs, or rather since I consent to lose her I have not lost her (that is the negation), I can recover her in language'" (43). In Lacan, the Real is the traumatic excess of Symbolic representation, which threatens the stability of the subject of language (as a whole and separate individual) and, therefore, of the possibility of representation itself. In Kristeva, the Semiotic is this excess, her real, *vreel*. It is the Imaginary which helps mediate the trauma of Symbolic castration (i.e., it is the necessary function as human beings are born into the world of language, "the home of Being," and therefore of representation). The return of the Real is a coping via *projecting* the "I" imago. This sense of projection sustains the mythological phantasy of return to the so-called origin, or *arkhē*, of the self. However, as we will see, it is not simply as projection, indeed Kristeva reads as inscription prior in advance of projection, the generativity of her *rejet*, with Freud; and building off Hegel, a fourth negation of this rejection, expulsion. Kristeva connects the forwarded concept of Force, via a "web of concepts," which includes Schelling's abyss of freedom, to Freud. Thus, Kristeva likewise posits that the Beyond in Freud's "beyond the pleasure principle" is Eros or Life; *Vereinigung*, binding, reunification, as well as *Vereinzelung*, individuation.

Lacan's *Seminar I, Freud Papers on Technique* (1953), which includes Hyppolite's guest lecture on *Verneinung*, captures Freud's papers on *rejete* (rejection) and *Ausstoßung* (expulsion) in *Beyond Pleasure Principle*. The point that is equivalent to this in Hegel is the cut, negation, but as well, the inversion, *Rückfrage*—of the direction, of embeddedness, the to and fro of the showing of the movement, *Bewegung* of the sign—as Hegel's dialectic would have it (1977, M152). The inversion (like trace, self-effacement, rebinding) is what interests us in Kristeva, and I dwell on this for a moment.

I can now trace more closely the relation to Hegel. Hegel formulates a master and slave recognitive dialectic, and, as Lacan notes with Bataille in *Seminar I*, urges that no safe death is left possible, no subjectivity beyond sacrifice, after the ambiguity of value, language as Culture, and alienation, overtakes the subject. Lacan asks that the imaginary, which is identical to introducing the shock of the intersubjective level in the experience of unsignifiable trauma, be taken into the explanation of intra-subjective or intrapsychic life as producing a discourse, and a discourse of trauma at the origin of history "itself." This movement begins classically in Hegel with the experience of self-consciousness as dependence, as "Unhappy Consciousness," which is the chapter title. But as Macdonald argues, Hegel privileges still the earlier movement in the book—"Force and Understanding," as the earliest encounter with the Other and the demand for a mediator, the third party. As Macdonald argues, the title chapter, "Lordship and Bondage," is a rerunning of the structures enabled in "Force and Understanding." Macdonald argues that the structure of the *Phenomenology* is a series of Spirit's Laws, "shapes of knowing" and is less hierarchical, not a Statism (Kristeva argues likewise).

As I argue, in *Revolution in Poetic Language*, the major achievement becomes not merely the view of negation as the arbitrariness of the sign, but the dialectic of mark and sign reinterpreted through the theory of the symbol as genuine negation—Kristeva's fourth negation (even as she says, Hegel does not have it). Generating the need for mediation is the signifying process, the movement of the concept as a mode of production of meaning, "moving forward" (M2). As Kristeva urges, the signification of the symbol (more than the cultural sign) is indebted to a pre-condition as psychic inscription and a dependency on the "corporeal responsiveness" of the maternal Other. Such an approach is premised on experience of intersubjective shock, genuine "negativity as the trans-subjective, trans-ideal, and trans-symbolic *movement* found in the *separation of matter*, one of the preconditions of symbolicity, which *generates the symbol*" (118). Note that what "generates the symbol" verges on the distinction between "negation" and "negativity." The former is not merely "the shadow of a false problem" but rather demonstrates a "logical inconsistency" which, through Freud, Kristeva says, we discover in "the movement that *produces* negation and of which negation is only an oblique mark in the presence of consciousness" (118). Kristeva deepens Freud, who states that negation "is already a lifting [*Aufhebung*] of the repression, though not, of course, an acceptance of what is repressed" (Freud, 1924–25, 235–36). Negation is a symbol, *Bejahung*, and as well acceptance opening to a welcoming, a receptivity to an anterior negativity, meaning, or text—thus, it alleviates. Freud: "With the help of the symbol of negation, thinking frees itself from the restrictions of repression and enriches itself with the material that is indispensable for its proper functioning" (236).

Kristeva adopts Freud's theory of the inscription of psychic processes, which she studied with André Green. The work of the negative, a tertiary processes model of psychic inscription is for Kristeva, energy or drive based. *Revolution in Poetic Language* is a development of the mechanisms of how negation functions, how repression, as found under the heading "the work of the negative" in Green is set up; and as corollary, how "through the lens of a Hegelian negation" it operates in "more affirmative, generative ways" (Macdonald 2014, 106). Kristeva demonstrates that Hegel's Unhappy Consciousness, which paradigmatically displays the essential dependency on the Other and the third party, the moment of mediator (cf. M231), is more affirmatively and generatively traced if we attend to the logical totality of the dynamics of the fourfold of Force, found in the earlier shape of "Force and Understanding." The point is that it is preceding but not in the sense of preexisting one after another in the extant order.

In backtracking to the shock of intersubjectivity initiated at "Force and Understanding" we recover the connection that ties the drive or instinct "to" desire as temporalization. It is, Kristeva argues, in this way "possible to see this stage of self-consciousness," which lies on the cusp of Reason, as not holding the "freedom of thought," and as not yet enriched with what Hegel sees as a "proper material for its functioning" (Macdonald 2014, 106).

The objective analysis of Force as structurally organized on the principle of the drives gives us Kristeva's study of the structure and management of the pure pleasure principle in Freud's tertiary psychic processes of inscription, a review of Freud's model of 1920 (cf. Kristeva 1984, 114). Structurally, in Freud, the psyche has within it the capacity for primary processes (i.e., the unbound unconscious, driven by the "pleasure principle") and secondary processes (i.e., thetic intentionality, bound in the conscious processes of "our normal waking life," governed by the "reality principle"). With the establishment of secondary processes, the puncturing of the primary processes will be necessary. Tertiary processes unbind—the death drive is this function. Kristeva is establishing what she will refer to as the "porosity" (102–3) of the semiotic *chōra* as threshold of signification, which she simultaneously posits as the possibility of creativity (energetic metaphysics), an indebtedness to malleability in the fixing of the pleasure principle.

In order for the pleasure principle to be fixed (the experience of infantile eroticism attaching to the libido), it must be breached. Fixing the pleasure principle is temporal in the logic of its essence, its establishing as being for itself (*Lustprinzip*, as ground) manifests as a body pointing beyond itself, a voracious negativity, and anticipation of anterior negativity. This is because, logically and chronologically, fixing operates in excess over the form of time as an ordered succession of signifiers, as we know it discursively (in *Vorstellung*, a signifier representing for another signifier).

The wish-fulfillment that represents the speculative nature of the death drive ("being for death"), as Kristeva argues, responds to anticipation of anterior negativity, an impossible to signify trauma (rather than merely biological instinct). Thus we say, the pure pleasure principle is dirempted in service of the death instinct, fixing a telos, inhibiting it. To inhibit the drive is to subordinate it, a function as recursive signifier, a speculative self-imposing on myself a desire for death (which will serve as the basis for aggression). The important insight is that the death drive both binds and unbinds, that is, its role is that it awakens, Kristeva says, reactivates as a response "to" trauma. In 1988 and 1987, Kristeva writes not about trauma *reel* but trauma *psychique*, adding to Freud and adding to Lacan. She adds a specificity of receptivity "to" a negativity anterior to factually true experience of injury leaving a trace. This restates that secondary processes constitute the life of the mind, mediated in and through telic repetition, what Freud calls the split (*Spaltung*) between inner and outer worlds. Surely, "as early as the *Project*, Freud associated the ego with bound energies. In fact, he offered the quality of being in a bound state as the very definition of the ego" (Boothby 1991, 80). Indeed, in order for the semiotic to make its way to the symbolic, the subject must accept and assume its position as a fundamental lack. However, for Kristeva, this position may only be fully assumed through metaphorical and unstable processes, reconceptualizing the semiotic dimension of language as investing a bodily limit—inscription of the maternal.

Access to the symbolic is predicated on assuming fundamental lack: in Kristeva this becomes, through "figuring" the productive tension—internal tension, which is semiotic, and depends on the semiotic-symbolic-thetic as a tripartite articulation. Two kinds of violence, then, claim inscription on the body: on the one hand, the symbolic is a foundation and violence, and as a "first" law it is powerless if it is founded but never enforced; on the other hand, the semiotic as a "second" law is fundamentally tyrannical if it is enforced, inscribed in bodily borders, the abjected maternal—and yet, the semiotic is never properly founded.

Kristeva takes up this direction in Hegel's "Force and Understanding" in 1974, this is the remarkable achievement of division 2, "'Kinesis,' 'Cura,' 'Desire'" (127–32). Here the completion of the virtual presence of a time that is near messianic, intimate revolutionary, is derivative of a relation of the splitting in the mother-child dyad, the inauguration of intersubjective shock as thematic of irreconcilable internal tension inscribed with meaning through the semiotic dimension of language.

How does Kristeva substantiate a generative, creative tension as temporality that is unavailable in Lacan and Freud? The signifying process is a result of an irrecuperable tension between inner (life of the mind) and outer (world of representation). The death drive, which stands for splitting as such, and will inaugurate desire, splits up the inner and outer worlds, for it sets up a barrier—as a protective (as well as projective) shield—which serves the function of *unifying*, by setting up boundaries. In contrast to Lacan, the symbolic order is preceded by a necessary separation between the subject and its primary bodily drives, in dependency on mastery by a third, or what Kristeva calls the "thetic phase" (43–46). The thetic phase is a necessary separation in order for a "subject" and an "object" to appear as such. Only if the preverbal subject and its drives is ruptured, can the thetic take place. Through the thetic as "deepest enunciation" (41, 105) the subject refers to objects through specific meaning production—namely, through metaphors or metonymies. Kristeva inserts into the thetic phase the negativity of inscribing the *chōra* and sets it up, similar to near messianic futurity, a present possibility of meaning so it may take place as a logical precondition of language. From this logic of precondition she argues for the virtual presence always-already of attribution of meaning to objects by the subject.

To summarize, temporally understood, unlike the mirror stage in Lacan, trauma inserts itself always already before the subject posited as ego. Kristeva, through the virtual presence of relation to the (m)Other, differentiates her view from the Imaginary in Lacan. Kristeva, alongside Klein, distinguishes between real Oedipal, and pre-Oedipal or psychic trauma, incurred through the split, its deep ambiguity, and the instability of the image other than the specular imaginary.[7]

The splitting of the self continuously distinguishes between negation and denial in Freud, and further, negativity, in Kristeva's fourth negation, which she adopts from Klein and Segal. As *Black Sun* notes, this set up of experience results very differently from there is "nothing there" to experience.

In Conclusion: Semiotic Inscription

Kristeva, along with Green, is a thinker with whom Macdonald agrees, citing *Revolution in Poetic Language*: "Force can be thought of in terms of energy" (Macdonald 2014, 108; Kristeva 1984, 114–16). "Force is the material expression of negativity" (Kristeva 1984, 114–16). Negativity, the fourth negation, equates to energy of the rupturing, presumably in Kristeva the negativity as inscription of the *chōra*. According to Hegel, once an idea is broken up into its elements, into moments, we have arrived at thought. It is, then, Understanding that has the power to dissolve again these thoughts, which in themselves are "familiar, fixed, and inert determinations further into their own self-movement" (1977, M18). Hyppolite, and Macdonald follows, distinguishes between two types of negativity: "genuine negativity" is different from an "ideal negation." Already at the recognitive dialectic stage in the development of self-consciousness in the classic chapter on desire and self-consciousness, "Lordship and Bondage," on Hyppolite's account, a weakening shift occurs, after Hegel's "Force and Understanding," in that "genuine negativity" is overtaken (e.g., capitalism as system) by the "destructive appetite which takes hold of desire" (Lacan, 1988, 293). That is, "ideal negation" just is the ending of master/slave dialectic (Macdonald 2014, 108).

First, Kristeva distinguishes against ideal negation—we begin with Frege's "*not* of negation in excess of judgement" is exactly this genuine negativity (119). "Behind affirmation [*Bejahung*] what is there? *Vereinigung*, which is Eros" (Lacan 1988, 293). Macdonald translates *Vereinigung* as "binding." As clarified above, Kristeva approaches Freud's doctrine of binding, the "beyond" as continuous with the pleasure principle. The Semiotic dismembers, Kristeva writes, by "decentering the transcendental ego, cutting through it, and opening it up to a dialectic in which its syntactic and categorical understanding is merely the liminary moment of the process, which is itself always acted upon by the relation to the other, dominated by the death drive and its productive reiteration of the 'signifier'" (38).

Second, the form of unbinding is closer to binding than we have thought. Kristeva follows "Eros, the life drive," for as Macdonald writes: "In positioning Eros, the life drive, as a binding activity, I am in a better position to understand what its relationship to the destructive drive as a form of unbinding will soon look like in Green's reading of Freud" (109). "For Freud, to affirm or to negate the content of thought is an act of intellectual judgement" (109). However, [. . .] "Judging is a continuation," along lines of expediency, of the "original process" by which the "ego took things into itself or expelled them from itself" (109).

Third, judging (*Ur-teil*) is a continuation of Eros, the life drive. Intellectual action is continuous with the binding and unbinding processes of psychic energy of the drives and cannot be otherwise. Hence, the importance of the fluidity of drive flows of the semiotic for the maintenance of the pleasure principle, as basis, whether taken or undergone, is a necessary condition of the productivity of the death drive; "In knowing itself, consciousness learns to take the other into itself and to eject this other from its internal world in order to keep the distinction between the two within the realm of its understanding. For consciousness, it is a process of defining itself by that which it is not" (109).

Fourth, *Force and Understanding* in Hegel lends itself to interpretation along the lines of *Innenwelt* and *Umwelt* as Lacanian signification, imputing internal tension between two, where the Thing of rebellion resists signification. On Kristeva's view, however, this is accommodating an account of "extended thinking" comprising the psychic processes of inscription active in the earliest mother-infant dyad for these serve as model to posit, transversal to judgment, a negative drive force at the pre-Oedipal narcissist formation. The psychic life of the ego, which structures itself around domination and independence avails itself of a meaning drawing from exteriority; it is the mother's body that expels (at birth) and unifies (welcomes the newly born life), both at once. The capacity to at once expel and welcome introduces a relationship between memory and Imagination, inner psychic life as capable of temporal differentiation, but as well, continuation, a receptivity to the address of the Other less than a "transcendental face to face" (Kristeva 2018, 232–33). Structurally, in Kristeva, this becomes the signifying process taken together with the social as a signifying space, "different from that of the symbolic law." Kristeva writes, "Though deprived of unity, identity, or deity, the *chōra* is nevertheless subject to a regulating process, which is different from that of the symbolic law but nevertheless effectuates discontinuities by temporarily articulating them and then starting over, again and again" (1984, 26).

It can be seen that through the means of idealization and inscription, the negativity of the bodily orifices is the earliest of self's encounters with the other and, out of this, the synchronous articulation of subjectivity becomes possible. It is thus a relation bounded on the drives of the sheltering, and shattering, the *chōra*. Kristeva increases the domain of reflectedness into another as more primary and dual foundation of the self, out of an enlarged "reflectedness-unto-itself" (Hegel, M154, cf. Kristeva 147, 150, 157–58) of the concept. The structured phantasy relation of the unconscious and hidden object-relations in Klein and Segal is then anterior to primary identification with the Law of the Freudian imaginary father of individual prehistory, which allows for signifying the heteronomy of the pleasure principle, with Bataille—within language. Accordingly, in Kristeva, the thetic, on which intentionality rests, is an unstable "threshold" (45, 48), mimetic of hidden maternal objects, and signifying processes succeed on the condition of cooperation of the thetic.

The symbolic (the Other), as Kristeva puts it, establishes itself after culture, tradition, and social groups have arrived; it cuts up the subject to pieces, it is in essence Law, a judgment, "we will reserve the term of symbol, the law, for later" (28). Kristeva posits that we look and see "what the law is doing to us" (28). "It is by the means of negation that this act of judgment finds meaning" (Macdonald 2014, 109). At the tail end of his paper, Freud writes, "Affirmation—as a substitute for uniting—belongs to Eros; negation—the successor to expulsion—belongs to the instinct of destruction" (239). Kristeva therefore posits that a dialectic of gaining access to language, speech as dialectic, as if realizing a substitution and displacement of subject and object, is premised on reactivating inversion (*Rückfrage*), as well as dropping Hegel's middle term of the mediator, as follows (M156–58).

In Hegel, then, dropping the mediator turns out creative: "I want to hold onto here this last idea of the destructive drive as giving birth to the very genesis of the thought and see what might be made of it in terms of the activity of vanishing" (Macdonald 2014, 110). As Macdonald notes, the vanishing that triggers the negative at work in Kristeva, would therefore lie specifically in abjection and the maternal object: "We must look for the 'other scene.'" Abjection of the maternal semiotic in Kristeva plays the role of constitution, an initial response at integrating the psychic life of the individual. In recognizing the authorship of that explanation (M155), consciousness becomes aware of itself for the first time—as in Hegel, but this is on condition of repression more anterior than in Freud, as Kristeva puts it.

To summarize, in 1974, Kristeva is exploring this exact possibility for emancipatory purposes. The process that leads to that point, which has been translated by *rejete* (rejection) without Freud having used the term

Verwerfung, is still yet more forcefully accented, since he uses *Ausstoßung*, which means expulsion. Here, then, in some ways one "finds 'the formal couple' of two primary forces: the force of attraction [*Einbeziehung*] and the force of repulsion, both, it appears, under the domination of the pleasure principle" (Lacan 1988, 293-94). I have sought to position Kristeva as an author of minimalist desire—not identical to the classic view of the recognitive theory of desire of recognition of self and other in Hegel.

Relating back to Hegel in Kristeva's fourth negation, Force can be known in the explanation, "in the law of it" (Macdonald 2014, 49, cf. Hegel M154). "Explaining [. . .] has the ability to facilitate the transition of the movement (of change), which was present only in the external world, into the inner world and thus to penetrate the supersensible world" (M154). The role of the maternal semiotic is indispensable as a mode of production of meaning, for its facilitation allows taking on the shape of cognition. Facilitating the movement of "change" corresponds to the production of the archaic maternal repressed in Kristeva. Alone on this precondition of Force as the material expression of negativity, energy as well as relation, Kristeva builds the possibility of the accession to the word. Unlike in Lacan, accession to the death drive is a passage to the position of enunciation in language, however, the introjection of the third, the smiling imaginary father of individual prehistory, is simultaneously enacting a nonnegligible cognition (intuition, action, the unconscious). This is in essence the ambiguity of more or less repression, "less repression than resistance" and inscription of the "other scene."

In Hegel's model of facilitation, consciousness makes the move "from experiencing its inner being as an object, but feeling no unity with this object, into the realm of the Understanding" (M154). Kristeva argues this move "from experiencing its inner being as an object, but feeling no unity with this object, into understanding" to be the leaping into the enunciating position, which is a qualitative leap in *Black Sun* (55). She therefore distinguishes this process of speech as the dialectic contrasting it to Kierkegaard, a "psychological ethics, kinesis" (1984, 128). Along with Hegel, and positing an ontological premise, desire/mood, including Heidegger, facilitation is where an "arduous and perpetual process" that is the "reconciliation of this split," will begin. The outcome of this significant change is that through "this process [of explanation] infinity is made an object for consciousness" (M154). That is, Kristeva argues that making "infinity an object for consciousness" is tantamount to investing speech—through investing the paternal metaphor of the third however, signification as we showed for her, passes via sublimation, inscription of the semiotic, and the perversion of the mother child-link.

Through the processes of normalization of psychic life, socialization, and so on, subsequently, consciousness "abolishes difference from its consideration of itself and its relation with the world," and thus becomes self-consciousness (M154). Detachment, in the psychoanalytic terms of Kristeva, is from the mother at the initiation of puberty—the equivalent of self-consciousness as "becoming" is passing through with immense social implications, of acceptability, norms, and expectations. Detachment and mood from Heidegger, through Kristeva, transform into means of formulating a thematic of ontic-ontological modes of production of meaning—excriptions. The argument in Kristeva is through reinterpreting Force as the relationality of the Other, Heidegger's term for "mattering." As Hegel will surmise, self-consciousness is now a "reflectedness-in-to-itself," because we see self-consciousness as holding the properties of Force, which is a "reflectedness-into-itself." In other words, "The unrest of self-movement, consciousness itself, has now become its own object. Force as a form of drive towards life" (Macdonald 2014, 54, cf. Hegel M101, 157, 163). As discussed above via the question of the death drive and the archive, this being a form of the drive toward life, Kristeva radicalizes the analogical model of desire and temporalization; and she posits, unlike Freud and Lacan, a tripartite signifying process—semiotic, symbolic, thetic. Kristeva, accordingly, identifies the difficulty at the heart of this project: these "operations" are "*pre-meaning* and *pre-sign* (or *trans-meaning, trans-sign*) [. . .] But since it is itself a metalanguage, semiotics can do no more than postulate this heterogeneity: as soon as it speaks about it, it homogenizes the phenomenon, links it with a system, loses hold of it. Its specificity can be preserved only in the signifying practices which set off the heterogeneity at issue" (32–33).

The new set of relations afforded through the inscription of the semiotic is a set of the ontology of relation in Kristeva, but which is irreducible to the anthropological and cultural linguistic ideas of the 1970s and is embedded in the system of inscription of meaning setting up the ethical relation to the Other. With the activity of Force, not only does "consciousness now know" of the difference between its internal and external realities, "but it also must now live with [. . .] this new set of relations as part of its own becoming. Hegel's ontology, then, is an ontology of relation" (Macdonald 2014, 55).

Did Kristeva recognize this ontology of relation in Hegel in 1974? I have sought to demonstrate that she did. Macdonald lays out a direct connection as she broaches via Kristeva this notion of Force. Hegel's notion of Force, alongside his notion of the negative, in Kristeva is a binding and generative dynamic entity that helps us to understand the "binding nature of both intra- and intersubjective states." Furthermore, in understanding the mechanisms of Force as a category of "relation," she posits the possibility of signifying practices as continuous with the ethical relation to the Other, in the earliest mother-child "taking an interest in the Other" (133–35), and provides one of the earliest unorthodox readings of Hegel. She reappropriates it as a "model for both recognition and desire," including for theorizing the latency of grief and relation to the mother—and the threshold of signification therefore does not equate to ontic assigned biological or cultural identity (transgressing law for the purposes of innovating it in the life sciences, cognitive sciences, legal sciences). Kristeva enjoins on Freud and Lacan, and through Klein, this theory of desire, double reversal, and negativity as a tool for recognizing in Force and in Hegel, an "epistemological and ontological weight that it is rarely given and creates an alternative economy through which the *Phenomenology of Spirit* can be understood" (Macdonald 2014, 19). The temporal latency of grief and the question of social conditions and foreclosure of proper mourning of the semiotic maternal repressed—in the situated environment of capitalism, critique, and oppression of nonbinary systems of inscription of the semiotic—these questions in Kristeva assume nonnegligible status with resistance as the injunction.

Notes

1. Beardsworth frames this sublimation in terms of tying the atemporal unconscious to symbolic history: "the world of signs must be tied to prehistorical corporeal responsiveness if mimetic relations are to have a history" (67).

2. Kristeva posits the semiotic sphere opens an entirely new realm of neuroses that could not be envisioned by Freud. "The fundamental predicament in this situation is not the preservation of infantile emotional ambivalence felt toward the father in the phallic organization of the libido, but that the loss of the mother can't be borne. The archaic mother is lost but the subject has failed to lose her" (Beardsworth 2005, 66).

3. See part of the argument for the "turn" in my chapter of Beardsworth (2020). Also see Söderbäck (2014).

4. Maternal passion is prototypical insofar as it is experienced by the child. It is in relation to the semiotic maternal body that the child first experiences emotions. Although these emotions are not reflexive, they do, according to Kristeva, contain *semiotic* meaning that is inscribed into the unconscious (Beardsworth 2005, 65).

5. Critchley's second essay on Levinas, titled "*Das Ding*: Lacan and Levinas," opens the discussion of traumatism with reference to Kristeva. "*Le traumatisme met à jour le rapport du sujet à la chose* (Traumatism illuminates the relation of the subject to the thing)." The citation is from the 1988 text appearing for the first time in English in the present volume, "The Impossibility of Loss." Cited in Critchley's *Ethics*, 199.

6. "[T]he subject of the semiotic metalanguage must, however briefly, call himself in question, must emerge from the protective shell of a transcendental ego within a logical system, and so restore his connection with that negativity—drive-governed, but also social, political and historical—which rends and renews the social code" (Kristeva 1984, 33).

7. The speaking, bodily, historical subject interacts with established meanings that (de)limit the linguistic world. "All functions which suppose a *frontier* (in this case the fissure created by the act of naming and the logico-linguistic synthesis that it sets off) and the transgression of that frontier (the sudden appearance of new signifying chains) are relevant to any account of signifying *practice*, where practice is taken as meaning the acceptance of a symbolic law together with the transgression of that law for the purpose of renovating it" (Kristeva 1984, 29).

References

Angelova, Emilia. 2020. "Abjection and the Maternal Semiotic in Kristeva's Intimate Revolt." In *The Philosophy of Julia Kristeva*, edited by Sara Beardsworth, 543–60. Chicago: Library of Living Philosophers.

Beardsworth, Sara. 2005. "Freud's Oedipus and Kristeva's Narcissus: Three Heterogeneities." *Hypatia* 20, no. 1: 54–77. muse.jhu.edu/article/177721.

———. 2017. "The Chiasmus of Action and Revolt: Julia Kristeva, Hannah Arendt, and Gillian Rose." In *New Forms of Revolt: Essays On Kristeva's Intimate Politics*, edited by S. K. Hansen and Rebecca Tuvel, 43–66. Albany: State University of New York Press.

Boothby, Richard. 1991. *Death and Desire: Psychoanalytic Theory and Lacan's Return to Freud*. New York: Routledge.

Critchley, Simon. (1999) 2009. *Ethics-Politics-Subjectivity: Essays on Derrida, Levinas and Contemporary French Thought*. London: Verso Books, 183–198, 199–216.

Derrida, Jacques. 1995. *Archive Fever*. Translated by Erin Prenowitz. Chicago, IL, and London: University of Chicago Press.
Freud, Sigmund. 1924–25. "Negation." *The Standard Edition of the Complete Psychological Works of Sigmund Freud*, vol. 19. Translated and edited by James Strachey. London: Hogarth.
———. 1924. "A Note Upon the 'Mystic Writing-Pad.'" *The Standard Edition of the Complete Psychological Works of Sigmund Freud*, vol. 19. Translated and edited by James Strachey. London: Hogarth.
Hegel, G. W. F. 1991. *Elements of the Philosophy of Right*. Translated by H. B. Nissbet, edited by Allen W. Wood. Cambridge: Cambridge University Press.
———. (1806) 1977. *Phänomenologie des Geistes*. Edited by H.-F. Wessels and H. Clairmont. Hamburg: Felix Meiner Verlag.
———. 1988. *The Phenomenology of Spirit*. Translated by A. V. Miller. Oxford, UK: Oxford University Press.
Heidegger, Martin. 2010. *Being and Time*. Translated by Joan Stambaugh. Albany: SUNY Press.
———. 1971. *On the Way to Language*. Translated by Peter D. Hertz. New York: Harper and Row.
Kristeva, Julia. 1984. *Revolution in Poetic Language*. Translated by Margaret Waller. New York: Columbia University Press.
———. 1982. *Powers of Horror: An Essay on Abjection*. Translated by Leon S. Roudiez. New York: Columbia University Press.
———. 1989. *Black Sun: Depression and Melancholia*. New York: Columbia University Press.
———. 2010. *Hatred and Forgiveness*. Translated by Jeanine Herman. New York: Columbia University Press.
———. 1987. *Tales of Love*. Translated by Leon S. Roudiez. New York: Columbia University Press.
———. 1993. *New Maladies of the Soul*. Translated by Jeanine Herman. New York: Columbia University Press.
———. 1988. "L'Impossibilité de perdre." *Les Cahiers de l'Institut de Psycho Pathologie Clinique* 8 (November). Special issue on "*Trauma réel, trauma psychique.*"
———. 2018. *The Passions of Our Time*. New York: Columbia University Press.
Lacan, Jacques. 1988. "The Symbolic Order." In *The Seminar Jacques Lacan: Book 1, Freud's Papers on Technique, 1953–1954*, edited by Jacques-Alain Miller and translated by John Forrester. New York: W. W. Norton.
Macdonald, Molly. 2014. *Hegel and Psychoanalysis: A New Interpretation of The Phenomenology of Spirit*. London and New York: Routledge.
Nancy, Jean-Luc. 1993. *The Experience of Freedom* (Meridian Crossing Aesthetics). Stanford, CA: Stanford University Press.

Nelson, Eric S. 2020. *Levinas, Adorno, and the Ethics of the Material Other.* Albany: State University of New York Press.
Oliver, Kelly. 2002. "Introduction: Kristeva's Revolutions." In *The Portable Kristeva.* New York: Columbia University Press.
Söderbäck, Fanny. 2014. "Timely Revolutions: On the Timelessness of the Unconscious." In *Journal of French and Francophone Philosophy* 21, no. 2: 46–55.

Chapter 13

Kristeva and Arendt on Language, Sanity, and the *Sensus Communis*

ANNE O'BYRNE

Introduction

In a well-known interview from 1964, Hannah Arendt reflects on the experience of returning to Germany after the war (Arendt 2013). She had left the country in 1933, after a period in prison for work on behalf of a Zionist organization, lived in France for several years, and then settled in the United States. The early years in New York were spent writing for the German-language *Vorwärts* and learning English, and by the mid-1940s her work was appearing in English-language publications. In 1949, she returned to Germany to the help organize the retrieval of Jewish books and artifacts and found herself once again surrounded by the sounds of her mother tongue. It was an experience accompanied by violent emotions.

Kristeva studies the interview in one of the final sections of *Hannah Arendt*, picking up the thread at the point where the interviewer, Günther Gaus, has asked what remains of prewar Europe and what has been irretrievably lost. It is an unscripted interview, with leaps and associations ripe for analysis.[1] "What remains?" Arendt responds. "The language remains." Though she was by then writing and speaking fluently in English, she felt herself at a certain distance from the language and continued to be consumed with German. "It wasn't the German language

283

that went crazy," she told Gaus. Kristeva notes Arendt's comments on what happens when one forgets one's mother tongue—"one cliché follows another"—and her agreement with the observation that this happens as a matter of repression and shock. Then, Kristeva observes, in the blink of an eye, she pivots to the question of Auschwitz. "What was decisive was the day we learned about Auschwitz. . . . It was really as if an abyss had opened up" (Arendt 2013).

For Kristeva, this is the decisive moment. In the course of the interview Arendt identifies herself repeatedly as someone who, above all, strives to understand. Now, Arendt-the-comprehender makes an unconscious association that, in Kristeva's diagnosis, reveals a logic in which three vital elements—primordial habitat, the mother language, and the thought of humanity as a whole—fall apart all at once (Kristeva 2003, 234). Arendt's own response to the shock is not to let go of the German language but to cling to it. She still speaks with a heavy accent, she points out, and still carries with her a great body of German poetry that she has learned by heart. She adds: "I can never do that again."

Here, Kristeva lets the thread fall, moving on to other texts. Picking it up now and following it further leads to more stumbles and into the heart of what concerns me here. Returning to Germany after the war meant confronting the terrible disloyalty of German friends, particularly the people in her intellectual circles who had fallen in line with the party right away. She captures the shock of that time: "[I]t was as if an empty space formed around one" (Arendt 2013). She would not confront them all. Anyone "who really became a Nazi" ceased to exist, as far as Arendt was concerned, and she did not speak to any of those people again (Arendt 2013). She continues,

> But they were not all murderers. There were people who fell into their own trap, as I would say today. Nor did they desire what came later. Thus, it seemed to me that there should be a basis for communication precisely in the abyss of Auschwitz. And that was true in many personal relations. I argued with people. I am not particularly agreeable, nor am I very polite; I say what I think. But somehow things were set straight again with a lot of people. (Arendt 2013)

How did this happen? How *could* it happen? Kristeva is unconvinced by the thought of the abyss as the scene where things get talked through and straightened out. In her view, this is where Arendt's thought reaches its limit, with all Arendt's responses traceable not to the *observation* that the German language did not go mad but to a transcendental conviction that language *cannot* go mad. Kristeva sees Arendt turning away from the logic that binds together the threefold loss of home, mother tongue, and the very thought of humanity, repressing knowledge of that logic in the name of renewed communication, somehow, after all.

I wish to examine this *somehow*. At the most obvious level, it refers to Heidegger, an unnamed presence in the interview. Arendt's references to a personal connection, an intellectual, someone who was a Nazi for "a year or two at most," who fell into his own trap, who made up ideas about Hitler, all point to him. The *somehow* acknowledges the reconciliation accomplished between them but also very clearly signals her refusal to go into any intimate detail. Besides, the details of the relationship may be beside the point, if not personally then philosophically. Even now, when we have access to a wealth of detail—in her published writing, in her *Denktagebuch*, in the Arendt-Heidegger correspondence—it is not clear how much light it can shed on *how* the former lovers made up, or what we could generalize from that experience.[2]

More promising, philosophically, is an examination of the *somehow* as part of a hermeneutics of reconciliation that includes certain sorts of empirical experience, on the one hand, certain commitments regarding the conditions for the possibility of those experiences, on the other, and repeated efforts and failures to stabilize the relation between the two. Somehow, there was forgiveness, and somehow, on the way to forgiveness, there was communication. The sort of communication that might allow a survivor and returned exile to go on after Auschwitz, that might hold open a public space where she could again engage with others politically, that might find a way to include forgiveness in the life of the *polis*, cannot be *grounded* in anything. Grounding would require bypassing or willfully forgetting the horror. Instead, communication has to begin again precisely in the un-ground, the abyss of annihilation. Where Kristeva sees Arendt making a surreptitious a priori commitment to the sanity of language, I see her making a turn in the Gaus interview that engages her in a long, manifest struggle to build an empirical and transcendental argument for a shared commonsense or *sensus communis* as the basis for renewed communication. In 1949, she appears to have already experienced a form of speech that was powerful enough to straighten things out with certain people, the ones whom Arendt finds herself describing in the interview as "not murderers," "not informers," temporary Nazis. We can follow Kristeva's analytic example and see Arendt catching herself in the midst of those descriptions, pivoting, and then making a series of rapid associations. She tells Gaus: "But the general, and the greatest experience when one returns to Germany—apart from the experience of recognition, which is always the crux of the action in Greek tragedy—is one of violent emotion. And then there was the experience of hearing German spoken in the streets. For me that was an indescribable joy" (Arendt 2013). As she approaches the greatest experience of her return from exile, she reaches for a familiar touchstone—narrative—as the form of language that reassures her that even this shock can be endured. Elsewhere, she quotes Isak Dinesen: "All sorrows can be borne if you put them in a story" (Arendt 1998, 175). The tragic moment of recognition is always frightful, but it is also the hinge of a narrative, a moment on the way to meaning. It marks the beginning of silence for some, and an onslaught of speech for others; after all, Jocasta has already left the stage, saying she will speak no more, when Oedipus recognizes himself and her, unleashing in him a torrent of speech. Recognition is the death of one and the tortured, blinded, exiled survival of the protagonist. But if recognition and all its aftermath are captured in the arc of a story, they can be made bearable as such to us, the spectators. For Kristeva, narrative is not precisely the triumph of the symbolic over the semiotic, but it is a distinctive form of the dialectic between them that insists on sense (Kristeva 1984, 24). Unlike the avant-garde poetry that most concerns her in *Revolution in Poetic Language*, narrative gives shape to experience; the disaster of recognition is repressed and recouped in the reassertion of a linguist form oriented to meaning.[3]

Arendt's own recognition of the horror happened in stages. The day in 1943 when she heard about Auschwitz was decisive, she said. But which day? "At first we didn't believe it. . . . Then half a year later we believed after all, because we had proof. That was the real shock. . . . This ought not to have happened. And I don't mean just the number of victims. I mean the method, the fabrication of corpses. . . . This should not have happened." Now, six years later, four years after the liberation of the camps, she was in Germany, in the grip of violent emotion, and forced to recognize the horror again. Her response? "I argued with people (*Ich habe mit Leuten auseinandergesetzt*)" (Arendt 2013). The symbolic rules of argument continued to apply. By *arguing*—in German, literally, sorting things out, making distinctions—one could hold off the emotion one feels in the face of what should not have happened.

Yet there, at the same time, was a joy beyond words. More than once in the interview, we hear about the violence of her emotions without further description of their content, until we are told also of the indescribable joy of hearing German spoken all around. Her discussions with the "not murderers" would begin in the grip of horror *and* joy, and would be conducted in their shared mother tongue. They would proceed by logic, argument, and disagreement, that is, by means of socially useful communicative discourse (Kristeva 1984, 16) that would "set things straight again [*wieder in Ordnung ziehen*] with a lot of people."

Forgiveness is key to Arendt's theory of action and her political theory, and Peg Birmingham has investigated how Kristeva sheds light on the psychological conditions it requires, an area into which Arendt herself—famously dismissive of psychology in general and psychoanalysis in particular—refused to go (Birmingham 2005, 130). Kristeva points to Freud's secular version of forgiveness, which is "not just a suspension of judgment but a giving of meaning, beyond judgment, within transference/ countertransference" (Kristeva 2002, 12); Arendt places forgiveness within the operation of judgment and in the context of the political obligation to judge. Yet the question of what brings one to forgiveness is answerable only abstractly in Arendt's schema; Kristeva turns our attention to the affective content of forgiveness. Birmingham suggests that the same holds true for another concept—"enlarged mentality," one of the three elements of *sensus communis*, which plays an equally important role in Arendtian political thinking. The investigation I undertake here follows the direction of that gesture. While I resist the specific psychologizing move in which Kristeva gives significance to Arendt's repressive response to her threefold loss, Kristeva's work does help us grasp the valences of Arendt's hope for *sensus communis*.

We know that both thinkers regarded the human condition of natality as the origin of human action (Birmingham 2005, 127). Even as Kristeva pursues this insight toward psychology and Arendt toward politics, they continue to address the same problems. While Kristeva sets the time of birth into to the timelessness of the unconsciousness, stressing the work that analysis does to reconcile us with it, Arendt concerns herself with natal newness as the source of, among other things, the anxiety of living between past and future like the figure in Kafka's parable, "He," who dreams of escaping into the peace of a *metaphysical* timelessness but must stay in the temporal fray, holding off the past and future that would otherwise annihilate each other (Hannah Arendt 1968, 10). While

Kristeva turns to literature because she sees the open possibilities of writing that reaches for non-sense—Mallarmé's ellipses and Joyce's polyphony, for example—a writing that finds its pulse in the realm that is no longer symbolic but semiotic, Arendt rejects anything she sees leading us toward the ugly sameness of the unconscious—the internal monologues of Joseph Heller's *Something Happened*, for example—in favor of the wholly externalized scenes of Natalie Sarraute or the narratives of Dinesen (O'Byrne 2020). She neglects the experimental modern poetry that Kristeva sees as engaging in a sort of "experimental psychosis," where meaning is unfolded to its limits and where the subject is lead into the hazardous regions where its unity risks annihilation, in favor of that reserve of canonical German poetry internalized in her youth (Kristeva 2002, 10). And while Kristeva identifies a certain resistance to analysis that springs from the human being's desire *not* to know, arguing that the human being prefers "sexual mystification to confronting truths that may place him in revolt," Arendt specifies her hesitation as emerging from a distinctively political resistance to transparency (Kristeva 2002, 11).[4]

Of all the challenges presented by Arendtian *sensus communis*, the most compelling may not be that it is based on an unwarranted transcendental conviction—a hope, in other words—that language cannot go mad. Instead, it may be the realization that, as she builds an empirical case and at the same time continues to speak in transcendental terms, she is showing the worry that, if language *were* to go mad, we might not be able to tell. The limits of language may be beyond our knowing.

"The only general symptom of insanity . . .":
Sensus communis and Political Communication

Sensus communis takes center stage in Arendt's *Lectures on Kant's Political Philosophy*, a course she gave at the New School in New York in 1970. The term has a history that stretches from Aristotle and the Stoics, through Cicero, Aquinas, Vico, Rousseau, and Voltaire, but Arendt's inheritance of the term comes exclusively through Kant. This is the source of most of the controversy surrounding the *Lectures*. For Kant, *sensus communis* is an additional human sense, something we have in common and that fits us into a human community. Communication, that is, speech, depends on it. Indeed, Arendt quotes, "The only general symptom of insanity is the loss of the *sensus communis* and the logical stubbornness in insisting on one's own sense (*sensus privatus*) which [in an insane person] is substituted for it" (Arendt 2014, s. 53). How are we to understand the *sensus* displaced in that movement? What does this symptom look like? Arendt continues to quote Kant:

> [U]nder the *sensus communis* we must include the idea of a sense *common to all*, i.e., of a faculty of judgment which, in its reflection, takes account (*a priori*) of the mode of representation of all other men in thought, in order, *as it were*, to compare its judgment with the collective reason of humanity. . . . This is done by comparing our judgment with the possible rather than the actual judgments of others, and by putting ourselves in the place of any other man, by abstracting from the limitations which contingently attach to our own judgment. (1989, 71)

The maxims that guide this activity are: (1) Think for oneself, or the maxim of enlightenment; (2) Put oneself in thought in the place of everyone else (the maxim of enlarged mentality); and, (3) Be in agreement with oneself (the maxim of consistency). Of these, enlarged mentality is the maxim of plurality and worldliness. The inability to enlarge one's mentality by stepping outside oneself is insane.

As early as *Revolution in Poetic Language*, Kristeva provides and elaborates the Kleinian structure that gives us a way to understand this symptom psychologically. It carries us beyond the subject as the subject of understanding, the user of language as a sign system that operates on the level of the symbolic. This means expanding analysis to the presymbolic and indeed pre-Oedipal functions within the subject. The drives are constantly in motion and are always ambiguous—assimilation/destruction, love/hate—but are not without direction and are not amorphous. Rather, for Klein, they are originally oriented toward the body of the mother, which "mediates the symbolic law organizing social relations." The *symbolic*—language—is a social effect of the relation to the (m)other, established through the objective constraints of biological differences and, Kristeva adds, concrete, historical family structures (Kristeva 1984, 27, 29).

The theory of abjection takes shape in other works (see *Powers of Horror* 1980), but in *Revolution in Poetic Language*, with its attunement to the literature of the late nineteenth century, this social effect unfolds as scission, separation, and rejection, that is, in Hegelian terms refracted through Freud (118). All three words signify "an event that moves through and is inherent in biological and signifying development [and] links them together" (146). Kristeva here prefers to emphasize *rejection*, using it to guide us through the rhythms of unity and fragmentation of the subject in a way that eventually allows us to see how it stalls in narcissism, which is the condition of the *sensus privatus*. This rhythmic movement is always under way. We cannot talk of a given, original unitary subject that is shattered under the experience of rejection, but we also cannot posit rejection as an origin. She writes: "Rejection rejects origin since it is always already the repetition of an impulse that is itself a rejection" (147). In Arendtian terms, it is not that we are born singular and then enter into the condition of plurality; we come to be in the natal condition of plurality (Arendt 1998, 8). When each of us was born, the world had never seen anyone quite like us before, and this character of uniqueness is shared by us all. In the terms of Klein's psychology, natality is marked by the movement of rejection—though not only rejection—of the mother's body. In terms of Kristeva's linguistic analysis: "*Rejection* is precisely the semiotic mode of this permanent aggressivity and the possibility of its being *posited* and thus *renewed*. . . . Rejection and sadism . . . return and disturb the symbolic chains." Constantly a matter of movement, rejection is a mechanism of reactivation, tension, life; it perpetuates tension and life (Kristeva 1984, 150–51).

In contrast to Arendt's therapeutic recourse to storytelling, Kristeva turns to avant-garde literature and its capacity to resist immobilization, to keep on shattering conceptual and subjective unities, and thus dissent from the dominant economic system—even as capitalism tries to assimilate it, incorporating rejection into itself (Kristeva 1984, 186). She writes,

> [Rejection even] works in the service of this assimilation to the extent that it is maintained by subjective narcissism, which is the refuge of the subject's unity and the necessary compensation for the violence of the death drive. The narcissistic moment tends to attach the process of rejection to the unity of the ego, thus preventing rejection's destructive and innovative vigor from going beyond the enclosure of subjectivity and opening up toward a revolutionary ideology capable of transforming the social machine. (Kristeva 1984, 186)

To have rejection captured and contained like this is a privation. *Privacy* is rooted in separation, bereavement, being robbed or stripped of something, being relieved of something. The narcissistic subject hides from itself the separation that terrifies it, and it does so by turning back into itself, enclosing itself. Deprived of others, it judges by its own lights, its own concern for truth, its own cleverness, and its own understanding, which "knows how to dissolve every thought and *always find the same barren Ego* instead of any content."[5] The narcissistic moment may be— ought to be—surpassed in the reactivation of rejection but, alternatively, it may generate the sort of comprehensive *sensus privatus* that will promptly grasp itself as sense as such. One's own sense comes to be experienced as the only sense, or the only sense that can possibly matter. In the Hegel passage above, it is a matter of the subject's burning zeal for truth, making it impossible for it to find any truth beyond the unique truth of vanity, that is, the truth of its own cleverness. This is Kant's *sensus privatus* or "*logische Eigensinn*," the logical "own-sense" that replaces *sensus communis* in the insane. Arendt adds: "The insane person has not lost his powers of expression to make his needs manifest and known to others" (Arendt 2014, 71). The difference is that others are relevant only in the context of unmet needs. For Arendt, privacy is privation and the intimate is private, so the realm of family, love, and emotion is essentially lesser—not only less valued or less important, but, as Cecilia Sjöholm points out, less real.[6] Arendt initially approaches enlarged mentality as a formal structure. She quotes Kant: "[U]nder the *sensus communis* we must include the idea of a sense *common to all*, i.e., of a faculty of judgment which, in its reflection, takes account (*a priori*) of the mode of representation of all other men in thought, in order, *as it were*, to compare its judgment with the collective reason of humanity" (Sjöholm 2009, 71, quoting Kant 1987, §40). What is in question here is not knowledge or understanding but specifically judgment, and Kristeva sees Arendt's reaching for transcendental human reason in this context as repression. If Arendt can sustain the comforting idea of the human community and hold to this formal requirement in the operation of judgment, it will allow her (as it allowed Kant) to evade the problem that the Other might have to be encountered in terms of "anguish and desire" (Kristeva 2003, 225). An a priori assessment that makes a comparison *as it were* preserves judgment from such entanglements. Yet such austere formality is not satisfying enough, and Arendt moves—I suspect willfully—toward a *sensus communis* that is more than formal. She is abetted by Kant's elaboration, which courts a measure of confusion (Norris 1996, 188). The quotation from the *Critique of Judgment* continues:

> This is done by comparing our judgment with the possible rather than the actual judgments of others, and by putting ourselves in the place of any other man, abstracting from the limitations which contingently attach to our own judgment . . . Now this operation of reflection seems perhaps too artificial to be attributed to the faculty called *common* sense, but it only appears so when expressed in abstract formulae. In itself there is nothing more natural than to abstract from charm and emotion if we are seeking a judgment that is to serve as a universal rule. (Kant 1987, §40)

Just as freedom entails the ability to leave one's home and talk to other people, as Arendt writes elsewhere, she thinks of enlarged mentality as an abstract structure but also as a practice of communicating with others. In this sense it has more in common with Aristotelian *phronesis*. She writes: "One can communicate only if one is able to think from the other person's standpoint; otherwise one will never meet him, never speak in such a way that he understands." The ability to occupy the position of the other is a condition for communication. "One judges always as a member of a community, guided by one's community sense, one's *sensus communis*" (Arendt 2014, 74, 75). Andrew Norris is right to point out that, in these last lectures in the Kant course, she effectively transforms a transcendental principle into an empirical criterion (Norris 1996, 188). The importance of this insight for my argument has less to do with a slippery, faithless reading of Kant, and more to do with the question of what the source of the criterion might be. If we are asked to entertain the *possible* judgments of others but told to ignore their *actual* judgments, what source can there be for the *possible* content of those *possible* judgments? What can be the basis on which we might establish a criterion of possibility? On the one hand, we could immediately apply the transcendental principle of human reason, but this would only allow us to distinguish between "good" judgments that conform to reason and are comprehensible and "bad" judgments that are not. This collapses the exercise of judgment into the realm of understanding and comprehensibility.

On the other hand, if the criterion is empirical, the question returns in another form: what *sort* of experience will be its basis? Will it be our individual experience, constrained as it is by private circumstances (Arendt), in other words, the experience of the narcissistic subject (Kristeva)? The very formula "enlarged mentality" suggests a starting point within a narrow mentality, the private mind where judgment is possible but limited in its exercise. Arendt writes: "Private conditions condition us; imagination and reflection enable us to liberate ourselves from them and to attain that relative impartiality that is the specific virtue of judgment." Yet if we can get trapped in self-enclosed subjectivity, we need reassurance that the diligent exercise of judgment has at least a hope of shaking off narcissistic constraints. At this point, Arendt again makes the transcendental gesture, taking a condition of deprivation (privacy) and applying further deprivation, stripping away the partial elements of private judgment and reducing it to an impartial abstraction, relieved of distinctive content (Arendt 2014, 73–74). In the reverse of the move described by Norris, she navigates from the empirical I to the transcendental principle. A criterion of communicability based on this reduction shows the difference between abstract judgments that have been scrubbed of idiosyncrasy and contingency, and others that remain tainted by the particular, but this does not guide us when it comes to knowing what judgments others can *possibly* make.[7]

Yet there is another method for overcoming partiality, and it is signaled here in the liberating promise of imagination. Earlier in the lectures she observes that "communicability obviously implies a community of men who can be addressed and who are listening and can be listened to," and *publicity* is the name she gives to the character our judgments take on when they are developed in a practice of testing our own thoughts in contact with other people's thinking.[8] We should understand this as an active, lively process. To think with an enlarged mentality means training one's imagination to go visiting, listening and being listened too, learning to put ourselves in the place of others. We can make progress in our practice, increasing our reach; "The larger the realm in which the enlightened individual is able to move from standpoint to standpoint, the more general will be his thinking." Yet, just as her description begins to gain traction as a worldly technique of being together, Arendt once again passes into abstraction. Visiting in imagination is a matter of "moving in a space that is potentially public, open to all sides. In other words, it adopts the position of Kant's world citizen" (Arendt 2014, 40–43).

The concern that drives Arendt to abstraction in these passages is the same worry each time: that listening and imagination will not be enough to spring the trap of private conditioning, that is, that my judgments will always be partial at best, insane at worst. Perhaps, when I go visiting in imagination, the prejudiced self comes along. If I am trying to be impartial, I will have made an effort to set my predilections aside, but how successful will I have been? Will I appreciate my own blind spots? Indeed, might what I experience as thinking from another's point of view in fact be a matter of putting myself in that person's position in the worst way, replacing their interests with my own? How will I know? How will I tell the difference between enlarged mentality and mere narcissism? Between my thinking from your point of view and delusion? The figure of the world citizen does not resolve the difficulty; its apparent worldliness may be the most comprehensive narcissism of all, its dreamed-of *sensus universalis* more akin to *sensus privatus* than *sensus communis*.[9]

What Arendt understands only in terms of privation, Kristeva unfolds as intimacy.

The Other *sensus communis* and the Place of Intimacy

The problem of transcendental conditions and empirical criteria, which Arendt keeps running up against and turning away from, is a long-standing concern in the work of Kant. Adrian Johnston puts it this way in his study of Kant and psychoanalysis: "The Kantian subject is basically split along a form-content divide: The transcendental subject is the formal possibility condition for consciousness, whereas the phenomenal subject is that which is made possible by the transcendental form. So, no conscious subject can have direct knowledge of its transcendental side, since to have such knowledge would mean that it stepped back behind itself as conscious in order to directly apprehend the very conditions for the emergence and functioning of this same consciousness" (Johnston 2005, 101). The same structure of split subjectivity undergirds both reason and unreason and, since there are regulative ideas of reason and unreason, can we tell which is which? The stakes are high, as Andrew Cutrofello notes:

> A deranged subject could well hold to a particular set of beliefs even in the face of what a "normal" person would call sufficient disconfirming evidence. How are we to explain such behavior. It is precisely here, of course, that the specificity of psychoanalytic questioning arises—and Kant clearly sees himself

as a "normal" subject capable of psychoanalyzing "abnormal" subjects. But Kant sidesteps the prior question of how I, the critical subject, can tell whether I am a normal or an abnormal subject. . . . Kant has very little to say on the topic. . . . The question that eventually emerges from this is not how we can tell who is really normal and who is really mad. The question, rather, is whether it is possible to distinguish normality from madness in a rigorous way at all. (Cutrofello 1997, 18)

Sensus communis—the lack of which is the only general symptom—was supposed to provide the criterion but, as Arendt's efforts show, turning to it merely moved the problem back another step in a logical regression. Just as the conscious subject cannot step back behind itself, *sensus communis* does not allow us to step back behind the sharing of a shared sense. It cannot tell us whether we belong among the sane or in the inner exile of the mad. At this point, we need the other *sensus communis*—more accurately, *a*nother, since the term has many histories—this one bound up with the accumulation of historically and culturally specific ways of being that frames actual communication in specific communities.[10] Its history runs from the Stoic thought of *koine ennoia*, or what all men have in common; through Cicero, where it becomes the basis for the rhetorical preference for everyday language, that is, the usage approved by the sense of the community [*communis sensus*]; to Vico, for whom *sensus communis*, as opposed to the *senso proprio* of the individual, was the expression of collective experience and was also what counted as knowledge. He writes: "One should live in continuous contact with one's community, let oneself be guided by its *sensus communis*" (Van Kessel 1987, 129). In the wake of Descartes, resisting the model of scientific certainty that was founded on the assumption of calculability and courted the risk of solipsism, Vico has a vision of what it would mean to "go mad rationally" by ignoring the fact that *sensus communis* guides everyday life in ways that defy the purely self-referential methods of mathematics, and forgetting that *sensus communis* is a historically and culturally determined phenomenon that does *not* presume that we can see from the point of view of all others.[11]

One element of what is missing is a robust account of publicity that would allow us to think in terms of *a* public, *one's* public, publics in the plural. (The other crucial element will return us to the conversation about intimacy below.) Kristeva identifies an intense satisfaction that Arendt gets from Kant's account of the process of reflection, which allows us to transform private feelings of pleasure and displeasure into public statements of approbation and disapprobation (Kristeva 2003, 226). Reflection means taking all others and their feelings into account. She is suspicious of Arendt's satisfaction, finding in it an unearned hope for the perpetual solution. For Kristeva, a settled solution would require the sacrifice of revolt.

Yet, despite the reference to "all others," Arendt on this occasion holds off the moment of cosmopolitan abstraction, asserting that one judges as "a member of *a* community (emphasis added)" (Kristeva 2003, 224, quoting *Life of the Mind: Thinking*, 72). In the practice of thinking publicly, our thinking must earn a level of generality, bit by bit. We see her holding off the moment once again in the *Kant Lectures*:

> This generality, however, is not the generality of the concept. . . . It is, on the contrary, closely connected with particulars, with the particular conditions of the standpoints one has to go through in order to arrive at *one's own* "general standpoint." . . . In Kant's own mind it was certainly the standpoint of the world citizen. But does this easy phrase of idealists, "citizen of the world," make sense? To be a citizen means among other things to have responsibilities, obligations, and rights, all of which make sense only if they are territorially limited (emphasis added). (Arendt 2014, 43–44)

The thought of rights is abstract and ideal under the heading of human rights, but it becomes concrete under the heading of civil rights, which are protected by state institutions; this is the import of *limited territory*, a state with borders. Note that, for Arendt, borders allow for the exclusion of the foreign and also allow us to imagine the exclusion of violence (Birmingham 2005, 137). But a limited territory is also a shared locale, requiring a mode of inhabiting a place together that is not determined by the institutions of state and cannot be captured by the anonymous cosmopolitan ideal. Being together with our fellow citizens as citizens is public life. There is satisfaction in this thought too, not dependent on the fantasy of achieved reason but bound up with the uncertain process of enlarging one's mentality; it involves the gratification of making one's way to other standpoints, the joy of talking with people, and the hermeneutic work of occupying and jointly creating and re-creating our publics.

When Arendt describes it in terms of abstracting one's way to impartiality, the process takes on the character of an exercise in reasoning; its success or failure will depend on our logical consistency and our imaginative agility. But, as a concrete, worldly endeavor, the activity of enlarging one's mentality takes on some of the character of action as per Arendt; it will be fraught with rejection and disappointment, and we will not be able to predict the outcome of our efforts. It will emerge from struggle since, as Kristeva warns above, the narcissistic subject will try to assimilate rejection, folding into itself the negativity that would otherwise drive the self beyond itself, toward transformation and revolution.

The other element missing from Arendt's schema is a conception of intimacy-without-privation, which Kristeva finds in a tradition determined neither by the Greek conjunction of speech and reason nor the modern faith in language as an exercise in effective communication—that is, in a Christian tradition of embodied meditation. In the work of Augustine and Loyola, the question of the relation between the word and the senses is central to the practice of meditation and to the soul's relation to God, and is experienced in or as intimacy. Cecilia Sjöholm writes:

> In the language of intimacy, the author is baring his soul through the unraveling of his senses . . . The intimate is a domain of affects, sensations, moods, and feelings, a domain in which the function of the mind is close to the body. Intimacy is the capacity of the mind to connect language to forms of sensibility. Intimacy, in this version, is not a description of a sphere of interiority but rather a description of a certain discourse of corporeality. (Sjöholm 2009, 191)

Kristeva understands psychoanalysis as having done more than any other modern practice to preserve this singularity of human existence without recourse to the divine. Freud allows us to recast the soul/mind dichotomy in an analysis that is not about learning to repress or release but to working out the psychical apparatus so that it will be capable of renewing itself with each new challenge (Kristeva 2002, 50). It is a renewal rooted in the condition of natality, prepared most explicitly in the intimate experience of transference/countertransference, and emerging in political life. She writes: "A laboratory is thus created where we test not only the 'enlarged mentality' dear to Kant, where through language I can universalize my peculiarities and communicate them to the other, to others, but a concrete, sensory link, mundane in the Greek sense of the term, understood as the seed of politics" (Kristeva 2002, 232).

Participating in Vico's *sensus communis* locates us in a specific network of meaning and has us participate in the generation of that meaning in language, but it does not eliminate the danger of absorption into a self-assured, narcissistic self or community. Arendt courts this danger too, so long as she leaves untested the relation between our commonness, on the one hand, and the alien or foreign in our midst, on the other. Birmingham argues that, for Arendt, the public space of speech and action is at the heart of the city, while violence and barbarism lie outside, beyond speech and beyond the walls. She is keenly aware that the violence inflicted by the city on its others—for example, in the history of European imperialism—eventually comes home, erupting within itself (Birmingham 2005, 137). What is needed is an examination of the confrontation of the familiar and the foreign in the self as well as in the city. By reading Freud through Melanie Klein, Kristeva opens up within the subject the scene of prelinguistic, presymbolic, semiotic functions. For Klein, the psychological element of rejection is sadism, which is subject to repression by the symbolic but also holds the possibility of articulating rejection in a way that allows it to avoid being subsumed by a Freudian superego, offering an escape from narcissism (Kristeva 1984, 27, 152).

Later, in *Strangers to Ourselves*, Kristeva will write: "We know that we are foreigners to ourselves, and it is with the help of that sole support that we can attempt to live with others. . . . Living with the other, with the foreigner, confronts us with the possibility or not of *being an other*. It is not simply—humanistically—a matter of our being able to accept the other, but of *being in his place*, and this means to imagine and make oneself other for oneself" (Kristeva 1991, 170, 13). In Arendt's work, this becomes most concrete as an intimate accomplishment that has everything to do with her status social and historical status. S. K. Keltner points out that, while Arendt may not be open to a revaluation of the sensory elements of intimate existence, the way she chooses to philosophize makes concrete thought itself. Keltner writes: "[In *Hannah Arendt*] Kristeva returns Arendt's concern for 'the value of human life' to an accomplishment of the positive dynamic of intimacy that is intimately joined to Arendt's *female* and *Jewish* subject position" (Keltner 2009, 175).

Conclusion: On the Street, in the Abyss

By 1949, Arendt had become a foreigner several times over—in her home country, on her arrival in France, and again on her internment there, in the United States, and back in her home country, which had been transformed and transformed again in her absence. On her return in 1949, she found her compatriots responding to the postwar world in a variety of ways, most typically with a "stubborn, at times vicious refusal to face and come to terms with what really happened" (Arendt 1950, 342). Describing her experiences in "The Aftermath of Nazi Rule," a report published in 1950 after her return to the US, she seems to have little hope. Important former Nazis were gleefully evading the denazification process. Those who had spent the war in a state of inner resistance found themselves struggling in another sort of loneliness. In between was a mass of "more-or-less compromised" people who were obsessed with just keeping busy and not thinking about what had happened. She writes: "The experience of totalitarianism has robbed them of all spontaneous speech and comprehension, so that now, having no official line to guide them, they are, as it were, speechless, incapable of articulating thoughts and adequately expressing their feelings. The intellectual atmosphere is clouded with vague pointless generalities. . . . One is oppressed by a kind of pervasive public stupidity which cannot be trusted to judge correctly the most elementary events" (345). The article points to encounters that made discussion seem hopeless. If Arendt was going to meet the "not-murderers" among her fellow German-speakers and talk things straight with them, then her interlocutors could not be like the woman in Southern Germany who told her that Russia had started the war by invading Danzig. They could not be people incapable or unwilling to distinguish fact and opinion (344). They could not still be mired in the habit of speaking in clichés. They could not be the ones caught up in guilt feelings that end in confusion about who really was guilty, on the one hand, and sentimentality about the shared experience, on the other. Perhaps there was some hope for those who had joined up late, after 1933, bowing to physical or economic pressure. Surely there were people who joined but continued to think otherwise. Arendt writes: "But curiously, very few Germans were capable of such healthy cynicism; what bothered them was not the membership card but the mental reservation, so that they often ended by adding to their enforced enrollment the necessary convictions, in order to shed the burden of duplicity" (345).

They could not countenance such strangeness to themselves. Since the end of the war, all had been assailed by rejection in Kristeva's sense, and almost all had set to work assimilating rejection into a collective narcissism. In an outburst of "blind self-centeredness," one newspaper would complain that "The world at large once again deserted us" (345).

There were many individual exceptions, Germans who were working to penetrate the stifling atmosphere around them, but they remained isolated (346). After all, Nazism had produced a mass shared delusion, and anyone who, under totalitarianism, had remembered how to think for himself had been like "a normal person who happens to be thrown into an insane asylum where all the inmates have exactly the same delusion" (348). In the asylum of the Third Reich, a viewpoint may be communicable in principle, but the conditions for publicity were absent and there could be no *sensus communis*, not even for the sane one. If every other available viewpoint is a token of the same official viewpoint, there is nowhere to go visiting. Now, postwar, the delusion had not vanished, and struggling to again expand one's mentality was the difficult work of reopening a public space.

Arendt found one functioning public in the case of Berlin, "whose people, in the midst of the most horrible destruction, . . . remained intact" (1950, 345). The city had been Arendt's home with her first husband, Günther Stern, from 1929 to 1933, and on her return, she found the Berlin customs, manners, speech and approaches to people unlike anything elsewhere in Germany. Berliners were able to pause in their busyness and show a visitor around the rubble-strewn city, reciting the names of streets that had been bombed to nothing. They were able to say what other Germans could not; without embarrassment or guilt, she writes, they would give a frank account of what had happened to the city's Jews at the beginning of the war. This was the essential starting point, the abyss; there might be hope for a conversation conducted in the language of Auschwitz if it could start from there.

The rhetors of Nazism made an art of creating clichéd winged words that simultaneously blocked thinking and inspired action. Eichmann spoke only in clichés. In postwar Germany, Arendt encountered people using one cliché after another. Likewise, those who have lost their mother tongue speak in a chain of clichés in the new language. If we hear *mother tongue* as *native language* or *national language*, we suspect Arendt of susceptibility to the worship of national language (which Kristeva warns against in *Strangers to Ourselves* [1991, 177]), on the one hand, or a nostalgia for a logic that could hold together a homeplace, a home in language, and a home in the world (which Kristeva also warns against in *Hannah Arendt*), on the other (Kristeva 2003, 185–86). But Arendt does not succumb to either, subjecting whatever hope she has to the risks of engagement. This is the form that her revolt takes. In 1949, as she traveled the country talking to people, her sense that it was not the German language that had gone mad might be understood as a hypothesis being put to the test. By 1964, after several more visits, it had taken the form of an assertion, suggesting an accumulation of evidence but also masking the uncertainty of inductive argument and the trouble (which we saw in Kant) of distinguishing the sane and the mad. If we ask, then: "Can language go mad?" the best answer will be: "Perhaps, but we don't have a reliable way to know if it has or not." And if we ask Arendt: "Could the German language go mad?" we might answer on her behalf: "Perhaps it could, but *it seems to me* that it did not."

We have seen Arendt describe herself arguing with her fellow Germans, saying what she thought, somehow setting things straight. For her, "it seems to me" is a matter of the *dokei moi* of Socrates, an opinion worked out on the basis of our observations of the world and in the back and forth of reflection and public discussion. Socrates spent his time engaging with citizen-practitioners of the back and forth of dialogue, committed above all to *logos*, the speech and reason that might be brought about between the best of citizen-friends. Speech and reason shared among us is the very antithesis of madness. Arendt's preferred Socrates is the one who draws thinking out into the public space of appearing; she was often dismissive of the Socrates, who withdrew into contemplation and cherished the state of being in harmony and agreement with himself. Dana Villa observes: "Her profound ambivalence . . . betrays her inability to conceive a self that is not a trap, that is not founded upon a narcissistic retreat from the world into the enjoyment of conflicting emotions and inner tensions" (Villa 1999, 253).

Kristeva's preferred Socrates is immersed in the world of experience, more concerned with living than knowing, engaged in dialogue that should not be understood as a matter of manifesting an inner self. Rather, she writes: "this speech practice is . . . organically linked to the man who created it (Socrates and his students), or better, speech *is* man and his activity" (Kristeva 1980, 81). This distinctively Greek moment held enduring appeal for Arendt (which sheds light on the difficulty Villa identifies) but also for Kristeva. Arendt cannot reassure us that we will know if and when language goes mad, while Kristeva points to the slips, neuroses, and experiments in poetic language that show us that language is never entirely sane. Both remain vigilant over the spaces where difference might appear. Kristeva writes the following in "Refoundation as Survival: An Interrogation of Hannah Arendt":

> Arendt envisages a political space and time where, as soon as it appears, "someone" will "open up," introduce himself, share of himself. These are the space and time of *Öffentlichkeit*, the opening (as the German language says) of the unthought, the forgotten, the repressed, the most interior, the intimate; the space and time of the public's Becoming, the space and time of "publicity," where the unspeakable and the invisible seem straightforwardly signifiable. . . . Opinion, as Arendt understands it, is the moment at which this worldliness, this publicity, this dawn of politics, appears. (Kristeva 2008, 356)

Notes

1. The TV broadcast of the interview is also available, and the interviewee's pauses—to stare at her fingernails, light a cigarette, look into space—are movingly eloquent (Gaus 1964).

2. Kristeva signals another bar to making generalizations on the basis of this relationship when she describes Arendt as regarding Heidegger as more deserving of forgiveness than most, not only because of love but because of respect due to a thought that is unique among all others (Kristeva 2003, 234).

3. Kristeva deals with Arendt's understanding of narrative in detail in "Refoundation as Survival: An Interrogation of Hannah Arendt" (Kristeva 2008).

4. S. K. Keltner sketches a historical trajectory that offers a historical trajectory leading to Arendt's and Kristeva's linked political projects and their divergent understandings of intimacy. Keltner traces both to the modern secular logic of the nation-state that culminated in nineteenth-century German nationalism. Kristeva sees Freud responding to this by revealing modern intimacy and developing analysis as "a journey into the strangeness of the other and of oneself" (Kristeva 1991, 98, 182). In *Strangers to Ourselves*, she describes this logic in political terms, noting that it is "amenable to improvement (democracies) or degeneration (totalitarianism)." Arendt, in contrast, regards Rousseau as the "first articulate explorer" of modern intimacy, and her response to the historical culmination of nationalism and its degeneration into Nazism is informed by Rousseau's

relentless excavation of intimate life and his vision of a politics of transparency (Arendt 2006, 1973). Keltner argues that nationalism "foregrounds the intimate as an interiority of what is most familiar as the organizing principle of modern society and political reality [understood in terms of blood, culture or language]. The intimate here marks the problems of race and nation in an expanding, globalizing world" (Keltner 2009, 167). Kristeva interrupts this version of intimacy, picking up the element of German Romanticism that is fascinated by what is strange and unexpected in language, just as Freud will become fascinated by slips in language. In *Eichmann in Jerusalem*, Arendt sees the perversion of German in the Nazi deployment of "winged words" and cliché, but also finds evidence for the resilience of language in very fact of those postwar arguments where she found reconciliation (Arendt 2006).

 5. Kristeva 1984, 187, quoting Hegel 1979, trans. Miller, 52.

 6. Indeed, Sjöholm argues that in Arendt's view, intimacy is modernity's the favorite form of escape (Sjöholm 2009, 193).

 7. Later in the same lecture, Arendt confronts this in a more promising way as the problem of the third term that would allow for the comparison of two particulars, that is, the *tertium quid* or the *tertium comparationis*. Acknowledging that the third term cannot be derived from outside but also cannot be derived from experience, she considers the use of examples to fulfill this role. "[The] exemplar is and remains a particular that in its very particularity reveals the generality that otherwise could not be defined" (Arendt 2014, 77).

 8. Despite making the distinction between *communicability* and *publicity* here, she often uses the terms interchangeably (Norris 1996, 187).

 9. For a feminist reading that excavates the violence in *sensus communis*, see Holthoon and Olson 1987.

 10. On the relations among the several histories of *sensus communis*, see Holthoon and Olson 1987.

 11. See "Giambattista Vico: Going Mad Rationally," in Crease 2019.

References

Arendt, Hannah. 1950. "The Aftermath of Nazi Rule: Report from Germany." *Commentary* 10 (January).

———. 1973. *The Origins of Totalitarianism*. New York: Houghton Mifflin Harcourt.

———. 1998. *The Human Condition*. 2nd ed. Chicago, IL: University of Chicago Press.

———. 2006. *Eichmann in Jerusalem*. New York: Penguin.

———. 2013. "'What Remains? The Language Remains': A Conversation with Günther Gaus." In *Hannah Arendt: The Last Interview and Other Conversations*, translated by Joan Stambaugh. Brooklyn, NY: Melville House.

———. 2014. *Lectures on Kant's Political Philosophy*. Edited by Ronald Beiner. Chicago, IL: University of Chicago Press.

Birmingham, Peg. 2005. "Political Affections: Kristeva, Arendt and the Space of Appearance." In *Revolt, Affect, Collectivity: The Unstable Boundaries of Kristeva's Politics*, 127–47. Albany: State University of New York Press.

Crease, Robert P. 2019. *The Workshop and the World: What Ten Thinkers Can Teach Us about Science and Authority*. W. W. Norton.

Cutrofello, Andrew. 1997. *Imagining Otherwise: Metapsychology and the Analytic a Posteriori*. Evanston, IL: Northwestern University Press.

Gaus, Günther. 1964. Zur Person: Hannah Arendt im Gesprach mit Günther Gaus Television. http://www.arendtcenter.it/en/tag/gunter-gaus/.

Hannah Arendt. 1968. *Between Past and Future: Eight Exercises in Political Thought*. New York: Penguin.

Holthoon, F. L. van, and David R. Olson. 1987. *Common Sense: The Foundations for Social Science*. Lanham, MD: University Press of America.

Johnston, Adrian. 2005. "Kant and the Conditions of Possibility for the Psychoanalytic Subject." In *Time Driven*, 79–119. Evanston, IL: Northwestern University Press.

Kant, Immanuel. 1987. *Critique of Judgment*. Translated by Werner S. Pluhar. Indianapolis, IN: Hackett.

Keltner, S. K. 2009. "What Is Intimacy?" In *Psychoanalysis, Aesthetics, and Politics in the Work of Julia Kristeva*, 163–78. Albany: State University of New York Press.

Kristeva, Julia. 1980. *Desire in Language: A Semiotic Approach to Literature and Art*. Oxford, UK: Blackwell.

———. 1984. *Revolution in Poetic Language*. New York: Columbia University Press.

———. 1991. *Strangers to Ourselves*. New York: Columbia University Press.

———. 2002. *Intimate Revolt*. Translated by Jeanine Herman. New York: Columbia University Press.

———. 2003. *Hannah Arendt*. New York: Columbia University Press.

———. 2008. "Refoundation as Survival: An Interrogation of Hannah Arendt Julia Kristeva." *Common Knowledge* 14, no. 3: 353–64.

Norris, Andrew. 1996. "Arendt, Kant, and the Politics of Common Sense." *Polity* 29, no. 2: 165–91. https://doi.org/10.2307/3235299.

O'Byrne, Anne. 2020. "The Ugly Psyche: Arendt and the Right to Opacity." *Research in Phenomenology* 50, no. 2: 177–98.

Sjöholm, Cecilia. 2009. "Fear of Intimacy? Psychoanalysis and the Resistance to Commodification." In *Psychoanalysis, Aesthetics, and Politics in the Work of Julia Kristeva*, edited by Kelly Oliver and S. K. Keltner. Albany: State University of New York Press.

Van Kessel, Peter J. 1987. "Common Sense between Bacon and Vico: Scepticism in England and Italy." In *Common Sense: The Foundations for Social Science*, edited by Frits van Holthoon and David R. Olson, 115–30. Lanham, MD: University Press of America.

Villa, Dana. 1999. "Arendt and Socrates." *Revue Internationale de Philosophie* 53, no. 208: 241–57.

———. 2007. "Genealogies of Total Domination: Arendt, Adorno, and Auschwitz." *New German Critique* 100: 1–45.

About the Contributors

(LISTED IN ALPHABETICAL ORDER)

Emilia Angelova is associate professor of philosophy at Concordia University, Montreal, Canada. She holds a PhD in philosophy from the University of Toronto. Her research is in nineteenth- and twentieth-century Continental philosophy, with special emphasis on themes such as selfhood, temporality, freedom, and the imagination, as raised by Kant and Hegel, and taken up by contemporary philosophy in Heidegger and French theory, especially Kristeva. Her publications include articles in *Idealistic Studies*, *Symposium: Canadian Journal of Continental Philosophy*, *Journal of Chinese Philosophy*, and multiple book chapters theorizing about Hegel in relation to Heidegger, Levinas, Deleuze, Nancy, and most recently Kristeva. She is also the editor of *The Necessity of Freedom in Hegel: Logic, Phenomenology and Aesthetics* (forthcoming).

Sid Hansen is associate professor of philosophy at California State University Northridge. Their writings have appeared in *Foucault Studies*, *Philosophy Today*, *Journal of French and Francophone Philosophy*, and *International Journal of French and Francophone Philosophy*. They are coeditor of *New Forms of Revolt: Essays on Kristeva's Intimate Politics* and codirector of the Kristeva Circle.

Alice Jardine is professor of Romance Languages and Literatures (RLL) and Studies of Women, Gender, and Sexuality (WGS) at Harvard University, where she cofounded and helped to develop and lead WGS. Her teaching in RLL focuses on twentieth- and twenty-first-century French/Francophone literature, and poststructuralist and feminist theory. Jardine's legacy of scholarship has been at the forefront of critical thought since the early 1980s. Her publications include *Gynesis: Configurations of Woman and Modernity* (1985), cotranslation of Kristeva's *Desire in Language* (1980), and several coedited volumes (e.g., *The Future of Difference, Men in Feminism, Shifting Scenes,* and *Living Attention*). Her most recent book, *At the Risk of Thinking: An Intellectual Biography of Julia Kristeva,* was published in January 2020.

Julia Kristeva is professor emeritus of linguistics at the University of Paris Diderot-Paris 7. She is a tutelary member of the Psychoanalytical Society of Paris and doctor *honoris causa* of a number of universities. She has taught regularly in the United States, Canada, and Europe. Commander of the Legion of Honor, Commander of the Order of Merit and the first laureate of the Holberg Prize in December 2004, Kristeva was awarded the Hannah Arendt Prize in December 2006, and the Vaclav Havel Prize in 2008. Julia Kristeva created the Prize Simone de Beauvoir for women's freedom in 2008. She is the author of some thirty works, including *Revolution in Poetic Language* (1974); *Powers of Horror* (1980); *Tales of Love* (1984); *Black Sun: Depression and Melancholia* (1987); *Proust and the Sense of Time* (1993); the trilogy Female Genius (*Hannah Arendt* (1999)), *Melanie Klein* (2000), *and Colette* (2001); *Hatred and Forgiveness* (2010); *The Incredible Need to Believe* (2007); *Possessions: A Novel* (1998); *Murder in Byzantium* (2008); *Seule une femme; Teresa, My Love* (2008); *Passions of Our Time* (2018); *The Enchanted Clock* (2019); and *Dostoyevsky, or The Flood of Language* (2021).

Elaine P. Miller is professor of philosophy at Miami University of Ohio. She researches and teaches nineteenth-century German philosophy, contemporary European feminist theory, aesthetics, and the philosophy of nature. Her books include *Head Cases: Julia Kristeva on Philosophy and Art in Depressed Times* (2014), *The Vegetative Soul: From Philosophy of Nature to Subjectivity in the Feminine* (SUNY Press, 2002), and an edited collection, *Returning to Irigaray: Feminist Philosophy, Politics, and the Question of Unity* (SUNY Press, 2006). She has also published articles in the *Hegel Bulletin,* the *Palgrave Handbook of German Romantic Philosophy, Idealistic Studies, Journal of Nietzsche Studies, Oxford Literary Review,* among other places.

John Montani is a doctoral candidate in Philosophy at the University of Oregon who holds an MA in Philosophy from Stony Brook University.

His research focuses on the notions of rhythm, sense, and world in the Continental tradition and in the history of philosophy.

Miglena Nikolchina is a Bulgarian poet, writer, and theoretician whose research interests involve the interactions of literature and philosophy. In English, her publications include numerous articles as well as the books *Matricide in Language: Writing Theory in Kristeva and Woolf* (2004) and *Lost Unicorns of the Velvet Revolutions: Heterotopias of the Seminar* (2013). She guest-edited a special issue of *differences* 32, no. 1 (2021), on "The Undead of Literary Theory." Her most recent book (in Bulgarian) is *God with Machine: Subtracting the Human* (2022).

Anne O'Byrne (PhD Vanderbilt, 1999) is professor of philosophy at Stony Brook University. Her work is in political philosophy and ontology informed by twentieth-century and contemporary European philosophy—Heidegger, Arendt, Dilthey, Derrida, and Jean-Luc Nancy. She works on radical democracy, identity, natality, embodiment, education, gender, race, and genocide. She is the author of *The Genocide Paradox: Democracy and Generational Being* (2023) and *Natality and Finitude* (2010); the editor (with Martin Shuster) of *Logics of Genocide: The Structures of Violence and the Contemporary World* (2020), and (with Hugh Silverman) of *Subjects and Simulations* (2014); and translator (with Robert Richardson) of Nancy's *Being Singular Plural* (1996), *Corpus II: Writings on Sexuality* (2013), and *Being Nude* (translated with Carlie Anglemire, 2014). Her current project is a book-length study of kinship, taxonomy, and the failure of democracies to resist genocidal violence.

Kelly Oliver recently retired from Vanderbilt University, where she was W. Alton Distinguished Professor of Philosophy. She is a past codirector of the Society for Phenomenology and Existential Philosophy (SPEP), and a founding member of both the Kristeva Circle and *philoSOPHIA*. She is a prominent author on Julia Kristeva (since 1991), and author of sixteen scholarly books, including *Earth and World, Philosophy after the Apollo Missions*; the editor of another thirteen books, including her most recent on *Gaslighting*; and the author of over 100 scholarly articles on a variety of topics, including refugee detention, capital punishment, animal ethics, sexual violence, images of women and war, psychoanalysis, and film. Her work has been translated into eight languages. She has been interviewed on ABC news, appeared on CSPAN Books, published in the *New York Times* and *Los Angeles Times*, among other appearances and publications in popular media. She is also the bestselling author of three award-winning mystery series, *The Jessica James Mysteries* (seven novels, contemporary suspense), *The Fiona Figg Mysteries* (five novels, the latest, *Covert in Cairo* came out April 24, 2023), and *The Pet Detective Mysteries* (three novels, middle grade).

Elisabeth Paquette is associate professor of comparative literature at the University of Buffalo (SUNY). She works at the intersection of social and political philosophy, feminist philosophy, and decolonial theory. Her book, titled *Universal Emancipation: Race beyond Badiou* (2020), engages French political theorist Alain Badiou's discussion of Négritude and the Haitian Revolution to develop a nuanced critique of his theory of emancipation. Currently, she is working on a monograph on the writings of decolonial theorist Sylvia Wynter. Her publications can be found in the following journals: *Badiou Studies*; *Philosophy Today*; *Radical Philosophy Review*; *Hypatia*; *philoSOPHIA*; and *Philosophy Compass*.

Surti Singh is assistant professor of philosophy at Villanova University. Her research interests include Frankfurt School Critical Theory, psychoanalysis, feminist philosophy, and aesthetics. She is coprincipal investigator of the research project Extimacies: Critical Theory from the Global South and currently serves as the president of the Association for Adorno Studies. Recent publications include "Adorno's Aesthetic Theory: The Artwork as Monad," in *The 'Aging' of Adorno's Aesthetic Theory: 50 Years Later* (2021) and "Dark Play: Aesthetic Resistance in Lukács, Benjamin, and Adorno," *Philosophy & Social Criticism* (2020).

Fanny Söderbäck is associate professor of philosophy at Södertörn University and the cofounder and codirector of the Kristeva Circle. She holds a PhD in Philosophy from the New School for Social Research and has held positions at Siena College and DePaul University. She is the author of *Revolutionary Time: On Time and Difference in Kristeva and Irigaray* (SUNY Press, 2019). She has edited *Feminist Readings of Antigone* (SUNY Press, 2010) and is a coeditor of the volume *Undutiful Daughters: New Directions in Feminist Thought and Practice* (2012). She is currently working on a book project on Italian feminist philosopher Adriana Cavarero, in which she puts her work into conversation with queer and trans theories as well as Latinx, Black, and decolonial feminisms to reenvision selfhood and human relations through the framework of singularity. She is also the editor of a special issue of *philoSOPHIA: A Journal of Continental Feminism* on the topic of birth. Her work has appeared in scholarly journals such as *Diacritics, Hypatia: A Journal of Feminist Philosophy, Journal of French and Francophone Philosophy, Journal of Speculative Philosophy, Signs: Journal of Women in Culture and Society,* and *Theory & Event*.

Index

For books and articles by Kristeva, seen under their English title.

abjection, 276. *See also* maternal; conditions of, 34; Kristeva's essay on, 33; maternal, 37, 69, 227, 272; retroaction, 35
action, and transgression, 47; delayed, 10
"Adolescence: A Syndrome of Ideality," 178
Adorno, Theodor W., 64
affect, in Fanon, 156; structure of, 59; tendential severance, 12
Ahmed, Sara, 116; foreigners, 129
alterity, asymmetry of, 8, 78
anality, and separation, 45; jubilatory, 45
anorexia, 68
Anzaldúa, Gloria, 123–133; ambivalent-ambiguous, 128; and skin, 131; *Borderlands/La Frontera*, 124; epistemic privilege of the oppressed in, 126; internal strangeness, 131; la faculdad, as consciousness raising, 131; liminality, 126; theory of subjectivity, 124
Aragon, Louis, 202
archaeology, archiving, 262; as Kristeva's method, 17

Arendt, Hannah, 14; enlarged mentality, 293; forgiveness and communication in, 285; Gaus interview, 285–286; German language in, 285; limited territory (vs cosmopolitanism), 296; madness vs sanity, 301; mother tongue in, 285; not-murderers, 299
Auschwitz (abyss of), 284

Badiou, Alain, 14, 203, 206
Bakhtin, Mikhail, 196
Bataille, Georges, 197, 261, 269, 276
Beardsworth, Sara, 254–255
Bejahung. *See* affirmation
Bergson, Henri, and time, 265–266
Birmingham, Peg, 287–288
Black peoples, assertion of, 146–148
Black Sun, 267
body, as semiotic, 42; consumption of, 16, 42; speaking, 10
Butler, Judith, 94–95

castration, 213. *See under* feminine castration; and unstable subject in Kristeva, 219; feminine (and narcissism), 47

cathexes, and pleasure principle, 36; unbounded, in a position of primacy, 36
Cavanaugh, Sheila, 21, 91
Celan, Paul, 65
Chanter, Tina, 95
chōra, 192; as originary process, 234–235; as prior to the imaginary, 217
colonialism, and violence, 148; coloniality of power, 147; crimes against humanity, 64; French, 152–153; history, in France, 165; in North Africa, 118; power structures (and internal strangeness), 119
consciousness, and activity of Force, 278; reflexive, as result, 79
contradiction, 170; objective, 148; paroxysmal, 267
Critchley, Simon, 257
Currah, Paisley, 101
Cutrofello, Andrew, 294

death, living dead, 48
depression, depressive position in Klein, 39; feminine, illustrations of, 31; undead mother, 38
Derrida, Jacques, arche-trace, 11; *Archive Fever*, 261; Kristeva's 1967 interview, 16
Descartes, René, 213
desire, and death in Lacan, 39; elaboration of, 215
Desire in Language, and rhythm, 249
disability, 67; affective meaning of, 84; solidarity with disabled, 83
Dreyfus affair, 163
drive, as instinctual, 235; death drive, 36, 40, 50, 261; in Kristeva vs Freud, 217–218; life drive, 45, 175, 278; maternal, 18; semiotic, 99

echolalia. See *under* semiotic

ego, as a construct, 214; as alienation, 214; in Kristeva, vs Sartre, 221; integration of in Klein, 39
"Engendering of the Formula," 201
Enlightenment, 66
ethics. See also feminism, herethics; asymmetry of, 78; autonomy, 228; of psychoanalysis, 83

Fanon, Frantz, 122, 156
feminism, and gender (limited plasticity of), 103; and racism, 151; herethics, 76–78, 85–87; liberation, 7
Foucault, Michel, 20, 95, 156, 255, 305
Fraser, Nancy, 20, 94, 105
Freud. See also cathexes; death instinct; affect, 259; emphasis on the paternal, 80; imaginary father, 178; imaginary father, as individual pre-history, 18; on sublimation, vs Kristeva, 174; patricide, 16; pleasure principle, 271; primary processes in, 271; unbinding, 274; uncanny in, 115
Freudian Thing, as cry, 44; metonymy of desire, 44; presence in language, 33; primary identification with, 43
fundamentalism, martyrs, 68; religious, and economic depression, 173; religious, in France, 155–156

Goldmann, Lucien, 3, 196–199
Grace, Laura Jane, 98–99
Green, Andre, 263

hallucination, in Kristeva, 226; psychical apparatus of, 226
Hansen, Sid, 6, 20, 124
Hatred and Forgiveness, 9
Hegel, and comedy, 258; and heteronomy, 257; dialectic, 4–5,

267–268; external world in, 168; "Force and the Understanding," 167, 254, 271; living nature as autonomous, 168; "logic behind consciousness," 168; ontology of relation, 278; role of the thing, 276; speculative logic, 249–250
Heidegger, Martin, 259–260; being-for-death, 35; Speech Being, 263
heterogeneity, as dialectical oscillation, 93; of language, 93; theorization of materiality, 93
Hôpital Cochin, 167–168
Hölderlin, Friedrich, 63

identity, and poetic language, 69; mimetic (as identification), 3; national, 69, 171; national, as antidepressant, 70; not a cult, as question mark, 69
image, as separation between subject and object, 216; in Kristeva, vs Sartre, 223; mental, 223–225
imaginary, in Sartre, 212; linguistic imagination, 4; loss of, 211; spectacular, 212; vs imagination, 220; vs second-degree thetic, 219
imagination. *See under* imaginary
intellectualism, 9
Intimate Revolt, 223
intimate revolt, relevance to trans studies, 98–101

Jardine, Alice, 2–3, 5, 8–9, 12, 19, 26, 149
Jean-Luc Nancy, and excription, 254
jouissance, 100; and archaic Thing, 45
Joyaux, David (son of Kristeva), 67

Kant, Immanuel, 32, 43, 182, 288–289; judgment in, 291–292
Keltner, S. K., 298
King, Martin Luther, 245

Kittay, Eva, 85
Klein, Melanie, 39; and proto-object, 177–178; and social relations, 289
Kristeva, relation to French philosophy, 14–16

"L 'Impossibilité de perdre," 19
Lacan. *See also* psychoanalysis
Lacan, Jacques, and the Real, 5–6, 269; lack, 11; metalanguage, 9–11; mirror stage, 216–217
language, 3. *See also* symbolic; *See under* human rights; and prelinguistic material, 53; and speaking body, 101; and the unconscious, 58; autopoeisis, 145; disorganization of, 53; exteriority of, 258; French (teaching of), 68; history of, 254; in Heidegger, 260; inner touch (*oikeiois*), 65–66; poetic, as trans-affirming, 100; power, 5–6; singularities in, 67; structure (as rise-fall), 247; transcendental dimension of, 17
"Language, Sublimation, Women," 263
Lechte, John, 229, 230
Lefebvre, Henri, 251
Leibniz, humanization (filter of), 190; theory of compossibles, 204
Levinas, Emmanuel, 256
life drive. *See also* affirmation
loss. *See also* mourning; archaic, impossibility of, 31; as atmosphere, 50; as unrepresentable, 43; grief, 256–257
love, critical, 79; debasement, 223; of others, 83
love-object, as hollow habitation, 79
Lukács, György, 194–199, 208

Macdonald, Molly, 271, 276
Margaroni, Maria, 229

Malebranche, intelligible extension in, 203
Mallarmé, Stephane, 15
masculine-feminine (dualism of), 7
maternal. *See also* Freudian thing; *See also* loss; abandonment, 46; ambivalence, 78; as passion and prototype, 79; as unnamable, 35; body, ordering of, 204, 276; conditions of mourning, 279; dead mother, 264; hold on culture, 80; hold on the child, 80; holding (psychoanalytic), 54; infant's relation to, 216; infantile event, 35; mother-child link, perversion of, 262–263; objectless love, 17–18; presence, traces of, 226; prior to mirror stage, 216; prohibition, eroticization, 264; separation, 226; structural experience of, 81; virtual presence of, 273
maternal semiotic, as precondition of language, 34; as production of meaning, 277
mathematics, and the maternal chōra, 204; nombrant (in number theory), 203–205
Mbembe, Achille, 180–181
McAfee, Noëlle, 111, 121
meaning, 5. *See under* symbolic; as retrospective, 4; collapse of, 13
metaphor, hallucinatory, 254; vs metonymy, 8
migrants (Syrian), 63
Miller, Elaine, 10, 17, 22, 155
Millot, Catherine, 91, 101–102
mirror stage, acoustic primacy, over the image, 226; Lacan, 213–215
modernity (digital), 67
Money, John, 96, 102, 103
Montesquieu, l'esprit général, and language, 120

mother. *See under* maternal
motherhood. *See* maternal
"Motherhood according to Giovanni Bellini," 205
mourning, 48. *See also* loss; diachrony of subject and object, 53
multiculturalism, 68
Muslim, French population, 117; head scarf, 117; immigrant youth, 167

Nancy, Jean-Luc, 14, 15–16
narcissism, 294; harm, 47
natality, 14; and temporality, 175; as renewal, 297; in Arendt, 290
Nations without Nationalisms, 129
Nazism, evading the denazification process, 299–300
"Need to believe," 68
negation, 270. *See also* fourth negation; fourth negation, 253, 269–270, 274; genuine negativity (as different from ideal negation), 274; rejection, 290–291
New Humanism, 2–3, 6
Nikolchina, Miglena, 23, 129

Oedipus (and narrative), 175–176
"Of What Use Are Poets in Times of Distress?," 19
Oliver, Kelly, 10, 20, 133, 255
Ortega, Mariana, 127

Palestinization, 181
"Passion According to Motherhood," 79
perlaboration. *See under* working-through. *See also* trauma
perversion, and depression, 48; economy of acts, 48
poetic, decentered, 8; naming, 145; travelling through writing, 64
poetry, 170–171; Arabic, 68

politics, identity, 8; of the least horrible, 69; precarity, 100
Polylogue, 205
postphenomenology, 221
Powers of Horror, 122
pregnancy, 79
Proust, Marcel, 163–167; time in, 174
psyche, and soma, 239; fear of heights, 50; inhibition, 47; intersubjective shock of, 269; investment, 177; libido (archaic), 37; primary processes, 238–239; structures, 13
psychoanalysis. *See also* psyche; as "counterdepressant," 16; listening, 83

radicalization, process of, 68
rationality (vs symbol), 5
rejection. *See under* semiotic, mark; speech, dead
rejection (of drives). *See* contradictions
reliance, and revolt, 80; maternal, 255
repassioning, as rebinding, 80; as reliance, 80
representation (task of), 80
revolt, 173, 226, 296. *See under* totalitarianism; *See also* intimate revolt; as psychic transgression-transformation, 131; intimacy-without-privation, 297; renewal (psychic), 11
revolution, 3. *See under* symbolic order; as oscillation, 101; language's potential for, 237; of the symbolic order, 143
Revolution in Poetic Language, 3; political themes in, 236
revolutionary practice (and political resistance), 171
revolutionary process, and social order, 144; as poetic language, 144
rhythm, 233–235; and articulation, 241–243; and drives, 235; and transposition, 234; as sociopolitical practice, 237; as transfiguration, 243; becoming practice, 236; instinctual, 238–239
Rose, Jacqueline, 163
Russian Revolution, 4–5

Salamon, Gayle, 102, 105
Sartre, Jean-Paul, 32, 212–213, 220–222; mental image, 213
semiotic, 4–8, 192; and relation to social plurality, 40; and symbolic, as non-oppositional, 98–101; and the symbolic, 142–143; art, 169; as non-opposed to symbolic, 234; as prior to language, 143; authority, 4; avant-garde, 202; binary logic, 34; carnival scene, 238; complicity of, 8; drive, 12–13; echolalia, 13; expenditure, 241; foundation, 14; mark, as rejection, 14; materiality (of linguistic signifier), 9; motility and fragmentation of in infant, 216; oppression, 236; vs symbolic, 236
Semēiotikē, 3, 23; and hybridity of terms, 192; major terms in, 192
sensus communis, 288–289; in Kant, 291
sensus privatus, 291
Serres, Michel, 203
sex, binary notion of, 97; biological, 96–98
sexual constitution, and prehistoric experience, 41
sexual difference, 153
significance, 198–199. *See also* signification; as break between signifier and signified, 219; as

significance *(continued)*
scission between symbolic and semiotic, 219; as transposition of praxis, 198; double bind, with semiotic, 17; dual authority of semiotic, 264; narcissism as condition of, 18; radical loss, 15; vs signification, 10–12
signification, 4. *See also* significance; *See also* humanization; as communication, 53; as process, 190–191; blank activity as exempt from, 47
singularity, ethics of, 81; of child, 78
Sjöholm, Cecilia, 291; intimacy of revolt, vs extimacy, 228
sociogeny, 156–157
Socrates, 301
Sollers, Philippe, 204
Souad (patient of Kristeva), 68
speaking being, as vulnerability, 85
speaking subject, and liberating the death drive, 262; and metonymy of desire, 219; at threshold of language, 235
speech (dead), 14
"Stabat Mater," 85
states of exception, 64
Stewart, Amy Ray, 91, 98–101
Stoller, Robert, 96, 102, 103
Stoyanov, Tzvetan, 195
stranger, as child, 78; as situatedness, 116; as uncanny, 78; cosmopolitanism, 115
Strangers to Ourselves, 298
Stryker, Susan, 101
subject, divided, 268; enunciation of, 12, 143, 245–246; fictional direction, 215; fictional direction of, 215; foreclosure of, 4; formation of, 276
subject-in-process, 158, 171; as negativity, 221; trial of, 144

subjectivity, 222
sublimation, and construction of the subject, 254; in Kristeva, 44; in Lacan, 32
sur-vival (of writing), 67
symbolic. *See also* language; affirmation of, 37; and sacrifice in Structuralism, 169; and the political, 154; aporia, 5; as sociopolitical, 4; as split unification, 219; as unstable process, 10; condition of possibility, 4–6; cultural space (vs religious dogma), 173; excription, 254; humiliation (and phallic power), 47; isolated individual (egoism), 14; justice (address of), 17; patriarchy and paternal law, 5; readability of, 11; reinscription, 143; separation from maternal, 12; structure of, 143; tension with semiotic, 143; thetic phase, 11, 169
Söderbäck, Fanny, 5–6, 8, 17, 18, 21, 92, 94, 98–99, 104

tenderness (and eroticism), 80
text, and discursive practices, 242; experience of, as trans-subjective and trans-phenomenal, 242–244
The Sense and Non-sense of Revolt, 15
"The State and Mystery," 198
The Text of the Novel, 197
thetic boundary, not reducible to personal threshold, 237
thetic consciousness, and semiotic rhythm, 235; as traversible boundary, 236
Thing (Freudian). *See under* Freudian Thing
time, hybridity of, 174; messianic structure of, 17; revolutionary, 5
Todorov, Tzvetan, 192

totalitarianism, 68; soft, 2
trans identity, 99; as intersectional, 103
transcendental, vs empirical criteria, 294–295
transference, forgiveness, 33; of affects, 82
transhumanism, 67
transitional nation, France as, 172
transphobia, 6
transposition, 238–239
transsexuality, terrain of sex, 96
trauma, vii. *See also under* infantile event; and hallucination, 54; as intersubjective shock, 42; as outside language, 52; as reactivating, 38; constitutive, 36, 51; integrating loss, 48; psychic, vs Lacan's real trauma, 52; repetition of, 38

unconscious, Arendt's rejection of, 288; as traversing consciousness, 221
unthought (publicity of), 302

values, renegotiation of, 8–9
Vincent, Jean-Didier, 79
violence (as founding), 11

Watkin, William, 14–16
woman (existential worth), 8
"Women's Time," 8
working-through, 1, 59
Wynter, Sylvia, 156; and the poetic, 145–147; episteme, 145–146; overlap with Kristeva, 148–149

Ziarek, Ewa, 154
Zionism, political, 165

www.ingramcontent.com/pod-product-compliance
Lightning Source LLC
Chambersburg PA
CBHW021647230426
43668CB00008B/546